# The World's Religions

Relief from Brauron showing Zeus, Leto, Apollo, and
Artemis, c. 400 B.C.E. National Museum, Athens.

# The World's Religions

## Ninian Smart

PRENTICE HALL
Englewood Cliffs, N.J.07632

*For Luisabel*

North and South American Edition first published 1989 by
Prentice-Hall, Inc,
Englewood Cliffs,
NJ 07632

A John Calmann and King book

ISBN 0 13 968 041-1

This book was designed and produced by
JOHN CALMANN AND KING LTD, LONDON

Designed by Andrew Shoolbred
Typeset by Composing Operations, England.
Printed in Hong Kong by Mandarin Offset International Ltd.

# Contents

# *Preface*

Though this book is written in a clear way for the general public and for students who wish to learn about the world's worldviews, it does rest on some theoretical foundations which may be of interest to historians of religion and others concerned with the analysis of human values. I use a seven-dimensional framework to analyze the religions—in terms of ethics, ritual, narrative or myth, experience, institutions or society, doctrine and art. Religions are placed in a historical context, and viewed in relation to their periods of formation and re-formation. I stress too the ways in which they blend with other movements such as modern nationalism.

I am most grateful to Laurence King of Calmann and King Ltd for proposing this book to me, and to Rosemary Bradley, Carolyn Yates, David Britt, Sara Waterson, Tracy Pinchman, and Andrew Shoolbred, who notably helped in the execution of the work.

*Ninian Smart*

# Introduction

## The Importance of Understanding the World's Worldviews

Understanding the world's religions and ideologies is important in three ways. First, they are a vital ingredient in the varied story of humankind's various experiments in living. The religions and ideas of ancient Greece or of the Maya are worth our recapturing, so far as we can, as part of the great heritage of human civilization. Second, and of more immediate importance, is the fact that in order to grasp the meanings and values of the plural cultures of today's world, we need to know something of the worldviews which underlie them. To understand the Middle East you need to know something about Islam, not to mention Christianity and Judaism; and to understand Japan you need some insight into Buddhism, Shinto, and the Confucian heritage. Third, we may as individuals be trying to form our own coherent and emotionally satisfying picture of reality, and it is always relevant to see the great ideas and practices of various important cultures and civilizations. To make judgments about philosophies and ways of life we need a comparative perspective—to know something of the quest of the Christian mystic and the Hindu yogin, and of the spirituality of the Hasidic Jew and the Mahāyāna Buddhist. In a number of ways, the individual cultures of the world contribute to human civilization, and the religions and ideologies permeating those cultures are not to be neglected.

In undertaking a voyage into the world's religions we should not define religion too narrowly. It is important for us to recognize secular ideologies as part of the story of human worldviews. It is artificial to divide them too sharply from religions, partly because they sometimes function in society like religions, and partly because the distinction between religious and secular beliefs and practices is a modern Western one and does not represent the way in which other cultures categorize human values. Essentially, this book is a history of ideas and practices which have moved human beings.

To understand religious and secular worldviews and their practical meaning we have to use imagination. We have to enter into the lives of those for whom such ideas and actions are important. As the Native American proverb says, "Never judge a person until you have walked a mile in his moccasins." Much of this book will be in a broad way informative; but it will also, I hope, convey something of the spirit of the human quest for crosscultural communication.

Once a Christian theologian complained to me in a public discussion because I had dealt among other themes with Buddhist attitudes to creation: "What need do we have to consider Buddhism, since it is incompatible with the Gospel, and the Christian Gospel is all the truth we need?" It seems to me inappropriate to be so defensive, and a limitation on this man's knowledge of the forces animating different parts of humanity. Anyway, I craftily replied: "You must indeed have read a lot, to know that Buddhism is incompatible with the Christian Gospel."

The voyage into other folks' beliefs and practices may turn out to be a journey into your neighborhood. It is common today for varieties of people to live together in the great cities. In London, New York, Los Angeles, Sydney, Singapore, Frankfurt, and Paris, most of the great religions and ideologies are present. This pluralism is the richer because each of the traditions includes many forms: Catholics, Orthodox, Lutherans, Baptists; Shi'a and Sunni Muslims, and Muslims from Morocco, Indonesia, and Egypt; Buddhists from Sri Lanka, Vietnam, and Korea, as well as Anglo converts; and so on. It often happens, then, that cities are microcosms of the whole world. This is an added reason why it is important to know something of others, so that mutual understanding, though maybe not agreement, may animate community relations.

Inevitably the Vietnamese migrant to Corpus Christi, Texas, and the Indian villager listening to a radio are affected to some degree by modernity and in a measure by Western values. The tremendous impact of the West has helped to shape the old religions in their voyage into the contemporary world. They have cherished their roots, but they have also adapted. The Hinduism of today bears deeply the imprint of its struggle against the imperial mentality, and the same is true, much more clearly, of the way smaller-scale cultures have bent to the winds of Western-dictated change. Consequently in this book the period of Western navigation, exploration, exploitation and imperial rule marks a watershed in the story. Before, there is the narrative of the rise and fall of religious cultures in differing parts of the globe; afterwards, we see patterns of interaction, and eventually the emergence of a global civilization, in which inevitably religious and secular worldviews have to learn to adapt to one another.

## The Nature of a Religion

In thinking about religion, it is easy to be confused about what it is. Is there some essence which is common to all religions? And cannot a person be religious without belonging to any of the religions? The search for an essence ends up in vagueness—for instance in the statement that a religion is some system of worship or other practice recognizing a transcendent Being or goal. Our problems break out again in trying to define the key term "transcendent." And in answer to the second question, why yes: there are plenty of people with deep spiritual concerns who do not ally themselves to any formal religious movement, and who may not themselves recognize anything as transcendent. They may see ultimate spiritual meaning in unity with nature or in relationships to other persons.

It is more practical to come to terms first of all not with what religion is in general but with what *a* religion is. Can we find some scheme of ideas which will help us to think about and to appreciate the nature of the religions?

Before I describe such a scheme, let me first point to something which we need to bear in mind in looking at religious traditions such as Christianity, Buddhism or Islam. Though we use the singular label "Christianity," in fact there is a great number of varieties of Christianity, and there are some movements about which we may have doubts as to whether they count as Christian. The same is true of all traditions: they manifest themselves as a loosely held-together family of subtraditions. Consider: a Baptist chapel in Georgia is a very different structure from an Eastern Orthodox church in Romania, with its blazing candles and rich ikons; and the two house very diverse services—the one plain, with hymns and Bible-reading, prayers and impassioned preaching; the other much more ritually anchored, with processions and chanting, and mysterious ceremonies in the light behind the screen where the ikons hang, concealing most of the priestly activities. Ask either of the religious specialists, the Baptist preacher or the Orthodox priest, and he will tell you that his own form of faith corresponds to original Christianity. To list some of the denominations of Christianity is to show something of its diverse practice—Orthodox, Catholic, Coptic, Nestorian, Armenian, Mar Thoma, Lutheran, Calvinist, Methodist, Baptist, Unitarian, Mennonite, Congregationalist, Disciples of Christ—and we have not reached some of the newer, more problematic forms: Latter-Day Saints, Christian Scientists, Unificationists, Zulu Zionists, and so forth.

Moreover, each faith is found in many countries, and takes color from each region. German Lutheranism differs from American; Ukrainian Catholicism from Irish; Greek Orthodoxy from Russian. Every religion has permeated and been permeated by a variety of diverse cultures. This adds to the richness of human experience, but it makes our tasks of thinking and feeling about the variety of faiths more complicated than we might at first suppose. We are dealing with not just traditions but many subtraditions.

It may happen, by the way, that a person within one family of subtraditions may be drawn closer to some subtradition of another family than to one or two subtraditions in her own family (as with human families; this is how marriage occurs). I happen to have had a lot to do with Buddhists in Sri Lanka and in some ways feel much closer to them than I do to some groups within my own family of Christianity.

The fact of pluralism inside religious traditions is enhanced by what goes on between them. The meeting of different cultures and traditions often produces new religious movements, such as the many black independent churches in Africa, combining classical African motifs and Christianities. All around us in Western countries are to be seen new movements and combinations.

Despite all this, it is possible to make sense of the variety and to discern some patterns in the luxurious vegetation of the world's religions and subtraditions. One approach is to look at the different aspects or dimensions of religion.

### The Practical and Ritual Dimension

Every tradition has some practices to which it adheres—for instance regular worship, preaching, prayers, and so on. They are often known as rituals (though they may well be more informal than this word implies). This *practical* and *ritual* dimension is especially important with faiths of a strongly sacramental kind, such as Eastern Orthodox Christianity with its long and elaborate service known as the Liturgy. The ancient Jewish tradition of the Temple, before it was destroyed in 70 C.E., was preoccupied with the rituals of sacrifice, and thereafter with the study of such rites seen itself as equivalent to their performance, so that study itself becomes almost a ritual

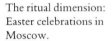

The ritual dimension: Easter celebrations in Moscow.

12

activity. Again, sacrificial rituals are important among Brahmin forms of the Hindu tradition.

Also important are other patterns of behavior which, while they may not strictly count as rituals, fulfill a function in developing spiritual awareness or ethical insight: practices such as yoga in the Buddhist and Hindu traditions, methods of stilling the self in Eastern Orthodox mysticism, meditations which can help to increase compassion and love, and so on. Such practices can be combined with rituals of worship, where meditation is directed towards union with God. They can count as a form of prayer. In such ways they overlap with the more formal or explicit rites of religion.

### The Experiential and Emotional Dimension

We only have to glance at religious history to see the enormous vitality and significance of experience in the formation and development of religious traditions. Consider the visions of the Prophet Muhammad, the conversion of Paul, the enlightenment of the Buddha. These were seminal events in human history. And it is obvious that the *emotions* and *experiences* of men and women are the food on which the other dimensions of religion feed: ritual without feeling is cold, doctrines without awe or compassion are dry, and myths which do not move hearers are feeble. So it is important in understanding a tradition to try to enter into the feelings which it generates—to feel the sacred awe, the calm peace, the rousing inner dynamism, the perception of a brilliant emptiness within, the outpouring of love, the sensations of hope, the gratitude for favors which have been received. One of the main reasons why music is so potent in religion is that it has mysterious powers to express and engender emotions.

Writers on religion have singled out differing experiences as being central. For instance, Rudolf Otto (1869–1937) coined the word "numinous." For the ancient Romans there were *numina* or spirits all around them, present in brooks and streams, and in mysterious copses, in mountains and in dwelling-places; they were to be treated with awe and a kind of fear. From the word, Otto built up his adjective, to refer to the feeling aroused by a *mysterium tremendum et fascinans*, a mysterious something which draws you to it but at the same time brings an awe-permeated fear. It is a good characterization of many religious experiences and visions of God as Other. It captures the impact of the prophetic experiences of Isaiah and Jeremiah, the theophany through which God appeared to Job, the conversion of Paul, the overwhelming vision given to Arjuna in the Hindu Song of the Lord (*Bhagavadgītā*). At a gentler level it delineates too the spirit of loving devotion, in that the devotee sees God as merciful and loving, yet Other, and to be worshiped and adored.

But the numinous is rather different in character from those other experiences which are often called "mystical." Mysticism is the inner or contemplative quest for what lies within—variously thought of as the Divine Being within, or the eternal soul, or the Cloud of Unknowing, emptiness, a dazzling darkness. There are those, such as Aldous Huxley (1894–1963), who

The experiential
dimension: casting out
demons in Zimbabwe.

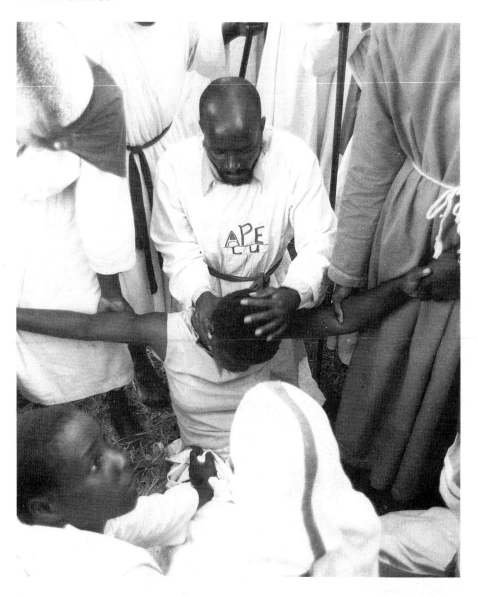

have thought that the imageless, insight-giving inner mystical experience lies
at the heart of all the major religions.

There are other related experiences, such as the dramas of conversion,
being "born again," turning around from worldly to otherworldly existence.
There is also the shamanistic type of experience, where a person goes upon a
vision quest and acquires powers to heal, often through suffering himself and
vividly traveling to the netherworld to rescue the dying and bring them to life
again. Shamans are common to many small-scale societies and peoples that
make their living by hunting, but many of the marks of the shamanistic quest
have been left upon larger religions.

### The Narrative or Mythic Dimension

Often experience is channeled and expressed not only by ritual but also by sacred narrative or myth. This is the third dimension—the *mythic* or *narrative*. It is the story side of religion. It is typical of all faiths to hand down vital stories: some historical; some about that mysterious primordial time when the world was in its timeless dawn; some about things to come at the end of time; some about great heroes and saints; some about great founders, such as Moses, the Buddha, Jesus, and Muhammad; some about assaults by the Evil One; some parables and edifying tales; some about the adventures of the gods; and so on. These stories often are called myths. The term may be a bit misleading, for in the context of the modern study of religion there is no implication that a myth is false.

The seminal stories of a religion may be rooted in history or they may not.

The mythic dimension: a brahmin worshiping Krsna.

Stories of creation are before history, as are myths which indicate how death and suffering came into the world. Others are about historical events—for instance the life of the Prophet Muhammad, or the execution of Jesus, and the enlightenment of the Buddha. Historians have sometimes cast doubt on some aspects of these historical stories, but from the standpoint of the student of religion this question is secondary to the meaning and function of the myth; and to the believer, very often, these narratives *are* history.

This belief is strengthened by the fact that many faiths look upon certain documents, originally maybe based upon long oral traditions, as true scriptures. They are canonical or recognized by the relevant body of the faithful (the Church, the community, Brahmins and others in India, the Buddhist Sangha or Order). They are often treated as inspired directly by God or as records of the very words of the Founder. They have authority, and they contain many stories and myths which are taken to be divinely or otherwise guaranteed. But other documents and oral traditions may also be important—the lives of the saints, the chronicles of Ceylon as a Buddhist nation, the stories of famous holy men of Eastern Europe in the Hasidic tradition, traditions concerning the life of the Prophet (*hadīth*), and so forth. These stories may have lesser authority but they can still be inspiring to the followers.

Stories in religion are often tightly integrated into the ritual dimension. The Christian Mass or communion service, for instance, commemorates and presents the story of the Last Supper, when Jesus celebrated with his disciples his forthcoming fate, by which (according to Christians) he saved humankind and brought us back into harmony with the Divine Being. The Jewish Passover ceremonies commemorate and make real to us the events of the Exodus from Egypt, the sufferings of the people, and their relationship to the Lord who led them out of servitude in ancient Egypt. As Jews share the meal, so they retrace the story. Ritual and story are bound together.

### The Doctrinal and Philosophical Dimension

Underpinning the narrative dimension is the *doctrinal* dimension. Thus, in the Christian tradition, the story of Jesus' life and the ritual of the communion service led to attempts to provide an analysis of the nature of the Divine Being which would preserve both the idea of the Incarnation (Jesus as God) and the belief in one God. The result was the doctrine of the Trinity, which sees God as three persons in one substance. Similarly, with the meeting between early Christianity and the great Graeco-Roman philosophical and intellectual heritage it became necessary to face questions about the ultimate meaning of creation, the inner nature of God, the notion of grace, the analysis of how Christ could be both God and human being, and so on. These concerns led to the elaboration of Christian doctrine. In the case of Buddhism, to take another example, doctrinal ideas were more crucial right from the start, for the Buddha himself presented a philosophical vision of the world which itself was an aid to salvation.

In any event, doctrines come to play a significant part in all the major religions, partly because sooner or later a faith has to adapt to social reality and so to the fact that much of the leadership is well educated and seeks some kind of intellectual statement of the basis of the faith.

It happens that histories of religion have tended to exaggerate the importance of scriptures and doctrines; and this is not too surprising since so much of our knowledge of past religions must come from the documents which have been passed on by the scholarly elite. Also, and especially in the case of Christianity, doctrinal disputes have often been the overt expression of splits within the fabric of the community at large, so that frequently histories of a faith concentrate upon these hot issues. This is clearly unbalanced; but I would not want us to go to the other extreme. There are scholars today who have been much impressed with the symbolic and psychological force of myth, and have tended to neglect the essential intellectual component of religion.

The doctrinal dimension: the Buddha in his form as teacher.

### The Ethical and Legal Dimension

Both narrative and doctrine affect the values of a tradition by laying out the shape of a worldview and addressing the question of ultimate liberation or salvation. The law which a tradition or subtradition incorporates into its fabric can be called the *ethical* dimension of religion. In Buddhism for instance there are certain universally binding precepts, known as the five precepts or virtues, together with a set of further regulations controlling the lives of monks and nuns and monastic communities. In Judaism we have not merely the ten commandments but a complex of over six hundred rules imposed upon the community by the Divine Being. All this Law or Torah is a framework for living for the Orthodox Jew. It also is part of the ritual dimension, because, for instance, the injunction to keep the Sabbath as a day of rest is also the injunction to perform certain sacred practices and rituals, such as attending the synagogue and maintaining purity.

Similarly, Islamic life has traditionally been controlled by the Law or *Sharī'a*, which shapes society both as a religious and a political society, as well as the moral life of the individual—prescribing that he should pray daily, give alms to the poor, and so on, and that society should have various institutions, such as marriage, modes of banking, etc.

Other traditions can be less tied to a system of law, but still display an ethic which is influenced and indeed controlled by the myth and doctrine of the faith. For instance, the central ethical attitude in the Christian faith is love. This springs not just from Jesus' injunction to his followers to love God and their neighbors: it also flows from the story of Christ himself who gave his life out of love for his fellow human beings. It also is rooted in the very idea of the Trinity, for God from all eternity is a society of three persons, Father, Son and Holy Spirit, kept together by the bond of love. The Christian joins a community which reflects, it is hoped at any rate, the life of the Divine Being, both as Trinity and as suffering servant of the human race and indeed of all creation.

The ethical dimension: Zen monks exhibit discipline and the desire for orderly work as they set out to tidy the grounds of their monastery.

### The Social and Institutional Dimension

The dimensions outlined so far—the experiential, the ritual, the mythic, the doctrinal, and the ethical—can be considered in abstract terms, without being embodied in external form. The last two dimensions have to do with the incarnation of religion. First, every religious movement is embodied in a group of people, and that is very often rather formally organized—as Church, or Sangha, or *umma*. The sixth dimension therefore is what may be called the *social* or *institutional* aspect of religion. To understand a faith we need to see how it works among people. This is one reason why such an important tool of the investigator of religion is that subdiscipline which is known as the sociology of religion. Sometimes the social aspect of a worldview is simply identical with society itself, as in small-scale groups such as tribes. But there is a variety of relations between organized religions and society at large: a faith may be the official religion, or it may be just one denomination among many, or it may be somewhat cut off from social life, as a sect. Within the organization of one religion, moreover, there are many models—from the relative democratic governance of a radical Protestant congregation to the hierarchical and monarchical system of the Church of Rome.

It is not however the formal officials of a religion who may in the long run turn out to be the most important persons in a tradition. For there are charismatic or sacred personages, whose spiritual power glows through their demeanor and actions, and who vivify the faith of more ordinary folk—saintly people, gurus, mystics and prophets, whose words and example stir up the spiritual enthusiasm of the masses, and who lend depth and meaning to the rituals and values of a tradition. They can also be revolutionaries and set religion on new courses. They can, like John Wesley, become leaders of a new denomination, almost against their will; or they can be founders of new groups which may in due course emerge as separate religions—an example is Joseph Smith II, Prophet of the new faith of Mormonism. In short, the social dimension of religion includes not only the mass of persons but also the outstanding individuals through whose features glimmer old and new thoughts of the heaven towards which they aspire.

The social dimension: a Jewish family celebrating their first Passover since arriving in Israel.

19

## The Material Dimension

This social or institutional dimension of religion almost inevitably becomes incarnate in a different way, in *material* form, as buildings, works of art, and other creations. Some movements—such as Calvinist Christianity, especially in the time before the present century—eschew external symbols as being potentially idolatrous; their buildings are often beautiful in their simplicity, but their intention is to be without artistic or other images which might seduce people from the thought that God is a spirit who transcends all representations. However, the material expressions of religion are more often elaborate, moving, and highly important for believers in their approach to the divine. How indeed could we understand Eastern Orthodox Christianity without seeing what ikons are like and knowing that they are regarded as windows onto heaven? How could we get inside the feel of Hinduism without attending to the varied statues of God and the gods?

Also important material expressions of a religion are those natural features of the world which are singled out as being of special sacredness and meaning—the river Ganges, the Jordan, the sacred mountains of China, Mount Fuji in Japan, Eyre's Rock in Australia, the Mount of Olives, Mount

The material dimension: the holy city of Banaras. Note that the Hindu temples are overshadowed by a mosque built by Aurangzeb as a sign of the ultimate triumph of Islam.

20

Sinai, and so forth. Sometimes of course these sacred landmarks combine with more direct human creations, such as the holy city of Jerusalem, the sacred shrines of Banaras, or the temple at Bodh Gaya which commemorates the Buddha's Enlightenment.

*Uses of the Seven Dimensions*

To sum up: we have surveyed briefly the seven dimensions of religion which help to characterize religions as they exist in the world. The point of the list is so that we can give a balanced description of the movements which have animated the human spirit and taken a place in the shaping of society, without neglecting either ideas or practices.

Naturally, there are religious movements or manifestations where one or other of the dimensions is so weak as to be virtually absent: nonliterate small-scale societies do not have much means of expressing the doctrinal dimension; Buddhist modernists, concentrating on meditation, ethics and philosophy, pay scant regard to the narrative dimension of Buddhism; some newly formed groups may not have evolved anything much in the way of the material dimension. Also there are so many people who are not formally part of any social religious grouping, but have their own particular worldviews and practices, that we can observe in society atoms of religion which do not possess any well-formed social dimension. But of course in forming a phenomenon within society they reflect certain trends which in a sense form a shadow of the social dimension (just as those who have not yet got themselves a material dimension are nevertheless implicitly storing one up, for with success come buildings and with rituals ikons, most likely).

If our seven-dimensional portrait of religions is adequate, then we do not need to worry greatly about further definition of religion. In any case, I shall now turn to a most vital question in understanding the way the world works, namely to the relation between more or less overtly religious systems and those which are commonly called secular: ideologies or worldviews such as scientific humanism, Marxism, Existentialism, nationalism, and so on. In examining these worldviews we shall take on some of the discussion about what count as religious questions and themes. It is useful to begin by thinking out whether our seven-dimensional analysis can apply successfully to such secular worldviews.

# The Nature of Secular Worldviews

*Nationalism*

Although nationalism is not strictly speaking a single worldview or even in itself a complete worldview, it is convenient to begin with it. One reason is that it has been such a powerful force in human affairs. Virtually all the land surface of the globe, together with parts of the world's water surface, is now carved up between sovereign states. Nationalism has given shape decisively to the modern world, because its popularity in part stems from the way in

21

A Japanese naval officer indicates his nationalist dedication by wrapping his country's flag around his head before donning his helmet for combat.

which assembling peoples into states has helped with the processes of industrialization and modern bureaucratic organization. Countries such as Britain, France, the United States, Germany, and Italy pioneered the industrial revolution, and the system of national governments spread from Western to Eastern Europe after World War I and from Europe to Asia, Africa, and elsewhere after World War II. Ethnic identity was sometimes demarcated by language and therefore cultural heritage, sometimes by religion, sometimes both, and sometimes simply by shared history. Examples of each of these categories can be seen in the cases of Germany (shared language), the two parts of Ireland (distinctive religion), Poland (both distinctive language and religion), and Singapore (shared history of Chinese, Malay, and other linguistic groups). Colonialism often helped to spread nationalism by reaction: the British conquest of India fostered an Indian nationalism, and there are signs of national awakening in parts of the Soviet Union, once colonized by Tsarist Russia, and in Tibet, conquered by China.

The nation-state has many of the appurtenances of a religion. First of all (to use the order in which we expounded the dimensions of religion in the previous section), there are the *rituals* of nationhood: speaking the language itself; the national anthem; the flying and perhaps saluting of the flag; republic and memorial days, and other such festivals and holidays; the appearance of the Head of State at solemn occasions; military march-pasts; and so on. It is usual for citizens to make secular pilgrimages to the nation's capital and other significant spots — Washington (the Lincoln Memorial, the Vietnam Memorial, the White House, and so on); Plymouth Rock; Mount Rushmore; natural beauties exhibiting "America the Beautiful." Memorials to the nation's dead are of special significance, and often religious language is used about the sacrifices of the young on the altar of national duty.

The experiential or *emotional* side of nationalism is indeed powerful — for the sentiments of patriotism, pride in the nation, love of its beauties and powers, and dedication to national goals, can be very strong. Especially in times of national crisis, such as war, such sentiments rise to the surface. But they are reinforced all the time by such practices as singing the national anthem and other patriotic songs.

The *narrative* dimension of nationalism is easily seen, for it lies in the history of the nation, which is taught in the schools of the country, and which in some degree celebrates the values of the great men and women of the nation — for Italians, such great forebears as Julius Caesar (Giulio Cesare), Dante, Galileo, Leonardo, Garibaldi, Cavour, Verdi, Leopardi, Alcide de Gasperi and others. History is the narrative that helps to create in the young and in citizens at large a sense of identity, of belonging, of group solidarity.

Of *doctrines* nationalism is somewhat bereft, unless you count the doctrine of self-determination. But often, too, nations appeal to principles animating the modern state, such as the need for democracy and the rights of the individual in a freedom-loving nation, etc.; or a nation may appeal to the doctrine of a full-blown secular ideology, such as Marxism. Or it may hark back to the teachings of its ancestral religion, and so represent itself as guarding the truths and values of Christianity, or of Buddhism, or of a revived and revolutionary Islam.

The *ethical* dimension of nationalism consists in those values which are inculcated into citizens. Young people are expected to be loyal people, taxpayers, willing to fight if necessary for the country, law-abiding, and hopefully good family people (supplying thus the nation with its population). There is of course a blend between ethical values in general and the particular obligations to one's own kith and kin, one's fellow-nationals.

The *social* and *institutional* aspect of the nation-state is of course easily discerned. It culminates in a head of state who has extensive ceremonial functions — especially with monarchy, as in Britain, where the Queen is an important ritual object — and on whom sentiments of patriotism also focus. The state has its military services which also perform ceremonial as well as fighting tasks. There are the public schools, with the teachers imparting the treasured knowledge and rules of the nation. Even games come to play an institutional role; loyalty is expressed through Olympics and various other contests, and the ethos of the athlete comes to be blended with that of the ideal citizen. In some countries loyalty to religion or to a secular ideology blends with loyalty to one's nation, and those who do not subscribe to it are treated as disloyal. State occasions are shown on television, which itself comes to have a role in transmitting and focusing the values of the nation.

Finally, there is of course much *material* embodiment of the nation in its great buildings and memorials, its flag, its great art, its sacred land, its powerful military hardware.

In all these ways, then, the nation today is like a religion. If you have a relative who has died for a cause, it is not like the old days when he might have died for his religion, maybe at the stake; now he is most likely to have died for his country.

It is, then, reasonable to treat modern nationalism in the same terms as religion. It represents a set of values often allied with a kind of modernism, which is natural to the thinking of many of our contemporaries, and which stresses certain essentially modern concerns: the importance of economic development; the merits of technology; the wonders of science; the importance of either socialism or capitalism, or some mixture, in the process of modernization; the need for the state to look after the welfare of its citizens; the importance of universal education; and so on.

There are some growing limitations on nationalism: the fact that in many countries which were once reasonably homogeneous there are now increasing ethnic mixes, the growth of transnational corporations, the developing economic interdependence of nations, the impossibility of older ways of conceiving sovereignty in the context of modern warfare, and so on. But nevertheless, nationalism remains a very strong and alluring ingredient in the world, and many of the trouble spots are so because of unfulfilled ethnic expectations and ethnic rivalries—in Cyprus, Northern Ireland, Israel and Palestine, South Africa, Sri Lanka, Kurdistan, Afghanistan, and elsewhere.

*The Dimensions of Marxism*
It is because Marxism has itself become more than a movement of ideas but has become embodied in many states that its analysis too needs to follow the general outlines I have sketched. It has a coherent set of *doctrines*, modified variously by leaders such as Stalin, Mao, Hoxha and Ceauşescu; it has a *mythic* dimension in the analysis of historical events in accordance with the principles of the dialectic (so that then the history of the Russian Revolution or the German Democratic Republic gets fitted into a more general salvation-history of the human race). Its *rituals* combine with those of nationalism but have their own symbolisms, such as the widespread use of the color red, the adoption of festivals such as May Day and the anniversary of the October Revolution, the adulation of the Party leader, etc. The *emotions* it encourages are those of patriotism, internationalism, and revolutionary commitment; its

*ethics* those of solidarity; its *institutions* those of the Party; and its *artistic* style is that of socialist realism, which glorifies the ideals of the Party, state, and country, with more than a hint of that pietism which can characterize religious painting. Its music is heroic and rousing. State Marxism, then, has a distinctly religious-type function, and moves men by theory, symbols, rituals, and Party energy. Like many religions it may not ultimately prove to be successful, for the people may not be inwardly and deeply moved by the embodied values of Marxism as an ideology: indeed much evidence shows the hollowness of Marxism in a number of Eastern European countries, and even in the Soviet Union. It is always faced with the struggle against local patriotisms, against religions, against the humanist desire for freedom of enquiry, and so on.

Some other secular worldviews are less clearly like traditional religions in so far as they tend not to wield the symbols of power: for instance, scientific humanism, which is influential in one form or another among many intellectuals in the West, and which in rather inarticulate form expresses something of the worldview of ordinary folk in secularized circumstances. It holds to human and democratic values, and it stresses science as the source of knowledge. It repudiates the doctrines of religion, especially of Jewish and Christian theism. It sees human individuals as of ultimate value. But it does not, as I have said, embody itself in a rich way as a religious-type system. Its *rituals* are slight, beyond those which reinforce other aspects of modernity. Perhaps the modern passion for games and sports is one sign of a kind of persistence of interest in activities pursued according to ritual rules. Its *myths* are not extensive, beyond a feel for the clash between science and religion during the modern period from Galileo Galilei (1564–1642) onwards. Its *doctrines* can be complex, especially in the formulations of contemporary humanistic (analytical and linguistic) philosophy. Its profoundest *experiences* are maybe those of culture, such as music and the arts. Its *ethics* are generally speaking those of utilitarianism, which sees morality as maximizing happiness and minimizing suffering. Its *institutions* are found in secular education. Its *material* symbols are perhaps the sky-scraper and the stadium. But it is hard to disentangle its manifestations from many other aspects of modern living.

Though to a greater or lesser extent our seven-dimensional model may apply to secular worldviews, it is not really appropriate to try to call them religions, or even "quasi-religions" (which by implication demotes them below the status of "real" religions). For the adherents of Marxism and humanism wish to be demarcated strictly from those who espouse religions— they conceive of themselves, on the whole, as antireligious. However, we have seen enough of the seven-dimensional character of the secular worldviews (especially nationalism and state Marxism) to emphasize that the various systems of ideas and practices, whether religious or not, are competitors and mutual blenders, and can thus be said to play in the same league. They all help to express the various ways in which human beings conceive of themselves, and act in the world.

## Roots, Formation, and Reformation

We are here concerned with the history of the worldviews of the world. It has been conventional to look at the founders and first scriptures as being the points of origin of the faiths: as though Judaism had sprung in all its complexity from the mouth of Moses, and as if Hinduism were all there in the Vedas; and as if Christianity had been fully sketched out, so to speak, in the mind of Christ. While it remains most important to evaluate founders and early scriptures, we also need to be sensitive to the ways in which religious traditions evolve and form. It does not take long to reflect that some vital features of Hinduism, for instance, are absent from the early Vedic writings, even from the great texts known as the Upanishads: for instance the whole complex of temple religion, the cult of images, pilgrimages, and so on. It may be that materials for the construction of the Trinity doctrine or the Eastern Orthodox liturgy are to be found in the New Testament, but formally speaking that doctrine and that liturgy are not there. In short, religions may be rooted in their early texts, but they do not form and develop simply on a scriptural basis. There may indeed be a later development—such as the Reformation in Christianity—that demands a return to absolute origins and seeks to base everything on scripture; but even here modern elements, undreamed of by Jesus' disciples or by Paul, are blended into the new and reformed patterns of religion.

We may be the more aware of this because of the way in which contemporary traditions, whether East or West or North or South, reflect attempts to deal with the revolutionary changes which have overcome the world—the rise of science, the emergence of nationalisms, Western-style imperialism and colonialism, the interplay of cultures. These events have led necessarily to changes in worldviews. To some extent nearly all of the religions of the world, except in the remotest spots, have undergone Western and modern influences. And so, even if the modern Western-educated Hindu, for instance, may draw upon ancient motifs and old philosophies, and quote texts of three thousand years ago, she will cast her exposition of the faith in forms which owe much to the seminal period of nineteenth- and twentieth-century thought and struggle. She will be influenced by Vivekananda (1862–1902) and Radhakrishnan (1888–1975), not to mention Mahatma Gandhi (1869–1948) (see Chapter 16).

Because of the evolving and changing character of the traditions and subtraditions of the world, I shall not oversimplify by treating religions as if there were a neat origin for each. Of course, there are some, such as Islam or Mormonism, where the founding Prophet and his period are of immense, even overwhelming, importance. But generally we may distinguish between the period or periods of *roots* and those of *formation*. Thus early classical Christianity of course had its roots in the New Testament and the theology of Paul. But it is not until the fourth century C.E. that its formation is (roughly speaking) completed, with the formulation of crucial doctrines, such as that of the Trinity, the full elaboration of the communion or liturgy, the creation of a complex priestly hierarchy, the beginnings of mysticism and the monastic impulse, the new ethos of being both a good Christian and a good citizen, the emergence of Eastern and Western forms based on linguistic and political differences.

Judaism had a similar period of formation, which culminated in the period of the Diaspora or dispersion of the people after the destruction of the Temple in 70 C.E. The classical features of rabbinic scholarship, synagogue worship, conception of the oral Torah, the study of the Temple rituals as a substitute for conducting them, dispersal of the community, belief in an afterlife, and so forth, had their antecedents before this period; but it was really not until the emergence of Christianity and the perceived need to regroup after the disaster of 70 C.E. and persecutions in the Empire that Judaism finally pulled together in a form recognizable still to us today. Then there was a second great period of formation, that of modern Judaism in its disjunct modes, as Orthodox, Reform, and Conservative (with other variations too), during the nineteenth century after the thrill and trauma of emancipation.

Of course, religions reflect on their own history, and it is natural to project supposed origins back onto roots. The oral Torah is ascribed to the time of Moses; the doctrines and rites of classical Christianity are seen in the New Testament. By contrast, modern scholarship tends to tug at these projections and cause them to disintegrate: and this is a potent source of tension between piety and scholarship. In so far as this book is a modern history, it has to be somewhat sceptical of some pious beliefs; but in thinking of a tradition as having a "root" period and a period of classical formation, as well as other times of major reformation, we may seek to avoid unnecessary conflicts.

In some degree traditions have to change in order to stay the same. This is paradoxical; but if you stay frozen in the customs and interpretations of a given period, then changed circumstances will make you look old-fashioned, when that was not your original intention. Riding buggies, like the Amish of Pennsylvania, means something quite different in an age before there are cars from what it means when there are actually automobiles to reject. So it is natural enough that, although some aspects of a tradition may indeed be traditional (like the mitres worn by Catholic bishops), not all of them can be ancient, for the tradition will have had to adapt in some degree in order to continue to be intelligible and meaningful.

There is also some variation in the time of the "watershed" which has altered the face of religious history. For the West it was the period of the Reformation and its scientific and artistic aftermath. For Judaism it was the period of emancipation, namely the first part of the nineteenth century. For the Hindu and Buddhist traditions it was the nineteenth century, with European penetration into the relevant cultures of Asia. For African religions it was likewise the nineteenth century, but a bit later. For the Native American religions of North and South America, it was essentially earlier, with the vast shock, especially, of the Spanish and Portuguese conquests in the sixteenth and seventeenth centuries. Basically, the countries of the world (and I have not here listed all regions or religions) came to be deeply affected by the expansion of Europe, and the subsequent spread of various political and scientific ideas, jointly with the spread of missionary Christianity. Of course there had been other shocks and watersheds: the Muslim conquest of much of India had, of course, affected Islam before the British Raj. Islamic forces also transformed parts of Africa before the European "scramble for Africa." The Mongol conquests of Genghis Khan and his successors had been a shock, from China to Europe. But nothing ultimately has matched the effects of European conquest, for it introduced a whole variety of challenges across the world and spread ideas as heady as democracy, liberation, modernity, and the need for higher education in the Western mode. It was impossible that religious and other worldviews could be unaffected. It is out of the turbulences born of these conquests and of the two great wars of the twentieth century that the contemporary world has been created.

## Patterns of the Present

Still vitally important and in many ways dominant is the civilization of the West. The countries of Scandinavia and Western Europe are all democratic and capitalist, though with socialist admixtures; and the same can be said of North America and Australasia. These countries have been deeply affected by Christianity and most of all by varieties of Protestantism, from the state-supported types like Lutheranism and Anglicanism to the radical kinds like Anabaptism and the Quaker tradition. But also vital in this bloc is the intellectual rejection of religion among scientific humanists, and in many countries the alienation of the working classes from religion. So we cannot simply call this Western bloc of countries Christian. (In any case there are minority faiths, from Jews to Hindus.) But it has had the imprint of Europe's major faith. We can call it the "Transchristian West," meaning that it contains and yet also transcends Christian values. As mother of so much in modern culture and knowledge it remains powerful, despite the end of the colonial period in which so many Western countries carved empires for themselves in Asia, Africa, America, and the Pacific (see Map 12, p. 338). The first then of our cultural blocs is what I have called the *Transchristian West*.

Another region which overlaps greatly with it in religious and political attitudes is the *Latin South*—namely Latin America from Mexico to the Argentine, and partly embracing the Caribbean. Though it is Catholic like Southern Europe, it has not had quite the same experiences, for it was born of the synthesis between Iberian and indigenous cultures, and underwent the colonial period. It thus has a different attitude towards capitalist democracy, and is often suspicious of its Northern manifestations.

Another region which has strong links to the Transchristian West is Eastern Europe and the Soviet Union. However, these countries are being formed into a Marxist civilization, together with others such as China, North

Korea, Vietnam, Laos, and Cambodia (and one or two outriders like Cuba). Religions are heavily controlled or suppressed, and Marxisms become the official worldviews of the various regimes. This *Marxist Bloc* is of great strength, but also shows moments of hesitation, and it is uncertain whether relaxations of control will restore religions to anything like their former cultural potency.

In South and Southeast Asia various countries have been able to maintain important parts of their traditions and to incorporate some elements too of modern capitalism and democracy—countries such as India, Nepal, Burma, Sri Lanka, Thailand. They may have Muslim minorities (very large in the case of India), but they are predominantly non-Muslim in character, maintaining the traditional religions of *Old South Asia*.

To the East is another area where indigenous traditions have maintained themselves, though with infusions of Western ideas and practices. Here we have Japan, South Korea, Taiwan, Hong Kong, and Singapore. They maintain in some degree the three religions of the old China, with that special evolution which is Japanese religion, including indigenous Shinto. They have in recent times had a spectacular economic success. We shall call this bloc *Old East Asia*.

Slicing through the South Asian region is that vast crescent which constitutes the Islamic cultures of the world: Indonesia, Malaysia, Bangladesh, Pakistan, Afghanistan, Iran, Iraq, and so on through the Arab countries to secular (but historically Islamic) Turkey and to the countries of West Africa as far as northern Nigeria. This region contains many smaller countries, and outside it there are further important Islamic populations. We can call it the *Islamic Crescent*.

East of it are the Pacific islands, from huge New Guinea to the Melanesian, Micronesian, and Polynesian groups. Very scattered and not heavily populated, they nevertheless constitute an alternative style. They are in many ways allied to other small-scale societies in the Philippines, Australia (the Aboriginals), North America (Native Americans), and elsewhere. We may refer to these as *Small-Scalers*; and they overlap into all regions of the world. They are important from various points of view, and we may sometimes have to draw attention to their plight amid the large-scale and often cruel forces of the modern world.

Finally, there are the multitudinous variations of Black culture in Africa south of the Sahara (roughly speaking). Here we have complex and differing kinds of classical African religions often in deep interplay with kinds of missionary religions, resulting in a whole flock of new religious movements and forms of independent Churches. This region we can call *Black Africa* (though it also contains that troublesome component, South Africa, with its potent white minority).

These regions—the Transchristian West, the Marxist Bloc, the Latin South, Old South Asia, Old East Asia, the Islamic Crescent, the Small-Scalers, and Black Africa—together constitute our world. They are woven together by modern communications and are coalescing into a single global economy. It is from this postcolonial perspective that we conceive the present and the past. But in now trying to see the way human spiritual and material history was before our time, we have to shake our heads and rid them of the knowledge we now have: for the civilizations as they grew did so in relative isolation, and they had no advance insight into how human history was to turn out. As the children of Israel entered the Promised Land they could foresee neither Pilate nor Yasser Arafat; and as artisans produced wondrous figures in the cities of the Indus Valley, they could not foresee the *Gītā* or Gandhi.

So now, in the first part of this book, we turn to plumb the depths of the past. We begin, speculatively, before history began. From the things which have been left to us from beyond the historical record—bones, red ocher, flint arrowheads, teeth, jawbones, skulls, fragmented animal skeletons, urns, ashes, and painted caves—we try to piece together societies and human beings whom we can but dimly imagine, and try to understand something of their philosophies and spiritual outlooks. From the jawbone to the feeling of awe there is a long, long jump.

PART

# Earliest Religion

## The Problem of Origins

It is most likely that the first humans came from Africa. Once that continent, together with Europe, was covered with forests. As it thinned out, and the trees were interspersed with grasslands and swamps, so its game became most plentiful; and in this favorable milieu there emerged hominids who became progressively closer to modern humans. There was *Homo habilis*, the tool-user, and *Homo erectus*, the upright type, walking like us on two feet; and then, perhaps 250,000 years ago, *Homo sapiens*, the knowledgeable one. Later we discover Neanderthal humans, of the same or parallel stock, with thick limbs and heavy bones. Their name, drawn from a valley in West Germany where the first remains were found, is sometimes associated with beetle-browed thugs, in the modern caricature; but they were bright people who, like other modern humans, gained their advantage through social cooperation, of which language is a key factor. And there is evidence—from red ocher used in staining bones, which has survived in some Neanderthal burial grounds—that they may have believed in some kind of survival after death. Even before this, in the deep reaches of the prehistory of *Homo erectus*, there are telltale signs of beliefs about the afterlife.

Naturally, as we push back our knowledge further into human prehistory, we speculate about the lives of these our predecessors; and so ultimately we speculate about the origin of human religion. But thoughts are hard to infer from bones, or feelings from chiseled flint, or wishes from fragments of animal skeletons partly touched by fire. Some scholars have wished to infer beginnings from the religions of hunter-gatherers today, like the Australian aboriginals or the Tierra del Fuegans. Yet such a move is risky, for every

*Opposite* Cave painting from Lascaux, France, c. 16,000–14,000 B.C.E.

people extant today has lived over many, many centuries and has necessarily undergone change. Once, too, such a move was likely to be part of a racist ideology that treated hunter-gatherers as essentially "primitive." There used to be a vogue for thinking that there was something called "primitive religion," and such a view implied that the contemporary aboriginal was at some kind of arrested stage of evolutionary development. This was a convenient ideology for those who came into their regions to deprive them of their lands.

Of course, we can learn something from hunting and gathering societies. If early humans lived in the same way, we can obviously hear the echoes reverberating into prehistory. Basically, however, early humans and ourselves are just alike in basic character and intelligence: where we differ is only in cultural style, and in the greater organizational complexity of the world today. Further, modern hunting and gathering societies are in some respects diverse, so we should bear in mind that the pursuit of something called "prehistoric religion" in the singular is no doubt misconceived. There must have been very divergent patterns of ritual and belief through the varied cultures that were developing after 30,000 B.C.E. in Siberia, Australia, Africa, Europe, and, a little later, in the Americas. In some of them, ranging in time and space from southwest France and northern Spain to the Urals and southern Africa, and from 20,000 B.C.E. to relatively modern times, there is a brilliant display of rock and cave paintings. Amber bison, black and white cows, horses, crows, and eagles vibrate off ancient surfaces, and so sometimes

One of the famous cave paintings of a wild animal, in this case a horse, from Ariège in France, from about 12,000 B.C.E.

do the figures and arrows of the hunters. These pictures are mysterious to interpret, and sometimes they are buried in deep recesses of the ground, like painted wombs in mother earth. Old wicker lamps dimly lit these wondrous exhibitions of the mimic skill of ancient humans. But we possess no records and can only guess at the ideas and rituals that underpinned these great artistic endeavors.

So it is that questions about the origin of religion are guesswork. It is no longer fashionable to create such theories at all, but in late Victorian times it was all the rage. Thus Sir James Frazer (1854–1941), famous author of *The Golden Bough*, saw a certain evolution of ideas, beginning with the use of magic, which used sacred formulae to try to coerce and bend the operations of nature, and leading on to religion proper, which sought to propitiate unseen forces rather than compel them. In his view these ways of dealing with the world were replaced in modern times by science, which is the most rational and effective way of harnessing the powers of Nature. Edward Tylor (1832–1917), an early anthropologist, saw primitive religion as consisting entirely in a belief in, and practice towards, unseen spirits: such religion he dubbed "animism" (a term which most scholars nowadays reject, but which is still used popularly and in censuses to refer to classical or indigenous religions in small-scale societies). Another anthropologist, R. R. Marett (1866–1943) proposed the idea of "preanimism" or "dynamism" as even more basic and early, in which nature is seen as pervaded by nonpersonal forces, to which humans can relate through various rites. Often these powers were referred to by using the Melanesian term *mana*, a kind of sacred power inhering in anything unusual—in a strange rock, a peculiar mountain, an unusual human, a chief, a beautiful woman, a ferocious bear, or whatever. It was theorized that religion first started with belief in *mana*, then progressed to belief in more personal spirits, then moved into polytheism, where the gods are even more fully personalized, and then into monotheism and (this extra option depended on the ideology of the theorist) atheism.

Such evolutionary schemes can be challenged. Wilhelm Schmidt (1868–1954), a Catholic priest and anthropologist, detected widespread belief in a High God existing "behind" or "above" the many gods, spirits, and powers of many small-scale societies. He thought that this indicated a substratum of theism—belief in a personal God—which derived from a primordial revelation and was subsequently overlain by belief in many spirits and gods. He wished to save the traditional idea of a revelation at the beginning of human history, reflecting the account in *Genesis* of God's dealings with the first humans.

There may be some truth in such ideas, but hardly anyone now would subscribe to any one of these accounts; nor would we adhere in any literal fashion to the account given by Sigmund Freud (1856–1939) in his *Totem and Taboo*, which made too much of totemism, that is, the belief in and practice of a sacramental relationship with some animal species or other entities on the part of diverse segments of a group. It is not anywhere near universal in small-scale religion as was once thought. Freud's account was based on his psychoanalytic theory, drawing on the dynamics of the nuclear family in modern Vienna.

## The Patterns of Prehistoric Life

If we are to speculate about motifs in prehistoric religion, we need to think about the differing ingredients in the life of the hunters and gatherers of Stone Age times and earlier. Such ingredients are: the need for group activity in hunting the larger and more agile animals, and in fishing; the discovery and use of fire, going back to the epoch of *Homo erectus*; the importance of stories in the cultural life of any group, with (moreover) quite a lot of leisure to while away in the periods between big chases; reflection on the inner life—the role of dreams and visions, and possibly early forms of meditation and yoga; the wondrous sky and its rhythmic relations to earthly cycles, e.g. the menstrual; the feeling that humans, who can talk and hunt so well, are a special breed apart from the animals with whom they live; the vital role of ritual and etiquette in interpersonal relations; the magic of representation and the success in painting and sculpture, where this occurred; the great human dependence on nature, and on the animals and plants in particular; the mysteries of birth and fecundity, both in human beings and elsewhere; the reality of sickness and concern with maintaining health; the universal character of death; storms and violence in the sky and environment; and the beginning powers of music.

### The Dimensions of Prehistoric Religion

From reflection on the above motifs, and from archaeological discoveries, it is possible to hazard some guesses about early humans' religious life. Let us begin with the *ritual* dimension. The first thing to consider is that religious ritual and ceremonious behavior is continuous with the kind of stylized actions and words which we use in treating each other as persons. Human language is replete with performance utterances, to use a word coined by the philosopher John Austin (1911–60): that is, by uses of language which perform or do things—such as cursing, promising, thanking, pleading, or saluting—rather than simply inform. Every fully fledged performative utterance has, in the broad sense of the term, a ritual aspect. It is thus when people say to each other "Good morning." Such a greeting is a little ceremony in which two persons acknowledge each other's presence at the beginning of a new day, and take up their relationship from previous days.

Early humans, making use of language and bodily gestures, were aware of how the coherence of each group was vital to its survival, since the human ability to deal with more powerful animals, for instance the bear, stems from cooperative effort. It is not unreasonable for humans to think of ceremonious behavior, so effective in keeping groups together and shaping their strategies of hunting and gathering, as effective beyond the group, in relationship to animals, natural forces and broadly the whole universe which lies unfolded before the human being. It is thus likely that rituals addressed to these entities formed part of the fabric of the life of early humans from the times of *Homo erectus* onwards, but especially among the Neanderthal strain and its relation, our own direct ancestor *Homo sapiens sapiens*.

We have evidence of this in remains of burials and in the cult of skulls and in the mysterious paintings in caves such as Lascaux in France and Altamira in Spain. In a cave in eastern Switzerland are various caves, including one with bear skulls in niches in the wall. It seems hard to explain this except in terms of some rituals directed towards the bear. Some have seen the paintings as having to do with hunting magic; and the brilliant depictions of bison and other beasts, both here and on bone decorations, suggest a connection with these people's source of food. And yet the inaccessibility of some of the caves, the discovery of beautifully made lamps, and the painting or engraving of various abstract signs, suggest something more.

Since it was not until much later in human cultural history that a purely nonpersonal idea of causation came to be established, it is quite probable that in speculating about their surroundings early humans thought of changes as brought about by personal causation of some kind. Early humans could not have known much about the past, save what was handed on in each group. Their cosmology had to proceed outwards from their own experience. It was thus reasonable for them to try to establish potent relations with various forces through ritual means.

Some of the burial rites suggest too a kind of ceremonial to somehow ensure safe passage to the next world: the bones of the Neanderthal dead, smeared with red ocher, may have reflected some ritual reintroduction of blood to symbolize revived flesh. There are hints of concern with human survival in the bones of *Homo erectus* at Choukout'ien outside Peking (Beijing). At Le Moustier in the Dordogne in France, a young Neanderthal man was buried, on his right side, with his head pillowed with flat stones; and by his body were charred animal bones and a hand axe. All this suggests some belief in life beyond death. But at any rate, here is evidence of ritual behavior concerned with reverence for and no doubt love for the dead.

An animal from the Vogelherd Cave in Germany, maybe indicating some form of magic associated with hunting and dating possibly from around 26,000 B.C.E.

The celebrated dancing sorcerer (if that is what it is) or shaman figure from Les Trois Frères Cave, Ariège, in France.

Another factor about which we may speculate is symbolic thinking. A symbol is something which stands for or represents something else. Among instances of symbolic thinking the most obvious and powerful is when one member of a species or kind is taken to stand for the whole. It suggests a shadowy but real collective being or spirit lying behind and pervading all members of that species or kind. The one bison stands for the collective; and by extension the image stands for what it is an image of. Such an attitude is echoed in modern times by what philosophers call "realism" as opposed to "nominalism" (nominalism being the idea that all that holds together individuals of the same kind is the common name; realism being the theory, stemming from Plato, that the individuals share the same "real" universal).

Such a conception allows people to think of their symbolic rituals as causing them to participate in the power inherent in the being towards whom their sacrifice or communion is directed. It may even be that the marvelous art of Altamira, Lascaux, and elsewhere was itself seen as a kind of offering to the sacred forces inherent in the herds of bison and in the other animal species represented.

There is a famous picture (left) in the cave at Les Trois Frères in France of a figure dressed, so it seems, in animal skins and antlers, who may represent a great sorcerer and possibly a shaman—that is a religious specialist who has great powers derived from ecstatic experiences in which he or she has contact with sacred forces. At Star Carr in England, by a lake, there has been found an antlered skull with holes drilled in it suggesting it was worn as a headdress. This is reminiscent of some forms of headdress worn by modern shamans in Siberia and elsewhere. To this question of shamanism in prehistory I shall return. Let us turn briefly to speculate about the worldviews held by ancient humans.

The hunter and gatherer has a lot of leisure, especially when resources are plentiful. It is not like the long drudgery of much of agricultural life, still less like the clocked-in hours of industrial humanity. With the invention of techniques for preserving and kindling fire, humans had a natural focus of warmth and sociability; it is thus inevitable that the telling of stories should occupy much of their time. Narrative has a powerful grip on the human imagination, and is a way of imagining the past, bringing to the forefront of imagination some selected contents of the past and explaining how things too in nature came to be. Again, it is reasonable to think that prehistoric thinking proceeded from the microcosm to the macrocosm, from the human situation to the delineation of the whole environment. Together with the notions to which we have already alluded—that personal causation works in nature as well as in human events, and that similar things are animated by the same substance—the preference for the story form will have generated a whole range of myths: how sky and earth perform together; the way the moon waxes and wanes, and how woman reflects this moonishness; how the spirit of the bison or the fox was created; how humans can turn into animals, and one species into another; the cause of the mountains over there; how the sea was formed; how a spirit below the sea brings the sole to multiply. The concern with fertility, and the analogy of the earth as a woman, no doubt grew in importance as settled agriculture developed in such regions as north China, Thailand, the Indus Valley, Mesopotamia, and Egypt.

The story form, laced with symbols, could be well integrated into the rituals whereby early humans celebrated and coaxed the powers about them. Underlying the stories however there could be speculative answers to questions of creation, and such thinking is reflected in some of humankind's early texts. There could be a Spirit who produced an egg, out of which other beings could come. Or it might be that the thought that the First Being needed an Other led to the evolution of the world. Or maybe the world was produced by a number of beings (but whence did they come, and whence came the one Spirit?—there were unanswerable riddles about ultimate origins). Or perhaps there was always something there, like water, which needed stirring up before the world could condense or form.

There were questions about pain and suffering, no doubt, too. How did these come to us? Where did Death come from? Perhaps it was because of some primeval alienation between humans and the Spirit. It was easy to think that humans had become distanced from their world, for they (we) were thinking about other beings, and *they* showed no signs of fully comprehending the future and the nature of death. But we humans faced that terror.

Was death, moreover, the end? This was another question which might rate as an expression of early humankind's *doctrinal* dimension. We have seen hints in practice of belief in some future life. There were rituals to send off the dead, and maybe for revering the ancestors. If so, early humans must have also been wondering about the other life: was it hunting in some other realm, or perchance rebirth in animal or human or spiritual form? And there may have been the beginnings of epistemology: reflection about how to know things, with a reliance on vivid dreams and bright visions induced in quests and dancing, and in self-control. It may have been that the visions of the shaman prepared the way for the later refined forms of yoga. Men and women noticed their own powers, and saw that with language they could think in ways that were locked away even from the divine and clever bear.

The hints of shamanism may tell us something of the *experience* of prehistoric humans. The special people who had strong visions and dreams would also have affinity with some animal kind or other—with the bison, the serpent, the crow, the tiger: and they would have special knowledge of which direction to go in the hunt. And they would, too, have knowledge of the cure of souls and bodies. In their visionary episodes they would skim into the lower world where dead people went, and would rescue the sick person by undergoing his pain and travail. This would rest on the perception that mind and body are intertwined, and rock and spirit, and tree and god. The spirit could be seen as the essence of the human or animal: but so also could bones. The shaman's fate was to have his bones de-fleshed (like the dead) and to be put back together again.

We may also accept that the feeling of awe before powerful sacred forces—the numinous experience—will have occurred, as described in the classic account of Rudolf Otto (1869–1937). This may have contributed to self-consciousness, human beings feeling themselves apart from the world around them; as they stalked zebra through the savannah, or plotted together the next hunt of the elephant, or lazily stirred by the side of the fire at the memory of how they had fared as a group. They would have felt terror and awe at the fierce thunderstorms round Mount Kilimanjaro or among the foothills of the Alps; and they would have cowered at great hailstorms. They would have felt, though, their own solidarity, and the beginnings too of affinity with other human groups. And so in self-consciousness they would have wondered at the Creation. Some of them, no doubt, would have conceived of the world as a whole, and made a myth about its origin: partly because having knowledge of origins is a way of having power over that whose origins you know.

About the *ethical* dimension we know scarcely anything. There are signs of human violence in some remains, and no doubt warfare between groups was not infrequent, though the landscapes were vast and human populations probably rather scattered and small. With the beginning of large settlements and cities, which depended on food surpluses and agriculture, wider systems of *social* political organization were required. Already such developments are starting to merge into history, in Egypt, Mesopotamia, the Indus Valley, northern China, and so on.

We can only guess at the nature of the ethical and institutional dimensions of the many societies which constituted early humankind; but we can see that some of the influential early theories were both right and wrong. They were wrong in imposing too orderly an evolutionary sequence upon events, and certainly wrong to think that so-called "primitives" were in basic constitution less developed than ourselves. They were wrong to neglect ways in which so-called "primitive" thought can be found among moderns. They often generalized too much, finding (for instance) totemism everywhere. There were probably here and there the various elements held at one time or another to be characteristic of early religion, but blended together into untidy wholes. Thus, it is plausible to think that prehistoric men and women in some groups combined the ideas of monotheism, belief in a High God, with ideas of many more or less personalized powers (polytheism and animism) and with notions of sacred forces with less personal attributes (dynamism). They may have believed in a life after death, and they may have begun to practice self-control in the transition to a form of primeval yoga.

What is sure is that in their engraved bones and cave paintings some very ancient groups produced some of the most splendid kinds of art. The *material* dimension of their life, in so far as it has come down to us, is spectacular. This is a further good indication that it is unwise to think that they were essentially different from ourselves.

They also pioneered the marks and signs which are the precursors of

A head from Jericho made from a real skull, plaster and shell, possibly indicating belief in the continued life of the individual.

writing. Some of these may record the phases of the moon, and others may have had some use in rituals addressed to ancestors. It would not be surprising if they had a relatively sophisticated knowledge of the behavior of the heavenly bodies. If there is an evolution in human beings it is a cumulative cultural advance, as the tentacles of language spread ever wider, and a gallery of concepts is built up with which to understand and manipulate our world.

There are other aspects of prehistory which I shall not touch on here—for instance the Megalithic culture of northern Europe and the enigmatic remains of the Indus Valley culture. I shall leave this urban and stone-building prehistory to be developed on a regional basis. This in itself will help to dispel the illusion of a single prehistory, to which it is easy to fall prey in the absence of much information to guide us in judging the spiritual life of early human beings.

We need also to remember that we are talking about very long periods—perhaps over two million years ago for the emergence of *Homo erectus*. Caves could be occupied and worked on for one or two millennia. In the evolutionary "rise" to *Homo habilis*, and through *Homo erectus* to *Homo sapiens*, and through Neanderthal humanity to ourselves, we have already the proliferation of cultures which characterizes later human civilizations. But there can be no doubt that human beings through all these developments had an awareness of that unseen world which they have in diverse ways striven to understand. They perceived their affinity with the animals, and yet were conscious of their distance from them too. If they could feel communion with the bear or stag whose flesh they ate, they also knew how to manipulate life somewhat, and to begin their long march towards the technological mastery of nature, including—in aspiration, at least—their own nature. But similar hatreds and loves, and a like sense of identity in a group, no doubt animated them as us; and we have become much more dangerous than they.

41

# South Asia

## India's Diversity

India is often referred to as a subcontinent. Its area is fairly well defined, because it resulted from the drift of part of the old continent of Gondwanaland northwards, where it slowly but inexorably collided with the southern part of what was then Asia. By consequence the great ranges of the Himalayas rose up, to form a barrier, scarcely penetrable except to the northwest, which was to enable Indian culture to emerge largely on its own. In thinking about the area we should not be mesmerized by modern political divisions. India, in the historical sense of the term, comprises everything now included in the modern states of Pakistan, India, Bangladesh, Nepal, Bhutan, and Sri Lanka. Also in this treatment it is convenient to include Tibet, for it was permeated by Buddhist culture from India.

The top and the bottom of the region—Tibet and Sri Lanka—are predominantly Buddhist. Much of the subcontinent at one time was also Buddhist; but over time, Hinduism has become the main force in Indian life, together with Islam. During the most glorious period of Indian civilization, roughly speaking during the first thousand or more years of the Common Era, there was a mixed Hindu-Buddhist Indic culture, with other smaller religious elements, such as Jainism and, in the far southwest, Christianity, woven into its fabric. This Indic civilization had within it fabulous diversity, made richer by the fact that only at certain periods was India under the domination of a single major empire, and that it was typically fragmented into various states and tribal enclaves. Its diversity partly came from its languages, ranging from the Indo-European tongues of north India (such as Gujerati, Hindi, and Bengali) to the Dravidian languages (Tamil, Telugu, Kannada, Malayalam) of the south. As these languages developed they became vehicles of differing

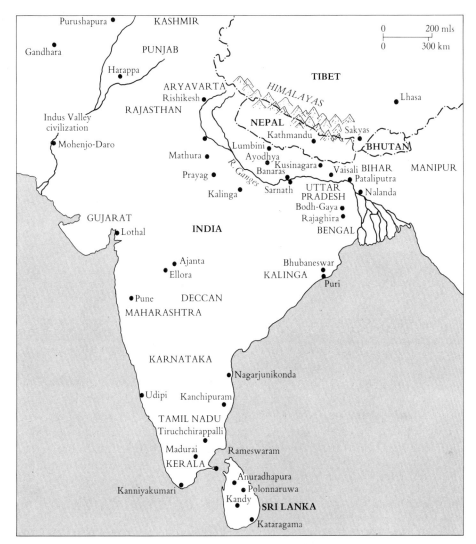

Map 1  South Asia

kinds of piety. And beyond the variety of tongues there were differences of climate and terrain, from the mountains and green forests of Sri Lanka and Kerala to the dry deserts of Rajasthan, and from the steamy heat of the monsoons to the colder drizzles and snows of the Himalayan foothills.

Even to talk of a single something called Hinduism can be misleading, because of the great variety of customs, forms of worship, gods, myths, philosophies, types of ritual, movements, and styles of art and music contained loosely within the bounds of the religion. Some scholars would like to jettison the term. Yet in modern times there is a much better defined sense than before of what is in the Hindu tradition. It is as if many Hinduisms had merged into one. It is now much more like the trunk of a single mighty tree; but its past is a tangle of most divergent roots.

Regarding the formation of religious ideas and practices there are periods into which the history of the subcontinent can be divided: the early period of the Indus Valley civilization and its aftermath lasted from about 3000 B.C.E. down to the culture reflected in the early sacred text known as the *Rig Veda*, around 1000 B.C.E.

The next phase, which may be called preclassical, covers the formative and creative recasting and development of worldviews, including the composition of the texts known as Upanishads (800–400 B.C.E.), the teachings of Mahāvīra the Jain and Gautama the Buddha (c.500 B.C.E.), and the spread of the religions of the Brahmins, the Buddhists, the Jains, and others. Roughly speaking, this is the period of a thousand years from 1000 B.C.E. to near the turn of the millennium (say 100 C.E.).

Then we come to the great classical period of Indic civilization, lasting until about 1000 C.E., which contains the development of most of the patterns of classical Hindu religiosity and the great flourishing and then the decline (in India) of Mahāyāna Buddhism and indeed of Buddhism generally. It was a Hindu-Buddhist civilization, with many other motifs woven into it.

Then, from 1000 onwards till the dawn of the modern period (roughly 1750), we have the formation of a Hindu and Muslim civilization in the Indian subcontinent. It saw the reign of the great Mughals from Delhi, the consolidation of traditional Hinduism, the final withering of Buddhism in India, the rise of the Sikhs, and the attempt by Akbar (ruled 1562–1605) to establish a pluralistic ideology accepting the truth of India's many faiths. This "medieval" period ended with the increased incursions of Europeans, above all the British, who came to dominate the area.

The modern era, after 1750, saw the coming of missionaries, the founding of the British Rāj, and the development of railroads, higher education, modern industry, and a relatively centralized administration. It saw the renewal of Hinduism, Islam, and other religions, and the struggle for independence which ended with the partition of India into the states of India and Pakistan, and the subsequent splitting of Pakistan into (West) Pakistan and Bangladesh. It saw the resurgence of Buddhism in Sri Lanka and the forcible modernization of Tibet by China. Above all it brought a new understanding of Hinduism.

During the various periods there arose empires which sometimes unified most of India and sometimes did not—such as the Indus Valley civilization which lasted till about 1500 B.C.E. in the early period; the Mauryan empire towards the end of the preclassical period, especially under the pro-Buddhist emperor Aśoka (reigned 269–232 B.C.E.); the Gupta and Kushan empires during the classical period; and the Mughal empire during premodern times. Especially during the Gupta period, the spread of Sanskrit culture across the whole of India helped unify the subcontinent. Even among the Buddhists, who rejected the authority of the Brahmins—the primary bearers of Sanskrit culture—the language was used in the composition of sacred texts and commentaries. In Sri Lanka the texts were written in Pali, and in Tibet they were translated into Tibetan. This linguistic difference came to be a chief marker of the difference between Indic, Tibetan, and Sinhala cultures.

In all sorts of ways, however, it is not possible to look on South Asia—the Indian subcontinent—as a single unit. Regional empires and monarchies and other groupings were quite as normal as the unitary state.

## The Ingredients of Indian Religion

If the history of India and its neighbors up to the modern period has been complex, so have the many doctrines, rituals, experiences, and customs which characterize Indian thinking. To a Western reader in particular, and to many South Asians who have been alienated from their heritage by modern education, they are in part unfamiliar. So it is useful to list some of the main ingredients of Hindu and Buddhist, and other, practices and beliefs during the classical period. This will make it useful to survey these ingredients in advance of our discussion of the history: it will constitute the grammar of Indian religions, just as the gods, holy figures, temples, and statues constitute their vocabulary.

If we were miraculously transported back to the sacred cities along the holy river Ganges during the classical age of Indian culture, we would be struck, doubtless, by the splendor of temples, the variety of human types, from proud Brahmins, with their partly shaved heads, to recluses with matted hair; from women in white, widowed and immersed in piety, to monks and nuns belonging to the Jain and Buddhist orders. Let us analyze the ingredients by reference to our seven dimensions.

Of the *ritual* and *practical* dimension, three important elements are: Yoga, or self-training; worship or *pūjā*; and sacrifice. The first is ancient in the tradition, and forms the basis of an inward search, and a training of the mind, taking somewhat differing forms according to the school or movement to which one belongs. Much later, during the premodern period, it was supplemented by that kind of gymnastics which in this century became popular in the West and which often is identified with Yoga, although it is in fact far less significant than the spiritual side. The inward search is to discover the true Self or to attain liberation. It has been one of the main preoccupations of the Indian spiritual tradition.

Worship was in classical India directed toward a large number of gods, of whom Viṣṇu and Śiva emerged as dominant. Buddhist *pūjā* was at first little more than the ceremonial remembrance of a great teacher, but later, as the faith flowered into the high Mahāyāna or Great Vehicle, it embodied fervent devotion or *bhakti* toward the Buddha conceived as a kind of God.

Sacrifices of all sorts existed in earliest India. Later, under the influence of Buddhism and Jainism—both religions with a deep respect for animal life—sacrifice came to be largely confined to plant life and melted butter (ghee) and the like. The people in charge of sacrificial ritual were the Brahmins, who were the highest of the four classes which supplied the

Bodnath stūpa in Nepal, in characteristic Nepalese style, shows the eyes of the Buddha gazing out from the stone, signifying his presence.

skeleton of the later fully elaborated caste system. From their expertise in sacrifices, the Brahmins came to dominate the rituals of temples, which did not exist in the earliest recorded Brahmin religion, i.e. in the Vedas. Temples were houses of the gods, in which their daily life was enacted, and where festivals abounded.

Pilgrimage is a less important element in the ritual dimension, but it was integral to Jainism, Buddhism and the religion of the Brahmins, taking the faithful to sacred rivers, to holy temples, to the birthplaces of the great, or to the Bodhi Tree under which the Buddha attained his great illumination. There were treks, too, to the great mountains, to the source of the Ganges, and to the places where holy persons would meditate and practice austerities.

The Sanskrit for austerity is *tapas*, literally "heat," for austere self-mortification creates heat in the body, and with it power. *Tapas* as a practice came to form a vital part of some religious movements, notably Jainism. It is the polar opposite of Tantra, which uses magical and esoteric means of gaining liberation, sometimes through the performance of that which is normally forbidden—extramarital sex, meat-eating, and so forth—to express the ways in which the Tantric adept is above ordinary social laws.

So we can list as important practices, among the welter of Hindu, Buddhist and other rituals, yoga, worship, sacrifice, pilgrimage, austerity, and Tantra. On the *experiential* and *emotional* level, the spirit behind such ritual practices varied. Poets and others expressed the feelings of devotional religion or *bhakti*, associated both with temple worship and with the fervor of pilgrimages and festivals. Behind yoga there was the spirit of meditation or *dhyāna*, with the hope of inner peace, bliss, insight, and what was called liberation. For the ascetic there was the sense of independence and power, so that the adept frightened the gods, according to myth: for the ascetic would gain more power than they.

The doctrinal dimension: for many centuries it was customary to represent the Buddha by his absence. Here the seat and the Bodhi tree signify his presence. This no doubt helped to convey the doctrine that after his decease it is neither correct to say that the Buddha exists, nor that he does not exist. Similarly, it is incorrect to state that he both does and does not, or that he neither does nor does not.

The *mythic* dimension of Indian classical culture revolves around a thousand themes. There are millions of gods (traditionally 330 million), but there emerged the famous trio of Brahmā, Viṣṇu and Śiva as the most important. Also vital are their female consorts, conceived as personal manifestations of *śakti* or creative force. In Indian civilization the female is thought of as active, the male more as passive. Sometimes, in the religious movement known as Śaktism (from *śakti*), the Supreme Being is conceived as female (Durgā or Kālī). Another theme is that of the *avatār* or human incarnation of God, mostly of Viṣṇu, a theme which plays some part in the vast epics known as the *Mahābhārata* and the *Rāmāyana*. It is thought that the *avatār* figure comes down to restore proper teachings and behavior at the end of a period of decline, a theme which is found in the three major traditions of the Brahmins, Buddhism, and Jainism. In the case of the Buddha, he is not precisely a "descent" of God, but rather a superhuman person who enters the world to restore the Truth to humans.

God is described in numerous narratives as taking many forms, and gradually there grew up the view that the different gods were so many manifestations of the One Divine Being. This idea, first expressed in the *Rig Veda*, was among other things a way of synthesizing the myriad myths.

In all the major systems of belief in Indian culture there prevailed a sense of decline. The present age, or Kaliyuga, latest of the vast and endless cycles of time which go to make up the fabric of human existence, is one of increasing chaos and evil; and in the Buddhist cosmology there is a sense that religion declines the farther you get in time from the age of the Buddha himself.

These ideas were to be interpreted in terms of the *doctrinal* and *philosophical* themes which characterize classical Indian culture. Pervasive is the theme of rebirth or reincarnation. Each individual living being traverses virtually endless time through many, many lives. The person's destiny is shaped by the deeds she has performed both before and in this life. This "law of *karma*" (action) binds living beings to the round of existence or *saṃsāra*. The desire to leave *saṃsāra*, or at least to overcome its cloying effects, calls for great efforts, which eventually may yield liberation or *mokṣa* when the individual leaves *saṃsāra*, or at least overcomes it by superior insight into the nature of the world. Such liberation is often called *nirvāṇa* in the Buddhist tradition, and is referred to as *kevala* or isolation in the Jain tradition.

God as creator is also implicated in the processes of *saṃsāra*: but he or she (or It) is often conceived also as lying beyond all description. This unspeakable Brahman lies beyond even God as she appears as a person. So in some philosophies there is that higher side of the Divine which has a correspondence with the inner side of the soul, the eternal *ātman* or Self which lies within every individual. By turning inwards and practicing meditation a person may come to experience that inner eternal Self and at the same time achieve unity with the one Divine Being, Brahman. Many forms of belief in India have not accepted the idea of God, and so in them liberation is not communion with God but a lonely disappearance from the round of rebirth.

So there are various dominant doctrines of Indian culture during the classical age: the idea of reincarnation or rebirth, the possibility of ultimate liberation, the idea of a personal God who creates and recreates the cosmos, and for that matter destroys and redestroys it, the notion of an indescribable Brahman lying so to speak beyond the personal God, and the idea of an eternal "something" within the migrating individual. The various philosophies of the Indian tradition are expressed through variations of the ways in which these ideas are put together.

As to the *ethical* dimension; the Jain and Buddhist traditions place much, though differently slanted, emphasis on the practice of non-injury to living beings. This had its effects on the Brahmins, who came to be vegetarian. It was part of an ethos of asceticism which permeated parts of classical Indian civilization. Such "giving up" often took the form of leaving the world to become a monk or nun; but an alternative was the system of four stages of life, which was often held up as the ideal of the pious householder. According to this scheme a man in his early life is a celibate student, learning at the feet of a Brahmin teacher; then he becomes a householder; thirdly, he begins to withdraw from family and public life; and finally he becomes a wandering, homeless recluse, or *sannyāsin*. This allows an ethic of compromise between living in the world and outside society. Increasingly, a person's moral and ritual duties came to be determined by his particular circumstances in life.

The pervasive belief in rebirth had its effects of course on the whole interpretation of moral life. It was typically thought in popular Indian traditions that one could improve one's position in life in the future—even to the extent of going to heaven—by accumulating merit. Such merit could be attained by charitable giving (to holy persons and for pious purposes, such as contributing to the beautification of temples); but above all by good deeds.

In brief, from an ethical angle, there are a number of fairly constant elements in Indian civilization: a tendency to respect the sanctity of all forms of life; a sense of the special character of the ascetic life; an emphasis on merit-making; and the idea that much, in the practical life, depends on a person's place in life.

All this was integrated into the *social* and *institutional* dimension of classical Indian culture, of which the caste system came to be the most striking and pervasive feature. Its skeletal structure was formed during the early days of the Indo-European invasion of India, around 1500 B.C.E. The invaders, like others of the Indo-European linguistic group, were divided into three classes: the priests (Brahmins), the warriors (Kṣatriyas), and the artisans and others who served the top two classes (Vaiśyas). As they conquered the indigenous peoples a fourth class of servants and underlings (Śūdras) was added. Eventually, even further down, a fifth class of "untouchables" came to be recognized. Because Hindu ritual was much concerned with purity, the four- or five-class system itself came to be reinforced by the practical application of the concepts of purity and impurity: the upper-class Indian could be contaminated by contact with those lower down, and especially by the untouchables. This last class came to include a whole variety of tribal peoples who were absorbed into the fabric of the wider society. The first four classes are known as the *varṇas* or (literally) "colors." This name probably derives from racial distinctions, the Indo-European invaders being originally of light complexion. This *varṇa* system was later reinforced and rendered much more complicated by subgroups known as *jātis* ("births" or "lineages").

The vast mosaic known as the caste system represents a great hierarchy into which Indian society is formed; but the Buddhists and others never recognized the system, especially because, when men and women entered the monastic order, the Sangha, they were supposed to leave social distinctions behind them. This Order was, with its Jain counterpart, an important ingredient in Indian society in the classical period. Monasticism had some place in Hinduism also, as in the organization founded by the great reformer Śankara (late eighth century C.E.).

Various other kinds of holy persons were socially important too: the priestly Brahmins, who were highest in the Indian hierarchy; Buddhist and other monks, dressed in brown, grey or pink robes symbolizing rags; naked holy men and Jain monks whose nudity indicated the absolute rejection of worldly things; gurus or teachers of various kinds; *sannyāsins* or recluses of varying persuasions. Also animals, above all the cow, could be a source of holy power and cleansing efficacy. Yet if many of these figures signified renunciation, erotic acceptance of the world was also part of the fabric of India. The family was a vital center of life and of domestic cults.

On the *material* and *artistic* level, the classical period saw the emergence of that typical feature of the Indian scene, the temple. (In the early period Brahmin religion used only temporary sacred grounds and structures.) As well as the shrines to the many gods, there were Buddhist and Jain temples.

There were also sacred rivers, sources of purity and founts of merit; and holy mountains, homes of gods and sacred teachers. In the temples were images and icons—images of the Buddha, of Mahāvīra and other great figures of the Jain tradition, or of Hindu gods—and in houses too there were little shrines. Some of the carvings of the classical period are sublime, whether of the Buddha preaching, teaching, and—in reclining pose—at the time of his decease, or of Śiva dancing. In Sri Lanka the golden ages of the cities of Anuradhapura and Polonnaruwa were particularly productive of great art. In Tibet there evolved wonderful paintings which depicted the great celestial beings of the Buddhist tradition. Many images were small and cheap, for the villager or the poor person; and some were made of clay and used temporarily for some great feast in the calendar of Indian religious life. They were "throwaway" sculptures. Perhaps most powerful of all symbols was a stone pillar with a rounded top, the *lingam*. In its simplicity and suggestive strength, it expressed and promised the fertile power of God.

We can schematize all this as follows:

| DIMENSION | ITEMS |
| --- | --- |
| Ritual, practical | yoga, worship, sacrifice, pilgrimage, austerity, and tantra |
| Experiential, emotional | *bhakti*, *dhyāna*, sense of empowerment |
| Narrative, mythic | myriad gods, the religious hero who restores the Truth, times in decline |
| Doctrinal, philosophical | rebirth, possibility of liberation, God as personal, Brahman as nonpersonal, an eternal soul or freedom-seeking nature within each person |
| Ethical, legal | reverence for animals, ascetic ethos, merit-making, ethics of one's station in life |
| Social, institutional | caste system, Sangha system, varieties of sacred or holy persons, sacred cow, family |
| Material, artistic | holy places (mountains and rivers), temples, images, *lingam* |

These ingredients, combined in differing ways, represent many of the varieties of Indian religion. It was out of this classical material that the idea of Hinduism as such was composed in the modern, colonial period.

## The Early Period

In 1924 there began a series of discoveries which has revealed a remarkable ancient culture, known as the Indus Valley civilization. It has deepened our understanding of Indian religions, for it contains suggestive features foreshadowing later developments. This great and uniform civilization stretched from Gujarat in the south to the eastern Punjab in the north and from Sind in the west to the edges of Uttar Pradesh in the east. Its chief cities were at Mohenjo-Daro on the Indus and Harappa on the Ravi (or near it, for the riverbed has changed its course). They were rather uniformly laid out in grids of streets, with villas, houses, and small lanes occupying the various blocks; and with a higher acropolis containing what seems to be a temple complex and a granary, dominated by a large tank or bath. The whole of each city was laced with an excellent sewage system. Outside the main walls of each city (walls designed no doubt to resist flooding) were areas for the farmers and others who supplied services to the merchants and priests who, we may infer, controlled the civilization.

There are affinities to, and there were some contacts with, the Elamite and Sumerian cultures to the west; and from Elam the Indus Valley civilization may have derived its writing system. Alas, this is as yet not deciphered, or at least not in any agreed manner. The most likely thing is that the language was an early version of Dravidian, and that Dravidian-speakers, probably pastoralists, had moved southwards from Central Asia to the Indus region, where on the basis of villages an urban and mercantile civilization had gradually been built up. The Indus Valley civilization lasted essentially from about 2500 to 1500 B.C.E. It ended rather suddenly, possibly through some great natural disaster combined with conquest by outsiders. Many scholars have held that it was destroyed by the invading Aryans, speaking an Indo-European language, who came into India around 1500 B.C.E.

From the Indus Valley culture we have a wonderful harvest of seals, inscribed clearly with the ideographic script whose decipherment remains controversial. The seals lead us into a world of goddesses, snakes, tigers, water buffaloes, a unicorn, sacred peepul trees, bulls, and elephants. There is a cross-legged figure sometimes thought to be a forerunner of the Hindu god Śiva. There are also small figures of gods and goddesses, sometimes dancing. But what these seals and figurines mean is obscure. There are some mixed animal-human figures, and a wonderful figure of a priest or shaman, perhaps, with a neat beard and a band round his head. Many of these figures are suggestive: they link up with later Dravidian conceptions of a fertility goddess with both benign and fierce attributes. There are suggestions that perhaps sacrifice on the high places in the cities was important. There may have been great processions of the goddess and other deities, and maybe pilgrimages to the mountains from where the inhabitants of the civilization had come. It may be, too, that the figure often identified with Śiva was a fertility god. Perhaps there were myths of the divine couple. The buffalo also seems to have been the consort of the Great Goddess.

We have too little evidence to be sure of anything about the worldview or political structure of this great civilization. We can imagine that once the streets and alleyways of the cities teemed with life, each household no doubt engaging in domestic rites before sculptured figures, and that religious life also involved ablutions and perchance, among the more prosperous, the sacrifice of animals. Out in the surrounding countryside there were wide fields of grain, part of which was tribute to the city granaries. All this is likely to have been organized through religious allegiance rather than force, for we do not, strange to say, find evidence of weapons. On great feast days doubtless the high platforms with their bathing tanks would witness a priesthood skilled in sacrificial ritual, parading before the Goddess from whom the earth and the prosperities of the farming life emanated. From her too, no doubt, came domestic animals, and she gave protection against the tigers and snakes who lurked on the earth and on the fringes of the villages.

# The Preclassical Period

As time passed, the Dravidians moved south, and in due course made other powerful contributions to Indian religion and culture. The great Indus Valley civilization died. In its place there slowly arose a new mixture, composed of Aryan and various other ingredients. The invaders came from the northwest and settled in the region between the Indus, flowing southwest, and the Ganges going east. Eventually the heartland of this Aryan culture, of which Sanskrit was the sacred and later the literary language, spread down along the Ganges, where, by the sixth century B.C.E., various mercantile cities arose, such as Banaras (or Varanasi) and Pataliputra (modern Patna). Republics and kingdoms were in the making; and in this exciting climate of economic advancement and political consolidation there was a creative welter of religious movements. The Aryan priests, the Brahmins, brought with them a repertory of sacred lore and hymns composed over a period of five hundred years. The ascetic traditions were revitalized in the same period by Mahāvīra and the Buddha; and other worldviews, typically propounded by wandering teachers, contended both with these and with Brahmin orthodoxy. Among these doctrines were materialism, rejecting all ideas of transcendent powers and goals, and skepticism, rejecting all positions.

## The Brahmins and Ascetics

Brahmin culture turned out to be the most persistent element in all Indian civilization. The Brahmins, who thought of themselves as animated by the power *brahman*, enjoyed tremendous prestige, and shared preeminence with other sacred persons, collectively known as *śramaṇas* or wandering ascetics. *Śramaṇas* thought of themselves as beyond ordinary social obligations: they had left the world behind. But the Brahmins were necessarily tied to the concerns of ordinary life in a rather direct way: many of them made their living by their expertise in ritual. This ritual, increasingly complicated, could bring for the person who paid for the sacrifice (in cows and other expensive commodities) prosperity and the assurance of worldly success. And the tradition of ritual which they brought with them was derived from the timeless past, from the beginning of the cosmos, from everlasting authority, from the age of the seers (*ṛṣis*) who heard the ultimate sacred sounds and brought them forth by a creative process to compose the collections of hymns known as the Three Vedas (to which a fourth, magical collection, the *Atharva Veda*, was added in the preclassical period, after 600 B.C.E.). Masters of the holy hymns and the sacred language, skilled in the intricacies and long performance of sacrificial rites, whether for kings and princes or for ordinary householders, the Brahmins were one of the main forces in the creation of Indian religion. So much so indeed that even today what we mean by "Hinduism" is largely their creation: Hindu orthodoxy is defined as the acceptance of the authoritative value of the revelation (*śruti*) which includes the Vedas.

## The Early Vedic Period

In voyaging to the ancient past we are necessarily indebted mainly to texts. We have seen how hard it is to interpret the rich archaeological findings of the Indus Valley civilization without the benefit of a deciphering of the script. In the case of the early Aryans in India, who infiltrated there in waves during the period from about 1500 B.C.E. onwards, having originated (probably) in the region of southern Russia, we have texts which reflect their existence during the period of settlement. There are of course problems, for the texts, orally transmitted over many centuries, were gathered together subsequently for ritual purposes, and not in order to give us an historical record of early times. We have to make inferences from the hymns, and it is not always easy to do so. Imagine trying to reconstruct American or British life from a Catholic hymnbook. We could pick up hints, but often the references to Zion and Calvary would baffle us: were they contemporary references or not?

The hymns look back to a time when the plains of north India were being subdued by those who called themselves Aryans or "Noble People." Arrogant with horses and chariots, aggressive and confident, these folk were able to conquer the native Dasyus, who were dark people, living in citadels, venerating *lingams*, tied in no doubt to a plethora of rituals to increase their crops and pastoral wealth. They were many of them descendants of those who had once occupied the Indus Valley cities. Much of their lore, and elements of their speech, were to enter the habits of the Aryans.

Some of the many gods of the *Rig Veda* reflect the period of aggrandisement. There is the fierce, towering Indra, great warrior leader, incarnated in the thunderstorm and the lightning bolt. Over a quarter of the hymns in the collection are addressed to him. His main function is in leading the warriors, the Kṣatriya class, the second of the fourfold list of Vedic society. Not only does he fight human enemies but also the wicked demons, the antigods, who support them. But Indra is also in some sense creator, for in primordial times he prises apart heaven and earth, and frees from a cave the cows imprisoned there, the main symbol of Aryan wealth. In his creative act he discovers the Sun, which brings light and vision to all creatures.

Indra in his violence and creativity—and his exuberance, too, in drinking great drafts of the sacred and hallucinogenic drink of *soma*—gives us a feel for the rough warriors who led the migrations out of the plains southward and westward in search of new pasturelands and places to conquer. It hints at the ethos of the distant past, before the Aryans became settled in and integrated into the landscape of north India, with its warm and rich forests, its cleared areas for cultivation, its expanding villages, and its cities in the making.

Indra's parting of the sky and earth sets the scene for conflicts between good and evil gods. The latter are often associated with human enemies; but even the divine Vedic world itself is riven with conflict, so that there are strains between a number of the mighty forces which are envisioned in the hymns. Even sacrifice, the central ritual, is seen as a mode of conflict: sacrificial rituals often incorporated contests of riddles and chariot races, as if inner combats were continuous with the ongoing struggle between the mobile horsemen of the Aryans and the settled culture of the despoiled indigenous inhabitants.

If Indra is rambunctious and somewhat chaotic, the god Varuṇa is, much of the time, the model of order. He presides over the orderliness of the cosmos, summed up as *ṛta*, an idea somewhat like the later Hindu concept of *dharma* as the sacred pattern underlying both cosmic and social life. He displaces Dyaus the old sky-god, who is the Vedic counterpart of the Greek Zeus and the Roman Jupiter. Varuṇa rules the heavens and especially the night sky, where the stars are perceived as his innumerable eyes. And so it is that he knows everything. He is the moral judge, since he knows all the secrets of human beings, and with his companion, Mitra, he presides over promises and contracts. He upholds truth. But he has dark and earthly associations too, and these become more vital in the later mythology of the classical period.

An important ritual god, personifying the phenomenon that is central to sacrifice, is Agni, god of fire. As the representative of earthly fire, Agni is the lowest of a threesome that also includes atmospheric fire or lightning (Indra) and the heavenly fire of the Sun (Surya). Alternatively, he may be identified with the fiery aspect of all three. By a splendid act of imagination, the people who defined their society through the Vedic hymns saw the continuity between the three levels of heaven, atmosphere, and earth. A night storm, especially in the warm climate of India, is numinous and terrifying; and earthly fire can be unpredictable and elusive, even hard to maintain, especially when people are on the move.

Fire is important sacrificially in many cultures. The reason is that it performs at least two functions: it consumes or (in the case of roasting) transforms that which is offered; and it wafts the offering upward to the gods, conceived as being "up there." When a person offers that which is valuable, it is important that he gives it away: it has to leave his zone and enter the god's zone. This is done by the smoke of offerings burnt as sacrifice. Already something is done, of course, in the case of animals; their life is destroyed, for instance by the letting of blood.

In the sacrifice, fire is created by one stick twirling in a hole in another. The sexual symbolism to be seen in this—phallus in vagina—makes the making of fire like the stimulating of fertility in animals and human beings. So in many ways fire is crucial to cosmic processes. But above all it is the consumer and conveyor of what is sacrificed, whether it be the horses of the ancient kingly sacrifices or the ghee and milk poured out daily in domestic rituals. It is the necessary adjunct of the long and complex Brahmin-controlled sacrifices that are made to bring prosperity. So it is not surprising that Agni the fire god appears so frequently in the Vedic hymns.

Another important god in Vedic times, who later faded in actual religious practice, was Soma, god of the intoxicating juice that was prepared and consumed as part of the ritual. It stimulated visions, and it may be that some of the imagery of the hymns comes from the contents of such visions.

By comparison the gods who are so great later—Viṣṇu and Śiva—are minor. But Viṣṇu's importance is foreshadowed in the myth in which he takes three steps across the universe, establishing its bounds; the last step is indeed beyond human ken, for it paces out heaven. Those who reenact this creative act in ritual attain to a mastery of the cosmos. His companion Rudra, the Red One, is uncontrolled fire, dwelling in mountains and jungles, wild. Later he is to become the great god Śiva.

The hymns indicate that within the framework of a given celebration many of the gods—the more important ones described above, as well as others—were regarded each as supreme. It is like a painting: the perspective and the frame isolate the painting from all others. So in a given hymn the given god is God. This has been called henotheism, from the Greek, meaning "one-God-at-a-time-ism." It is one way of combining a kind of theism or belief in God with the existence of different cults of gods; and it has been a characteristic of Indian religion since these early times.

The hymns of the *Rig Veda* and the other collections do not yield enough information for us to trace anything of the history of the early period, or indeed of anything before about 600 B.C.E. Their importance is less as historical data than as sacred texts, which came to be part of the later canonical revelation. Though there are continuities between the hymns and the more developed classical religion of India, there were also considerable transformations, which were brought about by the Brahmins' seeking control over, and being influenced by, non-Aryan forces in Indian society which brought with them new religious ideas. It was a series of blends between the Vedic tradition and such forces which prepared the way for the creation of classical Hinduism.

## A New Beginning

In the hundred years or so around 500 B.C.E., a whole new constellation of ideas and practices was moved into the forefront of attention. Most important was the idea of *saṃsāra*, the cycle of rebirth, which led to a quest for liberation through the practice of austerity or meditation or both. To be saved we need to wipe out the effects of our past actions or *karma*. It is this set of beliefs that formed the background of many of the new religious movements; and it was a set of ideas that penetrated into Brahmin religion as a new and great secret, in the teachings of the speculative texts known as the Upanishads.

This was a period when, evidently, many *śramaṇas* or wandering recluses and teachers had gained vast respect and were often coupled in the texts with Brahmins. The region of India in which this ferment was occurring was to the east of the area round modern Delhi which constituted the Aryan heartland. It was a region centered on the Ganges, and on such newly great cities as Banaras and Patna. Because of new economic and political forces, including the emergence of strong kingdoms and republics, a new mercantile class was becoming more important, and this was attracted to some of the new movements that were springing up, especially that of the Buddha.

## Buddhism

The Banaras waterfront is a tangle of temples, including the Visvanath Temple, shown here in the center.

All dates in early Indian history are the subject of scholarly debate. But it was probably in the sixth century B.C.E. that the Buddha was born and various other major figures flourished. Some scholars date such events later: the Buddha, for instance, in the fourth century. But we shall stay with a more traditional scheme.

The Buddha's story is legendary: onto some historical facts were glued some wondrous stories. This fact means that it is hard for us to get to what may be called the "historical Buddha." But the legendary account of the Buddha's life is important, for it is that on which the remembrance and piety of Buddhists through the ages has fastened. Moreover, it has served as a kind of model for analogous lives, such as that of his supposed contemporary Mahāvīra, who founded or refounded the Jain tradition.

Later Buddhists were to have the creed: "I take refuge in the Buddha; I take refuge in the Dharma; I take refuge in the Sangha." We can translate this as "I take refuge in the Enlightened One; I take refuge in the Teaching; I take refuge in the Order" (that is of monks and nuns). This summary of loyalty pinpoints the three most vital ingredients in the Buddhist tradition: the narrative of the Buddha; the doctrinal or philosophical worldview presented; and the institution that carried on the practical path to liberation, namely the body of dedicated followers of the Buddha. Beyond this simple credo Buddhism was to take many forms, and it is useful here to give a small sketch of that history of divergence.

## The History of Buddhism in Brief

First, there is the early period, in which the Buddha lived and the teachings and practice were consolidated. This period can be said to last from about 500 B.C.E. down to the first century C.E., by which time the Canon of scriptures was already written down in Pali, in Sri Lanka, and was taking a fixed form in the shape of what is known as Theravāda or the Doctrine of the Elders. This stream of Buddhism still carries on in Sri Lanka and Southeast Asia, though not without admixture from the other great branch, the Mahāyāna or Greater Vehicle. The Mahāyāna, which had roots parallel to those of the Theravāda in early Buddhism, emerged in India in about the third century B.C.E.

Second, from the first century C.E. onward, Buddhism spread into China and eventually into Korea and Japan. Both in Indian Mahāyāna and in the Theravāda, Buddhism achieved high articulation, and we can call this the classical period.

Third, from the seventh century C.E., there developed a form of Buddhism, sometimes called the Vajrayāna (Diamond Vehicle) and sometimes the Mantrayāna (Vehicle of Sacred Utterance), with much emphasis upon magical and sacramental rites, in which spiritual consequences were thought to flow from the recitation of *mantras* or sacred formulae. This was gradually assimilated into the Hindu practices of the era, and was one reason for the ultimate virtual disappearance of Buddhism from subcontinental India. On the other hand it became the dominant form of Buddhism in Nepal and Tibet, where the religion spread during this period. We may call the era from the seventh century C.E. till the eighteenth century the medieval period.

Fourth, there came the modern period, which eventually affected Buddhism not only in South Asia but in the rest of Asia whither it had spread. The impact of colonialism will be discussed in the second part of this book.

**Buddhism** some key terms

*Bodhisattva* Buddha-to-be who puts off his final liberation to work tirelessly for the sake of other living beings. The most famous bodhisattva figure is Avalokiteśvara who became Kuan-yin in China and Kannon in Japan.

*Buddha* An enlightened being who has seen the truth of dharma.

*Dhyāna* Meditation: usually in eight stages of ascending purity of consciousness.

*Nirvāṇa* Final liberation when the saint will no longer be reborn.

*Prajñā* Insight or wisdom concerning the nature of the cosmos.

*Pratītyasamutpāda* Codependent origination of events, the law which links together all the events of the world in sequences of samsāra.

*Saṃsāra* The living flux of existence in which individuals are involved in the process of rebirth.

*Sangha* The order of monks and nuns founded by the Buddha to carry on the teaching of the Dharma.

*Śīla* Virtue or a precept encouraging a virtue, such as the five precepts summing up Buddhist morality.

*Stūpa* A mound for containing relics, formalized into the central feature of temples and pagoda.

*Śūnyatā* Emptiness, the pervading characteristic of all events, in that they are empty of self-subsistence and are relative.

*Tantra* A ritual text or method in the so-called Vajrayana form of Buddhism (chiefly now in Tibet) for acquiring sacramental power, usually through the instruction of a guru.

All these periods—early, classical, medieval and modern—apply primarily to Buddhism in South Asia, and differing periodization will be used in regard to East Asia and elsewhere.

In sketching Buddhist roots, I shall deal with its different dimensions as follows. First, the *narrative* dimension, telling the story of the Buddha and the world out of which he came. Second, the *doctrines* he taught: these philosophical ideas are geared to the practical life, but are especially important in the Buddhist tradition, which has a strong emphasis—for reasons which will become clear—upon analysis of the world and of human nature. Third, the ritual or *practical* dimension, so central in the quest for liberation. With this we shall connect the *ethical* dimension. Then we shall look to the inward *experiences* of both the Buddha and his followers. We shall move on to sketch the *social* organization of the religion. Finally we shall look at the *material* dimension of early Buddhism.

## The Narrative Dimension

Where indeed should one begin to tell the story of the man who came to be called the Buddha? His life as an individual never really began, for, like us all, he was, in the Buddhist view, a beginningless wayfarer in the round of *saṃsāra*. There are many wondrous and edifying tales told of him in the scriptures about how he was a snake, or a hare, or a king, or whatever, in previous births. These so-called Jataka tales were a great source of instruction in social life and compassion for the peoples who came to follow the Buddha. Immediately before his birth in this world as a human and more-than-human teacher and liberator, the Buddha-to-be, or Bodhisattva, resided for millions of years in a heaven, called Tuṣita, enjoying great happiness like a god. But he had to give this up to help living beings to relieve and ultimately to get rid of their sufferings.

It was possibly in 586 B.C.E. that he was born into this world as Siddhartha Gautama, on the periphery of the new civilization emerging along the river Ganges. He was born into a people known as the Śākyas, and came to be known as Śākyamuni, the sage of the Śākyas. They were under the general suzerainty of the kingdom of Kosala. His father Suddhodana was a ruler, and his mother was Mahāmāyā. It was predicted at his birth that he was destined to become a world ruler, but it was uncertain whether this was to be in a political or a spiritual sense. The birth itself was miraculous, according to legend. His mother dreamed that the Buddha-to-be took the form of a white elephant and entered her womb, and she ceased to have any wish for sex. So though she was not a virgin, having borne other children, it was in a loose sense a virgin birth; and it occurred at the time of the full moon in May at a park called Lumbini.

The young Siddhartha grew up in some luxury, but eventually, after he married and had become father of a son, he was impelled to leave the worldly life, and to take up that of the wandering recluse. He had been struck by the four sights of a very old man, a sick person, a corpse being taken to the burning-ground, and finally a holy beggar. He left his wife and baby and lived a nomadic life of severe austerity and reflection. He studied and practiced for a while with a group of six fellow *śramaṇas*. Eventually, on his own, and at a place now called Bodh-Gaya, under a sacred fig tree or pipal, he attained full insight into the nature of the world and of the way to overcome suffering and tribulation. As Enlightened One, he was henceforth to be called the Buddha.

He returned to Banaras, to a deer park outside the city at a place called Sarnath, where he had left his companions, and delivered to them his first Sermon in which he expounded his insight. It was referred to as the Sermon of the Turning of the Wheel, in which he set the wheel of Dharma in motion. They became his first disciples and core of the new order of Sangha.

Thereafter, for forty-five years until he was eighty, he traveled about, teaching and consolidating the organization of the Sangha. He visited the great new cities of the region—Banaras, Uruvela, Rajagriha, Vaisali, Sravasti, Kausambi, and his own town Kapilavastu. According to Sri Lankan chronicles, the Buddha made three journeys to the island in his lifetime, one being to the peak of Sumanakata, later called Adam's Peak, where he left a huge footprint which became the focus of the island's most important pilgrimage. He consorted with princes and kings, courtesans and smiths. He preached his saving doctrine of the Way to Liberation.

At last, he died of a digestive complaint. As with other major events in his life there were heavenly and earthly portents—earthquakes and showers of flowers. His decease was one of insight and peace: all compound things are impermanent and sooner or later the death of the physical Gautama Buddha had to take place. He had fought off more than once the wiles of Māra the

The grief of his followers at the passing of the Buddha—he had told them, however, that all compound things are impermanent and that the Teaching would remain.

Tempter, who would have liked the Buddha not to have gained insight, and not to have kept on in the world to deliver his message. He had overcome the forces of death, and now he would be no more reborn. He came to be called the Tathagata, or Thus-Gone, and his final state was mysterious. He would not be reborn, but it was wrong to think of him as either existing or not existing, or both or neither. His followers cremated his body, and his relics were installed under cairns in various places.

This was the life of the most recent in the line of Buddhas. In the Pali Canon, various others are listed, such as the Buddhas Vipassi, Sikhi, Vessabhu, Kakusandha, Konagamana, and Kassapa. It is not thought that the Buddha founded the faith, but restored it.

## The Doctrinal Dimension

The Buddha's doctrines belonged to the general pattern of śramanic religion of the time, but he gave that a radical new interpretation. The primary questions turned round the problem of rebirth and how to gain liberation from an unsatisfactory world. Like the contemporary Jain and Ājīvika groups (see pp. 68–71), he was attracted to the practice of austerity; but in the end he found mere austerity too negative. He learned from others the arts of yoga, and evolved a system of meditation; but he thought that meditation without understanding was blind, and understanding without meditation was without fruits. You had to combine the two, and for this a right orientation to philosophical questions was vital.

His central insight was of the impermanence and interdependence of everything. He sought the causes of every event, and especially those which directly concern the human being: so we need to train ourselves in self-awareness to perceive the nature of events taking place inside us and their conditions. But he rejected determinism (as preached by the Ājīvikas, for instance). We are free to reshape our destinies, even though we inherit from previous lives tendencies which, if unchecked, will lead to other existences, each one impregnated with *dukkha* or illfare (usually translated as "suffering"). Indeed, in the popular view of the nature of the universe which Buddhism adapted and reshaped, there are many heavens—though even in these the good life must come to an end—and many purgatories of a horrifying kind; while humans could become ghosts, or worms or any other kind of living being, in accordance with their deeds.

Because nothing in the universe is permanent, no satisfaction can last for ever; and its disappearance is painful. All life therefore is permeated by suffering. This was the first of the Four Noble Truths which the Buddha enunciated. The second is that the cause of suffering is craving or thirst for existence (Pali: *taṇhā*). The third is that this cause can be eliminated. And the fourth is that the mode of doing this is by treading the Noble Eightfold Path.

This path has eight aspects, and is an expansion of a more fundamental idea, that there are three elements in the Way, namely trust, ethical conduct, and meditation. The first two aspects of the Path concern trust: they are Right

61

Belief and Right Attitude. The next three are to do with ethical conduct: Right Speech, Right Bodily Action, and Right Livelihood (that is, not engaging in an occupation which would necessarily cause the infringement of the Buddhist ethic, such as butchering). The last three, to do with yoga or self-training, are: Right Effort, Right Self-Awareness, and Right Meditation.

The Path was thought of by the Buddha as "Middle," that is, as centered between extremes: between the extremes of self-indulgence and self-mortification, and between the extremes of thinking that the soul is eternal and that it is cut off at death. It is in various other ways a moderate faith.

The Path leads to a condition in this life of complete insight and serenity, such as the Buddha himself achieved at his Enlightenment; on death the saint disappears like a flame going out or a spark disappearing in the darkness. It is not extinction, but it is not continued individual existence either. So the Tathagata was seen as having no further relations with this world. The best way to point to his transcendent condition is by silence.

The best way to go for salvation is by becoming a nun or a monk. Such a life of spiritual community, with periods of solitude, is best for meditation. Lay followers not yet ready for the relative severity of the Sangha might through ethical living and by giving to the order attain a future in some better or heavenly state, and might thereafter come back to earth ready to assume the ocher robe.

The idea of impermanence, the rejection too of a permanent soul in the individual, the concept of universal causation, and the goal of an ineffable ultimate state — nirvāna — are the bare bones of the Buddha's message. We shall

---

*Dependence and the Middle Path:  Saṃyutta Nikāya*

On ignorance depends karma;
On karma depends consciousness;
On consciousness depend name and form;
On name and form depend the six organs of sense;
On the six organs of sense depends contact;
On contact depends sensation;
On sensation depends desire;
On desire depends attachment;
On attachment depends existence;
On existence depends birth;
On birth depend old age and death, sorrow, lamentation, misery, grief, and despair. Thus does this entire aggregation of misery arise.

But on the complete fading out and cessation of ignorance ceases karma;
On the cessation of karma ceases consciousness;

On the cessation of consciousness cease name and form;
On the cessation of name and form cease the six organs of sense;
On the cessation of the six organs of sense ceases contact;
On the cessation of contact ceases sensation;
On the cessation of sensation ceases desire;
On the cessation of desire ceases attachment;
On the cessation of attachment ceases existence;
On the cessation of existence ceases birth;
On the cessation of birth cease old age and death, sorrow, lamentation, misery, grief, and despair. Thus does this entire aggregation of misery cease.

see later how these notions came to be developed. Underpinning the worldview was the thought of rebirth and the pervasive power of *karma*. It was original in its substance and presentation and had a strong appeal in the areas where the Buddha taught.

It rejected the appeal to revelation, and in particular Brahmin claims for the Vedas. The Buddha had directly experienced the truths he taught, and the Brahmins (he argued) relied on mere tradition and authority. They had not seen the gods they called upon. The true Brahmin was not the one born into a priestly class, but the person who followed virtue and self-control.

## The Practical Dimension

The most important practice invoked in the Buddha's teachings is that of Yoga, in which an individual, seated in some serene spot, tries to control his mind, and is eventually able to climb up through the various stages of *dhyāna* (Pali: *jhāna*). He might begin with some simple object such as a blue flower and learn to see it just as a patch of blue. Then he might discard such a device and ascend through various levels of increasing purity of consciousness. The adept does not by such exercises alone attain to *nirvāṇa* and sainthood; but they form an integral part of the earliest pictures we have of Buddhism. It is above all a faith of meditation and self-training.

The structure of the Sangha prevents, however, too great an individualism, since the Buddha envisaged his followers as living together according to the rule or *vinaya*. At each phase of the moon, they would make a mutual public confession of faults; and at the end of the rainy season there would be a larger and more formal occasion for such confession and mutual forgiveness.

Another important aspect of early life was that like other śramanic groups Buddhist monks and nuns would get their food by begging. It was an exchange: they received food, the lay folk got merit. This giving (*dāna*) was the primary lay duty towards the order. Early on, the important sites of the Buddha's life may have been thought worth visiting to gain merit: where he was born, where he gained his Vision, where he preached the first sermon, and where he died; at Lumbini, Bodh-Gaya, Sarnath, and Kusinagara. In the treatment of Gautama's relics, at his death, lay the germs of later devotion and indeed worship (though in a sense the Tathagata was "not there" to worship: only his memory served as a spur to good deeds and self-salvation).

## The Ethical Dimension

As a Middle Path, the Way emphasized that intentions count, rather than a literal application of the rules. Our actions should be controlled by the Five Precepts (*pancaśīla* in Sanskrit and in Pali). One should refrain from taking life, from taking what is not given, from wrong sex, from wrong speech, and from drugs (substances which obstruct self-awareness). To these basic rules were added a set for controlling more narrowly the life of the nun or monk: such rules about not using a high bed, or money, and following the conditions of the Order. Such morality was to be suffused by certain great

*Opposite* A twelfth-
century carving at
Polonnaruwa in Sri
Lanka, showing on the
right the Buddha
having attained final
*nirvāna*.

virtues, such as compassion. This was one of the Four Divine Dwelling Places in which the good person should reside—friendliness, compassion, sympathy, and equanimity.

### The Experiential Dimension

What kind of inner experiences did earliest Buddhism aim toward? We can learn something from the accounts of yogic practice. The supreme point in the ascending scale of purifying consciousness is a kind of tranquil bliss, from which height the adept looks down, when he comes out of trance, at ordinary experience as being mundane and yet itself, in tranquility, suffused by a kind of joy and assurance.

Such illuminated consciousness is sometimes referred to as mystical experience; but in the Buddhist case there is no question of seeing it as a union with the Ultimate, such as a personal God. Buddhism does not deny the gods, even the great god Brahmā, creator of the world according to Brahmins (though not according to the Buddha: he is merely the first god to come into existence at the beginning of a new cycle in the universe's existence). But the gods too, however splendid, are impermanent. So the supreme bliss and insight of *nirvāna* are beyond all words and all ideas of being united with Anyone.

This seems the central experience of the Buddha and of his saintly followers—that is, those who attained *nirvāna*. But such high consciousness is accompanied by an intellectual realization that all things are impermanent. Such a realization could occur in a flash, in a pregnant moment of understanding. We have accounts of such moments in some of the autobiographical poems of the early monks and nuns which were incorporated into the Pali Canon. It took time for a more fervent devotional religion aimed at celestial Buddhas to come about. But there is plenty of recognition in the early Canon of the keen appreciation of Nature and the poignancy of life, and such sentiments form a fine counterpoint to the depths and glories of Buddhist meditation.

### The Social Dimension

The Sangha was at first perhaps much more loosely brought together than it later became. Many monks and nuns were hermits over much of the year, camping in caves and by river banks in huts, save for the wet season when they would congregate and live in some of the centers given by rich laity in and around the cities and larger villages. Though the Buddha acted as monarch of the Sangha in his lifetime, thus being a spiritual world-conqueror and imperial figure, he made no provision for a successor. He preferred the republican model of some of the peoples now being absorbed into the kingdoms burgeoning along the valley of the Ganges. The new leader would be the Dharma, the teaching. After I am gone, said the Buddha, there will remain the Teaching.

Similarly organized were some of the other śramanic movements, notably those of the Jains and Ājīvikas, led by Mahāvīra Vardhamāna and Makkhali Gosāla respectively. So we can see the Buddhist Sangha alongside its rivals, and surrounded at the periphery by a miscellaneous population of wandering recluses, some shaven, some naked, some with matted hair, some weird and frightening, others gentle. It was also a rival to the hereditary priests or Brahmins. The civilization was mixed, and the Brahmins, recluses, and monks of the various traditions had to live together. Buddhism had lots of rich support, from kings and merchants. It was modernizing and subtle, and gave opportunities for lay people to use their wealth and clean living in ways which promised better things for the future, and possibly heaven.

It was also a period of political change. Some of the tribal republics were being absorbed into the kingdoms which dominated the region. The Sangha offered an alternative life when so many social changes were occurring.

*The Material Dimension*
The relics of the Buddha were distributed at his death. They were installed in cairns, which were the precursor of the great mound or *stūpa* of the classical Buddhist temple. Such concern with relics was to prefigure much else. But it was some time before Buddhist monasteries, with all their accompanying art, were to be created. Only later was there to be the wonderful development of statuary and paintings which made Buddhist art one of the glories of human civilization. In the beginning, there was perhaps a strong sense that by the doctrines taught by the Buddha there was "nothing there" to portray. The Teacher was trackless, like a rhinoceros or a bird in the sky.

# Śramanic Alternatives

From these early beginnings, Buddhism started to spread. We should note the success, too, of some of its rivals. In the period following 400 B.C.E. we have some consolidation indeed of all the major strands of religious practice. The Brahmins had developed far beyond the Three Vedas which were so severely chastized in the Buddhist texts. By the time of the Buddha, or not long after it, there were in existence the principal classical Upanishads. These discourses, originally handed down orally, contain ideas which became seminal for some of the innovative theologies of classical Hindu thought. Within the wider context of the consolidation of kingdoms, such as that of Magadha, the Brahmin class had new opportunities; and when the old Āryavarta or Aryan region around Delhi was absorbed by the vigorous mercantile states of the Ganges valley, the Brahmin theories were brought into direct conflict and coexistence with the newer śramanic ideologies. As we move on through a period which also saw the invasion of India by Alexander the Great in 327–324 B.C.E., with stimulating effects on Indian culture, we may survey the religious traditions which formed alternatives to early Buddhism. The major ones are Jainism, Ājīvika, and Brahmin thought itself, or Brahmanism.

*Opposite* A bronze figure from Nepal of the great Bodhisattva of compassion, Avalokiteśvara.

*Jainism*

Jainism, like Buddhism, claimed immemorial antiquity: the leader, Mahāvīra, merely restored an ancient faith and did not originate it. It has a more severe character than Buddhism, and its central virtue is *ahiṃsā* or non-injury to living beings, practised in a very comprehensive way. Monks should tread the ground softly for fear of squashing insects and smaller forms of life. They should sweep the terrain with peacock feathers to clear away such beings. They should strain their drinking water, wear masks, and so on, to prevent the accidental taking of life. For such actions, even when not intended, bring bad karmic consequences. The monks, nuns and dedicated lay followers practice severe austerity, or *tapas*. It is a religion which involves mental training; but physical austerities lie at its heart. The noblest ideal is for the saint, when he is ready, to starve himself to death.

---

**Jainism** some key terms

*Ahiṃsā* Non-violence toward all living beings, a virtue central to Jainism, and important in aspects of Hinduism and in Buddhism, as well as in Gandhi's thought.

*Ajīva* Non-living matter, including human and other bodies: everything which is not *jīva* (soul).

*Anekāntavāda* Perspectivism or non-one-sidedness: the doctrine that no one perspective gives you the whole truth.

*Angas* The earliest texts in the Jain tradition.

*Digambara* Sky-clad ones, that is, Jains who keep to the rule of nudity for monks, as a sign of ultimate lack of possessions.

*Jina* Victor or conqueror, the main title of the great Jain teachers, notably Mahāvīra: from it is derived the name *Jaina* or follower of the Jina.

*Kevala* State of liberation in which the *jīva* exists motionless at the summit of the universe, pictured as a colossal human.

*Mahāvrata* Great vow taken by a monk or nun, pledging to practice *ahiṃsā*, and to avoid lying, sex, stealing, or owning anything.

*Śvetambara* White-clad ones: those Jains belonging to the group which does not practice monastic nudity. Each monk or nun has three pieces of white cloth to wear.

*Tapas* Austerity, widely practiced in India, but especially by Jains.

*Tīrthaṃkara* Ford-maker, that is, a great leader such as Mahāvīra who makes a way across the stream of life to salvation.

---

## Non-Injury and the Path: *Sūtrakṛtāṅga*

This is the quintessence of wisdom: not to kill anything. Know this to be the legitimate conclusion from the principle of the reciprocity with regard to non-killing.

He should cease to injure living beings whether they move or not, on high, below and on earth. For this has been called the Nirvāṇa, which consists in peace.

Master of his senses and avoiding wrong, he should do no harm to anybody, neither by thoughts, nor words, nor acts.

A wise man who restrains his senses and possesses great knowledge, should accept such things as are freely given him, being always circumspect with regard to the accepting of alms, and abstaining from what he is forbidden to accept.

The ethical dimension: Jain ascetics wear masks so that they do not inadvertently inhale insects. This is part of their non-violent practice.

Jaina cosmology: the cosmos is seen in this Jaina manuscript as a huge human. Liberated souls eventually rise to the top of the universe and stay motionless forever.

Vardhamāna, or Mahāvīra ("Great Hero"), was born, according to Jain tradition, in 599 B.C.E.—but some scholars put his date fifty or more years after this—in a village near Vaiśālī in what is now the state of Bihar. At the age of thirty he, like the Buddha, renounced the world, and plucked out all his hair, to lead the life of the wandering holy man. After twelve years of fasting and penances he gained release and the sense of omniscience. He went on to gather disciples and refounded in a fuller form the religion of his predecessor, Pārśva, the previous Tīrthamkara (or "Fordmaker," i.e. person who shows the crossing to the other shore of existence), who may have lived in the eighth century B.C.E. At seventy-two Mahāvīra gained final *nirvāṇa*.

He was thought to be the last of twenty-four Fordmakers. The Jain religion came to be quite influential in medieval times, but its numbers now in India are less than three million. Because followers could not take up agriculture and other death-dealing professions they came to populate the merchant and artisan classes, and are a relatively prosperous community. They feel that the religion, as we get away from Mahāvīra's time, and as history goes on in a downward direction, is in decline. They are divided into two denominations, the chief difference between them being that one demands that monks and nuns be unclothed and the other that they wear robes. The one is called the Digambaras or "Sky-Clad" and the other the Svetambaras or "White-Clad."

Jainism has no doctrine of a creator. The universe is roughly in the shape of a huge person, we being at the waist. Above are various heavens and below are hells. The liberated *jīva* or soul rises, free of the weight of its depressing *karma*, to the top of the universe where it remains, free from pain and motionless. Every soul is in itself omniscient, but due to defilements it loses this knowledge; through emancipation its original omniscience is regained.

These beliefs, seemingly archaic, have provided the framework for the practice of a religion which through the centuries has had important influences on Indian civilization as a whole. In the Buddhist texts it comes out, with the Brahmins, as the chief rival to Buddhism.

## The Ājīvikas

The leader of the important Ājīvika movement was Maskarin Gośāla (Sanskrit) or Makkhali Gośāla (Pali), who conformed to the general śramanic pattern. He too was thought of as the twenty-fourth Fordmaker of the present age. Born in Magadha, he took up the mendicant life and for six years was indeed a follower of Mahāvīra. He claimed to have advanced beyond the latter in his practice of austerity and acquisition of magical powers, and set up his headquarters at Sravasti in northwestern Magadha. Eventually he died of self-starvation in about 487 B.C.E.

According to Ājīvika teachings, which we have to reconstruct from outside sources such as Jain and Buddhist scriptures, the Ājīvika monks and nuns underwent severe austerities. In the first two or three centuries of the religion's existence it was a primary rival to Buddhism and Jainism. In one of his inscriptions, the emperor Aśoka (after 268 B.C.E.) names the Ājīvikas third after Buddhists and Brahmins (maybe third in size or third in his approbation).

The Ājīvika teachings centered on the idea of *niyati* or fate. No virtuous act or austerity can help an individual to be released from the sufferings of this world, although such actions are presumably indications that a person is close to liberation. Every soul, indeed, must traverse eight million four hundred thousand lives. Even then it may be that she is not finally released but comes back from blissful existence to resume transmigrations. There is, then, nothing that an individual can do to alter his destiny or fate. This idea was most strenuously resisted by the Buddha and Mahāvīra. The Buddhists regarded the fatalism of the Ājīvikas as particularly threatening.

After about 100 B.C.E. their influence seems to have dwindled, though we have references to them in south India as late as the fourteenth century. In the Tamil country they seem eventually to have merged with the Digambara denomination of the Jains and with devotional Vaisnavas (followers of Visnu).

It is interesting to see the relative destinies of the three main śramanic movements. Buddhism died out in India almost completely, but established itself throughout nearly all the rest of South and East Asia. It became one of the three great missionary religions of the world. The Ājīvikas died out completely. The Jains flourished but eventually shrank, surviving significantly in India but not becoming a missionary religion like Buddhism. A major reason for Buddhism's success was its cultural adaptability; and that in a sense too was the cause of its demise in India, since it merged so successfully with Hindu culture that the latter took it over.

# Brahmanism, or the Religion of the Upanishads

Meanwhile, in the centuries up to the time of the Buddha, the religion of the Brahmins had been evolving. Long periods of settlement in the Āryavarta had made the thundering and conquering religion of Indra the Warrior less relevant. To the east of the main Aryan area, the new religious revival

Brahmins reciting a
fire ritual to ensure a
good harvest.

represented by Buddhism, Jainism, and other movements was a challenge
from a region where Brahmin control and presence were less fully felt. There
was in Brahmin life a certain dilemma. The reason why Brahmins were in
demand from kings and wealthy folk was their expertise in ritual: that
implied secrecy. On the other hand, their doctrines needed to develop in
debate with outsiders, such as these sophisticated new movements. They
were scarcely in a position to speak too openly, beyond instructing those
members of the community who belonged to the upper three classes (priests,
warriors, and artisans): the "twice-born" who were born again through an
initiation with the sacred thread and the status of full-fledged Aryans.

In some measure Brahmin ideas were opened up through the composition
of the texts known as Upanishads. The principal ones were composed
perhaps between 800 and 400 B.C.E., and in parallel with some of the new
ideas prevalent in the śramanic movements. These works, partly verse and
partly prose, were attached to the growing corpus of works in turn affixed to
the Vedic hymn collections, and known as Brāhmaṇas and Āraṇyakas (Holy
and Forest Treatises). The Upanishads are concerned essentially with the
meaning of the sacrificial rites, and in the process they introduce profound
metaphysical and religious ideas.

When we refer to "the Upanishads" we mean those original ones which
form part of the revealed corpus of the Veda. In fact, Upanishads as a kind of
literature continued to be composed right down to the sixteenth century. The
term means "Secret Teachings," and it is assumed that they originated in oral
interpretations of the sacred tradition imparted by gurus within the context of
initiation.

72

The central concept in the Upanishads is that of *brahman*. This is sacred or divine power operative in the sacrifice and indeed within the Brahmin class itself. What power? The new insight of these texts is that the whole cosmos is as it were a sacrifice, and *brahman* is the holy power which informs and animates the whole of reality. Consequently the word came to be used as a name of the divine Ultimate, or of God, and is commonly written in English with a capital, as Brahman. No longer was the sacred expertise of the Brahmins seen as something restricted to the operations of sacred liturgy. It was now seen in principle as knowledge about the whole universe. Some of the Upanishads see Brahman as a personal Lord or Īśvara, as in the *Īśa Upaniṣad*. Sometimes it is seen as without personal qualities, but lying "beyond" qualities and the reach of speech. Much of later Indian philosophizing concerns the question as to whether the Ultimate is personal or nonpersonal. Sometimes it is seen as both: nonpersonal in its own nature, but personal in relation to the universe and creatures.

Into the sacred world of Brahman and the Brahmin ideology there penetrated that other complex of ideas which I have called śramanic: ideas of reincarnation, liberation, yoga, and *tapas*. So many times we hear in ancient texts of Brahmins and *śramaṇas* as coupled together: they were the two classes of holy persons in the society of the sixth and fifth centuries B.C.E. It is not surprising that the Brahmins made a move towards synthesis. The results of such a move are to be found in the Upanishads.

First, there is presented as a new and secret teaching the idea of rebirth—or redeath as it is more grimly called—the thought that the individual who has not gained the Ultimate will be subjected to repeated death.

Second, in the Upanishads we find the remarkable act of identification in which the inner, yogic quest is coupled by implication to the rituals of

---

*Īśa Upanisad*

By the Lord all this universe must be enveloped,
Whatever moving thing there is in this moving world.
Renounce this and you may enjoy existence.
Do not covet anyone's wealth.
Even while doing deeds here
One may wish to live a hundred years;
Thus on thee – this is how it is –
The deed adheres, not on the person.

Those worlds are named after the antigods
Which are covered over by blind darkness.
Those people who kill the Self
Go to them, on descending.

Unmoving, the One is swifter than the mind.
The senses do not reach it, as it hurries on before,
Running past others. It goes, while standing still.
In it Mātariśvān places activity.

It moves, it moves not;
It is far and it is near;
It is within this universe
And it is outside of all this.

Now he who looks on all things
As in the Self, and on the Self
As in all beings – he
Does not shrink away from Him.

sacrifice through which Brahmins tried to control cosmic events. This act of identification is to say that Brahman is the same as the *ātman* or eternal Self which lies within the person. As the formula which is used has it, "That art thou:" in other words, that ultimate being out there, which lies behind and pervades the visible world as its ground and creator, is the same as that eternal something within you.

So the two paths, of ritual action and inner self-control, converge. The Upanishads, moreover, stress the unity of the world and with it the sacred Lord who controls it. But the many gods of the Vedic tradition are not simply swept aside: they are so many refractions of the One. The texts also make use of ideas which were later or at about the same time worked up into the philosophical system known as Sāṃkhya, which was closely associated with the practice of yoga and the Hindu tradition of thought known as the Yoga Philosophy. Though yoga in the general sense crosses the boundaries of tradition, a particular formulation of its philosophy came to be accepted as orthodox and Hindu; and it was this system which coalesced in the medieval period with Sāṃkhya.

Sāṃkhya thought had affinities with the śramanic systems. It saw the world in terms of a unitary cosmos, known as *prakṛti* or nature, and many souls wandering through transmigration and so impaled on suffering. There was no God as such in this viewpoint, but the Upanishads saw the quest for liberation in terms of the attainment of unity with or close communion with the One Holy Power or Brahman.

If the central ritual idea in Brahmanism was *yajña* or sacrifice, the central idea of the inner quest was that of direct experience through meditation. A third ingredient can be seen glimmering through the texts. The beginnings of devotion are to be seen as directed toward a supreme Lord. This motif was to be taken up much more powerfully later on in the Indian traditions, both Buddhist and Hindu, as *bhakti*. The reliance on the Lord also foreshadows the message of the *Bhagavadgītā*. And so the main themes of the Hindu tradition are perceived at least in principle.

In the *Īśa Upaniṣad* (Secret Teaching of the Lord) there is a famous vision of the cosmic Lord standing outside the cosmos, and a vision of the One somehow within us. The question which was later to exercise thinkers was whether Brahman and soul are strictly identical, in which case we all share the one Self, and the fact that we seem to be many individuals rests on an illusion; or whether we have separate selves in which the one Lord indwells. But we still have some way to go from the Upanishads to classical Hinduism.

## Theravāda Buddhism

### The Mauryan Empire and Aśoka

Of the states arising in the Ganges region in the period of the Buddha the most vital was Magadha, which eventually became the basis for the Mauryan empire, named after Candragupta Maurya, who came to the throne in 326

B.C.E. He expanded the empire to cover most of north India, defeating the Greek successor of Alexander, Seleucus, in the process and acquiring large swaths of territory in the northwest. Of those who followed him the most important was Aśoka, who came to the throne probably in 268 B.C.E. A few years later he conquered Kaliṇga, a troublesome eastern kingdom. The massacres and miseries consequent upon this action afflicted his conscience, and he became a lay follower of Buddhism. The rock edicts he inscribed in various parts of his dominions testify to his concern for religious tolerance and the values of the Dharma. This Dharma was an extrapolation from the full Buddhist teaching, but it enjoined virtue and discouraged practices such as meat-eating. The moderating effects of Buddhist values were brought into Aśoka's practice of statecraft. In 258 B.C.E. he celebrated a great festival of Buddhism in his vast capital of Pātaliputra on the Ganges (the largest city of its time in the world), and began to send out missionaries and ambassadors to distant regions, including Greece and the successor states to Alexander's empire. Partly thanks to his energy, Buddhism spread into Central Asia, whence in due course it was to be taken along the silk route into China. Aśoka gave an example of the virtuous king, which was to remain an important ideal both in Hindu and Buddhist tradition.

One of his most lasting achievements was the spread of Buddhism to Sri Lanka, carried there by his son (or nephew), Mahinda. It was in Sri Lanka that the Pali scriptures were written down, and there a major form of Buddhism, Theravāda, had its apogee in the civilization which flowered first and most strikingly in Anuradhapura.

## Classical and Medieval Theravāda

The coming of Mahinda, and the importance of Aśoka in the legendary past of Buddhism, added to the belief that the Buddha had set foot in Sri Lanka during his lifetime. For the Sinhalese people, who spoke a language derived from north India, it seemed as if their blessed isle was singularly favored to carry on the Dharma (Pali: Dhamma) of the Buddha. It was a rich place, especially because of the development of irrigation in the dry north-central region. In the capital, as Buddhism came to be firmly established as the royal religion, there arose the great monastic settlement known as the Mahāvihāra, with its huge relic mound or *stūpa*, known as the Ruanväli. Later another monastic settlement known as the Abhayagiri was established, which was more hospitable than the conservative Mahāvihāra to non-Theravādin forms of Buddhism. In the third century C.E. the penetration of too many unorthodox elements (as the rebels saw it) brought the hiving off of a third great settlement, the Jetavana.

Though some Mahāyāna and Hindu elements in the end got incorporated into the fabric of orthodox Theravāda—such as the use of Buddha statues (which for obscure reasons were not favored in early Buddhism) and the building of shrines to the gods inside temple complexes—Theravāda remained remarkably unchanged in the long period from King Dutthagamini in the first century B.C.E. until the advent of the British. It became a civilizational religion, both forming and being formed by the culture of the island. A solid bond related monarchy to the Sangha. The king was to keep an eye on the monastic community, in case moral and spiritual abuses became too widespread. The Sangha ensured the prosperity and order of the kingdom. Monarchy contributed in a worldly way to the spiritual health of religion, and religion in a spiritual way to the worldly health of monarchy. Such a pattern was to be followed in Thailand and other Buddhist societies of South and Southeast Asia. Theravāda of course also flourished over a long period in India itself; but it is convenient for us to trace its shape through the living tradition of an Indic civilization outside of mainland India proper. Let us look to its various dimensions.

## Theravāda: Ritual and Practical Dimensions

We have seen that meditation was a central part of early Buddhism. In theory this was a main occupation of monks and nuns. Also increasingly important, as the Pali Canon of scriptures came to be written down, was study, with a growing body of commentaries. The complexities of Buddhist analysis were considerable: there were analyses of the material and psychological constituents of the individual, from blood, pus, and semen to mental dispositions and states of consciousness; and of forms of perception; and of rules of conduct; and so on. There was, then, fertile ground for commentarial work. Monks also had a duty to preach to the laity and instruct them in the values of social life. Then, as time went on there were increasingly elaborate public festivals, for instance at Vesak, the full moon in May, celebrating the birth, Enlightenment and final decease of the Buddha. The clergy were also in demand to perform rites for the sick, and to protect households, and the like. In theory nuns and monks got their food by begging, but modern excavation has revealed arrangements for serving the monastic inhabitants with large quantities of food, doubtless ultimately supplied by the king and other laity. At the end of Vassa, the rainy season of retreat, lay folk presented new robes to the monks, and this was an occasion of joyful ceremonial.

What made the great monasteries possible was high income from food-growing, and orderly government to control a society which had to maintain large irrigation works. Naturally, over the centuries there were attempts at reform of a religion which risked becoming self-satisfied in a very rich environment. There were those who became araññika or forest-monks, and who revived the practice of the hermit life, dwelling alone in caves and huts in the jungle, and carrying on with strict meditation. They were relevant to outlying village life, for their reputation for merit made the villagers' offerings especially potent.

For the laity, various works of piety were the norm: feeding the monks and nuns, sending a son or daughter into the Order, going to the monasteries to circumambulate the stūpa or relic-mound, often huge and white, its plaster surface shining against the greens of the tropical landscape. There were gifts which the poorest and the richest might give to the Sangha. All such deeds brought merit which might help an individual to attain heaven next time, or at least a more favorable station in life. For the laity perhaps heaven was the dominant hope; but, as still today, they were able to distinguish between the desire for enjoyment, of which rebirth in one of the many heavens would be the greatest example, and spiritual growth, of which *nibbāna* (*nirvāṇa*) would be the culminating point. In their lives the monks and nuns stood as constant reminders of the ideal of "giving up" and looking to a goal beyond all ordinary goals.

Largely under outside (Mahāyāna) influence, there came to be shrines at the temples which included Buddha statues, some of enormous size. These became objects of piety, and again merit and mental purification could be had by making offerings to the Buddha. And surrounding Buddhist practice and commingling with it were the various gods and spirits, to whom the villagers still turned for help with harvest, possession, sickness, and other concerns. This interface with ordinary culture has been characteristic of Buddhism throughout its spread.

## Theravāda: the Experiential Dimension

One of the reasons why the classical Theravāda is so important in the history of religions is that it is the prime example of mysticism without God, and even without some all-pervading Absolute such as Brahman. The monk, nun, or pious layperson who follows the prescriptions of one of the famous manuals, for instance Buddhaghosa's *Visuddhimagga* (*Path of Purity*, fourth-fifth century C.E.), is doing something very like those Sufis and Christian contemplatives who empty their minds of thoughts and imaginings to make way for a divine vision. But here the ultimate experience is seen as realizing or (so to speak) touching *nibbāna*: coming in contact with that unborn, ineffable, transcendental state which for the Buddha is the Ultimate. The training of one who takes this path to the Highest includes much besides the purification of consciousness—it involves moral improvement, for instance—but at its heart is the practice of the *jhāna* (Sanskrit: *dhyāna*), to which we referred earlier. But since the Buddha did not believe in anything Beyond in the form of God or Absolute, mysticism in the Theravāda tradition does not involve any kind of sense of union, which many other branches of mysticism speak about.

Though the Theravāda has no place for a numinous Supreme Being, its practice has tended to invest its ceremonies and artifacts with something of that sense of the sacred. So the layperson might feel awe at a Buddha statue, as well as in connection with the lesser deities of daily life. In popular cults, too, there were aspects of shamanism in the healing ceremonies for those possessed by demons. But the gods and spirits were outside the Sangha's ambit of organization. For the spiritual path itself there was emphasis upon purity of life and self-training through meditation. It was through this that holy monks and nuns exuded a strange power.

Adam's Peak, Sri
Lanka.

### Theravāda: the Narrative Dimension

It became a commonplace that the story of the Buddha's life could be traced
through many generations. His previous lives were edifying; and after his
decease his influence still lived. For monks and laity alike in Sri Lanka this tale
was continued in the various chronicles, which saw the island as creating a
fine Buddhist civilization and as battling (against Tamil Hindu dynasties, for
instance) for the preservation of this spiritual heritage. This was reinforced by
the pilgrimage to Adam's Peak, which emphasized a sense of the holy
presence of the Buddha in the island. There was also the shrine at Mihintale,
recalling Mahinda's coming at the behest of the legendary great emperor,
Aśoka. In these ways, the story of the Buddha was extended to history,
giving the assurance of the central place of Sri Lanka, blessed island, in the
whole story of Liberation.

## Theravāda: the Doctrinal Dimension

Though there was plenty of the miraculous in the scriptural accounts of the Buddha, Theravāda saw him primarily as a great human being, who however in attaining a full understanding of the Dhamma came to embody it. So there was a transcendental side to his nature. But believers adhered to the view that it was unwise to go beyond what the Buddha had said, so that though analysis could be elaborated, no large-scale development of doctrine was possible. Little could be said as to the nature of *nibbāna*, except that it was Beyond the perishable events of this world. They stuck to the fourfold negation enunciated in this matter by the Buddha. As to the question of whether a Tathagata existed after death, he said: "It is not correct to say that he does, or does not, or both does and does not, or neither does nor does not." Such comprehensive negation pointed to the idea that the question was wrongly put: *nibbāna* as a condition escapes our ordinary language.

Great emphasis was placed on the *anattā* or nonself doctrine. Individuals transmigrate, but there is no permanent soul. What use is an unchanging soul? It can explain nothing by the very fact that it is unchanging: to cause something a thing has to change. It merely stands as a symbol for the possibility of salvation, and that was sufficiently taken care of by use of the concept of *nibbāna*.

The world of the Theravāda is vast: there are many world systems apart from ours, and each "galaxy" has its own heavens and hells and earth, its own gods, including Brahmā, and its own Satan, Māra, the death-dealing Tempter. The universe is virtually unending and beginningless, and exists in vast dimensions of space and time. The individual transmigrates through this vast system, now going to heaven, now assuming human, animal, or ghostly form, now suffering torments in one of the hells, now rising to the insect class, and so on and so on, till hopefully he may be reborn as a monk and approach final liberation: *nibbāna*. Then he will no longer be reborn. Pure selflessness in spirit will ensure that he will not regret the final disappearance of his individuality.

The Buddhist analysis of persons was designed to reinforce this sense of "selflessness:" a person was made up of five types of events—bodily events, perceptions, feelings, dispositions, and states of consciousness. These five groups of events were dispersed at death and reassembled because of the continued impulses contained in the dispositions. So if you still have a craving for this or that you will be reborn. What holds one part of your life together with another is just a complex chain of causes; similarly with what holds one life together with another. The person, then, is a temporary putting together of five kinds of impermanent events.

Much of the close doctrinal analysis in the Theravāda is in the third portion of the Tripitaka, that is, the threefold Canon of scriptures. This, known as the *Abhidhamma* portion (the name means "Analysis of the Dhamma:" Sanskrit *Abhidharma*), was the last to be assembled, after the two other portions, the *Sutta* (supposed discourses or *sūtras* of the Buddha) and *Vinaya* (Rule).

*Theravāda: Institutions and other matters*

The Vinaya rules control in great detail the daily life of the monk and nun. They can in theory be altered by majority vote, since the Sangha is constitutionally based on a republican form of government extant in the Buddha's time. But on the whole the conservative tendencies of the Theravāda have held the system fairly tight. The scriptures are shared, of course, by other Theravādin communities in other countries, such as Burma and Thailand, and there has been much interaction over the centuries between the Theravādin countries.

The brilliant capital of Anuradhapura came to be replaced by the glories of Polonnaruwa (p. 65) to the east, the center of a renewed irrigation-based civilization in the eleventh and twelfth centuries C.E. At this period there was greater integration between Buddhist and Hindu rites, and shrines to the gods were brought inside the temple complexes. We find, then, in Theravādin Sri Lanka a rich Indic civilization, which had a strong feeling of its glorious destiny in the spiritual life of the human race.

# The Rise of the Mahāyāna

In parallel with the full formation of the Theravādin tradition there came into existence a type of Buddhism which regarded itself as a Mahāyāna, a Greater Vehicle towards salvation than the more narrowly conceived Theravāda and other "Lesser Vehicle" schools. Its roots relate to the ethical, ritual and philosophical dimensions. At the ethical level, there was felt to be an increasing strain in the conventional interpretation of Buddhism: if a person strove through the practice of *dhyāna* and the like to better himself and ultimately to attain *nirvāṇa*, was not this essentially selfish and ego-oriented? The ideal of the serene *arhant* or Theravādin saint was in the final analysis as egoistic as the pursuits of the wealth-gaining merchant. The problem was the tension between insight and compassion, and was resolved, said the proponents of these ideas, in the ideal of the Bodhisattva, or Buddha-to-be, who out of compassion puts off his own final salvation till all are saved. This was a development of ideas implicit in the Jātaka stories and in the career of the Buddha himself, who was tempted to leave the world but stayed to preach the liberating, but subtle and difficult, Dharma.

In the ritual dimension, there was a growth in northwest India, from about the second century B.C.E., of the use of Buddha statues. It was not a long step from this to the idea that Buddhas continue to be present to us and so can be worshiped. This generated a type of Buddhism in which *bhakti* (warm devotion) came to supplement and even displace the austerer form of self-training, and mysticism. Out of this arose mythological innovations: stories about great Bodhisattvas such as Avalokiteśvara (p. 66), the Lord Who Looks Down (with compassion), and Amitābha, the Buddha of Infinite Light. Already about the third century B.C.E., a group known as the Mahāsanghikas had begun to break away from the Sthaviravādin (Theravādin) tradition in

India, arguing for a more open community, and for a less rigid adherence to the words of the historical Buddha. They regarded the Buddha as *lokottara*, beyond the world and transcendent, and yet somehow still present. All these tendencies came together from the first century B.C.E. onwards in the worship of a multiplicity of Buddha and Bodhisattva figures. This gave Buddhism a rich *bhakti* dimension. It also developed ideas of merit, so that the laity, and indeed monks and nuns, could gain merit by *pūjā*, the worship of these semidivine beings; and this in turn paved the way for a doctrine of grace, that is, salvation granted from above.

In some ways the philosophical changes were even more dramatic, though they are not always easy to grasp. Parallel developments occurred in the writings known as *Prajñāpāramitā Sūtras*, or *sūtras* of the Perfection of Wisdom, and in the writings of the philosopher Nāgārjuna of the early second century C.E. It may be noted that scriptures (*sūtras*) of various kinds were being composed in this period in Sanskrit or what is called Buddhist Hybrid Sanskrit. The writings are not cryptic and secretive, like Hindu parallels (there *sūtras* cannot be understood without a teacher or commentary); Buddhist writings are generally long and open, to the point of being prolix and repetitive. But the fact that new scriptures were being composed was important: it was a period when writing was becoming more universal, and something of the mystique which writing possesses for those who are still being weaned from oral traditions rubbed off on such literature. Texts were even to be put in *stūpas* and so reverenced like relics. The words describe the Truth and participate in the Truth; so in reverencing texts you reverence the Truth, and in doing this you reverence the Buddha, whose body is Truth. Naturally the Theravāda resisted the introduction of what it regarded as new and unwarranted "scriptures" into the canon. But the composers of the new texts thought of themselves as drawing out the essence of the Buddha's message, and so the writings could be ascribed to the Buddha himself.

The fundamental teaching of the Perfection of Wisdom is that all things in the world are relative to one another. They are mutually conditioned. Nothing has its own nature in itself. Intrinsically all things are "empty." If there is any ultimate truth it is this: the truth of emptiness, which is ineffable and can only be realized through direct experience—the mystical experience of the Buddhas.

Nāgārjuna's Mādhyamika or "Middle" philosophy is very similar and is argued in a more explicitly philosophical manner, refuting alternative theories. It can be shown, according to Nāgārjuna, that certain fundamental concepts which pervade all our thinking and talking, such as the idea of cause, are contradictory. If causes are short-lived events, then they go out of existence before their effects arrive; and this implies that the existent is caused by the nonexistent, which is absurd. And so on with all theories. If our fundamental ideas are vitiated by contradictions, so then are all accounts of the world. At best our language is a convenience, but it cannot "get at" the nature of reality, which is relative, empty, unspeakable. So we follow the Buddha, for he

*Opposite* The ritual dimension: Banaras, the greatest of India's holy cities, is a focus of pilgrimage and piety. Here, a Brahmin is washing in the river.

pointed the way through the contradiction, to the experience of liberation which can replace all philosophy, including the Buddha's own. This approach of Nāgārjuna's implies a two-level theory of truth: a distinction between ordinary pragmatic truth and ultimate, experienceable, Truth.

These notions from the Perfection of Wisdom and the Mādhyamika combined with religious ones. In attaining Truth we in effect become Buddhas, just as at the ethical level in treading the path of the Bodhisattva we are indeed Buddhas-to-be, and the Buddha nature resides in each one of us. In worshiping Buddhas and Bodhisattvas we are still at the lower level and, as it were, worshiping our future state. The whole apparatus of celestial Buddhas and belief in the earthly Buddha eventually can be discarded when we enter the Beyond, in ineffable enlightenment.

There was another twist to the tale. If you recognize with Nāgārjuna that our usual conceptual distinctions between one thing and another are merely provisional, then so is our conventional distinction between *nirvāṇa* and *saṃsāra*. In other words, we already are in the realm of *nirvāṇa*, but do not know it until we have the "higher" point of view. All this fitted together with a new role for the layperson who could as well tread the Bodhisattva path in the ordinary life of *saṃsāra*.

### The Mahāyāna Pure Land

Three centuries or more after Nāgārjuna's work there was the philosophy of the brothers Asanga and Vasubandhu, who propounded the so-called Vijñānavāda or Consciousness school. It is often thought to teach the unreality of the world out there and its origin in the mind. It is in the philosophical sense "idealist," according to this way of looking at it. But more strictly it teaches that everything which we claim as the truth or knowledge is qualified by consciousness: that is, it is reality as interpreted by consciousness and language. It is always seen through the lens of the subject-object structure of consciousness. In itself, however, reality does not have this subject-object character. We can seek to obtain a unitive consciousness without duality through the higher experience of Buddhism.

More important in the life of ordinary people was the Sukhāvatī or Pure Land school, which arose about the time of Nāgārjuna; it holds that the Buddha Amitābha has constructed a Pure Land far to the west, full of splendors and joys, such as rivers which run as deep or as warm as you want and trees composed wholly of jewels. This place is highly conducive to the ultimate attainment of *nirvāṇa*; but its glories tended to dominate the imagination and it became for many an end in itself, like the Christian or Islamic Paradise. Just by calling on the name of Amitābha, the faithful were assured of translation at death to the Pure Land.

We shall return to these forms of the Mahāyāna when we are dealing with Chinese and Japanese experience, for there they had their full flower. They and many other schools of Buddhism flourished in India during the first millennium C.E. They flourished in such study centers as Nalanda in the

LXXXVI

north and Nagarjunikonda in the south; and were interwoven with the fabric of growing Hinduism. There still remains one more phase of the life of Buddhism in South Asia, before the modern period; and that is its journey into Tibet and life there. This is tied in with those developments known as Tantra. Meanwhile let us turn to see how classical Hindu practices and ideas were taking shape just before and during the first millennium C.E.

## Classical Hinduism: its Main Shape

### Devotion

Various forces were coalescing to provide a shape for the heterogeneous religions over which the Brahmins came to prevail. The cult of gods and goddesses, probably always important in modest circumstances inside the home, began to acquire more permanent public form. Perhaps in part under the stimulus of Buddhism, the Hindu temple came to play a leading role in Indian life. It provided a focus for ceremonial and a place for meeting with the

---

**Hinduism** some key terms

*Arca* Image which is occupied by a God once it is consecrated.

*Ātman* The self of an individual which is eternal and in Advaita is regarded as identical with Brahman (see below).

*Avatāra* Descent or incarnation of God (notably Viṣṇu) in such figures as Rama, Kṛṣṇa and the future Kalki.

*Bhakti* Warm devotion to God.

*Brahman* The sacred Power which is both in the sacrificial process and in the cosmos: hence the term is used of the Divine Being.

*Dharma* The pattern underlying the cosmos and manifest in the ethical and social laws of humankind.

*Īśvara* The Lord, that is, God considered as a person and (typically) as creator.

*Jāti* Caste, a group with whom the individual identifies in marriage and in eating: the fabric of *jātis* makes up the caste system.

*Karma* The law which governs the effects of deeds both in this life and in subsequent lives within the operation of rebirth or reincarnation.

*Pūjā* Worship.

*Sannyāsin* Holy person who has left ordinary duties as determined by *dharma* and *jāti* behind, often as a wanderer.

*Yoga* Methods of meditation, sometimes involving physical as well as mental discipline.

---

*Opposite, above* The narrative dimension: an episode from the *Mahābhārata*, one of Hinduism's two great epics, and a vast source of entertainment and spiritual instruction. This scene shows Arjuna overcoming Karna, with various gods looking on. This was an episode in the great civil war depicted in the epic.

*Opposite, below* The doctrinal dimension: much of Hindu tradition envisaged the cosmos as being periodically created and re-created. In between were periods of rest, symbolized here by Viṣṇu lying on the serpent Ananta ("Endless"), representing eternity. Viṣṇu, accompanied here by his consort, Lakṣmi, awaits his next burst of creative activity.

great and lesser gods. The Brahmanical heritage in the old days had been without such ikons and buildings. The place of sacrifice had to be laid out, constructed, as befitted an originally nomadic way of life. There was no necessity that Brahmins should be involved in the *pūjā* of the temple; but it was an advantage to the priestly class that it should control so potent a means of focusing the people's piety and impulses to giving. So images and temples were the outer manifestation of a wider role for priests in the developing Hindu society.

This was a symptom of the growing importance not just of worship but more particularly that fervent sharing in the life of the God known as *bhakti* religion. Its features are already portrayed in one book of the great epic *Mahābhārata*, known as the Song of the Lord or *Bhagavadgītā*. This was composed possibly as early as 300 B.C.E. It has in it—as the most famed of India's philosophers, Sánkara, said—the essence of the Vedas. Its popularity gave it immense influence, and it inspired many imitations on behalf of Śiva and other gods. It came to be recognized as part of the sacred tradition or *smṛti*, which continues the more strictly authoritative *śruti* or revelation, consisting of the Vedic hymns and appended works down to the main classical Upanishads; in fact, in its conditioning of Indian religion, the *Gītā* is actually more influential than the Vedic hymn collections.

In the *Bhagavadgītā*, Viṣṇu as Lord and numinous creator of the universe

*Below* A typical southern *gopuram* or temple tower, decorated with the gods, near Kanchipuram.

*Below right* The descent from heaven to earth of the river Ganges, with various mythic figures, at Mahabalipuram in Tamil Nadu, South India.

reveals himself as also loving. His avatar Kṛṣṇa declares at the end: "Those who worship me with complete discipline and who contemplate me, whose thoughts are constantly on me—these I soon raise up from the sea of death and rebirth." Arjuna, awaiting battle against his relatives, is given a firmer mind after his confusions and despair about the dread effects of battling against his kith and kin. There are many riches in the *Gītā* ("song"), as it is often called for short; but the central value is that of loyalty and devotion to God, namely *bhakti*.

Viṣṇu, with his incarnations, and Śiva, great Yogin and destroyer of the world, stimulator of the divine *śakti* or power, emerge during this time as the twin great manifestations of the divine Being. They displace some of the older deities important in the Vedic scriptures. Followers of Viṣṇu were called *Vaiṣṇavas* and of Śiva were called *Śaivas* and included the important movements of Kashmiri and Tamil Śaivism. They are enclosed together in the world of traditional religion (*smārta*) as both rivals and cooperators. Viṣṇu is gentler, and much concerned with the periodic restoration of the Dharma through sending down his incarnations, of whom Rāma and Kṛṣṇa are the two most important—Rāma the ideal king, Kṛṣṇa the glorious lover. Śiva is more numinous, wrathful and destructive, but potent through yoga, and indissolubly linked to the Goddess.

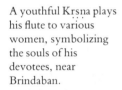

A youthful Kṛṣṇa plays his flute to various women, symbolizing the souls of his devotees, near Brindaban.

*Above* The mythic dimension: an eighth-century Pala bronze of Viṣṇu.

The third main divinity of later Hinduism, the Goddess was beginning to emerge into general recognition by the fourth century C.E., in such texts as the *Devīmahātmyam*. She was always there, of course: already in the Indus Valley civilization, and in the villages and undercurrents of life below the surface of the rather macho society of the Vedic hymns; and in the many myths of the consorts of the gods, above all of the great Gods. In Tantric Hinduism she was destined to flower further. But we may say that for much of the Hindu tradition the three great deities are Śiva, Viṣṇu, and the Goddess, under her various names such as Dūrgā, Kālī, and Parvatī.

Below the ultimate Gods are the many deities of the incredibly rich narrative corpus of the Hindus: the two vast epics; the *Harivamśa* (about Kṛṣṇa); the *Purāṇas*, and the oral traditions of the various regions of the subcontinent.

*Philosophies*

Behind the stories were erected the philosophies, above all those systems of belief known as Vedānta, which contains several great variations. There is the doctrine of the aphoristic scripture known as the *Brahmasūtra*, which sets forth Vedānta, "The End or Final Part of the Veda." Its doctrine is probably a version of that system known as Bhedābhedavāda or "Difference-in-Nondifference:" Brahman is both different from and not different from the world and souls. The most influential in modern times has been the Advaita, or Nondualistic Vedānta, of Śankara (eighth century C.E.) and his later followers, which sets forth the identity of the soul and Brahman, and the illusoriness, therefore, of the world as multiplicity. There was in the eleventh century the *bhakti*-oriented theism of Rāmānuja's Viśiṣṭādvaita or Qualified Nondualism, which sees the world and souls as God's body and instruments of his will. In the thirteenth century there was Madhva's Dvaita or Dualism, in which an eternal difference between soul and soul, soul and world, soul and Brahman, and world and Brahman is affirmed: again a kind of theism. These philosophies underpinned spiritual practice: Śankara could only assign *bhakti* to second place, as something fit for the unenlightened person still mired in the world of magical illusion (*māyā*). Mystical intuition of identity with the One is the fruit of the higher path.

Commonly these philosophies are held to conduce to liberation or *mokṣa*, which was the last of the four ends of life laid down in classical Hinduism—the others being *kāma*, pleasure (sex being the most intense of the pleasures, the word also stands for this as in the famous *Kāmasūtra*), *artha* or economic gain, and *dharma*, virtue or action in accord with the Dharma. This last was summed up in the law books of Manu, which set down the varieties of duties of Hindus within the structure of the caste system.

*Social existence in the classical period*

In the early classical period it was thought necessary to fight the challenge posed to orthodoxy by Buddhism and the other śramanic movements. There was evolved the theory of the four stages of life or *varṇāśramadharma*: student, householder, parent of adult son, ascetic; and Hinduism developed its own monastic orders, one of which was founded by Sankara.

Classical Hinduism saw the increasing articulation of the caste system. Caste groups married within each group, and ate only with that group. These practices of endogamy and commensality were the framework for various castes based upon occupation, traditional God, region, and history. The framework of the four *varṇas* was filled in with a vast mosaic of more refined distinctions, in a social hierarchy topped by the Brahmins and undergirded by the "fifth class" or untouchables, whose occupations were specially polluting (leather work, butchering, brewing, cleaning latrines, fishing, etc.).

And so during the Gupta period, a most florid episode in Indian history, from the fourth to the sixth centuries C.E., we can imagine the glories and complexities of classical Hinduism—the temples, the great rivers, the pilgrims, the parades of gods, the recitations of the epics, the fervor of *bhakti*, the wandering *sannyāsins*, the yogins in meditation, the pandits exploring metaphysics, the elaboration of caste, the sacrifices for princes and emperors, the chanting of vastly ancient verses, the household rites, the pomp of weddings, the countless villages, the wandering of sacred cows, the smell of cowdung burning, the hovels of untouchables, the pride of Brahmins, the rites of the Goddess, the lingam of Śiva, the tales of Kṛṣṇa—a great amalgam which yet through the Brahmins had a loose orthodoxy. Hinduism by now had a loose federal existence through the idea that those who accepted the *śruti*, whatever else they did not accept—God, Viṣṇu, *karma*, rebirth, virtue—accepted the primordial authority of the Veda, coeval with time.

And in our mental picture of the times we should recall too, mingled in with the Hindu conglomeration, the shaven-headed monks and nuns of the Buddhists, the various ascetics, the angular temples of the Jaina tradition, the stūpas and Bo trees of Buddhist compounds, the cells of monks, the flags of unorthodox festivities, the Buddha statues and the Jātaka tales, the moral discourses, the huge scriptures, the *bhakti* to Amitābha, the giving of protective spells, wives who followed the wise teachings of the Buddha, households of Jains gentle toward animals and insects—in short the whole mingling of the unorthodox traditions with the religion where the Brahmins held sway. India then was a glorious jumble of customs and beliefs, as indeed it is to a lesser extent today.

## Buddhism spreads North: the Tibetan Experience

The cultural region which stretches from Ladakh and Nepal up over the mountains into Tibet, and east beyond today's Tibet into western China, can conveniently be called the Tibetan region; it came gradually to absorb influences both from China and from India. In the end Indian, and in particular Buddhist, influence was predominant. The area assumed very great significance, for the destruction of Buddhist centers in north India by Turkish

*Left* In the Himalayan region, as in Sikkim, the Vajrāyana or Diamond Vehicle predominates: this old Buddhist woman uses a prayer wheel to express her piety.

*Below, left* A Tibetan painting of Avalokiteśvara as a meditation Buddha-to-be

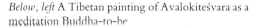

*Below, right* A *maṇḍala* or ritual diagram displaying Akṣobhya, the Eastern Buddha, one of the Buddhas of the five directions (North, South, East, West, and Center).

Muslim pillagers left Tibet as the great repository of Mahāyāna texts, as well as of a whole assemblage of esoteric or secret Tantric texts. The form of Buddhism which had developed in northern Bihar, Bengal, and Kashmir was naturally accessible to Tibet. And it included what is often referred to as the Vajrayāna or "Diamond Vehicle," sometimes also called the Mantrayāna or "Sacred Formula Vehicle." The reason for this last name was because of the great emphasis put in this form of Buddhism on the use of ritual utterances.

The Vajrayāna was concerned with new ways of transforming consciousness, typically in conjunction with the guidance of a guru, through the practice of relating both to sacred formulae and to the visualized figures of various Buddhas and deities. Equations between the different aspects of individual life, the cosmos, and the deities led to a fusion of inner and outer magical and psychological methods. Sometimes Tantric initiates used forbidden practices, such as meat-eating and sexual intercourse, to help them to rise "beyond morality" and so beyond the world. Such methods, by the use of secret rituals and the breaking of taboos in a ritual context, were pioneered also in the Hindu environment of north India. But though they were an element in the kind of Buddhism which came to be established in Tibet, Tibetan Buddhism could also more broadly be defined as Mahāyāna. The texts that they studied, much of the yoga they practiced, and much of the spirit of Tibet could be said to be "Greater Vehicle" in character.

The "Diamond" of the name of the Vajrayāna refers to the eternal Buddhahood resident in all beings, unsplittable and achieved through the cutting edge of wisdom (*prajñā*). The spiritual exercises of Tantra aimed at identification with this Buddhahood here and now, and conceived of the individual as being of the same nature as the universe. So by self-purification, usually using earlier Buddhist methods of meditation, an adept could visualize his chosen deity or Buddha-figure and thus attain unity with him. The use of magical diagrams or *maṇḍalas* combined the elements of sacred formulae, since the diagrams contained sacred syllables, and the internal use of the visual imagination. Various equations occurred: the five *skandhas* or groups of events which make up the individual (bodily events, perceptions, feelings, dispositions, and states of consciousness) were equated with five Buddhas—Vairocana, Akṣobhya, Ratnasambhava, Amitābha, and Amoghasiddhi (their names mean: Illuminator, Imperturbable, Jewel-Born, Boundless Light, and Infallible Success). These in turn correspond to the five directions of the cosmos (center, east, south, west, and north), and to five kinds of evil and five kinds of wisdom. By imagining brilliantly your deity, you gain unity with him and he with you. This nondual unification is often symbolized by the sexual bond, where two bodies become fused into one.

Female deities took on great importance as consorts or *śaktis* of Buddhas; the greatest of them, Tārā, the Savioress, is the consort of the great Bodhisattva Avalokiteśvara. Though gentler in nature and purer in appearance than the somewhat fierce representation of the numinous Goddess in the Hindu tradition, the Goddess here is part of a very old stream of sentiment going back to the beginnings of Indic civilization, but here translated to Tibet. Avalokiteśvara and Tārā, incidentally, are thought to have procreated monkeys who transformed themselves over generations into the Tibetan people. (No emotional problems here over the theory of evolution!)

The first monastery in Tibet was founded near the end of the eighth century C.E. There was some resistance to the new religion from the indigenous religion, commonly referred to as Bön (but to its nature and identity we shall return). It was in the eleventh century that there was a second and more vigorous diffusion of Buddhism. It was in this period that the great teacher Atīśa, who had been to Sumatra to advise the court over there, came to Tibet at the insistance of the Buddhist rulers of west Tibet. One of his disciples founded the religious order of bKa'-gdams-pa. In the same century, in consequence of the teaching of Marpa, a famous Tibetan monk who had studied at one of the great north Indian universities, the Sa-skya order was started. A third order, the bKa'-rgyud-pa, was host to Tibet's most beloved religious teacher, Mila Raspa (or Milarepa, 1079–1153).

On the whole the reason for the importation of Buddhism into Tibet by its secular rulers seems to have been political, to provide a "modern" ideology of rule and to open up to Tibet the advantages of literacy and philosophy. In the ensuing centuries it became more important due to the conversion of many Mongols, especially the emperor of China, Kublai Khan. The grand lamas of the Sa-skya order were nominated in effect as viceroys, under Mongol suzerainty; eventually, after political conflict, sometimes armed (so we have the spectacle of Buddhist orders fighting one another as monks of war, but overwhelmingly for political and not ideological reasons), the chief rule passed in the seventeenth century C.E. to the head of the reformed Dge-lugs-pa order, which had been founded by the great Tson-kha-pa in the fourteenth century. The succession of the Dalai Lamas, as they are still called, is by a process of identifying a reincarnation of a deceased Dalai Lama. This was a method of succession which had been used by other orders in Tibet since the twelfth century.

Thus we have established in Tibet a kind of theocracy—one could call it a Buddhocracy. Though it was a country thoroughly infused with varieties of the Vajrayāna, it also contained something of its own indigenous Bön tradition. But this too had undergone a transformation over the years as a result of Buddhist influence. Ascribing its founding to the legendary Gsen-rab, from a country far to the west, who was a fully enlightened being at birth and spent his life as a prince propagating the Bön religion, the religion formed its own corpus of scriptures corresponding to those of the Buddhists. Just as the Tibetan Buddhists believe that the scriptures in their corpus, the Tanjur, were expounded by the Buddha Śākyamuni himself, so the Bön-po think of *their* Tanjur as having been uttered by Gsen-rab himself. Also like the Buddhists, they have a body of commentaries and other works known as the

Kanjur. The Bön-po have their own monasteries, order, *stūpas*, and so on: they have produced a sort of mirror image of Buddhism. They circumambulate their *stūpas* and other holy objects counterclockwise, and likewise spin their prayer wheels; but they teach that the Buddha was a fraud, and that the coming of Buddhism to Tibet was a great disaster, the cause of evil *karma*. Even so, their aims and methods and popular piety are much the same as those of Buddhism, and the two religions live side by side amicably enough.

## The Goddess and Hindu Tantra

Though the roots of the worship of the Goddess go right back to the Indus Valley civilization, it was in the late classical and medieval periods that it achieved a central importance in the Indian tradition. It was especially important in the northeast, in Bengal and Assam; but everywhere in India, scattered through villages and in domestic rites, there were varieties of goddesses, who came to be seen as diverse manifestations of one Goddess, who represents the creative power or *śakti* of the Ultimate. There is of course no reason in doctrine why we should think of God as female or as male, since she/he is neither, strictly. It is only human imagery that needs to make the decision. But there are powerful connections with the idea of the supreme Female, with the earth as being our Mother, with fertility, with motherly love, with falling in love. A devotee could see the Goddess under so many disguises, as provider of food, of great creatrix of the world, as object of affection and devotion, as lover of my soul, as all-devouring Time or Death, as bringer of smallpox and cholera, and so on.

Śaktism could be connected in practice with Hindu Tantra. The main thoughts behind this magico-spiritual outlook have been in part touched upon in regard to Buddhist Tantra: but in the Hindu context it especially is expressed through the thought of harnessing magical and spiritual energy—the *śakti* which the female both personifies and wields. Another motif is secrecy, mimicking the restrictions which apply to Vedic knowledge, but here devoted to keeping apart the techniques and initiations of those adept in harnessing the energy. Like a number of other religious movements, Tantrism broke down caste barriers, as it indeed could violate other taboos.

## Islam in India

Though Islam came to Sind in the seventh century, and Muslim traders also settled in various places, it was not really till the eleventh century that substantial inroads were made into the traditional heartlands of Indian culture. Islam and Indic religions were on the whole in conflict. Islam rejected, with a kind of pious horror, the use of images; and this provided the excuse for invaders to smash up statues and temples, whether Hindu, Buddhist, or Jain.

A popular Muslim story tells of an ascetic visited in the desert by his former beloved—showing Hindu influences on Islamic spirituality.

However, Islam was by no means wholly alien. There were other movements in India which were largely without images; the *sant* tradition of poets and preachers emphasized devotion towards the *nirguṇam* form of God, that is, his nature seen as without visible attributes or images. Moreover, Islam had the great advantage that it was not fettered by the caste system. It was not spread chiefly by the sword, but by the conversion of men and women, and here missionary Sufis were important in India. Their mystical path was congenial to many Hindus, and their sanctity could combine with the more evident social justice in Islam to attract many to convert. The Islamic shaykhs and pirs as holy leaders had analogies to Hindu holy men; while the influential work of Ibn al-Arabi (1185–1240), with its emphasis on the unity of all being, had similarities to Advaita Vedānta. There were less orthodox holy men, *qalandars*, who closely resembled some of the wandering ascetics, going round smeared in ashes, begging, performing austerities, smoking hashish: they were inclined to sit loose to orthodox Islamic practice, but they could mediate belief in Allah to the Hindu population.

From the sixteenth century on, the pressures of state also moved toward conversion under the great Mughal Empire, ruled from Delhi. It is true that the emperor Akbar (1556–1605) tried to establish a new, syncretic religion, combining the best, as he saw it, in Islam and the Hindu and other traditions; but under his successor there was a rather rigid imposition of Islamic law.

Mughal culture gave much to India—a framework in which a new kind of piety could flourish, and the brilliance of architecture and art which provided a model for later princes, whether Hindu, Muslim, or Christian. But it was surrounded by a rich civilization that had its own new impulses to religious creativity, some of which had their roots in the classical period.

## Regional Movements

In examining the varieties of Hinduism in the medieval epoch I shall be necessarily selective, and shall choose four from differing regions; Śrī Vaiṣṇavism from Tamil Nadu; the Lingayats of south central India; Kashmiri Śaivism from the far north; and the Caitanya tradition from the northeast. To this I shall add the Sikhs, who though they became a separate religion displayed some characteristic features of *bhakti* Hinduism.

### Śrī Vaiṣṇavism and Tamil Poetry

The greatest thinker in the Vaiṣṇava tradition was undoubtedly Rāmānuja, who lived around 1000 C.E. His great synthesis reconciled the Tamil Vaiṣṇava and Vedānta traditions. His motives were not primarily philosophical but religious. He found the Nondualism (Advaita) of Śankara to be a great danger, mainly because with its theory of levels of truth and reality it assigned the Lord, and the worship of the Lord, to the lower level, below the mystical intuition of Oneness. It cut at the root of devotional religion. It also cut at the root of sacrificial Brahmin practice; but that was less serious. Rāmānuja wished to express a fervid devotion to the Lord which at the same time could be seen as a good interpretation of the *śruti* or revealed truth of the Hindu faith, notably as expressed in the Upanishads and the *Brahmasūtra*, and as shown forth in the *Gītā,* which was the jewel of *smṛti* or holy memory.

For five centuries the great poets of Tamil Nadu had been composing sacred songs to both Viṣṇu and Śiva. These poets were known as the Ālvārs (Vaiṣṇavas) and the Nayanars (Śaivas). Twelve Ālvār poets are found in the tenth-century collection known as "The Four Thousand Divine Verses." The works of the sixty-three Nayanars, of whom the most important was Māṇikkavāçagar, were incorporated in the Śaiva Canon (*Āgamas*) which expressed an alternative to the Veda (sometimes it was called a fifth Veda) for the followers of the Tamil movement known as Śaiva Siddhānta.

After Rāmānuja, Srī Vaiṣṇavism became a very powerful force in the south, splitting into two schools, based on Sanskrit and Tamil scriptures and sources respectively, and holding different views on the subject of God's grace. Both stressed that salvation from the ocean of rebirth flows from God's love; the debate centered on the interpretation of this—whether the devotee has to do nothing, like the kitten being transported by the scruff of its neck by its mother, or to reach out, as the little monkey uses its arms to cling to its mother—but the essence of the faith was loving devotion to and reliance upon the Lord. The Lord's mythic deeds and goodness were to be celebrated in song, in the rites of clothing and feeding him (present in his image), and in pilgrimage to the sacred sites commemorating his glory. Socially, Śrī Vaiṣṇavism was egalitarian before the Lord. Since it is not by works that you are saved, your status—arrived at through *karma*—does not matter. Thus, as elsewhere, *bhakti* could be a protest against the hierarchical nature of Indian society. The *bhaktas* or devotees of south India picked up some of the ethos of Buddhism and Jainism which they had done so much, by their fervid missionary spirit, to phase out.

Rāmānuja thought of the cosmos and the souls which transmigrated within it as being God's body. By "body" he meant that which subserves a soul. God, being perfect, perfectly controls his body; we do so with ours only imperfectly. He guides us also from within each individual soul as the *antaryāmin* or "inner controller." *Karma* is merely the working out of God's will; and if we call on God in faith we shall be rewarded by being born in God's glorious heaven, close to him. By the metaphor of the body Rāmānuja preserves the sense of intimate unity between God and the world, as expressed in the Upanishads themselves.

### The Lingāyata Contrast

Lingāyata was founded in the twelfth century by an intellectual and reformer called Bāsava. Its other name is Vīraśaiva or heroic Śaivism. It has a certain austerity, deriving ultimately from the Jain tradition. The Lingāyats are called "*lingam*-carriers," the meaning of their name, because each person is supposed to carry a small phallic symbol in a tube fastened round the neck or to the arm, and this is virtually the sole ikon in their faith. It is useless to go on pilgrimage or worship in temples or perform any other ritual actions, and for the major part of life the sole practice enjoined by Bāsava was the reverencing of the *lingam*, symbol of Śiva, twice a day. Some other rites and the use of holy water, ashes, rosaries, and so on also came into Lingāyata practice, which concentrates in other respects on the paying of homage to Śiva, through the formula *Namaḥ Śivāya*, and the inner recollection of the God.

Striking features of Lingāyata are its rejection of the caste system, its condemnation of child marriage, and its proclamation of the equality of the sexes. Though it has a hereditary priesthood of its own, it avoids all the rituals of the Brahmins, and in some respects seems a protest against Brahmin domination. Though it rejected caste at the outset, the inevitable of course happened: it itself was treated by the other castes as a caste. There is little escaping the embracing arms of the system in Hindu India. Its ethics are those of equality and humility, as befits those who follow the great God. Honesty and hard work in one's daily occupation were deemed important; and in some ways the group seems like a Hindu counterpart of Protestant Christianity.

## Kashmiri Śaivism: a Synthesis

Very different in emphasis from the two regional movements we have looked at is the so-called Trika (Triad) Śaivism of Kashmir, which started as a Tantric movement directed at absorbing and utilizing the energy of a threesome or triad of goddesses, later seen as three manifestations of Śiva's powerful consort Kālī (probably the most potent of all Indian representations of the Goddess). Mostly the movement had its base in Kashmir; and its chief exponent and theologian was the philosopher Abhinavagupta (975?–?1035). He wrote important works on aesthetics, partly because there was emphasis in the rites of this kind of Śaivism on dance, song and poetry. Abhinavagupta argued against various positions, though he was sympathetic to their general sense, such as Śaiva Siddhānta (the theology of south Indian Śaivism), the Yogācāra school of Buddhism, and Advaita Vedānta. In combining elements from the orthodox tradition of Śankara and the unorthodox Tantric Śaivism, which involved sexual intercourse as a means of attaining the highest state of interior bliss and knowledge, he claimed to teach the most catholic of Śaiva doctrines and practices. He saw the world as a triadic unity between the individual, the divine Śakti or Goddess, and Śiva as the underlying being behind the Goddess. This "new triad" was intended to give a positive view of the notion of Nondualism: the nondual experience could be had in ecstatic participation in the world, and not (as with Śankara) by some kind of withdrawal to a higher level of Truth.

## Kṛṣṇa Devotion and Caitanya

Late in the premodern period of Hinduism, in the sixteenth century, we have in Bengal and elsewhere in the northeast (Orissa and Assam) the revival of an intense form of Kṛṣṇa devotion and Vaiṣṇava *bhakti* through the life and work of Caitanya. At the age of twenty-two, while on pilgrimage to Bodh-Gaya to perform rites for the death of his first wife, Caitanya had an intense conversion to loyalty and love towards Kṛṣṇa. He changed his name to Kṛṣṇa-Caitanya ("he whose consciousness is Kṛṣṇa"—hence his modern followers refer to their movement as "Krishna Consciousness"). The chief practice of devotees, whether they be mendicants or householders—and the movement made powerful headway among the middle classes—was the utterance of Kṛṣṇa's name, calling on him for divine mercy. Love of Kṛṣṇa was often modeled after the loves that Kṛṣṇa himself had with the milkmaids of Brindavan or with his divine mistress Rādhā. Separation from him was pain, and the individual *bhakta* clung to Kṛṣṇa with passion. Persons were, as elsewhere in the main Hindu tradition, caught up in a cycle of rebirth; but by God's grace and mercy they would be delivered and restored to communion with Viṣṇu, from whom, like sparks, they had originally emanated. In this latter age, the Kaliyuga, it is not easy at all for people to undertake religious duties: it is fortunate that God in his love makes salvation available to those who throw themselves upon him in faith and love.

## Sikhism and the Bhakti Tradition

There were some obvious affinities between the *bhakti* movements—especially the *nirguṇam* form which stressed the imageless and formless God—and the Islamic heritage of devotion to the one God, Allah. The similarity was perceived with great clarity by Nānak (1469–1504), who came to be recognized as the first Guru in the Sikh tradition. In the traditional accounts of his life he underwent a dramatic experience when bathing in a stream, in which he received a call from God. When he reappeared after three days' absence, his first words were "There is no Hindu; there is no Muslim." Thereafter he became a wandering recluse and undertook long journeys, even according to Sikh tradition as far as Mecca. Before his experience, however, he had already moved in this direction of providing a faith which transcended

---

**Sikhism** some key terms

*Amrit* Initiation by baptism in sweetened water stirred by a two-edged sword, in which the initiate swears to abide by the code or Rahit.

*Granth* or *Adi Granth* or *Guru Granth* The sacred scriptures of Sikhism which, since Guru Gobind Singh, serve as the teacher or Guru.

*Gurdwara* or *Gurudwara* The Sikh temple housing, primarily, a copy of the Granth.

*Guru* One of the ten leaders and preceptors of Sikhism, from Nanak to Gobind Singh.

*Janamsakhi* Punjabi writings celebrating the life of Guru Nanak.

*Khalsa* The Sikh community or order, the "pure ones" started by Gobind.

*Mool Mantra* The "basic verse," a brief statement of belief composed by Nanak affirming the oneness of God.

*Panth* The community of the Sikhs, literally the "path."

*Rahit* The code of ethics and rituals laid upon Sikhs, including the wearing of the five K's: uncut hair, dagger, breeches, comb, iron bangle.

*Sant* A member of a devotional tradition of North India, picturing God as without attributes or *nirguṇan* rather than more personally as among Vaishnavas. The two most important members were founders of Sikhism, Nanak and Kabir. A Sant is a preceptor or guru within the tradition.

*Sat Guru* The name most given to God in Sikhism, "Being, the Teacher."

*Sikh* Literally "disciple," member of the Sikh Panth.

---

---

### Gurū Nānak's Japjī

There is but one God whose name is true, the Creator, devoid of fear and enmity, immortal, unborn, self-existent; by the favour of the Gurū.

The True One was in the beginning; the True One was in the primal age.

The True One is now also, O Nānak; the True One also shall be.

By thinking I cannot obtain a conception of Him, even though I think hundreds of thousands of times.

---

external barriers between religions. He and a Muslim minstrel called Mardana had composed hymns together, which became a vital part of later Sikh worship. On Nānak's journey to Mecca he is reported to have fallen asleep in error with his feet pointing toward Mecca, and so showing disrespect to the Muslim faith. A mullah had woken him angrily, but Nānak's comment was devastating: "Then turn my feet in a direction where God is not."

A feature of the religious movement set in motion by Nānak was the importance of the guru. The teacher, who is not thought of in any way as an incarnation or manifestation of God, is important for guiding people in the way of Truth or God. The framework of Nānak's theology was Hindu in that he affirmed reincarnation and that the best symbol of the divine was the mysterious syllable Oṃ, of Vedic origin. He referred to God as creator of Brahman and the Vedas. But he dispensed with the idea of a priesthood (he himself was a *kṣatriya*, of the warrior caste).

Nānak's successors as leaders of the new community were a line of nine further Gurus, culminating in Guru Gobind Singh, who died in 1708, and who nominated the scriptures of the community, the Ādi Granth, henceforth to be the Guru. Of the other Gurus perhaps Arjun is the most important. He led the community from 1581 to 1606. He founded the Golden Temple at Amritsar, collected the scriptures, and came into conflict with the emperor Jehangir—a conflict which led to clearer self-definition of the Sikhs as a militant and outwardly distinguishable group. But this side of the Sikh story comes later, in the modern period. It may be noted that there has long been fluidity at the edges of Sikhism. Quite a few followers of the Nānak tradition—and that of his elder contemporary Kabīr (1440–1518), some of whose poems were incorporated into the Sikh scriptures—remain within the definitely Hindu framework, as followers of a path which emphasizes *bhakti* and the unity of religions.

### Some Traditional Minorities

It must not be forgotten in drawing a picture of the mainstream traditions of the Indian classical and medieval periods that there were also some significant minorities—for instance there were the religions of the various tribal groups who peppered the subcontinent and who in many cases were gradually assimilated into the fabric of mainstream culture. We can ascribe some of the

*Opposite* The narrative dimension: Rāma, the avator of Viṣṇu and Lakṣmana shoot at Ravana, demon king of Lanka (Ceylon)—a scene from the *Rāmāyana*.

great richness of the Hindu mythic corpus to the assimilation of varied stories from such diverse groups.

There were also Christians in India throughout these later periods—the followers of St. Thomas the Apostle in south India. He is supposed to have preached there and to have been eventually martyred; his tomb is displayed in Mylapore, on the outskirts of Madras. Whether or not the tradition is true, the Thomas Christians are certainly very ancient, going back at least to the third century C.E.

There were two communities of Jews, so-called White and Black, on the coast of Kerala, and they claim origins going back to the fall of the Temple in 70 C.E.; but we have historical records only from about the year 1000.

Also settled on the west coast, from the eighth century onwards, were Zoroastrians (or Parsees, "Persians," as they came to be known), who remain a small but influential element in Indian society.

## The Indian Tradition in the Classical and Medieval Periods

The story we have told is only a sample of the full unfolding of events which are immensely complicated. If we look for a moment to the dimensions of religion we can rehearse some of the many patterns.

First, as to *ritual* and *practice*, we have seen varying types of yoga—Hindu, Buddhist, and Jain. We have seen the persistence of the Brahmins with their sacrificial rites and their takeover of the temples, which housed gods who were treated to worship and *bhakti*. We see how sometimes the inward devotion becomes much more important than any outward observance, as among the Lingāyats and in the Sikh religion of Nānak. We see India drawn together by great pilgrimages, at Banaras and at the vast Kumbh Mela fair at Prayag, where the rivers Jumna and Ganges meet the invisible river Sarasvatī. We see great regional divergences of practice, from Tamil Nadu to Kashmir and from Kerala to Assam. We see coming into this complex the Muslims, who helped to knock out Buddhism in north India and contributed to its demise in the whole of India. We see everywhere villages, and at a more basic level households. Each household was likely to have its little shrine, and such domestic rites remained a vital part of the fabric of Indian religions.

In *experience* we have the patterns of inner meditation and strenuously achieved bliss and equanimity; the numinous awe before great and fierce goddesses and gods; the devotion and sense of peace bestowed by loving deities; the securities bestowed by local and domestic gods; the sexual ecstasies of Tantra; and the luminous inner visions got in the Vajrayāna. There are mergings with Tārā in Tibet; there is the lofty path of inner purity in Sri Lanka; and there is still shamanism in villages and healing cults. All such experiences are impregnated with ideas and symbols drawn from doctrine and myth.

In *philosophy* there is Emptiness and the imageless (*nirguṇam*) Brahman, the creative Lord, dim liberation from the color and miseries of rebirth, there is

Śiva dancing and so
signifying the
effortless joy of the act
of creation.

Dualism and Nondualism and all the mysterious variations in between, there is the One Self of Advaita, the No-Self of Buddhism, and the many selves of the *bhakti* cults. There are the Six Viewpoints of the orthodox Brahmin schools, the semi-orthodox Śaiva Siddhānta and other systems, the many schools of Buddhism, the Jain metaphysics, and the negations of the Materialists. All these patterns of thought are woven into classical and medieval Indian civilization. To complicate further, there are the varied speculations of Sufis and Muslim philosophers.

At the *narrative* level, there are immense riches in medieval Hinduism: the great Sanskrit epics of the *Rāmāyana* and the *Mahābhārata*, translations in later vernaculars, the storehouse of myth known as the *Purānas*, the birth stories, of Buddhism and the tales concerning the various Buddhas and Bodhisattvas, the Jain narratives, the bewildering variety of local legend; and with all this there was *doctrinal* belief in many forms of God. The multiple manifestations of the gods gave the Hindu scene a confusing multiplicity, and as yet there was not yet the clear step to saying that the gods, however many, were really One; or at least this motif was only sporadically observed. Presiding over the many, though, were Śiva and Visnu and the Goddess, and as a strong and relentless rival conception the Allah of the Muslims.

By medieval times the *social* grip of the caste system was inexorable. With Buddhism fading and Jainism not so strong, it was possible for small rivals to be swallowed up and themselves treated as castes (this happened to Jews and Christians). The system imposed a kind of overall pattern on the varieties of customs and legal obligations and even ethical standards of the various groups: from those who sacrificed goats to those who were strict in harmlessness towards animals; and from celibacy to the glorification of sex; from those who searched for complete freedom to those who imposed the obligation of suicide for widows. There were also the types of holy persons on the fringes of society to consider—the naked ascetics, the *sannyāsins*, the wandering gurus, the monks of Hindu orders, and the monks of Buddhism and Jainism. There were the tribal groups trapped like islands within the sea of Indian culture.

And as a *material* sign of regional variety and religious plurality there were the many shrines, from the high temples of the South to the stūpas of Nepal, and from the Jain temples of Mount Abu to the wondrous painted walls of Ajanta. In all these outer manifestations of the spirit of Indian culture, perhaps the statues of the meditating Buddha and the dancing Śiva stand out—the one replete with lovely calm, the other expressing a dynamism of beauteous exuberance. These were the twin polarities of Indian civilization. One cannot any more quite go back to the Middle Ages, but the nearest thing perhaps is the Kathmandu Valley, with its medieval carved balconies and old streets, and its quiet blending of Buddhist and Hindu ways of life. It gives us a hint at least, amid the new diesel fumes, of what that ancient and diverse culture was like well before the British were poised to transform at least the surface of the subcontinent.

3

# *China*

## A General Perspective

Westerners have often been confused about religion in China. They have assumed that Chinese religious and philosophical ideas can be classified in a Western way, so that we can speak of three religions of China, namely Confucianism, Taoism, and Buddhism; but often these are not so much three as parts of a single functioning system. Also, the words themselves which we use can be misleading. Is "Confucianism" a word meaning the philosophical stream of thought that started with Confucius? Is Taoism the teaching of Lao-tzu? If so, then the religions labeled by these nouns are something very different from the "philosophical" teachings, though overlapping with them. Moreover, the state cult which is sometimes labeled "Confucianism," though it rested on an ideology of ritual which can be traced to Confucius—and though temples to the memory of the Sage himself were incorporated into it—was a rather artificial construction. It was not strictly speaking the religion of anyone, except that people were expected to observe it in connection with the ongoing welfare of the State. Also there is so-called "popular religion," meaning the general and usually very localized religion of the people, which also is sometimes loosely referred to as Confucianism, but is actually a set of practices and ideas which draws on various aspects and institutions of Taoism, Buddhism and the state religion. All this, from a Western angle, is rather messy and muddled. It seems clearer for us to make some stipulations about words.

First, what we are dealing with as a single roughly organic, but also very localized and varied phenomenon, is Chinese religion. Now because of substantial organizational facts we can point fairly clearly to Buddhism and Taoism, both of which have well defined monastic embodiment and a class of

Map 2 China and
Japan

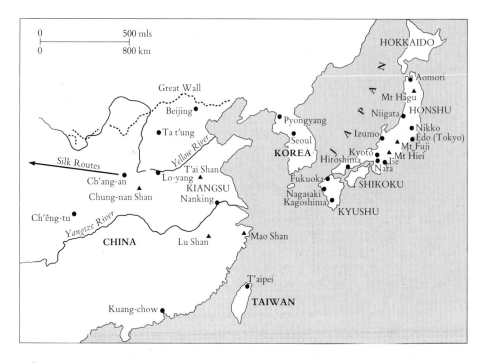

religious specialists; and when we refer to these traditions by these names, we
shall mean these religions as separately embodied. In parallel with this we
shall use "Confucianism" to refer to the official cult which disappeared with
the revolution of 1911, and has had no basic significance since then. To refer
to the philosophical tradition from the time of Confucius (and indeed before)
we shall speak of "Confucian thought." This includes a strong strand of
ethical theory and prescriptions, so one should not take the word "thought"
in too austerely intellectual a sense. Similarly we shall refer to the Taoist
intellectual tradition, which begins with the anthology known as the *Tao-te
Ching*, ascribed to the legendary Lao-tzu, and the treatise known as the *Book
of Chuang-tzu*, as "Taoist thought." Themes from Taoist thought were to be
incorporated, as one element, into "Taoist religion." But neither Lao-tzu nor
Chuang-tzu, even if they really existed as historical persons, was responsible
for the later faith, with all its complexities, which used the name of Tao to
describe itself.

Although the Chinese in fact managed to integrate rites from the three
strands into their local practice, there were of course also rivalries for state
patronage between the three organizations—the class of *ju* or Confucian-
trained scholars, the Buddhist order, and the Taoist monasteries. We may
also mention that at varying periods certain Western religions made some
impact on China: Nestorian Christianity, once quite powerful; Manichaeism;
Zoroastrianism; Judaism; and Islam. Of these Islam remains the most potent.
In modern times Christian missions have made an impact, especially in the
educational field.

## Important Periods of Chinese Religious History

Shortly before 1000 B.C.E. the old Shang dynasty came to an end, to be replaced by the Chou, under the regent who became an ideal figure in later times, the Duke of Chou. It was from the eighth century B.C.E., under the rule of the Eastern Chou (771–221 B.C.E.), that Chinese culture as we know it began to form. The classics which Confucius was to edit as part of his educational and philosophical task date from this time. Confucius himself, or Master K'ung as his name says ("Confucius" being a Latinized reflection of K'ung-Fu-tzu), lived from 551 to 479 B.C.E. The legendary Lao-tzu was supposedly an older contemporary of his; but the anthology which he is supposed to have composed is doubtless somewhat later. The succeeding centuries saw some important figures in the traditions of Confucian and Taoist thought, such as Chuang-tzu and Meng-tzu (Mencius).

By the first century C.E. Buddhism was starting to establish itself in China. In the second century Tao as a religious system was founded (or at least one main branch of it) by Chang Tao Ling. It seems therefore reasonable to look on the period before the second century C.E. as the formative or early period. Then we can look on the Sui and Tang dynasties, up to the tenth century, as the classical period, during which the three religious traditions took their main form, and when great contributions were made by specifically Chinese Buddhism to the corpus of Buddhist thought and practice. And finally, from the eleventh to the end of the eighteenth century we may nominate the medieval or premodern period, before the full and somewhat fatal impact of the West made itself felt in China.

During the classical period, particularly, the effects of Chinese culture were perceived abroad, especially in Vietnam, in Korea, and in Japan. China was the foremost world civilization, and was creating a new synthesis of cultures in Chinese Buddhism. In the nineteenth century substantial migrations occurred under the influence of a growing colonialist world economy, and in consequence Chinese culture and religion is to be found in the U.S.A., the West Indies, Indonesia, Malaysia, Singapore, and elsewhere.

### Confucius: Analects

K'ung said, "The ruler who governs the state through virtue is like the pole star, which stays put while the other stars revolve round it."

K'ung said, "All of the three hundred odes in the Classic of Poetry can be summed up in one of its lines, 'Have no wrong thoughts.'"

K'ung said, "If you control the people by government acts and keep them in line with law and order, they will refrain from doing wrong, but they will not have a sense of honour or shame. But if you lead them through virtue and regulate them by the laws of propriety, then they will have a sense of shame and will attain goodness."

K'ung said, "At fifteen my mind was fixed on learning. By thirty my character had been formed. At forty I had no more confusions. At fifty I understood the Mandate of Heaven. At sixty it was easy for me to hear the truth. At seventy I could follow my desires without transgressing what was right."

*Some Fundamental Ideas and Practices*

Since we are dealing with a single civilization which can be held to incorporate a single, but loosely knit, religion, it is reasonable to try to single out its chief ideas and practices. At the *ritual* level, there is that most general and important concept of *li*, roughly meaning due ceremonial behavior, or ritual at the broadest, including music. This *li* played a vital role in K'ung's whole philosophy. Of immediate significance also were the offerings directed toward ancestors—a kind of cult that occurred in the emperor's reverence toward his ancestors, in clan temples, and in the home. The cult of ancestors ties in with funerary rites, designed to transfer the dead happily to their resting-places, so that they are not consigned to the sad status of restless ghosts. A third important ritual motif was divination, extensively practised

---

**Chinese Religion** some key terms

*Ch'ān* Meditation (a Chinese version of Sanskrit *dhyāna*) and name of an important school known in Japanese as Zen.

*Ch'i* The idea of material energy, which combines with *li* or principle to make up things in the world, according to Neo-Confucian philosophy.

*Chiao* A religious movement, teaching or sect.

*Ching* A classical text, usually used for the ancient Confucian collection of five classics, but also applied to some other fundamental sources such as the Platform Sutra of Ch'ān tradition.

*Li* Principle or the spiritual substance or energy which combines with *ch'i*.

*Li* Rituals, ceremonial, rules of propriety, good behavior: a central concept in Confucian education.

*Ren* Human-heartedness, or loving benevolence toward other humans: a pivotal ethical notion in Confucianism.

*T'ai Chi* The Supreme Ultimate in the *I Ching* and in Neo-Confucianism or Source of all things.

*T'ai P'ing* The heavenly peace or eschatological kingdom looked forward to in some Taoist literature: the name given to the revolutionaries of 1850–64 who tried to establish a new order in central and north China.

*Tao* Way or principle through which nature works.

*T'ien* Heaven or personalized God residing above, whose cult was that of the Emperor.

*Yang* The male principle in the world, whose interplay with Yin forms the basis of much Chinese thinking.

*Yin* The female principle in dialectical interplay with Yang.

The doctrinal dimension: here various motifs important in Chinese thought are symbolized—the Yin and the Yang, the Buddhist swastika, the basic trigrams which when combined form the hexagrams of the *I Ching*, and stylized dragons, alluding to the fertility of nature and the Imperial.

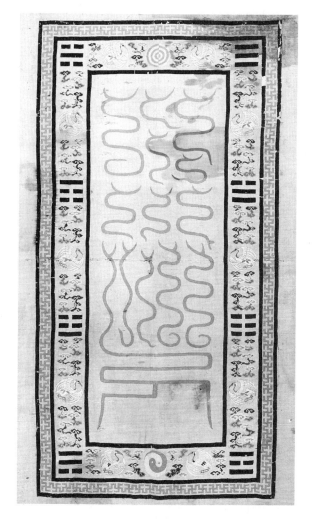

from before the time of the classic *Book of Changes* or *I Ching*. Geomancy, or the practice of harmonizing human activity—such as building a house—with the spirit (and the spirits) of the landscape, is worth mention too. Chinese religion also made its contributions to forms of mysticism and Yoga, through Taoist breath control and the novel methods of the Ch'an or meditation school of Buddhism.

At the *experiential* level, a characteristic idea was the goal of experiencing harmony or identity with nature through following the Way of Nature, the Tao. Mediumistic religion in the form of being possessed by the god was important in popular religion, and much attention was paid to visions of the divine realm.

*Doctrinally*, importance was always attached to the concept of Heaven, sometimes treated rather abstractly as Providence, and sometimes more personally as God. Rulers were thought of as receiving, or not receiving, the

The social dimension: Chinese women mourning at a grave, and burning imitation money as an offering. Ancestors remain important members of the society they have left behind.

Mandate of Heaven which justified (or failed to justify) their governance. In later thought there was also the notion of the Great Ultimate, a sort of God beyond God. In cosmology much was made throughout Chinese history of the interplay between the Yang and the Yin (the male and female principles, and active and passive polarities). There was a whole system of classifying phenomena according to the Yin and Yang and Five Elements or processes: wood, fire, earth, metal, and water.

The *narrative* and mythic dimension of Chinese culture was peculiarly rich. From our perspective we need to note the story of K'ung's life, the tale of Lao-tzu and the stories of the divine immortals as especially significant. *Socially*, the ideal of the scholar or *ju* was important; but still more vital was the figure of the sage. Much of Confucian *ethics* revolved around family relationships, but at the same time Buddhist and Taoist monasticism provided an escape from the family's structures, through the monastic vocation. Throughout there is a corresponding ethical contrast between the morality to be displayed by the benevolent person in the world, summed up in *jen* or human-heartedness, and that of the Taoist or Buddhist who is concerned with *wu wei*, that is not-acting, or acting through not acting.

These then are some of the principal motifs of Chinese religious culture. If one were to point to anything at the *material* level it would perhaps be the painting scroll. For the Chinese painter there is no frame. It is not as if nature can be framed: the scene painted wanders off beyond the dimensions of the scroll itself. And it is common to bind together the arts: the poem or inscription is an integral part of the painting and vice versa. A certain dynamic boundlessness gives fluidity to Chinese culture: it is less concerned with analysis, than either Western or Indian philosophy and religion.

## The Early Period

### K'ung's Life and Teachings

Because of the total imprint which he placed upon Chinese culture, it is right for us to start with K'ung, whose discourse has come down to us in the book known as *Analects* and whose spirit was to be followed by many generations of China's scholars and administrators. K'ung was born, probably in 551 B.C.E., in what is now Shantung Province, in the small state of Lu. He was perhaps from a minor aristocratic family. At any rate, he received an education, which until his time was normally reserved for the elite. One of the revolutionary aspects of his teaching was to throw open his academy to everyone; this helped, with his teachings, to create the notion of the true gentleman (*hsün-tzu*) whose high class is not a matter of birth but rather of moral behavior. K'ung was perturbed by the chaotic state of political and social life in his times. In theory the royal house of Chou was supreme in north China, but in fact there was a variety of independent feudal rulers. He saw that good rule should occur not by force but by moral suasion: and for this reason he paid a lot of attention to rites and ceremonies, since he perceived in them the characteristic way of inculcating right behavior and loyal service. He pondered the meaning of tradition, and though he was a reformer he was also highly committed to older ways. He had a vision of the past, refined and redefined, as playing a vital role in shaping the nonviolent means whereby the good ruler maintains his power.

At about the age of fifty, by which time, so K'ung avers in the *Analects*, he "knew Heaven's decree," he took service as a minister or official in the state of Lu; but in the event his political intervention was not a success. He left Lu in wandering exile for some thirteen years in neighboring states, with a band of his disciples. He went back to Lu about his sixty-eighth birthday. By seventy, he said, "he could follow his heart's desire without overstepping the line." He had reached full maturity of judgment. He died at seventy-three, saddened by the loss of his son and two disciples who predeceased him. But his influence lived on; and eventually his ideal of the scholar as administrator became the norm for about two thousand years.

He is credited (probably wrongly), with having edited the Six Classics, actually now five: the *Shi Ching* or Classic of Poetry, the *I Ching* or Classic of Changes, the *Shu Ching* or Classic of History, the *Li Chi* or Book of Ritual, the *Ch'un-ch'iu* or Spring and Autumn Annals, and the now lost *Yüeh Ching* or Classic of Music. At any rate, his name came to be associated with these major literary works, which together with some other writings came to form the curriculum for the imperial civil service examinations. And so, indirectly at least, K'ung was responsible for the creation of a class of bureaucrats who had deep literary skills, knew about the ceremonial side of life, and were brought up in the ideals not only of correct formal behavior but also of the necessary sincerity which has to lie behind it. They were also infused with the moral ideal of *jen* or human-heartedness. The official ruler must be correct, sincere and humane. It was a fine vision, which placed classical education at the heart of politics. The Confucian ideals were to serve China well.

There was nothing greatly speculative in K'ung's thought. It is clear from various references that, although he did not talk about it much, he respected belief in Heaven as a kind of personal God. He did not talk about miracles and such events, it is reported; and he was not without a gently rationalistic tone in what he said about religion. It is partly from this that later "official" Confucians were often dismissive of what they saw as the superstitions of popular religion. There came to develop an elitist poise about the scholarly gentleman in China; but this seems to have been foreign to K'ung's own thinking. He underlined the importance of treating all people well and the sanctity of ancient rites, including offerings to ancestors and to Heaven. His was not a combative nature, but one of humility and grave courtesy, not without a sense of humor. A nice touch is that when out shooting he would not shoot at a sitting bird, thus showing a sense of fair play.

K'ung set the agenda of much later Chinese thought, concerned as he was with political rule, right conduct, and human nature. In the following century we see the pendulum swinging toward a much less formal view of virtue and government. Mo-tzu argued vigorously for the importance of universal love and applied utilitarian tests to all policies, which should be in the interests of the people, conducing to their wealth and safety. He found a sanction for his doctrines in the will of a Supreme God, Heaven (T'ien), who had under his command a host of lesser spirits. His personalist ethic and frugality in living did not appeal to all, and the movement which he founded gradually died out, though there was a revival of interest in the eighteenth century C.E.

### Meng-tzu, Hsün-tzu, Han Fei-tzu

The greatest of the successors to K'ung-Fu-tzu was Meng-tzu, known in the West as Mencius, who lived *c.* 371–289 B.C.E. or perhaps two decades earlier. He advocated rule by a kingly sage, whose policies would be informed with virtue. His path should be the Wang-tao or Emperor's Way; and people were entitled to rise up against an evil monarch who would have forfeited the Mandate of Heaven. Despite this he was strongly pacifist, partly because of the disturbed and bloody period during which he lived. Conquest should only proceed by the desire of other peoples to join the country of a supremely benevolent ruler. The most important part of his teaching, however, has to do with his concept of *hsin*, or "heart," "mind." This is the power within each person which contains dispositions, which should be encouraged to sprout and grow, towards *jen* or humaneness, *i* or dutifulness, *li* or proper behavior, and *chih* or knowledge of right and wrong. This inner sense is essentially oriented therefore toward goodness. In other words human nature is essentially good. In this Meng was defending the Confucian tradition against those—Taoists, for instance—who saw the human heart as egoistic and obstructive of harmonious living, and on the other hand against those like Mo-tzu who had a superficial idea of goodness, defining it in outer and material terms. It followed also from his idea of *hsin* that both moral education and political policy should be designed to bring out the innate tendencies toward virtue.

By contrast Hsün-tzu (third century B.C.E.), who lived to see the unification of the states of China under the Ch'in regime (221 B.C.) and was upset to observe its harsh nature, especially since two of his own disciples served as officials at court, took a different and more pessimistic line from that of Mencius. In his view human nature was inherently chaotic and bad and needed the forces of education to tame it. He strongly emphasized the *li* aspect of the Confucian tradition: ceremonial and behavioral propriety was something that involved both inner feeling and outer act, but it was instrumental in teaching individuals how to act well, and was crucial therefore in moral education. In practice, then, Hsün-tzu, though breaking with the moral optimism of the earlier Confucian tradition, adopted a very similar view of the shape and point of education. Some of his writings also give *li* a cosmic role. Thus he says:

Indeed it is through *li* that Heaven and earth are in harmony, that the sun and moon are splendid, that the four seasons succeed each other, that the stars follow their motions, that the rivers and streams maintain their flow, that all things and creatures enjoy prosperity, and joy and wrath are controlled.

He also rather movingly writes, in defence of reverence for the dead, so central a value in Chinese culture:

When man's end and beginning are both well treated, the Tao of humanity is fulfilled. Hence the superior individual respects the beginning and attends to the end. To treat them alike is the Tao of the superior individual and the refinement of *li* and *i*. To exalt the living and belittle the dead is to respect one who has consciousness and neglect one who has lost it—this is the way of the evil man . . .

Hsün-tzu came at the end of a creative period, that of the so-called "hundred philosophers." There were various schools apart from the Confucian, of course—Taoists, legalists or authoritarian writers, and others. The Confucian tradition had already established itself as an educational force, and it was not long before Confucian literature became the staple of a centralized education system through the establishment of a Great Academy. Yet this was after a traumatic period for Chinese thought and scholarship, when in 213 B.C.E. all controversial books were burned.

Legalism (Fa-chia) had as its chief exponent Han Fei-tzu, who had studied with Hsün-tzu but rejected the latter's Confucian morality. The main point about Fa-chia was what it rejected: it saw written law as opposed to traditional moral values as the best way of controlling people. Han Fei-tzu's book is a witty exercise in expounding for a ruler the best methods of dominating people and controlling a bureaucracy. A person's title should be defined in terms of the work he was expected to perform and his actual success in this should be measured. The central fact about government is the use of power, and Han Fei-tzu has a lot of good advice on this front. For instance, the effective ruler should not make his desires or prejudices known, or otherwise his ministers will distort information and advice to him. He should delegate action, and so should sit at the center of power not acting (somewhat in the Taoist manner). The two handles of government are reward and punishment, and these should be used systematically. Method will triumph over virtue: you do not need to wait for a sage to get effective rule, since heeding Han Fei-tzu's methods will accomplish much, and mediocre talent will be able to make good use of them. But his rather cynical way of writing and his emphasis on human-created law rather than traditionally sanctioned morality gave him a Machiavellian reputation.

### Lao-tzu and the Taoist Tradition

Meanwhile the main anti-Confucian tradition of this early period had already begun to take shape in the book known as the *Tao-te Ching*, the Classic of the Way and its Virtue. This wonderful and mysterious text has exercised a fascination down the centuries, and not for nothing are there over forty English translations published. It is ascribed in the Taoist tradition to the sage Lao-tzu or Lao Tan, who supposedly was an older contemporary of K'ung, whom he instructed in various matters, including *li*, so claim later texts. Modern scholars are sceptical as to whether there was such an historical person; but he is vivid nevertheless in Chinese imagination, and for vast numbers of Chinese through the ages he has been real enough. Eventually he was seen as an incarnation of a transcendental Lao-tzu, supreme Immortal. But of such legendary developments we shall speak later, when we come to describe Taoism as a religion during the classical period. For the moment we are dealing with Taoist thought, in the *Tao-te Ching* and the later book the *Chuang-tzu*.

The justly famous opening words of the Classic of the Way and its Virtue have many resonances. They read:

The way that can be followed is not the eternal way;
The name that can be named is not the eternal name;
That which is without name is of heaven and earth the beginning;
That which is nameable is of the ten thousand things the mother.
He who is eternally without desire perceives the spiritual side of it:
He who is permanently with desire perceives the limit of it.
These two things are the same in origin but different in name;
Calling them the same is a mystery—
Indeed it is the mystery of mysteries; of all spirituality it is the gate.

The mythic
dimension: the
legendary Lao-tzu,
"founder" of Taoism,
with his disciples en
route to the far West
(some Taoists thought
of Buddhism as a
distorted form of
Taoism brought back
into China).

These words suggest that the underlying but ineffable principle which pervades the universe (and is indeed the origin of the cosmos) is the Tao, the Way. It is a fundamental idea in the classical work that this Way is something to which we should conform: but since nature acts with complete spontaneity, so in conforming to her we need spontaneity and complete naturalness. It is not something which can be striven for. That is why it is not a way which can be followed. It is not a way which can be taught. From this perspective Confucian thought with its stress on complex and learned *li* was on the wrong track. This is why according to the legend K'ung needed instruction from Lao-tzu. So the person who lives in accord with the way of all things sees the way in all things—and so the nameable world is also an unnameable Reality. As later was to be realized, there are profound similarities between these teachings and those of Buddhism, especially Mahāyāna Buddhism in the works of the *Prajñāpāramitā* and of Nāgārjuna. These resemblances were to be exploited both by Buddhists, in their evolution of Ch'an or Zen Buddhism, and by Taoists, who saw Buddhism as deceptive and derivative.

There is in the *Tao-te Ching* an array of analogies which were used to suggest the power of the empty Tao, the power of *wu-wei*, of "acting through not acting:" there is the valley which is the "active" space between the mountains; there is water which is so strong in its formless fluidity; there is the space in the pot—the whole point of a pot is that its space should be filled, but that point is constituted by a kind of nothingness. In brief, Taoist thought emphasizes not-acting, naturalness, spontaneity, passivity. It is a quietist tradition, emphasizing peace and meditation and it looks, in its experiential dimension, to the achievement of a contemplative inner stillness. By contrast Confucianist thought is active, pragmatic, conventional. Taoist thought is quietistic, anarchistic, and intuitive: in fact, ultimately it is not thought.

These motifs were carried on in the book known after its supposed author Chuang-tzu. He is supposed to have lived from about 369 B.C.E. to about 286 B.C.E. There are not many details of his life available, but we do have the fine and poetic book named for him. Again, he sees the Tao as the quiet spirit pervading everything. Since all the dualities which we use, such as health and sickness, life and death, pleasure and pain, brightness and darkness, are artificial—made up by us, and not ultimately true in telling about the Tao the way it really is—we should overcome them: we should treat sickness and health, good and bad, alike. We should cultivate utter serenity. This mystical quest is finally something very private. Chuang-tzu's doctrines were thus viewed by Confucian thinkers with deep suspicion as being subversive.

We may note that Taoist thinking was important in later Chinese contexts in its providing an ideology of rebellion, so maybe the Confucians were right in pointing towards its subversive nature as a movement. Chuang-tzu also, in describing the freedom of the Tao-conforming sage, writes of great flights through the air and immense longevity. Later in the Taoist tradition much attention is paid to the search for an elixir of life to stave off death, and to other miraculous powers that the Taoist follower might acquire. In these ways Chuang-tzu foreshadows later developments.

We have sampled some of the thinkers of the early period. China was moving towards unification. Buddhism was expanding into Central Asia. Various forces were arising which together would help to form religious Taoism. The scene was set, therefore, for what we have called the classical period, in which the three religions of China came to coalesce with varieties of local religion to produce the system which served China for a long time until its breakdown in the nineteenth century.

## The Classical Period

*Confucianism Becomes Official*

Despite the espousal of Legalism by the emperor Shih Huang-ti (reigned 221–210 B.C.E.), there were greater attractions for a ruler in taking up Confucian thought—partly its traditionalism, which was important in the legitimation of rule; partly its ritualism, which could be taken up into the practices of the central government; and partly too its moralism (it is, for one thing, unwise to act the Machiavelli if you parade that that is what you are doing; it is better to conceal cynicism behind a mask of morality). And Confucian thought was believable. At any rate, it was under the Han Dynasty, from the first century C.E., that Confucianism came to be an officially sponsored ideology and cult. Offerings were to be made to K'ung, and these were linked to state ceremonies in which the emperor made sacrifices to Heaven. Much later, in the seventh century, Confucian temples were established throughout the administrative system of the empire. Tablets inscribed to famous disciples and other prominent figures were included too, so that Confucianism came to be a kind of "civil religion" or national cult honoring those who had served the empire well.

The kind of Confucianism that became a state orthodoxy was the kind of view espoused by the highly influential thinker Tung Chung-shu (c. 179–104 B.C.E.). He expounded the doctrines of Confucian thought in terms of the generally accepted Chinese cosmology of the time, making use therefore of the notions of Yin and Yang, the Five Elements, and T'ien or Heaven, which he saw as a personal Lord. He made use too of the idea of the Mandate of Heaven, and evolved a theory of the succession of dynasties. If a ruler does not follow the Mandate by acting morally and wisely, then sooner or later the dynasty will break down. The Yin-Yang theory was applied by him to crucial human relations, especially the three bonds between ruler and ruled, father and son, and husband and wife. In each of these the Yang (ruler, father, husband) is superior. This hierarchical theory of human relationships was pervasive in Confucian China.

In effect, official Confucianism began the process of treating K'ung as an honored ancestor, together with other notables and the ancestors of the emperor. This was parallel to the cults which emerged systematically in classical China, especially in the south, of clan lineages. All this was in addition to domestic shrines in which the names of forebears inscribed on tablets came to be the norm.

### Taoism Emerges as a Religion

The early Taoist thought which we have looked at became an ingredient, though only one ingredient, of religious Taoism. Another was supplied by the experiences and organizational initiative of the legendary Chang Tao-ling. In 142 C.E. he received a vision of Lao-tzu, deified, who bestowed on him the title of T'ien-shih or Heavenly Master. A new scheme of worship was ordained, blood sacrifices were banned, and the faithful were to eschew their old gods. The movement became a highly organized sect, to which adherents were supposed to contribute five pecks of rice (so the nickname of the movement became "The Way of Five Pecks of Rice").

A similar movement in eastern China was inspired by a prophetic book which was later included in the Taoist canon, the *T'ai P'ing Ching*, or Classic of the Great Peace. This idea of a future heavenly state in which harmony was

A priest's robe depicting the heaven of Taoism, with the immortals.

*Opposite* A Tibetan figure of the Buddha, bringing the earth to bear witness of his Enlightenment.

to be achieved on earth was the inspiration of a number of messianic uprisings in Chinese history. The Yellow Turban, a religiously motivated rebellion, was eventually violently suppressed, but Chang Lu, Chang Tao Ling's grandson, who was also in conflict with the government, negotiated a surrender, and resided at the court of the Wei Emperor, receiving patronage and protection for the Heavenly Master sect. The organization among other things supplied free food and lodging over a wide area, and in some respects replaced the official government. By now Lao-tzu was treated as the supreme god as Lao-chün, Lord Lao; as a human being he was an incarnate manifestation of the Supreme One. This form of Taoism has lasted until the present day, with the chain of Heavenly Masters continuing through the centuries. But other ingredients as well went to make up Taoism as a religion.

One was a consequence of the failure of utopian rebellions. The T'ai P'ing or heavenly peace was to be sought within the individual through the practice of a shamanistic type of meditation which might result in a vision of heavenly beings, and even of Lao-chün. Meanwhile the traditional concern with longevity got combined with the techniques of alchemy, a kind of magical chemistry which sought to find some substance which would prolong life. Also important was the process of healing, it being thought that sickness was due to some moral fault or other. Some of the more practical concerns of Taoism were incorporated into a book by the important writer Ko Hung (283–343), the *Pao-p'u-tzu* or "The Master who Embraces Simplicity:" by the

*Left* A protective board with Yin and Yang and hexagram motifs to ward off bad spirits which might come into the house.

*Below* The mythic dimension: the Chinese transformation of Avalokiteśvara, Kuan-yin, guide of souls and savior deity. Tenth-century painting on silk, British Museum, London.

The ritual dimension: inside a Chinese temple in Taiwan.

pursuit of good deeds, breathing exercises, care not to lose sperm, and taking a sufficient amount of the elixir of immortality, one might aspire to become an immortal.

As a final main ingredient of religious Taoism we might mention the movement associated with Mount Mao or Mao Shan in Kiangsu, and based on revelations to Yang Hsi in the latter part of the fourth century: he was visited by supreme immortals. This visionary material was incorporated into further scriptures.

So what we have in the Taoist movements, increasingly coalescing into a single definable religion, is a combination of ancient quietism; a strong and fervent devotion to a heavenly Lord, believed to be incarnate in Lao-tzu himself, and to a lesser extent to other immortals; and the belief that the essence of divinity also resides in each individual where it can be cultivated by meditation, breathing, diet, and alchemical experiments. Eventually the contemplative practices of Taoism became highly complex and bore some resemblances to high Tantra in Buddhism.

Indeed, in a sense Buddhism became a fifth ingredient in Taoism; its coming into China was a challenge to Taoism in particular. One of the ways the Taoists hit back was by describing how Lao-tzu went west and actually taught a kind of Buddhism to the Indians. But also to some degree Taoism created a kind of counterpart of Buddhism: by arranging its scriptures into

## Shinto: Kojiki, *Preface*

Now when chaos had begun to condense, but force and form were not yet manifest, and there was nought named, nought done, who could know its shape? Nevertheless Heaven and Earth first parted, and the Three Deities performed the commencement of creation; the Passive and Active Essences then developed, and the Two Spirits became the ancestors of all things. Therefore did he enter obscurity and emerge into light, and the Sun and Moon were revealed by the washing of his eyes; he floated on and on plunged into the sea-water, and Heavenly and Earthly Deities appeared through the ablutions of his person. So in the dimness of the great commencement, we, by relying on the original teaching, learn the time of the conception of the earth and of the birth of islands; in the remoteness of the original beginning, we, by trusting the former sages, perceive the era of the genesis of Deities and of the establishment of men.

The experiential dimension: a Zen teacher draws a circle, symbolizing the emptiness and completion of ultimate realization—the experience of *satori*.

into secular pursuits such as martial skills and flower-arrangement; and the blending of Neo-Confucian and Zen motifs. In the modern period there were other novelties, which we shall come to later. The strength of Japanese aestheticism, the deliberate and highly committed following of artistic endeavors, was also expressed in a religious way, so that the boundaries between religious and other activities are peculiarly hard to define.

## The Early Period: *Kami* and Foreign Influences

The main center of Japanese power in the misty early centuries of the Common Era was the central region occupied by differing clans in a loose confederation under a Yamato kingship. Differing clans had differing *kami*, but gradually a central core of myths of origin came to play a role in the centralizing ideology of the Yamato emperors. This group of myths in part focused on the great goddess of the Sun, Amaterasu, divine ancestress of the royal family. The complex myths drew their sources from differing cultures, from Polynesia, China, and elsewhere, and were in due course codified in the books *Kojiki* and *Nihonshoki* in the latter part of the seventh century. They helped to justify imperial rule, granted absolutely to her descendants through the goddess. There was no Japanese theory of the "Mandate of Heaven" in relation to the royal family, and the fact that for many centuries actual rule was exercised by shoguns, while in theory deferring to the emperor, is a significant comment on the ultimate sanctity of the imperial lineage. In the early period there was also a gradual penetration of cultural elements from Korea and China. The Japanese fought and settled in southern Korea in the fourth century, though disastrously defeated by the northern state of Koguryo. The foundations, however, were laid for the decisive entry of official Buddhism into Japan in the mid part of the sixth century.

The multitudinous *kami* of mountains, streams, rocks, and the sea blended with ancestral and tutelary *kami* who were integrated into the life of particular clans. Broadly, the *kami* occupied differing planes of existence: Takamanohara or "high heaven;" Nakatsukuni or "middle land," i.e. roughly the earth; and Yomi, the underworld. Though the heavenly *kami* were important, the *kami* of the middle region often had more immediate interest in human and clan affairs. There were shrines to various spirits, which later in the early imperial period multiplied significantly as a result of state patronage.

The *kami* were important for agriculture and hunting, and ancient practices of shamanism, both male and female, persist right through Japanese religion. Later commonplaces, such as the use of clapping in worship, and purification with water, seem to date from prehistoric times.

## The Preclassical Period

*Prince Shotoku and the Buddhist Revolution*
Traditionally Buddhism is held to have been brought into Japan in either 538

## The Lotus Sutra

The World-honoured One, in his tactfulness, told of the Tathāgata-wisdom; but we, though following the Buddha and receiving a day's wage of nirvāna, deemed this a sufficient gain, never having a mind to seek after the Great Vehicle. We also have declared and expounded the Tathāgata-wisdom to Bodhisattvas, but in regard to this Great Vehicle we have never had a longing for it. Wherefore? The Buddha, knowing that our minds delighted in inferior things, by his tactfulness taught according to our capacity, but still we did not perceive that we were really Buddha-sons.

Now we have just realized that the World-honoured One does not grudge even the Buddha-wisdom. Wherefore? From of old we are really sons of Buddha, but have only taken pleasure in minor matters; if we had had a mind to take pleasure in the Great, the Buddha would have preached the Great Vehicle Law to us. At length, in this sutra, he preaches only the One Vehicle; and though formerly, in the presence of bodhisattvas, he spoke disparagingly of śrāvakas who were pleased with minor matters, yet the Buddha had in reality been instructing them in the Great Vehicle. Therefore we say that though we had no mind to hope or expect it, yet now the Great Treasure of the King of the Law has of itself come to us, and such things which Buddha-sons should obtain we have all obtained.

The material dimension: the largest wooden structure in the world—the Todaiji temple containing a huge bronze Buddha statue, in Nara, the ancient capital of Japan.

or 552 C.E.; but it was primarily during the regency of Prince Shotoku Taishi (574–622) that Buddhism took root as part of the fabric of Japanese official life. In the second year of his regency, while still a young man (he was nineteen when he became regent), he issued an edict which commended the Three Jewels of Buddhism—the Buddha, the Dharma, and the Sangha, which were to be seen as indissolubly united. Later, in the Seventeen Article Constitution which he promulgated, he stated that these three treasures were to be revered by all beings. So he regarded Buddhism as the spiritual message which gave moral shape to the country. He sent to China for *sūtras* and other documents and himself wrote commentaries on three important Mahāyāna texts, including the Lotus Sūtra. This last work is preserved in the imperial archives, and it is claimed to be in Shotoku's own writing. Shotoku is credited with founding one or two important temples, notably the Horyuji Temple in Nara, later the imperial capital. But he also made use of the Confucian tradition, in establishing various ranks of officials at the court; and he did not see any incompatibility between his favoring of Buddhism and support for the cult of the *kami*.

After his death a brief period of chaos and bloodshed preceded the consolidation of his reforms, and a more centralized empire somewhat on the

The practical dimension: the austerity of Buddhist monastic life, seen here at Mount Koyosan, headquarters of the Shingon branch of Japanese Buddhism.

Amaterasu, Sun Goddess and greatest divinity of the Shinto tradition. Disturbed that the Storm God had destroyed her crops, she withdrew into a cave, thus depriving the world of sunlight and was lured out only by the clamor of many *kamis* outside the cave. This print is by Kunisada. Victoria and Albert Museum, London.

Chinese model was established. Law was proclaimed by imperial rescript—in other words, written law, rather than immemorial custom was what counted, and the emperor himself was treated as a living *kami*. The emperor Temmu, who reigned from 672 to 686, ordered the writing of the *Kojiki* and *Nihonshoki*, and this helped to give a traditional justification for the new set-up. He is supposed also to have made Amaterasu's shrine at Ise the sacred focus of the cult of the imperial house.

The favoring of religion also meant its control. A law governed the activities of monks and nuns, and a ministry of *kami* was organized, which registered *kami* shrines and priests. Temmu also ordered the compilation of collections of traditional poetry. In 710 the court was established at Nara, which blended the glories of Buddhist faith and the pomp of imperial governance. In 741 the emperor Shōmu ordered the building of a state-financed system of provincial temples, and in 749 he had a vast statue in

136

bronze of the Buddha Vairocana installed in the great Todaiji Temple in Nara. Vairocana is especially associated with the Hua-yen (or in Japanese, Kegon) tradition, being the personalized form both of the universe and of what lies beyond it.

## Saichō and Kūkai

The close identification of religion and government, and the lavish subsidizing of monastic life, had cloying effects. As a radical move at reform, the emperor Kammu (reigned 781–806 C.E.) moved the capital from Nara to Heian (Kyoto). The bonds between politics and religion were cut, and government by legal edict was revived. Various economic and military reforms gave the Heian period an energetic start. The severance of Buddhism from the affairs of state was healthy, and led to the creation of two new forms of Buddhism through the activity of the two most famous monks of the Heian period, Saichō and Kūkai.

Saichō, also known by his posthumous title Dengyo Daishi (767–822), was sent as a student to China, after having studied at the Todaiji in Nara. He brought back to Japan the teachings of the T'ien-t'ai, somewhat amplified, and known in Japanese as Tendai. Saichō established the headquarters of the denomination on Mount Hiei, not far from the new imperial capital, and eventually after his death it was recognized as a place for the training of monks (the monopoly for this had been held by one of the Nara centers). His Tendai teachings were more syncretic than the Chinese, as he wove into them important Tantric motifs and the use of sacramental acts.

There was a place in the Tendai scheme of things for *kami*; and there was also a nationalistic flavor— Saichō believed that the Japanese were fully mature in their spiritual life and therefore ready for the consummate teachings of the Lotus Sūtra. He also elaborated his world-affirming theory of *hongaku* or "original enlightenment," which stressed the nondifference between the Buddha's enlightenment and that in ordinary men and women, and the identity between liberation and living in the world. Various new patterns of meditation were worked out, such as sitting ninety days in front of a statue of Amida (Amitābha), and circumambulating a sacred statue for ninety days, and so on. These practices were introduced from China by Saichō's disciple Ennin.

Tendai, because it found a place for all stages of religious development, was popular; but its emphasis upon the magical and spiritual effects of ritual were sometimes to be a weakness. This ritualism was even more marked in the other new movement, Shingon, or Mantra Sect. Kūkai, known posthumously as Kōbo Daishi, had initially sought government service and studied Confucian classics, but switched as a young man to Buddhist studies; he had the opportunity moreover to go on a delegation to China and there spent three years studying Shingon in the then capital of Chang-an. He introduced this form of Buddhism into Japan, on his return. He set up at Kongobuji, south of Nara, and also at Toji in Kyoto, as a springboard for propagating his message. He was influential in various directions: he founded the Imperial Academy of Arts and Knowledge, and was a senior religious adviser at the court. He had a warm attitude toward the way of the *kamis*. His teachings prepared the way for later syncretism between Shinto and esoteric Buddhism. He established the headquarters of the new denomination at Mount Koya, and after his death he was thought by his followers still to abide at Mount Koya, awaiting revived manifestation at the time of the coming of the future Buddha Maitreya.

The scheme which he evolved is a complex one. At its apex is the figure of the Buddha Mahāvairocana, conceived as identical with the Truth-body of the Buddha. That Ultimate Reality is described in typical Buddhist terms as emptiness and as the "Suchness" of the Buddha as Tathagata. But his emptiness is, so to speak, a full one. The truth-body is the creative force which is behind phenomena, and which embraces phenomena. In this Kūkai takes up the thought of Hua-yen. But because inner and outer are correlated (phenomena and ultimate Suchness; mind and body; and esoteric and exoteric Buddhism), the approach to attaining realization of one's essential Buddha-hood is sacramental in character. Realization therefore occurs not just through mental meditation but through the use of mysterious powers—the *mudrā* or bodily gestures which also play a vital role in Tantric thinking in India; the sacred *maṇḍalas* or diagrams which he brought back from China with him; and the sacred syllables or formulae, *mantrás*. For Kūkai, exoteric Shingon Buddhism was the highest form because it reflected the eternal Truth of the Body of Mahāvairocana and not the provisional and introductory teaching of the time-bound Buddha Śākyamuni.

The schools of Saichō and Kūkai represent the most solid achievements in the Buddhism of the preclassical period. They involved some adaptation of ideas and practices prevalent in the great T'ang capital of Ch'ang-an, which the two sages had the opportunity of visiting together. But it was basically at a later stage, after the coming of the Kamakura period, that Japanese originality in Buddhist religion really flowered, stretching Buddhism in the directions of fervid piety in the Pure Land interpretations, back toward the centrality of meditation in the Zen schools, and in a powerful nationalist direction in the teachings of Nichiren.

## The Classical Period

### The Pure Land Movements and the Mappō

Fundamental to the revolutions which took place from the twelfth century onward was the conception that we have reached the days of the final Dharma, the *mappō*. The present could be viewed from the standpoint of Buddhist orthodoxy as being a degenerate age in which the more rigorous path could not be trodden effectively, so poor had people's commitment and merit become; but according to the new viewpoint it was a period of optimism and a more democratic way of looking at the Buddha's path. For the tradition had of its nature tended to exclude certain people whose occupations grated against the Buddhist ethic—fishermen, warriors, hunters, peasants, prostitutes, and so on. But in the new age the faith was open to all. The success of the Pure Land movements in Japan was in great part due to their social widening of ultimate hope. The same, but in a rather different way, could be said of Zen.

The greatest figures in the Pure Land movements were undoubtedly Honen (??–1212) and Shinran (1173–1263). Honen involved himself in extensive studies within the Tendai tradition, but was especially drawn to meditation on the Buddha of Infinite Light, Amida. He followed the sacramental method of meditation in which by visualizing Amida he would become unified with him; but through much arduous meditation, in the years he spent in the retreat of the saintly monk Eiku on Mount Hiei, he nevertheless felt dissatisfied: he could not attain a sense of utter liberation. Honen turned to the idea that those who cannot be freed by strenuous meditation can nevertheless gain Amida's favor and assure themselves of rebirth in the Pure Land simply through the repetition of his name in the formula *Namu Amida Butsu*, or "Homage to the Buddha Amida." This simple formula was for those who had to rely, as Honen came to put it, on *tariki* or "the power of the other," rather than upon *jiriki*, "one's own power." Salvation had to come from another if one could not in this degenerate age rely on one's own strenuous efforts.

All this was in accord with the great vow of Amida Buddha to help all living beings in the world of suffering. His compassionate nature led to his projection of the Pure Land, where individuals could be reborn in conditions which were particularly suitable for the attainment of final liberation. In so far as this doctrine undercut the rationale for the extensive monastic training of the Tendai and other influential forms of Buddhism, Honen's rivals saw his new teaching as a threat. While they did not deny his own saintliness, they sought to suppress the new movement in 1204 and then again in 1205. Eventually the indiscretion of two of Honen's monks, in leading court ladies in an all-night worship service, enraged the emperor: they were executed, and Honen was banished for four years from the capital, from 1207. He returned in 1211 and died in early 1212, proclaiming his faith in Amida.

Honen's devotional pietism contained some possible inconsistencies which were the reason for the even more radical transformation of Buddhism that was to be attempted by Shinran. For one thing, Honen taught that *Namu Amida Butsu* should be continuously repeated by the faithful: but why so? Surely it was enough simply to turn once to Amida in faith. Repetition was no doubt creating a new form of practice, easier than traditional *jiriki*, but still a kind of *jiriki*. Second, Honen the monk had adhered to the forms of traditional Buddhism. His knowledge of the scriptures was intense. His adherence to the monastic rules had been severe. But such practice was a hangover from the *jiriki* mentality. Pure Land Buddhism, or Jodoshu, ought to go in an even more radical direction. The man who imparted this new

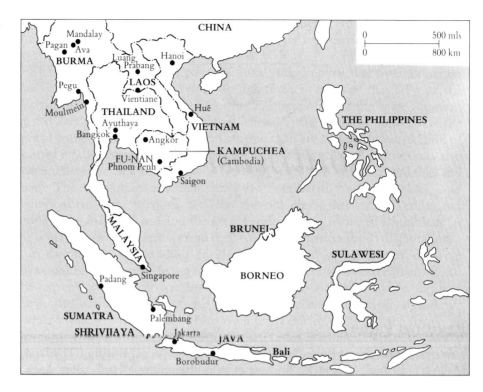

Map 3  Southeast Asia and Indonesia

the spread of Islam into many of the Indonesian islands and into the southern Philippines. Meanwhile the north Vietnamese state of Dai Viet had fought off Chinese invasions, designed to reannex it to the Chinese empire to which it had at one time belonged, and expanded southward to take over the kingdom of Champa, forming an empire roughly the same as modern Vietnam. In addition to the major faiths to be found in the area, various smaller-scale religions belong to the various tribal groups existing right across the region.

It must be emphasized that despite Indian influences and the fact that some Indian Brahmins, merchants, and Buddhist monks must have migrated and settled in the region, the cultural importation of Indian and Chinese elements was just that: it was convenient to borrow the Indian ideology of kingship, for instance, or to use Buddhist ideas in justifying political rule. The substratum of peoples upon which such a culture was grafted were a mixture, but neither Indian nor Chinese in the proper sense. So the imported great religions lived in symbiosis with home-grown popular religions.

It is convenient to look upon the period up to the seventh century C.E. as the early period; the time from the seventh century C.E. to the shaping of Theravādin orthodoxy and the coming substantially of Islam—i.e. to the thirteenth century—as the preclassical period; and the thirteenth through sixteenth centuries as the classical period. Thereafter we are in the modern period and witnessing the varied responses of the region to the impact of the colonial times.

## The Origins of Indian Influence

There have been differing theories as to why Indian cultural influences, both Buddhist and Hindu, crossed the Bay of Bengal and established themselves in Burma and other regions of the area. Whence ultimately came those vast monuments at Angkor Wat in Kampuchea and Borobodur in Java? Was it a matter of trade, or conquest, or religion, or what? There might have been elements of all three. But the evidence seems to have moved against what may be called the *vaiśya* and *kṣatriya* theories, that is, those views which look to the merchant and warrior castes, respectively, as the most important in the transmission of Indian cultural forms. The fact is that already there were kingdoms forming themselves in Southeast Asia, of an indigenous kind. But contact with south India (which must have involved some measure of trade, and to this extent the merchant theory has force) presented these smaller kingdoms, on their way to the creation of empires, with a model of ideology and theory of rule which was greatly attractive. The agents of Indianization were similar to those which saw the spread of north Indian ideas and practices into south India: basically we are back with that old formula so common in the Pali texts and elsewhere, the Brahmins and the *śramaṇas*—Brahmins and recluses, many of the latter being organized into the Buddhist and Jain orders. Holy persons were the bearers of a new civilization and theory of government. Not only that, but Brahmins, who had long acted as skilled advisers, could transmit the theories of government and of architecture. It seems then most likely that the "conversion" of much of Southeast Asia was a religious and ideological one, in which a new theory of rule was deliberately imported to consolidate the power of local princes and empires. All this was superimposed on a basis of the mingled agricultural religious practices of the varied indigenous peoples, who were now being organized by political means into more formidable wealth-producing units through the creation of irrigation schemes to enhance wet rice cultivation on a grander scale.

## Kingdoms and Empires

An early empire mentioned by the Chinese was that of Fu-nan, which is probably a representation of the Khmer (Kampuchean) word Phnom, meaning "mountain." No doubt, even as early as the second century C.E., its rulers adopted the title (reflecting practice in south India) of "king of the mountain." This was part of a mythic theory. The capital was built in the shape of a *maṇḍala*, in which the central feature was a stone representation of the sacred mountain at the center of the world on which dwelt the God. So the king's palace was a representation of the sacred center, and he was seen as divine representative on earth. It was he who through his organizational power did the earthly work of creation, bringing order out of chaos and ensuring the fertility of the realm. So in a way, as far as the people were concerned, there was a fair exchange. In exchange for the rice and other agricultural products and artifacts which served as taxes on the population they were given civil order and richness of harvests. A similar ideology was

151

*Opposite* A statue from the famous Buddhist complex at Borobudur, which reflects cosmologically the structure of the world. Borobodur combines the idea of the *stūpa*, the *maṇḍala* or ritual diagram, and the cosmic mountain. As you ascend, you pass scenes illustrating karma and its effects, to the life of the Buddha, and ultimately *nirvāṇa*.

probably used in the kingdom to the east of Fu-nan, namely the state of Champa in the southern part of what is now Vietnam. The northern part of Vietnam was ruled as a Chinese province down to about 900 C.E. In distinction from the rest of Southeast Asia this part was subject to Chinese, rather than mostly Indian, cultural influences.

Eventually, in place of the old state of Fu-nan, a Khmer empire was established, especially under the ruler King Jayavarman II in the ninth century. Their capital, Angkor, came to be a wonderful repository of great buildings; the most important was the Viṣṇu sanctuary of King Suryavarman II (1113–50), known as Angkor Wat. It later was overgrown by the jungle, to be discovered and restored in modern times. The chief sacred focus of the

Apsaras or singers, whose heavenly music and dance give pleasure to men and gods, carved on a main building of the Angkor Thom complex at Angkor in Cambodia, built by King Jayavarman VII about 1200 C.E.

Khmer kingly cult was Śiva: the *stūpa* or sacred mountain is in many cases surmounted by the *lingam*. In such a setting it was important to have Brahmins to perform the essential rites.

Meanwhile, with the decline of Fu-nan, there rose the power of the extensive maritime kingdom of Srivijaya, which probably developed from Indian trading settlements in southern Sumatra, and flourished because of its control of the convenient sea routes between India and China. Its capital was at Palembang, and it ruled over much of Sumatra, parts of Borneo, and the Malay peninsula. There were also Buddhist states to the east, in Java, especially remembered through the vast and beautiful temple complex at Borobodur (p. 153), a *stūpa* complex fashioned like a *maṇḍala*. Up to the thirteenth century, Srivijaya, united to the Sailendra kingdom of Java, was undoubtedly the dominant power in Southeast Asia, and showed the effectiveness of a sea-based empire. It was long an important center of Mahāyāna Buddhist Sanskrit learning.

During the eleventh and twelfth centuries there arose a powerful state in Burma, based on the holy city of Pagan. Its power was destroyed by Mongol invasions, but to some degree it profited from the Islamic conquest of north India, which led many learned refugee monks from the Buddhist university city of Nalanda to flee to Pagan.

*The Significance of Islam*
The advent of Islam in north India had a profound impact on Southeast Asian culture. The reason was that India under the Mughals cut the region off from the holy places of Buddhism and the traditional heartlands of the Buddhist faith. As Mughal rule extended south, it made some of the older Hindu models of kingship less attractive, and indeed opened up the question of the viability of a Muslim model for the region. At the same time it helped to turn the kingdoms of Southeast Asia in the direction of Sri Lankan Theravāda as a model ideology for rule. The consequence is that basically the region is now divided between Islam and the Theravāda, with the Philippines divided between Islam and Catholicism, and Java still retaining some Hindu elements.

At the beginning of the fifteenth century the state of Malacca was founded as an Islamic entity, and because of its strategic position it took over the earlier mantle of Srivijaya. Though at the beginning of the next century it was itself taken over by the Portuguese, it had a profound influence on the establishment of the Malay sultanates and served as a center of influence which helped the Islamization of parts of the southern Philippines and much of Borneo and Sulawesi.

# The Theravāda and the Classical Period

What I have termed the "classical period" of Southeast Asian culture overlaps with colonialism. But though toward the end of the period, in the sixteenth century, Portuguese and other powers from Europe were making their

*Opposite* The ritual dimension: the vast Buddhist shrine of the Shwedagon Temple in Rangoon, Burma. There is one immense *stūpa* surrounded by many small ones.

presence felt in the region, this was also the time of the flowering of a Theravādin civilization which has left its imprint on modern societies in the region. Burma, Thailand, Kampuchea, and Laos became predominantly Theravādin, and maintained a continuity of trade and scholarly exchange with Sri Lanka.

In Burma the way to a thoroughly Theravādin model of monarchy and civilization had been prepared by the conversion of King Anawrahta (Pali: Aniruddha), who came to the throne in 1044. His conversion to Theravāda by a famous monk, Shin Arahan, led to the wide influence of the religion, especially under his successor Kyanzittha, who caused the erection of the vast Schwezigon Pagoda in the city of Pagan. Anawrahta had sent for a Buddha relic from Sri Lanka, which was installed there, and a copy of the scriptures, the Tripitaka, to check out against scriptures that had been gained from the conquered Mon people. These contacts with Sri Lanka are significant and heralded much closer ties later on. Hitherto a prevalent variety of Buddhism was Tantra, which Anawrahta set out to replace.

The theory of kingship which the Burmese and others in Southeast Asia acquired partly from the Sinhalese, whose Buddhist civilization had its heyday in the twelfth century under King Parakramabahu and after, was that the king follows the myth of Aśoka Maurya, the ideal Buddhist emperor. A monarch might have to use evil means in coming to the throne or in expanding his empire, as did Aśoka, but ultimately he is a good king and pious Buddhist, who promotes vegetarianism, brings about justice, and encourages the spread of good religion. Such an ideal also sees the king as *cakkavattin*, the "Wheel-turner" (Sanskrit: *cakravartin*), the worldly counterpart to the spiritual role assumed by the Buddha Śākyamuni. He is seen too as a *bodhisatta* (*bodhisattva*) or Buddha-to-be, and this links up with the myth of the future Buddha, Metteyya (Maitreya). The king incarnates the future Buddha, and thus links past to future, as well as the spiritual to the worldly life. This ideology was a useful one: it assigned parallel roles to political power and to the spiritual force wielded by the Sangha, in a new synthesis which tried to ensure both material prosperity and moral virtue in the state.

This model was perhaps at its most successful in the Southeast Asian mainland nations. In the fifteenth century Burma was ruled from Pegu, in the lower part of the country, by King Dhammaceti (reigned 1472–92), who sought to unify the Sangha; monks from Burma itself and surrounding countries such as Kampuchea and Thailand came to receive ordination. There were missions to Sri Lanka, and Sinhalese monks visited the center at Pegu. This period was represented as being the golden age of the Theravāda political system in the Burmese context.

Thai culture owed something to Kublai Khan's extension of Chinese boundaries and the forcing of many Thai-speakers southward to conquer areas that had been under Mon and Khmer dominance. They learned from these cultures and, under able monarchs, established Theravādin polities in differing parts of what is now Thailand, at Chiangmai in the north and at

Ayuthia in the south, which dominated much of central Thailand. Buddhism continued to flourish, and to maintain links with the Sinhalese.

The Buddha reflected in a pool at Maha That in Thailand.

Widespread Thai influence in Laos and Kampuchea was one factor in ensuring that the "Theravādin revolution" spread to these kingdoms. In the case of Kampuchea, the older Hindu polity was undermined both politically and spiritually. The Theravādin monastic ideal kept the monks and nuns in close relationship with the people, and their life of relative poverty was impressive. Moreover it was possible, as throughout the region, to blend local cults of spirits relevant to the agricultural life with orthodox Theravāda, so that a happy symbiosis could be effected.

In these various Theravādin countries there is a similar worldview, but with some divergences of atmosphere and the contents of local religion where it is integrated into the Buddhist structure (there are also tribal cultures which lie partly outside the patterns of Theravāda influence). In the cosmology, the king is seen as a central figure, whose task is to protect the Dhamma (Dharma), assure the prosperity of his people, and encourage the ethical life. The round of rebirth is a generous one, for it includes heavenly possibilities of existence for the faithful layperson who gives generously to the Sangha. The monks and nuns are kept to their role of meditation and learning, as well as preaching to the people and assisting at ceremonies to ward off evil and the like. The capital city itself may become an important center of pilgrimage due

The That Luang Temple in Vientiane, capital of Laos, with the monument of King Setthathirat, who built the temple in 1566.

to the building of splendid temples and the importation of prestigious relics from Sri Lanka and elsewhere. The local area will have its temples too, and they will incorporate shrines to local spirits, such as the *nats* in Burma.

### Religion in Vietnam: the Chinese Influence

Unlike the other regions of mainland Southeast Asia, Vietnam was mostly under the influence of China, having indeed been part of the Chinese empire for a thousand years after its annexation in 111 B.C.E. by the Han Dynasty. Subsequently, except for a short time in the early fifteenth century C.E., when it was again under Chinese control, it had its own independent existence; but as the kingdom of Dai Viet it mirrored the Chinese system. Confucianism was the ideology of the court and the basis of the examination system; Taoism and Mahāyāna Buddhism were woven into the triple worldview. It was probably the Taoist element in this mix which was most closely integrated into indigenous folk motifs, partly through mediums, both male and female, who exercised shamanistic powers of healing, and partly through local and national tutelary deities who would preside over the affairs of each village or larger community. But Mahāyāna Buddhism, too, was firmly rooted in the soil of Vietnam, and though there remained some Theravādin monasteries, it was chiefly Chinese-affiliated Mahāyāna that predominated in the country. Thus we have a marked divergence in official religion between the Vietnamese and the rest of mainland Southeast Asia, especially in the classical period, just before the advent of the West.

## Islam's Spread into the Region

Though Islam was relatively a latecomer to the region it spread with great effectiveness. From the time that Islam had come to dominate the Arab world it also had a grip upon the trade across the Indian Ocean. It was indeed partly for this reason that the Portuguese and others were impelled to seek a way to the East through voyaging round Africa (and Columbus was to take his momentous short cut by going west). This brought Muslim merchants and sailors to the region, and it was doubtless mainly through their efforts that the religion was first planted there. In the thirteenth century the state of Pasai on the Malay peninsula already had an Islamic ruler. Around 1400 there was the foundation of Malacca, to which I have already referred, and from this time on Islam made strong progress. It is clear from a number of sources that Sufi orders took a prominent part in spreading the religion, as they had on the mainland of India, from whence a number of such itinerants came.

In Java and elsewhere in the region, two forms of Islam emerged: one being regular and orthodox, the other being syncretic, blending with older local and Indian motifs. Moreover, there remain places where a version of medieval Indian religion, combining both Hindu and Buddhist motifs, persists, most notably in the island of Bali. So Islam in the region has strong South Asian infusions, both from these forces, welling up as it were from below, and in the provenance of many of the mystics who helped Islam to spread in the islands. As we shall see later the great mix of different religious motifs made the encounter between Indonesian religion and the Westerners during the colonial period a rich one.

## Beyond the International Religions

As well as the various forces which we have been concerned with here—Confucianism from China, the Theravāda from Sri Lanka, the various forms of Mahāyāna from India and China, Hinduism from India, Islam from the Middle East—there have of course been numerous smaller-scale religions among the various peoples, from the hunters and gatherers of central Borneo to the rice-growers of Sulawesi and from the minorities of Burma to the hill peoples of Laos. Sometimes they have assimilated or succumbed to the larger culture-bearers; but sometimes they have retained their own identity. They too have a part to play in the richness of Southeast Asian life, and they too had to contend with the enormous impact of the colonial period.

# The Contribution of Southeast Asia to Religious History

It is worth reflecting briefly on how this cultural complex which we have been surveying imparts any new directions to religious history. The first point that it makes to us, especially if we think that the Brahmin theory of the transplantation of Indian cultural forms to Southeast Asia is right (or at least the theory that the coupled Brahmins and monks were the primary transmitters), is that Hindu culture has or had great mobility. It did not need the substructure of the Hindu caste system to uphold it. It contained an ideology of kingship which was in its day useful and important. Second, the ultimate use of the Indic base in the region to build on it a succession of Sinhala-influenced Theravādin states helps us to redress a certain balance in our perspective. For because Buddhism largely vanished from India proper, and with it forms of the "Lesser Vehicle" of Theravāda, which is also weakly represented in East Asian culture and in the religion of Tibet, it is easy to overlook the Theravāda as a force, save of course that it became a notable one in Southeast Asia. It too had a theory of kingship which was relatively benign and could replace the more florid Hindu and Sanskritic models.

Southeast Asian Islam is interesting not merely for its relative openness to cultural forces of a non-Islamic origin but because its importation seems so much to have been at the grassroots level. Basically Islam spread here in a way quite differently from its mode of outreach in much of the rest of Asia, which was always initially by political conquest. Here was a more intense form of its appeal of piety which had proved vital in the Indian subcontinent, beneath the palladium of Mughal rule.

In the colonial period there came the establishment of the only overwhelmingly Christian country in the East: the Philippines. Perhaps it is no coincidence that this was the one country in Asia which had failed to feel the influence of Buddhism.

Finally, in relation to the dimensions of religion, we see two of them as having an especially prominent role in Southeast Asia. First there is the central *institutional* idea of the divine or to-be-enlightened king, who preserves the Dharma of the realm, and who cooperates (in the case of Buddhism) with the Sangha, and so incarnates the myth of the great Aśoka. And second we can look to the amazing translation of such ideas into *artistic* form in the Angkor complexes, at Pagan, in Borobodur, and elsewhere. Architecture here speaks much louder than texts.

# The Pacific

## The Pacific Experience

The vast reaches of the Pacific Ocean were the scene of some of the most ambitious navigational feats in human history, especially in the settlement by Polynesians on islands as far apart as Hawaii and Easter Island, and Tahiti and New Zealand. The Polynesians, though vastly scattered, have a certain consistency in their culture which makes generalization possible. It is however not absolutely easy to delineate it, because for the most part the culture which was in being before the advent of Europeans during the eighteenth and nineteenth centuries has vanished. It seems clear that they originated ultimately on the Asian mainland, in Southeast Asia and south China, before embarking on their great voyages.

To the southwest of the large triangle which roughly speaking bounds the Polynesian Pacific, with its corners in Hawaii, New Zealand, and Easter Island, there is that region which is known as Melanesia. Sometimes Papua and New Guinea are included in this area and sometimes not: our habit will be to include it here. It contains various groups of islands, such as the Solomons, Vanuatu, and New Caledonia, as well as Fiji (though the Fijians are marginal in that they share characteristics too with the Polynesians). Roughly, Melanesia comprises a crescent of islands north and northeast of Australia. North of Melanesia and west of Polynesia are the clouds of tiny islands which comprise Micronesia: they cover the area of the continental United States and contain in all about one thousand square miles of territory and about 150,000 inhabitants.

Finally, the Pacific area includes, of course, the island continent of Australia: there exist the various groups of so-called Aborigines. Their religion has been the focus of intense interest and has attracted much writing,

Map 4 Oceania

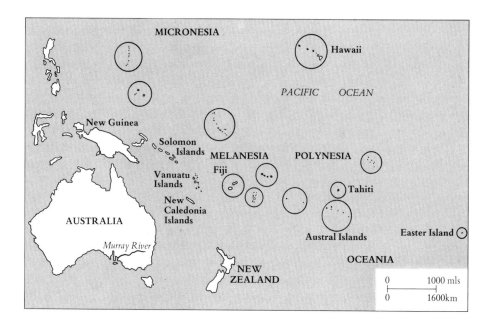

but it has also been under heavy pressure from Western culture, as indeed have all the religions of the Pacific region.

The geography of the Pacific—the breaking of the world into islands, the high mountains and deep valleys of New Guinea, and the very great distances in Australia (again, it is about the size of the continental United States)—have conspired to break folk up into small cultural units, and small groups have notoriously found it hard to stand up to the impact of larger cultures. The problem for us then is to penetrate beyond modern conditions in order to present some picture of these Oceanian cultures before the menacing dawn of the European day.

As to the cultures themselves, we shall look at them in the order laid out above: first, the Polynesians, next the Melanesians, then the Micronesians, and finally the Australian Aborigines, or what I shall call "classical Australians." In a way, it is of course artificial to group the four main cultures together (even internally they are largely groupings of convenience without a necessary basis in cultural homogeneity of any extent). Their sisterhood lies in their occupying the Pacific region. In any case my way of describing them will necessarily have to be greatly selective and indeed impressionistic. But they represent important branches of human experience, as they emerge today into the postcolonial light.

## Tabu *and* Mana

Before we embark on a description of some features of Pacific religion, it is worth noting that it is from its vocabulary that have been drawn two highly important words which have been prominent in the comparative study of religion—*mana* and *tabu* (or taboo). The latter indeed has passed into the stock

162

of ordinary English usage. The term *mana* came to prominence through one of the major theories of the origin of religion formulated by the anthropologist R. R. Marett (1866–1943) in a book published in 1909, *The Threshold of Religion*. He drew upon the reported finding by a fellow anthropologist in a book on the Melanesians published in 1891 that the fundamental concept of their religion was *mana* or power: for instance the power residing in a chief, or a rock, or in some sacralized object. It came to be noticed that similar ideas were to be found in a variety of small-scale cultures across the world; and the idea was taken up by some major theorists, notably Gerardus van der Leeuw

---

### Smallscale Religions  some key terms

*Atua* (Polynesian) a god or supernatural being, from the creator Tangaroa to local deities.

*Calumet* French term now applied to all smoking instruments of Native and South American peoples. Smoking is a ceremonial act, and the pipe is a microcosmic model of the universe.

*Corroboree* Aboriginal festive occasion with ceremonial rituals and dances, often reenacting myths.

*Kachina* Masks and other representations of mythic beings used among the Pueblo Indians of the American Southwest.

*Mana* Sacred and numinous power associated with gods, breach of tabu, holy forces in nature, etc.; used by anthropologists and others as a key notion in religions.

*Marae* (Polynesian) sacred area with shrine.

*Masalai* (Melanesian word from Papua New Guinea) animal spirits and demons liable to haunt human beings.

*Mizimu* (Bantu) the spirits of the dead: ancestors.

*Nganga* Specialist in dealing with illnesses and various evils: a so-called witch-doctor (Southern and Central African traditions).

*Shaman* (Tungus word from Siberia) a visionary who can, in sharing experimentally in the vicissitudes of the sick, help to cure them and who can locate resources (such as fish and game) in a hunting society; often experiences death and rebirth.

*Tabu* or *Tapu* (Polynesian) that which is forbidden and dangerous; great mana generates tapu.

*Totem* (Algonquin word from North America) a natural species of animal or plant life connected especially with a clan, who do not hunt or gather that species: key concept in many anthropological and psychological theories about the nature of religion.

---

modify it. Maui for instance stole fire from the gods, so that humans could cook and use it in other useful ways. He fished up various islands with his fishhook, including the North Island of New Zealand, according to Maori myth. He is supposed to have slowed down the sun so that humans could have a day of decent length to prepare food and make things, including nice images for the gods. He is credited with being the ancestor of the human race. He was not worshiped as such, but the stories of his tricky humiliation of pompous gods (who *were* worshiped) were told with relish.

Humans preexist in the "other world," and each enters this world through her or his mother. A woman, likewise, is the conduit of death. The tale is told that Maui intended to kill off Hine-nui-te-po, Great Hine of the Underworld, the personification of Death, by entering into her through her vagina and eventually coming out of her mouth. He slipped off his clothes, bound his strong club to his right wrist, and told his bird companions to stay absolutely quiet for fear of waking Hine: and so he started to climb into her vagina. The birds naturally thought this a scream and laughed raucously, all of which commotion woke Hine. She saw Maui climbing into her and crushed him to death between her thighs.

Naturally there are vast resources of myth available in the Polynesian world, and these few examples will suffice for a glimpse into this narrative world. The stories of the gods, from another angle, help as metaphors of society and social norms, and it is within the ethos of Polynesian religion that morality has its meaning. But in the nature of the case the pattern of values is heroic and greatly male-dominated. The battles which often engaged the peoples of the Pacific, the great deeds of navigation and fishing, and so on, led to a system of ethics which prized manliness and courage, and the kind of success which was exhibited in *mana*.

As for *experience*: the very pattern of belief about the gods prevalent across the Pacific, seeing everywhere the hands of hidden forces, meant that ordinary life had to be read all the time for omens, hints as to what the gods were up to. As you looked out to the deep blue Pacific waters you could almost see the gods of wind and water and storm; and as you scanned the white beach you could wonder whether the gods were secretly crossing it towards the abodes of human beings. And there around the village, in the curling smoke and in the shadows, were the hints of gods of disease, of the village, of carpentry, of all kinds of secret forces in human affairs. They were like the *numina* of ancient Rome. They lent an air of awe, of the numinous, to the wondrous environment in which human beings had their beautiful and dangerous existence. The murmurings of *tabu* reinforced fear. As the thunder might mutter in the distance, so might the unseen forces of the gods be mobilizing themselves for their own purposes, which yet would bring sorrow or joy to humans. So it was needful to read the sky and the plants and the animals, birds and fish.

Some people were specially deep in their dreaming and in visions, and they might become specialist diviners and healers. Dreams especially were significant events. But the whole world of Nature was after all part of the behavior of the gods: their bodies were thunder and rain and pigs and earth. Strange behavior in anything might provide a clue to the gods' intentions, and reinforced the sense of the numinous and of awe-inspiring *mana* which drenched the world of the Polynesian.

In the *material* dimension, masks, dances, carvings, and *maraes* or sacred enclosures were artifacts which helped to attract the gods and so canalize their powers in contact with the human race. The carvings of Polynesian art represented likenesses of the gods, or things congenial to them, so that they might be induced to come, regaled with song and chant and immemorial rituals, and then in due course sent on their way.

As far as the *organizational* dimension of religion went, although the preparation of *maraes* or sacred enclosures was a communal activity, Polynesian cultures had specialists in ritual, and also those especially skilled in healing, divination, and other arts. There were those also who used sorcery, and there was a dark underside of religion, in which the wrong uses of ritual were greatly to be feared.

## Melanesian Religions: Some Patterns

If there are variations in the Polynesian world, there are even more so in the whole range of Melanesia. The island of New Guinea, comprising what are now Papua New Guinea, an independent state, and Irian Jaya which is part of Indonesia, contains more than 1000 languages, some spoken by less than 200 people. The islands have diverse cultures, some heavily influenced by Polynesian motifs, as in Fiji. But if one can generalize, then one might say that the Melanesian religions have more confidence in the manipulative power of ritual, and they feel less dependent on the gods. Gods there are, and all kinds of spirits; but they are closer to the earthly realm and not too difficult in many cases to control. The importance of primary power or *mana* can be seen from this perspective, for it is this energy that humans would like to manipulate, and it is the ritual system which manages to do this that is important to Melanesian culture.

Were there a clear distinction to be made between magic and religion, then Melanesia exhibits more of magic than of religion. But it is not a distinction which bears much fruit. Suffice it to say that for many Melanesian societies ritual is at the heart of things, and the unseen forces with which ritual deals, and which it may create, are the most vital part of the fabric of events. Thus no major calamity and virtually no death fails to be explained either as a result of sorcery or the action of spirits, or as the result of the breaking of some taboo. It follows that disease itself has similar causes, and it is the job of specialists to be able to direct counter-ritual to work against the dangerous forces at work against the afflicted individual.

The range of unseen forces is great. There are deities, often associated with particular activities such as fishing or warfare; they often seem remote from

The ritual dimension: in Papua-New Guinea and New Ireland masks and headdresses are ceremonial means of assuming the identity of gods and spirits.

human activity, though they may play a role in myth. But even remote culture heroes and gods may be important in another way, as the ultimate sources of various spells and incantations, and knowledge of this will have been handed down secretly from generation to generation of ritual specialists. There are other spirits, or at any rate mythic beings, who are not gods but nevertheless attract fear: demon monsters who inhabit the wild parts of the bush which lie outside the relative order of human settlements, with their vegetable gardens and places for rearing pigs. Closer to the settlements are the hungry ghosts: the newly departed may still have nostalgia for those whom they knew, although they eventually drift away to their own world where they do much the same sort of thing that humans do, but in a rather pleasanter way, probably.

Belief in ghosts ties in with the general Melanesian belief in souls. Souls can be disturbed and even captured by sorcery. Human leftovers, such as cut hair or the remains of what you have been eating, can be used to control a soul. Where this happens the only recourse is counter-magic. In some places, for instance in the highlands of New Guinea, the souls of ancestors play an important role in religion in that they are thought to be able to promote the welfare of the community—through the fertility of crops, for instance. They exist as part of a wider society in which the visible community is embedded.

On the whole, then, Melanesian religion thinks of the spirit world, both divine and human (in the form of ghosts and the souls of ancestors), as being rather close to the visible community in which humans have their primary being. Some features of religion, while not unique to Melanesia, are nevertheless emphasized there. For instance, sometimes complex taboos surround men's dealings with women, who are generally thought to be inferior. Thus often a man is not supposed to be below a woman: he should not drink from water in a stream downstream from women; and in some societies villages are built in such a way that men's quarters are built on ridges to ensure physical superiority. Since contact with women is regarded in many places as itself polluting, boys' puberty rites involve vomiting and the letting of blood in order to rid them of the polluting contacts with food cooked by women, menstrual blood, and so on. Sometimes initiation takes the form of entry into a men's secret society, where adepts are eventually shown how to make sacred masks and conduct séances with spirits.

### The Meaning of Death

Very strong in the Melanesian context is the regard paid to the proper treatment of the dead. Elaborate feasts and burial ceremonies are the norm, and the corpse is sometimes cross-questioned to check on the cause of death. The extent of a widow's austere seclusion and expression of loss is held as an index of how she was not involved in poisoning her mate. The ceremonial may extend over a long period: first the ritual disposal of a corpse by burial or on a platform, then the collection of the bones, once the flesh has decayed away, and further rites. During this stretch of time it may be that the kin and in particular the widow remain in utter seclusion.

There are indications in the mourning of a deeper layer of ritual in the past when widows were killed, as in New Britain, and sent on with their deceased husbands to the afterlife. The possessions of the departed may also be destroyed, or ultimately consumed as part of a ritual of reintegration of the kin into society.

Even after the round of mortuary observances has been completed, the dead are not necessarily utterly gone: their ghosts may be summoned and consulted in future times, and shrines where their bones are kept may come to function like ancestral temples.

### Art and Religion

Especially in lowland New Guinea, but also elsewhere, Melanesian art and especially the making of masks for ceremonial purposes, is spectacular. Very often the construction—made out of barkcloth, say, and decorated with colored leaves and feathers, or painted with traditional designs—are short-lived, being made just for some ceremony, such as a funeral. Usually the making of such masks is a highly secret matter, to be kept secret in particular from women. There are other statues or masks of a more permanent kind, representing spirits. There are rites for the introduction of spirits into the masks and for dismissing them. Sometimes the painting of the eyes has special significance. The creation of such art would not of course be classified as such, since the aesthetic as a separate category is itself largely a Western phenomenon: but nevertheless is a testimony to the brilliant imagination of Melanesian societies and the intuitive realization of wonderful ways of representing and expressing the sense of the numinous.

We do not come across much, in the wide spectrum of Melanesian religion, which points to belief in a single Supreme Creator or High God. The *myths* of beginnings tend to deal with the bringing of some order out of a chaos of calamities. The small scale of most societies, and their being surrounded by a space which was largely unknown or fearful (ocean or bush), gave Melanesians a sense of contrast between man-made order and a somewhat spooky periphery, relevant to human affairs but somewhat threatening. The main feature of religions in the area is the highly developed sense of the practical efficacy of ritual, both for good and ill. Thus of all the dimensions of religion, ritual is here the most highly worked out and prized, and with it the physical manifestation of ritual, namely the body-painting, masks, and icons constructed for the ceremonial life.

## Micronesia

The worlds of the Micronesians are varied too; but they have somewhat more concern than the Melanesians with the creation, and the emphasis on female deities is greater. This may be in part because, while males are involved in fishing, navigation, housebuilding, the martial arts, etc., women are in charge of the gardens and agricultural work. Nevertheless, typically women are thought of as inferior and polluting, because of menstrual blood and giving birth. Sometimes, even so, the High God and Creator is thought of as female, and goddesses are frequently credited with the creation of differing food plants. In the Carolines the Great Goddess, Ligoupup, always existed, and made the world. She is conceived as lying beneath the islands, and when she stirs then there are earthquakes. Her son became god of the underworld and the sea and all that pertains to it; her daughter rose to heaven and wed a deity, by whom she had a son, Aluelap, who is the source of all knowledge. Elsewhere the High God is nominated as Anulap, who is ancient and white-haired, and so very weak that two servitors raise his eyelids so that he can see and raise his upper lip so that he can eat. He is a very colorful representation of what historians know as the *Deus otiosus* or "Superfluous God," who is

inactive in regard to human affairs (often being so high and numinous that humans cannot think of how he could come to be concerned with the trivial worries of the human race), and is consequently no longer worshiped. Still, he is creator, knows all, and is Supreme Being.

*Opposite* The ritual dimension: Maori body-painting.

In many ways the Micronesian religious world is like that of the Polynesians, and there has been some Polynesian cultural influence in some of the islands. They are a part of the great mosaic of religions of Oceania, opened up eventually to Westerners from the sixteenth century onwards, as navigators from an alien world discovered the often idyllic-seeming islands.

## Australia: the Land of the Dreaming

Finally, in our survey of the Pacific religions, we come to the classical culture of Australia before the Whites came to settle the land, some two hundred years ago. The societies which inhabit the vast reaches of Australia, from the snowy mountains of the southeast to the red plains of the west, are varied, but they display some traits in common, which we can look on as classical features of Australian religion and society. The two most striking of these are totemism and the concept of the Dreaming.

The Dreaming (or Dream Time) is that period long ago (yet still somehow present to us in everyday life) when the deities moved about on the earth, giving shape and substance to the land, generating human beings, and arranging the rules of society. It was in its own way a creative epoch, but it is much more than some generalized period of cosmogony. The Dreaming helps to explain the most particular items in the environment. That environment is—for the most part—a rather harsh one, in which ingenuity is needed to live successfully. It is a hot land, with red deserts and glittering eucalyptus trees, half dried watercourses and dry gullies, sparse rains and elusive high clouds, grand rounded rocks and strangely contoured hills: a land populated sparsely with ingenious animals—the kangaroo and the wallaby, the ant-eating echidna, the lizard goanna—and bright birds, from the small kooka-burra to the flamboyant galahs and bright-colored parrots, and many insects, notably the creators of great anthills and the ever-present flies. It is this environment that received its particularities in the phase of the Dreaming.

Important in the cycles of Australian myth are the routes which the protagonists took across the countryside in the Dreaming. These tales indicate places which are sacred, either because of events described in the myths or more intensely because they relate to the fertility of some relevant species. For instance there is the story of Ngurunderi, in the Murray river region of south Australia. He went down the river in a canoe, after the great Murray Cod, which swished its huge tail to and fro and splashed the water around. Thereby it formed the many bends in the river and the swamps which line it here and there. Eventually Cod was caught by his brother-in-law, and he strewed the chopped up bits into the lower Murray and the lakes at its mouth, to make many species of fish for later humans to gather. Or again, there is a myth from the far north which concerns a famous and widespread mythic figure, the Rainbow Snake. She came from the sea, but at first only found dry—very dry—land. She traveled underneath the earth and came to a waterfall. She went downstream, and when the water disappeared she dug out a large billabong (a pool in a river which is cut off from the flow) and produced an egg, which she set out to harden in the sun, and then slept in a cave. An old man came along and cooked the egg. She grabbed him and dragged him under the water, vomiting up his bones, which hardened. She made two more eggs which hardened there in the pool. She looks after them from the cave above the billabong. This is a highly particular myth, relating to a highly particular sacred site, with its spirit presences, the Rainbow Snake and the old man, frozen as it were into immortality by the tale.

The desert is the great area of mythic tracks where the gods and spirits went on their travels. You cannot know all the stories, and differing tribes characteristically knew different parts of the meaning of the overlapping sacred geography. In such ways the whole land was haunted by divine presences, projected into the Now from the time of the Dreaming. But the Dreaming of course does much more than present us with a sacred cartography: it accounts for social custom, for clan organization, for inventions—in short for the whole of arrangements for living. It explains rituals which in turn are designed to canalize the Dreaming to us so that we can benefit from its powers.

### Creation and Fertility

There are various stories of creation and sky gods, who nevertheless tend to fade into insignificance compared to the sacred events of the Dream Time. There is a story in central Australia, among those who speak Aranda, that there was a great emu-footed Father who lived in a paradisal place with many wives and children. These beings were not worried about the earth. Beneath the earth slept many other supernatural beings, who eventually awakened and started their wanderings. Human beings were created by them and taught the various arts which they would need to live in the region. The stories of this Dreaming period became much more vital for the Aranda than any high and "otiose" God. Their existential religion was a matter of communication not with the great Father but with the supernaturals of the Dreaming, and so rituals had to be used, themselves prescribed by the supernaturals, for recreating the ancestors in the present.

Some myths of origin concern fertility, and a famous one of these is the cycle of stories of Djangawwul, who landed on the coast from the hazy island of Bralgu with a male companion and his own two sisters, whom he kept in a state of perpetual pregnancy with his very long and potent penis. There was no question of incest here, as marriage customs had not yet been invented. The offspring of the sisters were the ancestors of the present-day Australian Aborigines. They also created various fertility rituals, in which women are often engaged. The sisters brought with them a cult object or *rangga*, symbolizing the penis. The men stole it and started their own cultic activities.

Fertility is often connected, too, with the system of totemism which is widespread in Australia. The supernaturals of the Dreaming become linked to clans, a clan being a group which is constituted by patrilineal descendants of a supernatural hero. These ideas can be illustrated from the case of the northern tribe of Walbiris, now some 1,400 in number. They are divided into about forty clans, each connected with a totem or personified version of some natural species or object—Kangaroo, Opossum, Yam, Rain, Fire, and so on. These heroes had their stories which told of the localities associated with them—sometimes marking enormously long tracks (one going as far as South Australia) and sometimes quite localized. These sacred places were infused with sacred particles which were the relatively dormant supernaturals. They had to be activated by human rituals, performed by the men's lodge of the relevant clan. Without the carrying on of such rituals the land and the people would not stay prosperous. The land, the heroes of the Dreaming, the former ancestors, and the present-day people thus formed an organic web, easy to rupture but happy in its wellbeing if all went well.

### Ecopsychism

That organic web was indeed ruptured by the coming to Australia of people who had very different views of the relation of land to people and of supernaturals to society. But we must first make the imaginative leap to that world which has lasted some 30,000 years or more. We know little of its ancient styles when it first came to the Australian mainland. But we can reach

Aboriginal art in Australia: this depicts an episode in a story of Western Arnhem land, with fragile spirits enticing a hunter.

175

back to view Aboriginal culture before the coming of the Europeans. We see a remarkable experiment in living in which diverse social groups crisscrossed the same land, managed between them in a segmented way the sacred places and tracks of a unitary landscape, and saw with the inward eye beyond the rocks and trees and leaping animals to the spirits that infused the creation around them and gave sanction and meaning to their customs. From the outside: dusty humans. From the inside: complicated social divisions and initiations and rites which meshed in with the hunting and gathering, across a changing daily scene. They pioneered a form of ecopsychism, a kind of gently effective way of living in a Nature which was itself conceived as infused with spirits.

It is rather different, this Australian world, from that of Melanesia, Micronesia, and Polynesia, where the sea is often dominant, and the land rich. Here there is a different, drier scene, and one where much more so than elsewhere the diverse social groups are more open to one another, for they share somewhat an interwoven system of sacred tracks and places. The Rainbow Snake's eggs have hardened in the sun, and there are unseen persons hovering round, and in, the billabong.

# The Americas

## A Wide Scene

It seems probable that all or virtually all the ancestors of the Native Americans in both North and South America migrated there from the Asian landmass by a northerly route, via what is now the Bering Straits. There may be some slight influence of Polynesian settlement, and it could be that in the period before Columbus there were Chinese landings; and we know of a small Viking presence. But, given the relative homogeneity of a largely Asian immigrant population (and even there, as today, there may have been great variations), the patterns of culture which were created in the regions of the Americas are extremely diverse. Among other achievements was the creation of some great urban civilizations in Central and South America.

There are five cultural areas which we shall consider here: first, the Andes; second, the rest of South America, comprising differing regions, such as Patagonia, the Pampas, the Gran Chaco, the Amazon Basin, Eastern Brazil, and the Caribbean coast; third, the islands of the Caribbean; fourth, Central America; and fifth, North America. In most of these we deal with very varied phenomena in the pre-Columbian period, and the best we can do here is to be selective in relation to differing types of religions and social values.

In terms of urban culture we can count 1000 C.E. as a watershed, in that it was in the tenth century that the Toltec empire in Mexico, a powerful predecessor of the Aztecs, collapsed, and at a somewhat similar time the Tiahuanaco empire in the Central Andes also disappeared. It was after this time that we see the rise of the great states which were so unsuccessful against the Spaniards. The Maya civilization also disappeared as a viable system in the tenth century. In many ways we might look upon the period before the tenth century as exhibiting classical forms of urban culture in Central America,

177

especially because of the delicacy of Maya art. But on the whole we know too little, even about the Maya, to decipher their religions clearly. With the subsequent period, and the Aztecs and the Incas, we are on somewhat firmer ground. As to cultures outside of Central America and the Inca region, we know relatively little about their forms before 1000. In many cases we have to describe classical religions in small-scale groups as they exist now, for lack of sufficient historical or archaeological knowledge.

## The Religion of the Incas

The empires which preceded the Incas in Peru were various—from the Chavín (eighth century C.E. onwards) through to the Chimú (1200–1400 C.E.). Unfortunately, we do not know too much of their religious ideas, because, like the Incas, they lacked a written language. The temples seem to have been used for sacrifices, including human sacrifice, and there is good evidence of complex rites related to calendars describing the movements of various heavenly bodies. The Sun and Moon seem to have been important deities, and there are images of gods in the form of animals, such as the puma.

The Inca religious system of the fifteenth century was an amalgamation of preceding cults, and in a way that emphasized and organized imperial rule. Roughly, the empire was a centralized federation in which local chiefs were summoned periodically to the capital Cuzco (or "Navel," that is, center of the

Map 5  Latin America

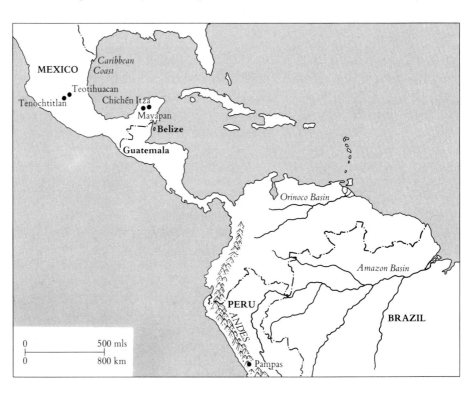

earth). The central Temple of the Sun at the junction of the rivers may also have been linked to the Milky Way, also seen as a river. At any rate here was the center of empire. From here radiated theoretical lines along each of which was placed 428 shrines. There were reciprocal relations between Cuzco and the approved sanctuaries of the provinces (but many local cults were suppressed, no doubt through having supported resistance to the greatly expanding Inca empire). The imperial ideology represented the emperor (the Inca) as responsible for the welfare of the empire, and so he was the chief point of intersection of his subjects and the great gods. He had to preside over earthly affairs during the present cosmic cycle; so he was himself a god, the offspring of the Sun, which was the great deity at the heart of the ritual complex at the temple of Cuzco.

The Sun at Cuzco had to share his temple with the Thunder God, whose sphere of operations was lower than the heavens; the Moon Goddess, who was especially important to women; and the Stars. Together they regulated time and the change of seasons. The Father of the Sun, and the Supreme Being (though not the only god), was Viracocha. He it was who formed and arranged things at the beginning of the era, and he was the recipient of prayers, especially from the aristocracy. One such prayer has survived:

You who are without equal, and span the ends of the earth: you who gave life and force to human beings, saying to one, "Let this be a man," and to the other, "Let this be a woman," you gave them being: Let them live without danger, in peace and health. You who are in the heavens and in the thunderstorm, grant them long life, and accept this our sacrifice.

Beneath the great gods were a cloud of other numinous beings, the *huaca*, and the hierarchical imperial system was also reflected in a hierarchy of gods, down to the village level.

Doctrinally, some great store seems to have been set by the binary oppositions of the cosmos: male-female, Sun-Moon, and so on. Likewise, villages were divided into two halves, and the whole earthly and cosmic system was seen as both in conflict and capable of being harmonized. It was the Inca's chief function to contribute to this harmony, by relevant offerings and by the maintenance of the cycle of public rituals. There are echoes of the Chinese search for harmony amid the polarities of Yin and Yang.

The glories and complexities of the ritual year must have been great. The ceremonies at Cuzco were dazzling, with the Inca on a gold throne presiding over sacrifices in the gold-plated halls of the temple. The ability to control so large an empire in part depended on these rites; but it must be remembered too that everywhere in the villages and homesteads of the vast region men and women celebrated their divine ancestors and had relations to lesser *huacas* to help them with their gardens and food-growing, and in the fight against illness and death. But the weakness of the system was its intense centralization, which is why in 1532 a few adventurers under Francisco Pizarro could strike in such a deadly way at the heart of the system.

## Small-scale Societies in South America

The conditions of existence in South America outside of the Andean region are of course very varied. Many of the groups in the tropical forest regions of the Amazon and Orinoco basins (sadly depleted, by the way, in population since the first culture contact with Europeans, so that also there may have thereby been great socioreligious changes) do not seem to have anything but occasional belief in a High God or Supreme Being. However, such a belief is very widespread in the regions of the Pampas and Patagonia. The rituals related to ancestral cults and the preservation of the dead are much more common in the Andes than elsewhere—perhaps because climatically such practices as mummification become feasible, whereas in steaming forests the dead decompose alarmingly fast. Fertility cults and vegetation deities are important in the northwest Amazon region and elsewhere, but not in the Grand Chaco. So we can point to considerable variety, reinforced of course once one begins to look at the content of the varied mythologies.

One element, however, is almost universal outside the Andes: shamanism. In many areas, the shaman identifies with the jaguar, which can act as his or her *alter ego*. This is probably for a number of reasons. First, the jaguar can swim and hunt in water and so has access to the (generally watery) underworld. Likewise the shaman can visit this region, in the course of saving spirits of humans from death. Second, a jaguar can climb and, like the shaman, has access to upper regions, the heavenly world. It is in any case a numinous creature, and full of ambiguities.

A mushroom-shaped stone from Central America. This may have represented a shaman who was influenced by hallucinogenic mushrooms.

The shaman testifies to the importance of religious experience, for it is by visions, ecstasies, and dreams that he or she receives a vocation. It may be that in many such societies the actual training with an expert is arduous: but at root there is the capacity for vision. This can be and is aided by hallucinogens. It appears as if the use of the San Pedro plant is attested for nearly three thousand years, from ancient pottery of the Chavín culture in Peru, where it is depicted. Such hallucinogens were often also combined with tobacco.

The shaman was important because by his experience and ritual powers he could project himself into the invisible worlds. He could thus effect cures in the case of those who might in a sense have died. But he could also enter the worlds of the spirits whose manifestations were in this world—as fish, animals, birds, and so on—and thus he could give guidance to hunters and gatherers (as many of these smaller-scale societies were).

## The Caribbean

The major peoples of the Caribbean islands were the Arawaks and the Caribs. After the settlement of the islands by Europeans, the aboriginal inhabitants were wiped out by imported diseases and the hardships of slave labor; they survive only in the descendants of interbreeding with Europeans or with the hardier slaves brought in from Africa. With them went the pre-Columbian religions of the islands. Traces of their beliefs and rituals are, however, to be found in Afro-Caribbean religion, and we shall see something of these developments in the second part of this book.

Both the Arawaks, who migrated about the beginning of the Common Era, and the Caribs, came from the mainland. As with the South American peoples we have just considered, shamanism was an important phenomenon. There were beliefs in High Gods, and among the Arawak importance was attached to the cult of ancestors. The Caribs were said by Columbus to have been cannibals (the English word derives from the word "Carib"), but this may well have been an unjustified accusation.

## Civilizations of Central America

### The Maya

The classical civilization of the Maya in Southeastern Mexico and in Guatemala and Belize still survives in a fragmentary way, not only in the great ruins of

The ethical dimension: a Mayan relief from Yaxchilan in Guatemala, showing a penitent mutilating his tongue before a priest. British Museum, London.

the area, such as at Chichén Itzá and Mayapán, but also in the cultures of people who still speak Mayan languages. Their cultural achievements in art, writing and mathematics were considerable; and they invented an ingenious calendrical system which was used to calculate and foretell auspicious days. It was based on units of 20, and so on a 360-day year, being the closest multiple of 20 to the real length of the year. Years were calculated according to a Short Count of 256-year cycles or a Long Count which started at the year 3114 B.C.E. The use of the Short Count persisted among the Maya until the eighteenth century, one of a number of long survivals of the culture after the Spanish conquest.

Time became the fundamental preoccupation of Maya culture, and this was tied of course to the revolutions of the Sun. The Sun God became the main focus of religion: he was also the creator and the first priestly figure who invented writing. The cosmos was arranged vertically in seven layers of heavens and below the earth were the five layers of the underworld, which was the realm of the dead. At the centre of the cosmos stood the First Tree, the *axis mundi*. This is reminiscent of many other cultures, and may reflect some shamanistic motifs as having entered into early Maya thought. But it seems that the sacred character of time which could be calculated by an esoteric arithmetic was the chief occupation of the priestly class.

## The Aztecs

For the Aztecs their wonderful capital, Tenochtitlán, was the chief marvel of civilization. In its immense size and beautiful architecture it was modeled on the older Toltec city of Teotihuacán, the "Abode of the Gods," some thirty miles to the north, and in its division into four quarters it reflected the Aztec understanding of the cosmos. These four directions together with the center are the typical five directions of Central American (as of Chinese) cosmology. The cosmos had its axis or invisible center in the vertical line which ran through the City, with thirteen heavenly levels arranged above and nine layers in the underworld. The number five was also important for time as well as space. The universe has five major periods, each ending with various calamities. In modern time, we are now embarked on the period of the Fifth Sun, when the sun rises in the East.

But the universe is gravely unstable, for the continuation of order requires continuous sacrifices. Indeed, before the start of the Fifth Sun the gods had to combine to energize the Sun, which did not rise above the horizon, by sacrificing themselves collectively. This myth provided justification for the continuing sacrificial cult which was centered in Tenochtitlán. The Aztec emperor was also the highest priest, and so there fell to him the task of maintaining not only the order of the empire but the order of the whole cosmos as well. So the Aztecs had this rather haunting and terrifying thought that indeed the Sun might not rise tomorrow, that the onward harmony of the world was something which was for ever in jeopardy. There was therefore a deep resonance between the cosmic and human worlds. The Sun

## The Tasks of the Wise Man (Aztec): Bernardino de Sahagún

The wise man: a light, a torch, a stout torch that does not smoke.

A perforated mirror, a mirror pierced on both sides.

His are the black and red ink, his are the illustrated manuscripts, he studies the illustrated manuscripts.

He himself is writing and wisdom.

He is the path, the true way for others.

He directs people and things; he is a guide in human affairs.

The wise man is careful [like a physician] and preserves tradition.

His is the handed-down wisdom; he teaches it; he follows the path of truth.

Teacher of the truth, he never ceases to admonish.

He makes wise the countenances of others; to them he gives a face [a personality]; he leads them to develop it.

He opens their ears; he enlightens them.

He is the teacher of guides; he shows them their path.

One depends upon him.

He puts a mirror before others; he makes them prudent, cautious; he causes a face [a personality] to appear in them.

He attends to things; he regulates their path, he arranges and commands.

He applies his light to the world.

He knows what is above us (and) in the region of the dead.

He is a serious man.

Everyone is comforted by him, corrected, taught.

Thanks to him people humanize their will and receive a strict education.

He comforts the heart, he comforts the people, he helps, gives remedies, heals everyone.

---

required human blood: this was the ideology of human sacrifice, itself a great stimulus to warfare, which was waged to capture fodder for the gods.

But the mythic cosmology was more than a depiction of the directions and epochs. It was filled in with pictures of the various gods and spiritual beings who animated and controlled the universe, beginning with the ultimate creator, Ometéotl, all-powerful, and a blend of male and female, who fused oppositions in her/his own person. There was Tezcatlipoca, Smoking Mirror, vigorous and frightening in his powers of transformation, identified with the Knife, a divinity vital (or one might say fatal) in sacrifice. There was Xiuhtecuhtli, the fire deity, important too in the priestly cult, where fires had to be maintained at all times and ritually renewed: every fifty-two years, at the end of a calendar cycle, a new fire was kindled in the hole in a sacrificial victim's chest, whence his palpitating heart had been plucked. He was also, as in other cultures, the god of the hearth, basic to domestic daily rites. There was the female Coatlícue (Snake Skirt), powerful in fertility, fierce, decorated with skulls, sacrificial hearts, and other appurtenances of monstrosity.

A god with a special importance was the skillful Quetzalcóatl (Feathered Snake), important also in pre-Aztec civilization and among the Maya, where his name was Kukulcán. He was the recreator of the world, inventing agriculture and the various human arts, and dived to the underworld to regain the bones of death; himself dying, he was resurrected, and saved the dead whose bones he reanimated. Around him there developed a dramatic myth, concerning his miraculous birth, his avenging of his father's death, his

*Right* The messenger of the gods, on whose stomach the hearts of victims were offered up: Chichen Itza, Yucatan.

*Below, right* Quetzalcóatl figure and a standard bearer on Temple of the Warriors. Later Quetzalcóatl played a highly important role in Aztec culture.

*Below* The mythic dimension: Tzazolteotl, a fertility goddess of rather fierce expression, here gives birth; she dealt with sexual transgressions.

training for the priesthood, his rule as sacred king, the fall of his empire, his flight, and his promise to return one day from the east to restore his rule and universal prosperity. It was this narrative which reportedly made Moctezuma II, the Aztec emperor, think that Hernán Cortés, coming in his feathered ships, was Quetzalcóatl returning to reclaim his kingdom. But that of course is a later story.

Then there was the fierce warrior god Huitzilopochtli, Humming Bird of the South, who together with Tláloc—the Rain God and source of fertility for the Aztec empire and the whole earth—was enshrined on top of the great temple pyramid, the Templo Mayor, in the capital. He was recipient of numerous sacrifices. He was the son, mysteriously conceived, of the goddess Coatlícue. All this indicates the close relation that war and fertility had in the Aztec worldview, where the pursuit of prisoners for human sacrifice was itself a force for political expansion.

As we have indicated, the central rites of the empire, presided over by the emperor himself, were human sacrifices in which a victim's chest would be opened and the still quivering heart torn out and presented to the gods. It was a grim rite, and may blind us to the beauty of the city itself, in its fertile valley amid lakes, with towering mountains in view (where Tláloc generated rain), its hanging gardens and intense cultivation of vegetables and fruits, its geometric layout, its white houses and great pyramidal temples, and its ready sunshine. Its weakness lay in its centralization and its commitment to warfare, which was bound to bring countervailing military forces to bear sooner or later.

Here then was a remarkable civilization, with a rather pessimistic worldview, which rested in part on the achievements of preceding cultures—the Toltec and others—and had relations with that now decayed civilization of the Maya. It is clear that mastery of the art of growing maize, which became the most vital staple of the Americas, gave the chance to use agricultural surpluses to create great urban centers, beautiful and elaborate artworks, and extravagant religious cults.

## North America

As we move north from the scenes of the great urban civilizations we encounter cultures which are also based on sedentary agriculture, with maize being the central product: notably there are the Pueblo peoples of the Southwestern U.S.A., who used irrigation techniques to shape their intensive agriculture. There are other groups, such as the Apache and Navajo, who blend agriculture and hunting; and some peoples who are still very much hunters and gatherers. To the West, in California and in the Pacific Northwest, there is a variety of cultures, some very much oriented towards the sea and the catching of the abundant sea life of the area. In the Southeast there is rich agricultural land lining the alluvial rivers, and the region was broken into chiefdoms, some sizeable. Life in the Northeast had a predominantly hunting character, where the area was rich with life in luxuriant woodlands, but there too was the cultivation of the "three sisters"—maize, beans, and squash.

In the Plains, reaching up into what is now Canada as well as the great central part of the United States, the introduction of the horse by the Spaniards considerably altered the economy as it facilitated a new and effective way of rounding up and hunting the buffalo. Before that there was a mix of horticulture and nomadism, involving hunting and gathering. The various groups in the area were somewhat more cooperative than elsewhere, in so far as they developed extensive trade and a sign language which enabled interlinguistic communication. Finally there are the varied groups of the Far North including the ingenious Inuit of the Arctic, who had mastered a highly problematic environment.

Now it is obvious that with so varied an economic spread, and so many different language groups, the cultural variation is immense. But it might be useful just to consider four of the groups as a sample: the Hopi of the Southwest; the Iroquois of the Northeast; the Lakota of the Plains; and the Inuit of the North. In the Hopi I shall emphasize the *social* organization of religion and the *material* dimension, in the Iroquois the *experiential, doctrinal,* and *ethical* dimensions, in the Lakota the *ritual* dimension, and in the Inuit the *mythic* dimension.

## Hopi Society

In this exposition the Hopi can stand as an example of the wider group of people settled in small towns and villages (*pueblos*) and known as the Pueblo peoples. It is interesting that they are organized, for ritual purposes, in a rather domestic manner, through the existence of a number of different societies each of which has to realize a particular type of ritual. In each of these groups there are priests and lay folk, and because their presentations are integrated into an annual cycle it means that a certain degree of cheerful competition ensures a high level of ceremonial. The ritual societies themselves are at different levels, so that a young person may graduate through them to senior status. At sixteen, males are initiated into the four main male groups, and the women into the women's society. There is a more exclusive male society which organizes the highly complicated and important ceremonies at the time of the winter solstice, when the direction of the sun needs to be changed, and plants, animals, and human life need to be renewed and reintegrated in the general cosmic harmony.

Central in Hopi concerns is of course maize. Corn is the substance of life, and corn meal is sprinkled as a santifying force, much as water is used in Christian ceremonial. Prayer is accompanied by the sprinkling of corn. When a child is born it is presented with two perfect ears of corn. And so on.

One of the most important features of Hopi ritual life is the *kachina* or mask, with accompanying clothes and body paint, through which a Hopi "performer" mediates the spirit inherent in the mask. It is a kind of ikon animated by a dancer. The *kachinas* embody a whole range of supernatural

Kachina masks in operation among the Hopi of the American Southwest.

spirits, the dead, and clouds (seen in their own way as spiritual beings); and in this way it is possible to enact the sacred narratives of the people, make social comment, celebrate the gods, and bring blessings on the people. There is a special period, from the winter solstice onwards, which is the *kachina* period, at the end of which the sacred masks and other paraphernalia are returned to their home in the mountains until the next season comes round. In this way the material and iconic side of religion is given a living form, since the masks themselves become operative only when they are worn by individuals who are during the ritual possessed by the spirits assigned to them. It is a kind of sacred ballet, and requires material manifestation through the masks.

## Iroquois Cosmogony, Experience, and Ethics

For the Iroquois the world was the creation of twins, one good and one evil. The Good Twin not only made that which is beneficent in the cosmos, but he also laid down human customs, which were modeled after the excellences of the sky world. The Bad Twin created what is distorted and horrid and against life. He is like ice, hard and cold. Both Twins made spirit forces which exist, both good and bad, in the world. It is the thrust of Iroquois religion, therefore, to fend off the effects of the Bad Twin and to promote the good forces which the Good Twin has made.

These spirit forces can be experienced directly, and for this reason great attention is paid to visions and dreams. Dreams especially are regarded with great seriousness and attention, for they may reveal some of the good and bad things that are in store for the individual or for the group. In this connection, as elsewhere in North and South America, shamanism is important: the shaman is simply a person with extra insight and dream-capacity. Through

*Opposite* The city of
Machu Picchu, high in
the Andes—one of the
startling remains of
Inca civilization.

dreams an individual will come to be related to some spirit who will act as his friend or guardian. It is important to stay in good relationship with such a force. Very often, illness is the consequence of a disruption of the friendship. It may also be the consequence of alienation within the individual between his body and his spirit. Dreams could be a clue to the secret desires of one's soul, and these have to be fulfilled. So their diagnosis is important, and is the subject of dream-guessing rituals.

Iroquois lived in longhouses shared by a group of families. This made for a strong emphasis on cooperative enterprises. It is perhaps not surprising that on the larger scale there was the formation in the eighteenth century of the League of Six Nations among the Iroquois (Mohawk, Oneida, Onondaga, Cayuga, Seneca, and Tuscarora). The dualistic cosmogony also emphasized the importance of moral values, as being on the side of life, and evil and bad intentions, on the side of death. There was, as with many other Native Americans, a sense of the harmony of Nature and humans as something which needs to be promoted and enhanced. Something of the ethical feeling underlying this is revealed by the fact that most of the Northeast woodlands people made apology to Nature for killing animals or cutting plants. Apologies would be directed at the animal killed, or rather to the collective spirit which the individual animal manifested, and similarly to the tree-spirit when one cut down a tree.

The ethical outlook of the Iroquois is further revealed by the fact that their most basic form of worship centrally involves thanksgiving directed to a spirit or force. The good manifestations of the Sacred Power which pervades the world must be thanked for the fact that they bring blessings on human beings. By contrast the evil use of ritual through sorcery is to be opposed.

The sense of community is enhanced by rituals for the dead. For instance, at the annual Feast for the Dead food is shared with the ghosts, and song and dance are put on to entertain them. There is a sense of the sacramental character of sharing food. Apart from such a high feast there are numerous family meals for the dead.

### Ritual among the Lakota

The Lakota originally dwelt in western Minnesota, but moved further West to the Plains in the first part of the eighteenth century C.E. This was a period of great movement and disruption among North American groups, especially in the Northeast and Plains regions. As a result of their move their economic life changed: they were now mainly concerned with hunting buffalo on horseback. The transition from a settled lakeside existence to this nomadic life led to alterations in their cosmology and values. However, they retained their seven great rituals, some of which are importantly representative of kinds found much more widely in the North American scene. I shall describe three in particular.

The first of these is the Sweat Lodge ceremony. The Sweat Lodge is a small domed structure built of saplings and covered with skins, which also

*Sacred Song of the Shaman  (Kwakiutl Indians)*

"I was taken away far inland to the edge of the world by the magical power of heaven, the treasure, ha, wo, ho.
Only then was I cured by it, when it was really thrown into me, the past life bringer of Naualakume, the treasure, ha, wo, ho.
I come to cure with this means of healing of Naualakume, the treasure. Therefore I shall be a life bringer, ha, wo, ho.
I come with the water of life given into my hand by Naualakume, the means of bringing to life, the treasures, ha, wo, ho."

Then Lebid sang his other sacred song:
"He turns to the right side, poor one, this supernatural one, so as to obtain the supernatural one, ha, wo, ho.
Let the supernatural one be the life bringer, the supernatural one, ha, wo, ho.
That the poor one may come to life with the lifebringer of Naualakume, ha, wo, ho.
The poor one comes, this supernatural one, to give protection with the means of giving protection of Naualakume, ha, wo, ho."

represents the shape of the Lakota universe. Heated stones are placed in it, and the water poured on them turns to steam. The person who sits in the structure is greatly heated up, and so he sweats: but also this revitalizes his spirit and he is visited by supernaturals and given visions which provide clues to communal or individual concerns. So a medicine person may gain the understanding which can lead to cures of the sick individuals in his or her care.

Not unrelated to the Sweat Lodge ceremony is the concept of the Vision Quest, the second of the Lakota main rites. A person sets forth and stays on a hillside in a shallow hole for a few days, without food or water. He is typically given a vision which is then interpreted for him by a medicine man.

The third ceremony is the Sun Dance, which is the most significant of the Lakota rites. A tree is ceremonially cut and used as the central pole of a lodge which represents the universe. During a whole day the dancers move round the periphery of the lodge gazing at the Sun as continuously as possible. Some of them are given hooks which are tied to the central tree and planted in their chests. They are encouraged in their sacrificial act by the martial songs and drumbeats of musicians. The families and groups from various tribes are seated round the lodge to participate in the sacred spectacle. The symbolism of the affair is important, and connects to fertility, for which the Sun is a source, while the central axis of the lodge (the *axis mundi*) has phallic meanings. The dancers bind themselves to the heart of the cosmic mystery, in preparation for the great midsummer hunts which will replenish the food and life of the whole group. The ceremony is also a great coming together of nomadic groups—or was in the old days—and so has a cheerful social significance.

These ritual themes of Sweat Lodge, Vision Quest and Sun Dance have a much more general manifestation among Native Americans. They have a shamanic substratum: a pervasive theme in the Americas.

*Opposite* The ritual dimension: the figure of Xipe Totec clad in the flayed skin of a sacrificial victim. Gladiatorial combat signified his warrior status and his insignia constituted the regalia of the Aztec emperor. The feast, in the spring, also related to fertility and the garb symbolized the breaking forth of the maize cob from its skin.

A shaman's mask from the Tlingit of Alaska.

## Myth among the Inuit

The life of the Inuit of the Arctic regions was traditionally a difficult one, which had to be closely interwoven with the seals and other sea animals on whom their living depended. So it is not surprising that among at least the Eastern Inuit there is the widespread story of the Mistress of Sea Animals, or the Sea Woman. There are a number of cultures in which the figure of the Master or Mistress of Animals is important (consider Śiva [p. 87] and Orpheus [p. 231]). Here there is a strange tale of how the sea animals, such as seals, whales and walruses, originated. The Sea Woman when still a girl had been tricked into marrying a Petrel who took her off to his land, where she was miserable. Her father went off to rescue her and, bringing her back in a canoe, was threatened by the Petrel who stirred up a big storm. To quieten the Petrel the father threw his daughter overboard, but she clung to the side of the boat, and he began cutting off her fingers: first the tips, then when she clung again at the next joint and so on. The bits of finger became the various species, small seals, bearded seals, and so forth. The Sea Woman sank to the sea bed, where she still lives.

The moral of the story is that if you do anything offensive to the Sea Woman she will withhold your catch of animals. Sometimes it was thought that the transgressions of humans would create dirt which would lodge in the Woman's hair, and because she had no fingers she was unable to comb it, and it would become uncomfortable. A shaman would be needed to go beneath the sea to her abode. After a struggle with her he would comb her hair and she would release the animals. In some Inuit cultures there were also symbolic sacrifices to the Sea Woman every year to ensure a good harvest.

Such a myth as that of the Sea Woman attests to the idea that behind a species or a set of species (the animals which the Inuit hunted) lies a Spirit, so that we have to enter into propitious relations with that Spirit if we are to have success in the anxious business of getting food through the year. Here as elsewhere, the shaman is important.

If anything is close to being a universal theme in the Americas it is that of shamanism. The sacred center of Tenochtitlán and the pole erected in the Sun Dance both attest to the symbolism of the *axis mundi*. The Sweat Lodge and the drugs of ancient Peru both attest to the Vision Quest. The figure of the priest and healer who also has the secret of fertility is one of the great symbols of the archaic world.

CHAPTER

8

# The Ancient Near East

## An Overview

Both Mesopotamia—roughly the region of modern Iraq—and ancient Egypt
produced dazzling urban civilizations. In the former region the pioneer was
Sumer, but the glory belonged first to Babylon, and then to its successor
Persia. To the west the Canaanites and Phoenicia flourished, and from
Phoenicia were planted the North African colonies which became the
Carthaginian state. There were other actors on the scene: the Assyrian
empire, some Indo-Europeans such as the Hittites to the north, and, folded in
between the great powers, the Israelites.

Sumer, Babylon, and Assyria belong to the same sequence, since the latter
two empires borrowed their religious forms from Sumer. Basically, too,
Canaanite and Phoenician religions were the same. To simplify our story we
can imagine little Israel as a center surrounded by Canaanites, Mesopotamian
religions, and Egypt. Israel is important to us because its religion proved to
be significant for both Judaism and Christianity, and to some degree Islam
too. So, whereas the religion of Phoenicia and that of Carthage are buried
under the sands of time, and Egyptian culture of the ancient period is to be
seen in museums and as great stone monuments in the desert, and much of
ancient Mesopotamia has disappeared, there remains a living stream which
runs down to us today from the Jordan Valley.

But dead religions deserve respect also: for that reason we shall at least
sketch briefly some of the features of ancient Near Eastern religions outside of
that of Israel. We have some literary records and to some degree we can travel
into these ancient minds; but this survey will necessarily be highly selective.

Some of the basic dates to keep in mind are these. First, it was around 3000
B.C.E. that urban culture was formed in Sumeria, at the lower part of the

to exist. It is worth noting, too, that though Judaism, Christianity, and Islam project themselves back in time to Abraham and to the religion of the Israelites—so that it is tempting to think, for instance, of Moses as the founder of Judaism—strictly speaking what we know as Judaism did not yet exist. There is some historic or other connection between Jews and their predecessors the Israelites, of course: but in the period we are talking about, from 1200 B.C.E. or so down to the time of Alexander (say) around 330 B.C.E., what existed was a stream of religious development which swelled into Judaism much later, at about the time that Christianity took its first classical form, three or four centuries after Jesus.

Most of our sources for the story of Israel come from the Bible, supplemented by fairly extensive archaeology. From the perspective of the history of religions we can use the Biblical narrative to establish a fairly clear account of the evolution of beliefs among the Israelites; but we have to use it judiciously as a source, the way we have used other scriptural traditions in this book.

The earliest period of the religion of the Israelites is a kind of prehistory: the period of the Patriarchs, beginning with the narrative of Avraham (Abraham), who came from Ur of the Chaldees in Samaria. His God is described as El (also the name, as we have seen, of the highest god of the Canaanites). His son Yitshaq (Isaac) was father of Ya'akov (Jacob), who had various adventures: during one he had a dream of a ladder leading up to Heaven, and named the place where he had it Bethel or House of God, which became the cult center, before Jerusalem, in northern Israel. On his return from a visit to Mesopotamia he had a wrestling contest with a mysterious being and his name was changed to Yisra'el. His twelve sons bore the names of the twelve tribes of Israel, and these became a confederacy which struggled successfully to dominate both northern and southern Palestine.

Many of the stories of this shadowy earlier period have become vital in the living faith of those who look back—the story of Avraham's willingness, in obedience to God, to sacrifice his only son; how Lot's wife turned into a pillar of salt; the destruction of the evil cities of Sodom and Gomorrah. But we know very little really about the religious shape of the period before the revolution that, it appears, was effected by the leader of those Israelites who were working as slaves for the Egyptians before they escaped through the Sinai peninsula. They conquered the land of Canaan in the name of a new religious ideology of commitment to one God, whom they called YHVH or Yahweh (and who, in the West, is often named Jehovah, a partially Latinized rendering of the Hebrew name). Scholars are not certain at all when Mosheh or Moses lived, but it was perhaps soon after 1300 B.C.E.

*The Mosheh Revolution and the Entry into Canaan*
The whole story of Mosheh seems to be a composite one, with differing traditions and ideas being woven together in the narrative as we have it, which derives from four or maybe three sources: the Book of Deuteronomy;

## Exodus

And the Lord said to Moses, "Say to the people of Israel, You shall keep my sabbaths, for this is a sign between me and you throughout your generations, that you may know that I, the Lord, sanctify you. You shall keep the sabbath, because it is holy for you; every one who profanes it shall be put to death; whoever does any work on it, that soul shall be cut off from among his people. Six days shall work be done, but the seventh day is a sabbath of solemn rest, holy to the Lord; whoever does any work on the sabbath day shall be put to death. Therefore the people of Israel shall keep the sabbath, observing the sabbath throughout their generations, as a perpetual covenant. It is a sign for ever between me and the people of Israel that in six days the Lord made heaven and earth, and on the seventh day he rested, and was refreshed."

the source which scholars call "J" (for Jehovah) because it stresses the concept of Yahweh; the closely related "E" (which uses the name Elohim for God rather than Yahweh), and the so-called Priestly source or "P". These were probably composed between about 700 and 400 B.C.E. Much is speculative in these discussions of origins and the composition of texts. But it may well be that Mosheh was indeed the revolutionary leader who did in fact cause the strict adoption of loyalty to Yahweh which became the hallmark of the official religion of the Israelites, and won out as a clear form of monotheistic faith, and so left a great mark on the whole historical process.

Mosheh teaching the people of Israel the Ten Commandments, from an early medieval Bible.

Mosheh is depicted as having escaped death as a baby by being put in a boat of reeds, which was found by the Pharaoh's daughter, so that though he was an Israelite he was brought up at court as a prince. But, because he struck and killed an Egyptian for oppressing an Israelite worker, he had to flee into the region beyond Egypt, in the deserts to the east. He there dwelt with a priest of Midian and worked as a shepherd. During this period he seems to have adopted in some modified form the religion of Midian, focusing on the God Yahweh. When later he led the Israelites out of Egypt, in that great event which later Jews would know as the Exodus (Greek for "departure"), he took them to Mount Sinai. Moreover, during his period in Sinai he had experienced the numinous vision of a bush which was burning and yet was not consumed by the fire, and he heard the voice of Yahweh, calling him to a leading role in the life of his people and the service of God. It was like a number of the prophetic visions of a much later period.

It was under his chief leadership, though in conjunction with his elder brother Aharon (Aaron), that he led the Israelites out of Egypt in a miraculous fashion according to the Biblical narrative, with events such as the plagues on Egypt, the Passover and the parting of the sea, saving the Israelites and then swamping the Egyptians. These events are commemorated of course at the great Jewish family feast, the Passover.

Most important were the events on Mount Sinai, when Mosheh ascended the mountain to have converse with the numinous Divine Being and to receive the agreement or covenant, including the Ten Commandments which were to become the basis of the Torah, or Law. (I translate Torah by "Law," though some Jews prefer some other appropriate translation such as "Teaching": they wish to avoid a translation which might reflect what is to their minds an unfortunate Christian stigmatizing of Law as opposed to Grace, in the New Testament.) It was henceforth the loyalty of official Israelite religion to the idea of One God, with no other gods, which brought it into conflict with Canaanite religion.

### The Temple

The process begun by Mosheh led to the domination of Canaan by the Twelve Tribes, so that a substantial part of the land was under their rule by as early as 1200 B.C.E. Eventually the pattern of leadership changed to kingship. The second king and great hero, David, captured Jerusalem and created the capital there. He had the ambition of building there a central temple, but it was left to his son Shelomoh (Solomon, 965–925 B.C.E.) to do this. His wonderful construction, known as the First Temple, lasted till its destruction in 586 B.C.E.

Its building was a means of centralizing all the cults of Israel in one focus. The advantage was both political and spiritual. It meant that the monarchs had greater control (though on Shelomoh's death political power was split and the Northern and Southern Kingdoms of Israel and Judah emerged: Israel did not survive the destruction of its capital Samaria in 721 B.C.E., the

overrunning of the region by Nebuchadnezzar of Babylon, and the subsequent period of Persian rule). The spiritual effect of having the central rites at Jerusalem was that it was easier to wipe out unacceptable forms of practice at the shrines scattered through the land. The Temple came to be a monopoly. It is of course true that, by the lavish care that Shelomoh bestowed on the Temple and by his desire for a glorious cult, there were elements in the worship which went beyond the more austere requirements of Yahwistic worship.

The building consisted of a large high hall, with cedar beams and cedar doors decorated with gold. At the west end was a windowless shrine inside of which was lodged the most holy object of ancient Israel, the Ark which contained the stone tablets on which the Ten Commandments were inscribed. Above were two gold cherubs. In front of the building was the altar used for sacrifices. Gradually round about it various outbuildings were erected, housing priestly implements and clothes and the like. It was ultimately enclosed in two great courtyards, approached by three sets of gatehouses and three flights of stairs.

After its destruction in 568 B.C.E., fifteen hundred of the elite of Judah, the Southern Kingdom, were taken in exile to Babylon. When some of these exiles returned in 538 B.C.E. they began to rebuild the Temple on the same site. It was dedicated more than twenty years later. Much later still, after many modifications and additions, King Herod the Great in 20 B.C.E. began the reconstruction of the entire complex, creating a beautiful building partially on Roman lines. Such rebuilding in fact continued more or less throughout the period, culminating in the destruction of the Second Temple in 70 C.E.

The altars of sacrifice in front of the Temple must have presented a busy sight, not altogether in harmony with modern feelings. Many animals and birds would be killed, and their blood drained, many functioning as burnt offerings in which the whole of the animal would be burnt. There would be offerings of grain and other foods too. Since the Temple came perforce to be a place of pilgrimage, in times of prosperity when many people could afford to pay for sacrifices, the daily killing must have been great. Many of the sacrifices were expiatory in character, where a person gave up something of worth, for instance a goat or a sheep, in a concrete manifestation of his feeling of sin or guilt at something he had done. So the sacrificial aspect of the Israelite religion, like its general worship, was focused on an ethical God.

## The Prophetic Tradition

In many religions we can contrast prophetic and priestly types. If the Temple was the heart of priestly religion, something else was the heart of prophetic faith. It was a mixture of vision, vocation, and ethical values. The true sacrifices to God should be, as one prophet remarked, a broken spirit and a humble heart. The inwardness of religion is the vital essence of it. Later Judaism always had something of this polarity: the very complexity of the

*Opposite* The death of Mani. Mani's doctrines, known as Manichaeism (see Chapter 9), were of wide influence, having an effect on Gnosticism, and indeed reflecting some Gnostic ideas.

Law meant that there were many, many externals in the Jewish religion, but like ancient Chinese *li* they were useless without the sincerity of inwardness.

There were "official" prophets in Israel and Judah, whose job it was to make predictions before military campaigns and the like. There were others attached to cult centers. But the great Prophets, who came to be rendered orthodox by the incorporation of their teachings into the sacred writings of the tradition, were detached from such organizational ties and were more individualistic in their utterances. Because their proclamations and criticisms were on the side of what became the official religion, their turbulence tended to be vindicated after their deaths. Their critical awareness, based upon personal religious experience, provided an indispensable element of renewal in a tradition which had its heavy investment in the expensive rites of the Temple and a detailed understanding of the provisions of the Law.

There are many prophets to choose from, but let us just briefly mention three or four: Amos, the two (or three) Isaiahs, and Jeremiah.

The Book of Amos dates from around 750 B.C.E. and incorporates an account of the prophet's inaugural vision. He saw the Lord at the altar, and so his criticisms of ritual do not stem from a rejection of the sacrificial cultus. But he is highly critical of those who think in a period of prosperity that these riches are the result of the rituals, and are a sign of God's blessing. It is too simple a view in an age of social injustice. God's relationship to Israel is founded on Israel's social and moral duty. The ruling class had better beware. The day of the Lord is not sweetness and light, but darkness. In such ways the prophet attacks the smugness of his time and demands that the externals of worship be tied to inner worthiness of aim and compassion for the poor.

The prophet Yesha'yahu or Isaiah lived not very long after Amos. But the Book of Isaiah is a composite work, which includes a major second part or Deutero-Isaiah (Second Isaiah), and maybe a third bit tagged on at the end. The first part belongs to the eighth century BC, the time of the Assyrian invasions, while the second refers to the Persian period. I shall refer to the two prophets as Yesha'yahu and Deutero-Isaiah respectively.

Yesha'yahu reports his inaugural vision as having happened while he was in the Temple, and it is a majestic and numinous experience:

In the year King Uzzi'ah died I saw the Lord sitting upon a throne high and lifted up; and his train filled the temple. Above him stood the seraphim: each had six wings — with two he covered his face, and with two he covered his feet, and with two he flew. And one called to another and said: "Holy, holy, holy is the Lord of hosts; the whole earth is full of his glory." And the foundations of the thresholds shook at the voice of him who called, and the house was filled with smoke. And I said "Woe is me! For I am lost; for I am a man of unclean lips, and I dwell in the midst of a people of unclean lips; for my eyes have seen the King, the Lord of hosts!"

Then flew one of the seraphim to me, having in his hand a burning coal which he had taken with tongs from the altar. And he touched my mouth and said "Behold, this has touched your lips; your guilt is taken away and your sin forgiven." And I heard the voice of the Lord saying "Whom shall I send, and who will go for us?" Then I said "Here am I! Send me." And he said "Go and say this to the people . . ."

There are various themes here. First, the vision which inaugurates the prophet's career is numinous and colorful. This is not that still inward light that illuminates the mystic or the Buddha but rather the exterior and dualistic vision of an Other. The very vision makes the prophet feel his unworthiness, and the guilt of the people to whom he belongs. But the vision is also a calling: the mysterious seraph comes and burns the uncleanness away from his mouth. And Isaiah responds willingly to the call after this: "Here am I!"

Yesha'yahu is concerned particularly with two political developments of his day: the attempt by the Northern Kingdom to replace the Southern monarch Ahaz with a favorite who would conform his policy to the strategy of the North (which involved an alliance with Syria or Aram against Assyria); and the Assyrian war against Jerusalem. For Yesha'yahu, historical and political developments are never merely so, but they have to do with the designs and will of God. For him also, Ahaz and the Davidic succession are important. The present troubles of Israel are the result of ethical misconduct. Assyria is God's means of punishing his people, but there is no need for ultimate worry. At the last moment Jerusalem will be purified and a remnant will return.

The unknown prophet known at Deutero-Isaiah had a tremendous influence on later religion, through his idea of the Suffering Servant of the Lord ('eved YHWH)—probably a metaphor for the people of Israel, but Christians read it as a reference to Jesus—who is rejected by his fellowmen, yet bears God's message and has a mission to restore justice. The 'eved YHWH represents an ideal which places value on faithfulness rather than prosperity. Yet in the end all will be well: Deutero-Isaiah looks forward in Chapter 11 to the time of the Anointed One, the Māshīah (Messiah), destined to restore Israel and to usher in a period of cosmic peace, when the wolf will lie down with the lamb, and the leopard with the kid, and the lion with the fatling. And then the earth will be full of the knowledge of the Lord.

Third Isaiah—the last section—presupposes the restoration of the Temple. It affirms the importance of the Sabbath, it criticizes foreign cults rather harshly, and it opposes the Temple rituals. In this it is somewhat different in emphasis from other prophets' writings.

In the stormy days which led up to the taking of Jerusalem by the Babylonians under Nebuchadnezzar, Yirmeyah (Jeremiah) called on the people to submit rather than resist. He naturally got into trouble as a traitor; but as he saw it neither the Northern Kingdom of Israel nor the Southern Kingdom of Judah had been able to live up to the covenant with God. He did not point his finger at any one class, but at all. Once Israel had entered into the Promised Land, the nation had become unfaithful. Yirmeyah called the people to repentance; but if his call remained unanswered then inevitably the destruction of the land was assured.

As a person Yirmeyah seems to have been depressive. He was unmarried, lonely, a person of strife who stirred things up, at the call of God. He wished, indeed, he had never been born. But he felt the prompting of the Lord to speak the gloomy truth to the populace. There was hope, even so; and Yirmeyah predicted that God would make another covenant which would be so written into the hearts of people that they would stay loyal.

In being so convinced that the old Israel would in effect be destroyed, Jeremiah paved the way for a more individualistic understanding of relationship to God. This was already implicit in the Torah at Sinai, in that its ethical requirements are placed in a personal framework. Much of the religion of the Israelites is based on the idea of a chosen people: but it also relates to individual acts and choices.

In the latter part of the sixth century B.C.E., following a decree of the Persian king, Cyrus the Great, in 538, the restoration of the Temple in Jerusalem was permitted and the exiles returned from Babylon. Under the leadership of Ezra, a large group set out from Babylon, with great financial resources, and arrived in the holy city. Amid the devastation they found that many Jews had married Gentiles and had given up their strict adherence to the lifestyle that had sustained the people before. All mixed marriages were dissolved, and, at the feast of Sukkot, Ezra read out the Torah from a great book at the ceremony in which the notion of a scriptural basis for the religion became an official doctrine. After a period of fasting and the confession of sins, the people undertook at another ceremony some months later to renew the covenant by supporting the Temple and observing the *Shabbat* (Sabbath) and the various laws of the Torah.

Maybe the book which Ezra read out was the Pentateuch or First Five Books of the Bible, which thus at this early date became the sacred scriptures. Or maybe it was something less. But in due course it was these Five Books that became regarded as the Written Torah. The so-called "Oral Torah," handed down verbally since Mosheh, was looked on by later orthodox Jews as authoritative also. It was an important buttress of Rabbinic Judaism, which we shall come to later.

### The Dimensions of Israelite Religion

This brief highlighting of some events in the Israelite experience, down to the Second Temple and the jelling of Jewish culture which took place before the coming of the Greeks and Romans and the absorption of the Jewish people into the Graeco-Roman experience, may enable us to understand some of the main features of the varied dimensions of this religion.

First, regarding *doctrine*: God is seen as supreme and then as alone. It became a monotheistic religion, and so apart from neighboring faiths and rituals. This development was doubtless due to the revolution in practice associated with the name of Mosheh. Second, as far as the *narrative* dimension goes, ancient Israel had the memory of the Exodus, the homelessness of the desert, and the conquest of Canaan. This narrative held a major place for the idea of the covenant with God. Third, in regard to *ritual*, there was a ban on graven images, which helped to separate Israel from many of the fertility and other cults of the area, though this separation seems to have been a constant struggle. The foundation of the kingship, leading to the centralization of worship at the Temple, was an important factor in maintaining the separateness and imageless character of Israelite worship. But the experience of exile also meant that an important elite became committed to maintaining the rituals even without the Temple. For this and other reasons, the restoration of the Temple also saw the beginnings of the idea of synagogue worship, in which congregations could take part.

As to the *experiential* dimension, the call of the Prophets became an important counterpart to the conservatism of the priestly tradition, intent on the niceties of sacrifice. The call blended with a sense of ethical destiny, which gave the Prophets their special edge as critics of the kingly and priestly establishment. The visions, too, reinforced the sense of the numinous presence of God.

In *ethics*, the law code which is already encapsulated in the Ten Commandments gave Israelites a clear vision of the conduct expected of those in a treaty relationship with God. Organizationally, the fact that by the end of our period there was the conception of written scriptures prepared the way for the rise of a scribal class whose job was to interpret the written texts. These were in parallel with the hereditary priests, whose main tasks related to the Temple liturgy.

The *institution* of kingship was important politically, even if finally not successful; but it came to be even more important in the mythic imagination of the people, who might look forward to an Anointed One who would restore the kingship and usher in a time of great peace and solemn prosperity. This vision was in part the result of the realization of the fragility of the Temple in political terms.

Finally, as to the *material* dimension, the Temple of course was the great big artifact on which Israel spiritually depended. Its glory under Shelomoh was great, and its restoration with the return of the exiles from Babylon was a reassurance. But there were other artifacts, such as the scriptures. They could—and eventually did—replace the tablets in the Ark of the Covenant. Perhaps the greatest material thing for the people in the end was the land of Israel. But the land was very much at the crossroads of great powers—the Assyrians, the Egyptians, the Babylonians, the Persians, the Greeks, the Romans.

Israelite religion was not altogether unaffected by the religions of the area. In particular it blended with Canaanite religion as well as separating itself out. The surrounding cultures could easily understand the slaughter of sheep and pigeons on the altars before the Temple; the glories of kingly power expressed by the pillars in front of the Temple; the importance of sacred writings; and the visions of the Prophets. But Israel's blend was very specific, and it had a great capacity for survival; for many of its customs, and many of its great ideas, were taken up by later peoples.

# Persia and Central Asia

## The Unification of Medes and Persians

The military genius of Cyrus the Great, king of the Persians, resulted in the defeat of the Medes in 550 B.C.E., and the bringing together of the Iranian peoples into the single most important power in the Near and Middle East. The dynasty which he founded, the Achaemenids, lasted until it was defeated and taken over by Alexander the Great and his successors the Seleucids, two centuries later. The period from the second century B.C.E. until 24 C.E. was dominated by the Parthians. After a period of disorganization Persia was, from 224 until 637, again a major power under the Sasanid dynasty, which finally collapsed under the onslaught of the Muslims from Arabia.

Iran was importantly the source of various major religions which have influenced world culture. First there is Zoroastrianism, which can be held to exist in six phases. Its early period lasted until the sixth century B.C.E., when it entered its second phase as the official religion of the Achaemenid dynasty. Then there is a period of flux until the third century C.E., when it was reconstructed as the official religion of the Sasanid dynasty. Then there is the persecution under the Muslims, and its migration in part to India. Finally there is the modern period when it has flourished within a modest population.

Also there was an important current within Zoroastrianism which some count as a separate religion; but it is perhaps better considered as the main stream of reconstructed Sasanid religion. This current is known in the modern West as Zurvanism.

Then again there was a dynamic and marvelously syncretic religion which was founded by Mani (early third century C.E.) and is usually known as Manichaeism (sometimes as Manichaeanism); it remained widespread and influential until the ninth century in China, Central Asia, Persia, and the West. Also with a Persian background was the mystery religion called

Mithraism, which was active throughout the Roman Empire, but which we shall discuss in Chapter 10.

# Zoroastrianism

## The Life of Zarathustra

The name Zoroaster is derived from a Greek mangling of the name Zarathustra. This great prophetic figure lived at some time before 600 B.C.E. Late Zoroastrian sources say that he lived 300 years (or less) before Alexander the Great, which might place him around 630 B.C.E. But most scholars think that he was older than that, and there is a rough consensus that he probably was of the tenth century B.C.E. He probably came from the region of what is now

---

**Zoroastrianism** some key terms

*Adur* or *Atar* Sacred fire. All fire is considered purified and is ritually tended in temples and holy places.

*Ahura Mazda* The Wise Lord, the creator God: later Ohrmazd.

*Amesha Spentas* The seven (later six, since Ohrmazd is identified with one of them) Holy Immortals, regarded as offshoots or emanations of God.

*Angra Mainyu* The Hostile Spirit, source of all evil, destined eventually to be overcome by Ahura Mazda: later Ahriman.

*Bundahishn* Creation of the world arising out of war between the Good and Evil Spirits.

*Chinvat* The bridge of separation and judgment: if the good in a soul predominates, it is led across the bridge by a beautiful maiden. Otherwise, it is led across by an old hag. The bridge is like a razor-blade, and the soul slides into hell.

*Frashokereti* The act of creation, the occasion of resurrection, and of the final judgment.

*Fravashis* The eternal spirits of human beings, which exist in heaven rather like angels: the implication is that humans have freely chosen to assume material form.

*Manthras* Words of power: prayers drawn mainly from the earliest scriptures attributed to Zarathustra.

*Yasasna* Temple rite, or worship generally.

*Yazatas* Heavenly beings or angels thought worthy of worship. The most popular is Mithra.

*Zurvan* Time, the focus of a deviant but important movement in later Zoroastrianism, known as Zurvanism: both Ohrmazd and Ahriman are supposed to derive from this one Being, who is beyond good and evil.

---

Map 7  Central Asia

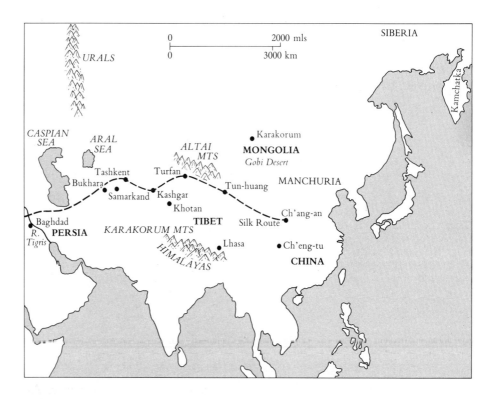

Afghanistan, or maybe from just inside the modern Iranian border. It was a region of East Iranian culture.

About his life we have few reasonably hard facts, though later legend was to fill in the spaces and see his career as that of an ideal human being, wise and good. Five songs or *Gāthās* in the scriptures are ascribed to him, and in these he mentions that he belonged to a priestly class. The East Iranian or Indo-Iranian culture had many affinities with the Aryan culture of the Vedic period in India, and so his position was analogous to that of a Brahmin. According to tradition he left home—possibly having already experienced the arduous training necessary to the priesthood—at the age of twenty, and at thirty had a powerful inspiration and vision which led him to begin to preach his new and highly original message.

The main component of this was his monotheism, seeing Ahura Mazdā as the One God: the Wise Lord, as his name says. He fathered twin spirits, Spenta Mainyu and Angra Mainyu (Beneficent Spirit and Hostile Spirit). They each make a primordial choice, the one for *asha*, goodness (which corresponds to the *ṛta* of the Veda) and the other for *druj*, the lie—in a word between good and evil. That primordial choice faces each person in her or his life. Zarathustra also seems to have taught the existence of six semi-independent abstractly named entities, the beneficent Immortals: Good Thought, Best Truth, Desirable Power, Great Devotion, Wholeness, and Immortality. Were they a kind of concession to the prevailing polytheism?

Perhaps not enough: for opposition from other priests led Zarathustra to leave his native area and advise at the court of King Vishtaspa, a convert to the new religion. This was supposedly at the age of forty-two. He was married twice and had a number of children: one of the *Gāthās* celebrates his third daughter's wedding. He died at the age of seventy-seven, assassinated by a priest.

His religion also protested against some features of the prevailing warrior religion of his time, which involved the sacrifice of bulls and the use of the hallucinogenic *haoma* (the same doubtless as the Vedic *soma*). In various ways, then, he was a threat to established ways. The question which is unclear is how this distant and somewhat hazy tradition came to be adopted as the imperial faith of the Achaemenids. In this the Magi seem to have played an important part.

### The Role of the Magi

The Magi are of course most famous as having come to Jesus' manger in Bethlehem, wise men from the East. Possibly they were a priestly tribe or caste originating in the west of Persia, among the Medes. They practiced marriage between close relatives, a custom which later spread to Zoroastrians; and they were responsible for dealing with the dead: their characteristic mode of disposing of them was by exposure of the corpses to animals and birds—a method which has become standard in Zoroastrianism, involving *dakhmas* or Towers of Silence where the vultures can pick the flesh off the bones. As priests who were thought necessary to ritual functions, the Magi played a role analogous to the Brahmin class in India, and with the unification of the empire in 550 B.C.E. they assumed an important role. In any event it seems that they came to adopt Zoroastrian beliefs, though not without embroidering and modifying them, in the service of the imperial state. Their learning enabled the corpus of ancient Zoroastrian texts to be handed down to us, as assembled by them from the fifth century B.C.E. onwards. In the Sasanid period they were responsible, it seems, for the reformulation of the religion and its doctrines.

The scriptures divide roughly into three phases: the original poems of Zarathustra, the *Gāthās*; then the rest of the *Avesta*, compiled around the sixth century C.E. but based on collections made about a thousand years earlier; and then the texts in the Pahlavi language, written in the ninth century C.E., during the Islamic period, when the Zoroastrian community was under threat. These last are of a commentarial nature, with summaries of knowledge, replies to Christian, Islamic, and other doctrines, and so on.

### The Drama of the World in Zarathustra's Teaching

In the original teaching of Zarathustra, so far as we can make out, the history of the cosmos is conceived as a drama. If Ahura Mazdā is perfectly good, then evil must come from some source which is both dependent on him (as Ahura Mazdā is the Creator of all things) and yet independent of him (for he is

Angra Mainyu, the spirit of Evil, in his struggle against Ahura Mazda, decides to tempt the ancestors of the human race. This fourteenth-century illustration shows a late Zoroastrian view of the fall of the human race, doubtless influenced by Christian ideas. Angra Mainyu here speaks with the primordial couple, offering them two fruits.

absolutely good). The idea that Angra Mainyu, the adversary, is evil because of a wrong choice, is a fine solution to the problem, though the source of the idea of evil still remains mysterious. The evil in the world struggles against the good, and humanity, which is capable of choices, must side with the good in the drama which will culminate in a third age when good and evil will be separated and the good will be rewarded with judgment and immortality. All this picture provided a monotheistic frame, but at the same time was realistic to the experience of human beings, which sees the world as a mixed place.

This threefold drama, and especially the concept of the future age when human beings will have pure bodies in a state of resurrection, has been very influential in the history of religions. The idea spread to Judaism, to Christianity, and to Islam. There will at the end of time be a wonderful refreshing of existence, making it splendid again. The Lie will be defeated and humbled: the Hostile Spirit will be driven away and finally annihilated. And in the process human beings will be made immortal. These ideas were already there in the beginning of Zoroastrian religion, but they became considerably elaborated as time went on.

### High Zoroastrianism of the Achaemenid Period

As Zoroastrianism developed into a state cult under the priestly guidance of the Magi, it began to reabsorb features of surrounding religions. Thus, the gods began to reappear within the fabric of the faith, though not the evil *daevas* or demonic gods denounced by Zarathustra. First of all the shadowy and abstract Immortals (Amesha Spentas) became personalized. Perhaps for the Prophet they were unseen forces which could possess the good person, but later they were as gods. In the *Yashts*, a section of the Avesta, we find various divinities being nominated as being "worthy of worship" or *yazata*. Among these are the Sun and the Moon; a rain god, Tishtrya; Anāhitā and Mithra (to them I shall return in a moment); Vayu the wind, the personified Haoma, and various other beings and entities, including the angel-like figures which guard individuals, the *fravashi*. There are also Saosha and Rashnu, who with Mithra judge the souls of the dead. If we define a god as a being whom people worship, then we have here in the *yazatas* the wholesale reintroduction of a kind of polytheism, even if the many gods are subordinated to the One God. It is a little like the situation in the Indian tradition.

In the first state of creation Gavaēvōdāta and Gayamaretan are the prototypes of animals and men; and the latter forms with Zarathustra and Saoshyant a triad of great figures relevant to the times. Eventually three Saoshyants were postulated, one each for the beginning of a new millennium (incidentally this imagery of a thousand-year cycle gained a strong grip on Western imagination, and it reappears, for instance, in Hitler's notion of a Thousand-Year Reich). The last Saoshyant will bring immortality to humans and fight a last battle with the forces of evil who will be destroyed.

This idea of a future summation of history had to be combined with a somewhat different piece of imagery, that of the Chinvat Bridge, which stretches from the great cosmic mountain at the center of the universe to Paradise and becomes as narrow as a razor's edge. When the individual soul reaches the Bridge it is judged by Mithra and the other judges, and is confronted by its image: if good, this image is like a beautiful young girl; if not, like a hag. The bad souls slip off the razor's edge into the fires of everlasting torment, and the righteous proceed onward to Paradise. Eventually this imagery was combined with the other, when Saoshyant looks on the world and restores it to imperishable glory, and the souls of the just are united to glorious bodies, and the sacrifice of a cow drink made of blended *haoma* and fat from the cow will confer immortal life upon them.

But despite the reinsertion of gods and goddesses into the religion, on the whole Zoroastrianism retained its imageless state and did not erect statues or have temples for individual deities. There were some exceptions: King Artaxerxes II (reigned 404–358 B.C.E.) put up temples of Anāhitā in the chief cities of the empire. But on the whole the battle against anthropomorphism was successful. The Zoroastrians in effect combined the ancient Indo-Iranian, nomadic, imageless, type of religion with the rejection of "pagan" gods in the name of monotheism: they arrived at the same conclusion but from another direction as the official religion of the ancient Israelites.

Many of these ideas, and their accompanying practices, were a good deal

219

more elaborated during the Sasanid period, from the third to the seventh century C.E., which also saw the growth of the Zurvanite myth and theology. To that I now come.

### Divine Time: Zurvān

Already during the Achaemenid and Greek periods there had evolved a series of ideas which later were to be elaborated in the Pahlavi literature which looks back to the glorious days of Sasanid times. It was an idea which in some ways reversed the thrust of the original dualism of Zarathustra. He had postulated a personal Supreme God and twins below him, one good and one evil. In Zurvanism the dualism was between Ohrmazd (Ahura Mazdā) and Ahriman (Angra Mainyu). These were twin offspring of a higher force, namely Time or Zurvān.

The reason for this way of modifying the original pattern was doubtless that, both in the late Achaemenid period and during Greek rule under the Seleucids, the notion of Time had an attraction, partly because of the influence of Babylonian astronomy on Persian culture and the derived astrological means of forecasting good and evil futures, and partly because of Greek notions of Fate. At any rate Zurvanism arrived at a new metaphysical interpretation of the world by sacrificing the ultimacy of the ethical good. Zarathustra had elevated the perfectly good God to the supreme place but sacrificed his power, setting up an evil principle from primordial times who would struggle against him, even if destined ultimately to be defeated. In Zurvanism, a morally neutral Time was elevated to the governing position, with both combatants on an equal footing in the cosmic struggle. Although the good God, Ohrmazd, ultimately wins, metaphysically he is not ultimate.

### Sasanid Zoroastrianism in its Dimensions

Zoroastrianism was refounded in the third century C.E. under various leaders, most importantly Kerder. Some of the *narrative* elements to which we have referred become more elaborate. Thus the Saoshyant or Savior who was to come in the final age was supposed to have been born of a virgin who was impregnated while bathing in a lake where the seed of Zarathustra was preserved—and where it had indeed been guarded by no less than 99,999 *fravashi* over the ages. Time, an increased preoccupation, was divided into segments. The age of the cosmos was supposed to be 12,000 years. This was in four stretches of 3000 years. During the first age, the mental age, Ohrmazd starts his creative activity and begins the war with Ahriman. They do a deal and agree to mingle for 9000 years. The next stage sees a shift from the mental to the material state. The third sees Ahriman's assault on the creation of Ohrmazd. At the end of that period the good God prepares for the coming of the Prophet, whose revelations begin the fourth age. There are three thousand years left; at the end of each thousand years a savior appears, and the last savior ushers in the revitalized cosmos. All this combined history and myth in an interesting and influential way.

In the *doctrinal* dimension, as we have seen, we have the experiment of Zurvanism as a counterpoint to the monotheism of the more orthodox tradition, which had however made compromises with polytheism. As for *ethics*: this dimension was integral to the fabric of Zoroastrian thinking, which focused on the struggle between good and evil. On the whole Zoroastrian ethics were highly world-affirming, even if the figure of Ahriman was influential in later world-denying creeds such as forms of Gnosticism and Manichaeism.

Regarding the *ritual* dimension, the main feature was the very complex fire ceremony, with the sacrifice of *haoma*. Fire was thought of as purifying in essence, and the rites attached to it required considerable time and knowledge. The calendar was also dense with festivals, such as celebrating the *fravashi* on the day of Nō Rūz, or New Year's Day, and at six other great festivals: at the middle of spring, at midsummer, at the corn harvest, in the fall, and at midwinter. Vital, too, were the feasts of Mithra and of the star god Sirius.

The *institutional* dimension in post-Sasanid times of course no longer involved state participation; but over the periods when the religion flowered

For the Sasanids, Zoroastrianism was a powerful State religion, and the emperor combined religious and political functions. Here Shapur I receives the submission of the Roman emperor Valerianus.

the priesthood was tied to the imperial system. The Magi, as we have seen, made up an hereditary caste, and they assisted with social affairs, such as the initiation of the young, marriages and funerals. Whether any among the Magi were religious specialists in some further sense, as prophets or ecstatics, is open to some question. Although Zarathustra himself was a visionary, we do not have much evidence on the *experiential* dimension of the religion.

Finally the main *artifacts* of Zoroastrianism were the fire temples and the *dakhmas* where the dead were exposed. In art the winged disc came to represent Ahura Mazdā; but as an aniconic or imageless religion Zoroastrianism had less to offer in art and statuary than most other faiths.

But the mental imagery was most powerful. The imagination of other traditions was haunted by the Chinvat' Bridge, and the resurrection of glorified bodies, and the coming of a Savior, and the thought of life as a struggle between good and evil. Though Zoroastrianism was only to survive in small numbers—maybe 150,000 people today—the religion has had vast influence and is a noble mode of organizing belief in one God.

## Mani and Another Use of Dualism

The prophet Mani was born near the city of Ctesiphon in Mesopotamia around 217 C.E., just before the establishment of the Sasanid dynasty. He had a visionary experience when he was twelve, and a few years later, when he was twenty-four, he received an angelic order to preach the truth in public. He spent his life in energetic missionary work, committing his teachings to writing and to painting. He had a high regard for pictorial art and thought it ought to be part of religious communication; he compiled a book of *Images* to illustrate the doctrines. His missions took him to Baluchistan, and he was granted permission by King Shapur to preach throughout the Persian empire. But after Shapur's death Mani fell from favor: the Magi were intent on reconstructing Zoroastrianism after the Parthian period. He was arrested and died after interrogation and being kept in chains, probably in 277 C.E. when he was sixty.

It seems that Mani thought of his religion as a suitable new state religion for the Sasanid dynasty, and this explains some of the hatred between the Magi and him. He genuinely seems to have seen his doctrines as universalistic, for he held that in part they made up the essence of the teachings of the three great founders, Zarathustra, the Buddha, and Jesus. He himself was raised as a Christian, in a Baptist denomination influential in his region, and so it became common for Christians to think of Manichaeism as a Christian heresy. But its dominant doctrine, of the separation of good and evil, light and darkness, seems to have owed much more to the Zoroastrian tradition.

Despite the persecution of the new religion for a while in the Persian Empire, it persisted there right into Islamic times. It had great success in going West, spreading through much of the Roman Empire in the century after Mani's death. Its most famous adherent, who then however converted to Christianity, was St. Augustine. It was also persecuted by Roman emperors, both before and after the Christianization of the Empire. In 527 C.E. an edict threatened death to followers of Mani, so it must have still had some vigor then.

The basic doctrines of Manichaeism were that the soul has fallen into the material world; that unless something happens it will remain trapped in the round of reincarnation; that God, the Father of Greatness, sends a savior who will rouse those asleep in darkness; and that the way to salvation is by knowledge—direct experience of the Light.

The war which exists between the Father of Greatness and the Prince of Darkness has much to do with sex, for the latter wants to produce as many bodies as possible to house and trap the light. Light lives in the seed, and Mani seems to have woven some Tantric ideas into his religion, about the importance of the retention of sperm. Those who were adepts were expected to refrain altogether from sex; the married laity should observe strict monogamy. The Manichaean Church was built along somewhat Buddhist lines, with the clergy living in monasteries and being supported by the lay folk. The clergy were supposed to practice truth-telling, nonviolence, celibacy, abstinence from meat and other impure foods, and poverty.

The myths of origin in the Manichaean scheme are somewhat lurid. As a result of the first clashes between the Father of Light and the Prince of Darkness the world is created, the lower regions being caused by the Prince of Darkness and the sun and stars by the offspring of light. These contests also generate some monsters. Primordial matter causes the demons Ashaglun and Namrael to eat the monsters and then to mate, and they bring Adam and Eve into being. But the Savior is sent from above, who arouses Adam from his ignorant sleep and shows him the light within, which ultimately has heavenly origins.

Manichaeism's ethics were strict and humane, abjuring all kinds of violence for lay and clergy alike. People were expected to give to the church either a tenth or a seventh part of their earnings. They were to fast on Sundays and during a month before the annual Bema celebration. They were to confess their sins weekly and annually at a collective ceremony. They had to pray four times a day. The Bema festival was a remembrance of Mani's suffering and death. The Bema itself was an empty throne, and this was a little like the early Buddhist practice of not showing the Buddha.

No doubt the Manichaeans encouraged meditative practices which would bring out the light within. At any rate it is through such a direct knowledge of the Light that the adept could finish the round of rebirth and ascend back to the Light which was the soul's source.

This was a vigorous but pessimistic religion, which may have spread in part because of its claims to universalism in bringing together themes from Christian, Buddhist, Zoroastrian, and other sources. In part it may have appealed because of its gentleness. Alongside its pessimism there was also hope, for the faith in a Savior pointed to a way out. With its austerity it may have looked good at a period when State religions were showing their corrupt side and harshness.

We have followed the story of Persia until the close of the Sasanid period. Persia was destined to be overcome by the forces of Islam, and entered on a quite different period of its civilization. Meanwhile let us glance briefly at Central Asia, from the edges of which the Prophet Zarathustra had come.

## The Geographic Significance of Central Asia

The region to the northwest of India, reaching up into what is now Afghanistan and Soviet Central Asia, for long had a special meaning for the world cultures, since it was through there, north of Tibet, that the trade routes ran which joined the West to China and to India (see Map 7, p. 216). Because this area lies open to invasion from the great northern plains that stretch from Europe to Eastern Siberia, it has also been a channel for the entry of relatively untamed peoples into the lives of the various major areas. In early days it was the place through which the Aryans migrated into India. Later, it was the area where Buddhism spread outwards from the north Indian plains. From there Buddhism was to have special influence to the east. Oddly, it never had much impact in a western direction.

It may be noted, too, that it was Buddhism which spread, rather than Brahmin culture and religion. Here was a contrast with developments in Southeast Asia. By about 650 C.E., when Islam had begun to explode out of the Arabian peninsula, various religions were living together in great tolerance in Central Asia: Zoroastrianism, Buddhism, Nestorian Christianity, Judaism, and Manichaeism.

In the seventh and eighth centuries Islam became lodged in the region, and in the end it was to become dominant. A crucial victory was the defeat of the T'ang emperor of China at the battle of Talas in 751 C.E. The rulers of the different Turkestani areas in the region were converted to Islam, and in consequence other religions came under pressure: the Buddhists, seen as idolaters, were especially condemned.

In the early part of the thirteenth century the region was conquered and its cities sacked by the Mongols under Genghis (Jinggis) Khan, and for more than a century the rulers were tolerant shamanists or had a leaning to Nestorian Christianity and Buddhism. But, as it happened, the Mongol rulers eventually converted to Islam, especially under Timur (1336–1405). We shall return to these events in dealing with Islam.

### Shamanism from North Asia
Central Asia has also been a conduit for shamanistic ideas and practices. In early times it may be that the śramanic tradition in India was affected by the shamanism of northern and central Siberia. Again, the Mongol religion incorporated strong shamanistic ingredients.

Till modern times shamanism has been a main feature of the great area stretching from European Russia to Kamchatka. The shaman is a spiritual specialist who has to undergo initiation; but prior to that he may have to undergo a great sickness. He will emerge from this experience, and from initiation, a vigorous and creative person, who will be able to help others, and who possesses visionary powers.

Often his ordeal is imagined as the extraction of his bones from his body and their reassembly—a kind of death and resurrection—brought about through the agency of shamanic ancestors or other hidden and spiritual forces. His vision may mean that he is able to discern where it is best to hunt or fish, and this is a valuable characteristic for his group. He may be repository of the tribe's poetical tradition and be an enactor of myth and legend. But above all he will be a healer, who helps others to go through death and resurrection like himself. He will be able to go into trance, where he is possessed by some powerful god or spirit. He can fly up to heaven and descend into the underworld, both to conduct souls to their final home and to rescue those who are so sick they have already entered into the realm of death. The shaman will often wear special dress and carry a drum, which helps to create through its beating and rhythm an altered state of consciousness, important during the public seances conducted by the shaman.

The type of cosmology associated with shamanism is of a cosmos which has as its center a sacred axis, what Mircea Eliade has called the *axis mundi*. This sometimes is a high mountain where the gods live, which reaches down into the underworld. There will be many gods and spirits, including those of ancestral shamans (who often take the aspiring shaman through the pains of his visionary death and resurrection). In the case of the Mongols, there was a supreme god called Tengri presiding over the sky; and shamanistic rites were adapted to the ideology of imperial rule, in a combination of ancestral rites with a seance—such a rite still continues in Inner Mongolia, addressed to the spirit of Genghis Khan.

Since the shamans of North Asia seem to have pioneered techniques of ecstasy, they may thereby have laid the foundations for two different directions in which religious experience has developed: in the one direction there is the inner, nonvisionary but highly technical attainment of higher states of consciousness, as in Buddhism; in the other direction, there are the numinous and visionary experiences of prophets and others, where the Other appears, apparently spontaneously, to the subject.

# The Greek and Roman World

Various cultural currents mingled together in the Mediterranean world to form Graeco-Roman civilization. But the two broadest streams were those of Greece, with its splendid but politically fragmented civilization, and of Rome, with its genius for conquest, law, and synthesis. A stepping-stone to the unification of the Mediterranean was the unification of the Greek East and various Levantine cultures through the conquests of Alexander the Great in 336–323 B.C.E. Another was the Roman defeat of the major rival power of Carthage in the three Punic wars of the next two centuries. With the Roman conquest of the East and the final stabilization of the empire under Augustus Caesar after 30 B.C.E., there came into firm existence a new Graeco-Roman civilization of great power, beauty, and spiritual vigor.

Certain dead civilizations also contributed obscurely to the later creativity of Rome and Greece, such as the Etruscans in Italy, absorbed by Rome in early days, and the Minoan civilization of Crete and its mainland offshoot, Mycenean culture, which was overtaken by conquest by Greek-speakers. The Roman Empire later synthesized and absorbed many streams of thought and practice from the subjugated peoples, and nowhere was this more obvious than in the case of religion: the cults of Isis from Egypt, Mithras from Persia, Cybele from Asia Minor, and Astarte from Syria; Jewish religion from Palestine; Manichaeism from Persia; and Christianity, also from Palestine, are prime examples, to set alongside such homegrown religiosities as the older paganism of Greece and Rome, the mysteries of Eleusis, Orphism, the intellectual faith of Platonism and its daughter Neoplatonism, Stoicism, and Epicureanism (see Map 8, p. 254). The empire was a great melting-pot of spiritual notions. In this chapter we shall sample some of these riches.

First there are the traditional religions of Greece and Rome, up till the flowering within these societies of wider ideas and philosophical movements.

So we are dealing with Greece up to the fifth century B.C.E., and Rome virtually till the first century B.C.E. We shall then look at the philosophies and new religious movements of Greece and the Hellenistic world down to the first century C.E. We shall then do the same for Rome before looking at the ebb and flow of religions in the early Roman empire, including Jewish religion and Christianity but in the wider context of other movements, such as Gnosticism, Mithraism, and other philosophies and mystery religions. We shall leave later developments to the next Chapter, which will see the emergence of classical forms of Christianity and Judaism.

# Greek Religion

## The Pattern of Gods

The system of classical Greek religion is, in terms of belief and worship, polytheistic. There are many gods, and much later this idea was itself castigated by the monotheistic Christians and Jews. It is true that there was a supreme god, a first among other immortals, a chief. And impressive he was too: the mighty Zeus, ruler of the sky, sometimes joined in a triad with

---

**Graeco-Roman Religion** some key terms

*Cosmos* The universe as an orderly whole.

*Holocaust* A whole burnt sacrificial offering.

*Hubris* Overweening pride and the desire to gain equality with the gods, which typically proves disastrous.

*Logos* Reason within humankind, sometimes treated as the principle governing the cosmos, as in Stoicism and in Philo and Christianity (where Logos is also creator and mediator).

*Manes* The spirits of the dead: the collective ancestors.

*Mysteria* Mysteries or mystery religions, such as those of Isis, Eleusis, and Mithras, involving the revelation of truth in dramatic form by initiation.

*Mythos* A story and in particular an authoritative story about the gods.

*Numen* Spirit, e.g. in a stream, a copse, a mountain or other sacred spot or force.

*Philosophia* Love of wisdom, or a system of ideas which helps us to understand and cope with life, such as Stoicism or Neoplatonism.

*Religio* That which binds us to the gods, religion.

*Temenos* A sanctuary or sacred area often including a temple.

*Theos* God, or God as supreme being, as in Aristotle's philosophy.

---

Poseidon, god of the sea, and Hades, god of the underworld. Zeus had destroyed a previous group of deities, the mighty Titans, and their leader Kronos. He was not just god of heavenly light, but also a just and kingly god, who was concerned with justice for human beings, and who supported good rulers. He was father of gods and men, the final ruler; but like a chief, he had his advisers and friends around him, and he could not fully control them. Various of his wives and consorts indicate some of the powers and ideals that he had gathered round his person. His great wife, Hera, helps him to sanctify the institution of marriage. When coupled with the earth goddess he represents the male fecundation of the world. In his mating with Themis, goddess of order, he brings regularity into human and cosmic affairs. They engender the Fates which rule over human destiny. And so on. If Zeus's frequent espousals and couplings were sometimes criticized later on as giving a bad example to men, they were from one perspective merely a sign of his various powers. And gods were different from us: they were the immortals, and it was *hubris*, or overweening presumption, even to compare ourselves to them.

Another deity we can sample among the clouds of spirits in the Greek world came from Cyprus, where she may have been stimulated by the example of the Semitic goddess Astarte. Aphrodite is the spirit of fertility and love, wed to the beautiful Adonis. In Homer she turns out to be the daughter of Zeus and Dione. She was to inspire the great sculptor Praxiteles (active c. 370–330 B.C.E.) to produce the greatest portrayal of her nude. She was a serious goddess, but she could have her wild side, for in the city of Corinth she was served by sacred prostitutes.

A god of uncertain origin but great influence was Apollo, an ideal young man in appearance and the patron of music, healing, prophecy, and the safekeeping of cattle; he was also, and most importantly, the god of the Panhellenic (all-Greece) shrine of Delphi. He may have been non-Greek in origin, in that he was supposedly the offspring of a Titan, which may reflect some old struggle between the Hellenic gods under Zeus and their predecessors. On the whole Apollo stands for orderly inspiration and creative prediction. He can be contrasted with the much more disorderly Dionysos. The main gods of Greece lived on Mount Olympus, the great mountain of central Greece and once considered to be an *axis mundi*. But Dionysos was not an Olympian, although it came to be said that he was the offspring of Zeus and Semele. He was the god of wine and the leader of orgiastic feasts and revels. Dionysos was associated with the religious origins of drama, in ritual performances in which sacred narratives were enacted. His cult forms the centerpiece of what is in many ways the most powerful play by the dramatist Euripides (480–406 B.C.E.), *The Bacchae*.

The many gods had a national meaning, but each was also rooted in the individual city-state or *polis*. In the heyday of Greek culture, around 600–400 B.C.E., the *polis* was the typical unit, even if Athens, for example, gathered round it an empire of subordinate cities and their territories. Each little region had its own shrines and gods, so Greek religion was an interplay between the localized cults and the Panhellenic religion which most of the culture shared: not only the Olympians, but central holy places like Delphi, where Apollo's oracle was; not only the great poets, above all Homer, who became the foundation of Greek education (and to a lesser extent Hesiod, about 700 B.C.E.), but also the Panhellenic games such as the Olympiad.

### The Importance of Sacrifice

The central ritual activity of Greek religion was the making of sacrifice to the gods. For the most part it involved the slaughter of animals. It is said that the first sacrifice was brought about by Prometheus. He was a primordial hero and trickster. He tried to deceive Zeus by making the portion he set aside for the gods look good: actually it was the animals' bones covered in fat; the good meat was concealed by rather revolting entrails and the like. He thought this would be good for the human race; but Zeus, who saw through the deception, cunningly took the bones and failed to reveal to Prometheus that a carnivorous life is one of death. So Prometheus unknowingly chose death for the human race. The institution of sacrifice thus drew the line between the gods, who were the immortals, and the mortal humans.

Animal sacrifices were well integrated into ordinary living, for they were the times when Greeks ate meat; so enjoyment and pious duty were thus harnessed together. Similarly, the priesthood for civic purposes were the magistrates, so again there was no divide between religion and the life of the *polis*.

Sacrifices to the earthly gods, the chthonian deities who belonged to the soil and the underworld, were holocausts, burnt whole. The blood, instead of spurting up toward heaven, as the sacrificer slit the animal's throat, poured downward through a hole in the ground. Instead of a high altar, there was a low altar.

### Heroes

Though the Greeks distinguished sharply between gods and humans, there was nevertheless a kind of transitional being or demigod who was important for cities, for families, and sometimes for all Greeks: the hero, who was celebrated after his death with a shrine, and who had attained legendary status. Perhaps he was the father of a colony, or a great ancient hero like Achilles or Heracles. He might be associated with the civic past, or with a profession (as was the legendary doctor, Asclepius). To a limited extent their existence formed an ancestor cult. At any rate the heroes, though not divine, were nearer to the gods than other humans; many were thought to be the offspring of gods, and some attained immortality.

## Religions Within Religion

In the complexity of the melange of cults which existed in the Greek world, certain movements had a more personal meaning, and these formed religions within the greater religion. (In some degree this description applies also to movements started by philosophers such as Pythagoras and Plato.) They included the Dionysian movement, turbulent and orgiastic; Orphism, purificatory and in search of release from rebirth; and the Eleusinian mysteries, sacramental and dramatic.

Let us begin with this last. It centered on the sacred complex of Eleusis, some distance outside Athens. The annual celebration of the rites or mysteries (from *mustai* meaning initiates, based on a verb meaning to keep silent, for the initiates were sworn to secrecy) involved a public procession from Athens, bathing of the initiates in the sea on the way, and the secret goings-on in the cave and temple of Eleusis. The drama there, the rites, the spoken words, the presentation of sacred images by the light of flaring torches, were said to be profoundly moving. As Aristotle said, you went there not to learn anything but to have an experience (a rhyming jingle in Greek: *ou mathein alla pathein*). The sacred drama concerned the descent of the distraught corn-goddess Demeter into the underworld, to which her daughter Kore or Persephone has

Some of the most powerful rituals were those of initiation, especially at Eleusis. Here we see a relief of Demeter and her daughter Persephone, whose myth was integral to the Eleusinian rites or "mysteries."

been abducted to marry the infernal god Hades; eventually Zeus imposes a solution: Kore is to spend half the year in the world and half below. This agricultural myth was transmuted into a higher meaning, to do with the changing of the life of the initiate. Those who were initiated were then able to feel extra depth to their religious life amidst the daily routines of the *polis*.

Orphism was a loosely defined movement named after the primordial singer, whose voice can enchant the beasts and the plants and rocks. Orphism has its own priesthood, who traveled about advocating a pure way of life, involving vegetarianism and other means of self-purification. The Orphics saw the cosmos as having started perfectly, as a Cosmic Egg (according to one version), and then progressively becoming more chaotic. The soul is entombed in the body, the Orphics said, and is doomed to transmigration if salvation is not sought. The whole movement was something of a quietist rebellion, in that the ban on meat meant a ban on partaking in sacrifices and therefore in civic life. In a culture in which nothing of importance was ever decided without a sacrifice, the Orphic message must have seemed disturbing and revolutionary.

In some degree there was an overlap between it and Dionysian religion, which encouraged rather the opposite behavior. The myths were connected, and in Orphism there was the conception that Dionysos had been eaten by the Titans who were burned up by Zeus and whose ashes provided the material for creating the human race—so each person contains within himself the divine spark of Dionysos. Dionysianism encouraged women's orgies in the wild places, and frenzied dancing, and the consumption of the raw flesh of animals torn apart—an accepted breach of its own taboo. Or, in its tamer, civic form, it provided for a sort of Mardi Gras as a counterpoint to the solemnity of many other civic religious occasions.

Next, there is the movement, periodically revived, of Pythagoreanism. Here we begin to make the bridge between religious and philosophical visions. Pythagoras (570?–500 B.C.E.) came from Samos in the Aegean, but his main work was conducted in Croton, a Greek colony in southern Italy. There he founded a religious order which also took political control of the city. Pythagoras died in Metapontum, in Asia Minor, exiled from Croton for some reason. His order proliferated and was influential for more than fifty years in the area. This order looked on Pythagoras as a holy man, perhaps divine, who taught various spiritual, practical and philosophical things. According to his view the ultimate constituents of the world were numbers— an idea which was ultimately to have a profound impact on Western thought. The discovery of the mathematical ratio involved in musical harmony had a large effect on Pythagorean thinking. The world somehow flows from the relationship between the bounded, symbolised by numbers, and the unbounded. The soul was held to be involved in reincarnation; and by a process of purification, by following the precepts of Pythagoras, including food taboos —for instance on the eating of beans—the adepts could free an individual from this round of rebirth. So the Pythagorean message was a blend of theoretical, mathematical learning and practical spirituality: and all this was related to political action. As we shall see, all these three motifs were important for Plato.

### The Love of Wisdom and Religious Goals

Already there were connections between what we would call religion and that activity which was known as the love of wisdom (the literal translation of the term *philosophia*). In modern times, in the West, philosophy has become increasingly technical and theoretical. It is true that sometimes it incorporates a worldview—often that of scientific humanism, in the English-speaking world in particular—but it tends often to define itself in opposition to religion and indeed to the idea of wisdom. But this was not so in ancient Greece.

Apart from Pythagoras, some thinkers, known now as the Presocratics—Thales, Anaximander, and Anaxagoras among them—pioneered speculative thought. Heraclitus (c. 540–c. 480 B.C.E.) said that everything is in flux, and that you cannot step into the same river twice (a doctrine reminiscent of those of his contemporary, Buddha Śākyamuni). Parmenides saw reality as unchanging Being. Socrates (c. 470–399 B.C.E.) concentrated on seeking the definition or essence of things, asking questions like "What is courage?" and generally stirring his contemporaries to reflect about moral issues—for which he was condemned to death for corrupting the young. The teachings and methods of these men prepared the way for Plato, and thence for Platonism and later Neoplatonism, which often took a highly religious form.

Plato (429?–347 B.C.E.) was influenced somewhat by Orphic and Pythagorean thought and argued, in his delightful dialogue, the *Phaedo*, for the doctrine of reincarnation. He held that human souls were unable to retain their splendid original state of immortality and so sank down into bodies, to wander through life from existence to existence. But knowledge enables them to rise again to a state of liberation. Knowledge involves knowing essences, which for Plato are defined by the Forms which earthly things imitate and participate in. The World of Forms is where the soul came from, so acquiring knowledge is really remembering. And this, according to Plato, is how Socrates' method of arousing thought managed to work: as Socrates himself said, he was a midwife of knowledge.

The World of Forms is a great hierarchy, with at the top the Form of the Good which informs all other Forms because each is ideal. So the soul through knowledge can climb up to the Form of the Good and perceive it in a vision. Plato's intuition was thus both mystical and intellectual, and part of the rigorous training of the disciple had to be in mathematics. In his school in the grove known as Akademos (hence the words "academic" and "academy") he had written over the entrance the words *Mēdeis ageōmetros eisitō*—"Let no one ignorant of geometry enter here."

Plato was not only concerned with theory and vision but also with politics. He made some fruitless visits to Sicily at the behest of the dictator Dion of Syracuse. But most of his life was devoted to education, and it was one of his pupils, Aristotle (384–322 B.C.E.), who took Plato's philosophy in a different direction, bringing the essences down to earth, and developing marvelous analytical treatments of biology, psychology, physics, metaphysics, ethics, politics, and logic which were to have a profound effect on European thought.

Platonism provided a noble and unified vision which could be set alongside the religion of the mysteries and the new movements, and, up to a point, alongside traditional religion and civic cults. But Plato was very critical of the poetic tradition of Homer and Hesiod and the low morals ascribed to the gods. In Greek religion, around 350 B.C.E., there was a mixture of differing levels of public and private religion, with certain high philosophical speculations woven into the fabric of life. In a way Greek religion was like that of the Indian tradition of the same period—not yet synthesized in a cohesive system, but full of potentialities which were to be realized later.

### Alexander and After: Some New Philosophical Movements

Greece was unified, and the city-states tamed, by Philip II, king of Macedon (382–326 B.C.E.) and his genius son Alexander the Great (356–323 B.C.E.)—a pupil, by the way, of Aristotle. In a series of brilliant campaigns, Alexander swept aside the Persian empire, Greece's vast neighbor, which had long been its polar opposite in politics, thought, and religion. He laid the foundations of Greek-influenced regimes in Egypt, Syria (including Palestine), Persia, and Bactria in Central Asia. In Greece itself he brought to a close a turbulent but wonderfully creative period and ushered in the age which we know as "Hellenistic." During this time some new philosophies were pioneered which became influential both in the Greek East and the Roman West of the Mediterranean world.

Epicurus (342–271 B.C.E.) taught most of his life in Athens, and made use of the atomic theory of his predecessor Democritus: he argued that everything in the world is composed of atoms in emptiness. The soul too is a composite, and so when a person dies his atoms are dispersed and that is that. The gods are made of refined atoms but exist outside of our world, and they are not concerned at all with what we do or do not do. The best thing is to cultivate moderation in the pursuit of reasonable pleasure and to cultivate the virtue of *ataraxia* or equanimity. Later this worldview was put into poetic form by the Roman poet Lucretius (c. 96–c. 55 B.C.E.), who in his *De rerum natura*, "On the Nature of Things," sought to dispel fear of the *numina*, gods and spirits.

About 300 B.C.E., Zeno of Citium founded the school which was known, after the cloisters or *stoa* where he taught, as Stoicism. He demythologized the gods, treating them as natural forces. The universe was controlled by mind (itself a material entity, though of a superior, refined nature—and poetically this could be called Zeus). On death we exist no more: but we are superior to animals because we possess reason. The wise person steels himself in the face of ultimate extinction, and bears himself with courage, self-control and realism in the face of evil and death, which are unavoidable ingredients of

233

the way things are. This austere doctrine had an appeal to Roman nobility, and was taught in Rome by the Greek slave Epictetus in the first century C.E. and in the famous *Meditations* of the emperor Marcus Aurelius (121–180 C.E.), who became emperor in 161.

The latter part of what is called the Hellenistic age saw the conquest of the Greek East by the Romans and the fusion of the Mediterranean world into a single multicultural empire. In order to see the religious character of this new age, we need to retrace our steps to look at the nature of early Roman religion.

## Roman Religion

### The Numina and Civic Virtue

Roman religion was focused on deities and spirits who can collectively be called *numina*—mysterious spirits who roused reverential fear. Its gods ranged from the great Jupiter, with his consort Juno, through Mars or War, Venus or Love, and Ceres of the grain harvest, to such specialist deities as Sarrator, the god of weeding, and Januarius, the god of the threshold. The whole of reality and of human activity was punctuated and pervaded by the *numina*.

The aim of public worship in the early Roman system was to ensure that the gods remained or became benevolent. The calendar was a mosaic of feast days for worshiping varied gods. March, for instance, started off with a sacrifice to Mars, after whom it was named; and there were days for the blessing of horses, arms, trumpets, and so on. In addition the various games had religious significance—chariot races, wrestling, boxing, and later on (borrowed from the Etruscans) gladiatorial combats. To administer all these public events there were different classes of priests, headed by the supreme priest, the *pontifex maximus* (a title later to be taken over by the Popes), and including the Vestal Virgins, appointed each for thirty years and enjoying great prestige, who had to maintain the sacred fire in the court of the goddess Vesta. There were also differing kinds of diviners, such as the augurs, who predicted the future on the basis of the flights of birds—a custom which has a vestigial hangover in European countries where people may be superstitious about seeing an odd number, but not an even number, of magpies.

The public rites had their complement in household ceremonies, addressed to the *lares* or household gods, and to the ancestors, honored as *di manes* or divine shades. All this system made the Romans a very religiously observant people. As they grew outwards, absorbing other cultures, the pantheon expanded. Since, too, the Romans were increasingly exposed to Greek culture, both because of the overrunning of Greek cities in the south of Italy and through the importation of educated Greek slaves as tutors and so on, the tendency was to identify Greek and Roman gods freely—Jupiter and Zeus, Venus and Aphrodite, Juno and Hera, and so on. This prepared the way for a blended Graeco-Roman civilization when ultimately the Romans overran

The numinous figure of the great Greek god Zeus is tempered by the increasing realism and humanity with which the Greeks depicted their gods.

Greece and the Hellenic East. This they did effectively from the mid-second century B.C.E., when they annexed Greece, having shortly before razed Carthage; and in 66 B.C.E. Pompey organized the whole of the East, as far as the Persian border, into provinces subsidiary to Rome. Not long after that, Julius Caesar conquered Gaul and started the subjugation of Britain. By the time he died, in 44 B.C.E., the Roman empire was more or less in place. It was taken over, after wracking civil wars, by Caesar's adopted son, Octavian, who assumed the title of emperor (*princeps*) and, in 27 B.C.E., took the solemn, rather religious name of Augustus.

## The Spread of Mysteries and Philosophies

Perhaps because of the pluralism of the new empire, and because of the abatement of civic concern in the states which it had absorbed, religion became more individualized and was seen more and more as a matter of choice. The imperial ideology, it is true, required sacrifice to the emperor, as a means of expressing loyalty. But within that limit there was a remarkable flux of beliefs and practices. Among these movements were many mystery religions, which, like the cult of Eleusis, gave dramatic shape to the initiation

235

of those who wish to pursue purity or immortality and to take part in the power of the god or goddess.

Already some of the Oriental deities had taken root in Rome, such as Isis of Egypt who had had a temple on the Aventine hill since the second century B.C.E. She brought feminine powers to bear on faith. Isis, of course, restores Osiris to life, and likewise the initiate is given new and restored existence by the goddess. She was regarded as the supreme deity; and the initiate's vision of her is movingly depicted by the writer Apuleius (second century C.E.) in *The Golden Ass*. The hero, who has unfortunately been turned into an ass, is ultimately redeemed from his brutish existence by the goddess.

A mystery cult that had special appeal to the Roman soldiery was that of Mithras. Mithras was credited with slaying the bull which would renew life, in alliance with the Sun: this myth was celebrated with the sacrifice of a bull in the half-underground temple which was characteristic of the cult. The worshipers present at the action partook of a subsequent feast. (Or, at least, this is a prevailing interpretation of our archaeological evidence.) Mithraism became a kind of initiatory club, its rites engendering the feeling of renewed life and comradeship.

At a higher level educationally there came the development of the Neoplatonic movement, especially through the writings and teaching of

The mythic dimension: popular particularly among Roman soldiers was Mithras. This offshoot of Iranian religion related to the myth of Mithras as the unconquerable Sun. London Museum.

---

### Neoplatonism: Iamblichus on the Mysteries

No sacral act can be effective without the supplication of prayer. Steady continuance in prayer nourishes our mind, enlarges the soul for the reception of the gods, opens up to men the realm of the gods, accustoms us to the splendour of the divine light, and gradually perfects in us [our] union with the gods, until at last it leads us back to the supreme heights. Our mode of thinking is drawn gently aloft and implants in us the spirit of the gods; it awakens confidence, fellowship, and undying friendship [with them]; it increases the longing for God; it inflames in us whatever is divine within the soul; it banishes all opposition from the soul, and strips away from the radiant, light-formed spirit everything that leads to generation; it creates good hope and trust in the light. In brief, it gives to those who engage in it intercourse with the gods.

---

Plotinus (205?–269 C.E.) and his successors Porphyry (232?–303) and Iamblichus (250?–330). Plotinus was from Upper Egypt and studied with the teacher Ammonius Saccas in Alexandria before setting off on an expedition to eastern Persia in the hope of learning something of Eastern thought. Later he started teaching in Rome, gathering about him some influential disciples. He greatly modified the teachings of Plato.

At the summit of Plotinus' system is the One—known simply as the One, without any further way of talking about it except that it is the supreme God and emanates in the form of the Intellect or Nous. This contains within it the intelligible Forms of Plato's system. Beyond that, Intellect has a further emanation, the Soul, in which the Forms are seen in space and time. The Soul is on the brink of becoming the material world, into which the human soul descends. The world has many beauties, though it is a kind of prison that entraps the human soul. The One spreads love or passion (*eros*) for itself to the souls of human beings who begin the ascent back, through intellectual, ethical, and mystical endeavor, to the One. As he lay dying, Plotinus is supposed to have said: "I am trying to bring back the divine in me to the divine in the All."

Such teachings ultimately had a lot of appeal to Christians who were trying to make a blend between their monotheistic Jewish tradition and the classical culture of their environment in the Roman Empire. Neoplatonism could be detached from paganism and its ideas made use of in formulating a deep Christian theology. Their emphasis too on contemplation gave Neoplatonic writers an edge at a time when monasticism was growing, after the Christian takeover of the Roman Empire in 330 C.E. and the consequent need to reaffirm commitment and purity of life in a world gone easy.

So we find in the Hellenistic world and the early centuries of Rome a variety of mystery religions, some from the East, and of philosophies which could make special appeal to the literate elite. There was also something else brewing, and that was a challenging religion which also had some appeal across the whole empire: the religion of the Jews. To understand this we need once more to retrace our steps a little.

# Religion in Palestine

## The Vicissitudes of the Jews

The period from the reconstitution of the Israelite tradition under Ezra to the period of the Roman Empire saw Palestine under Greek rule, that of the Seleucids. It also saw some Persian influences, through the notion of the resurrection, and an increased emphasis upon apocalyptic prophecies, with concomitantly the elevation of the figure of the *Mashiah*, Anointed One of the House of David, who would come to restore the kingdom of Israel. All this emerges in the Book of Daniel, replete with dazzling imagery. After many attacks on the people of Israel by foreign adversaries, God sends a great leader to lead them in defeating their foes and establishes an everlasting kingdom. The wicked are condemned to perish, and the good live on.

Various parties emerged before the time of Jesus, and it was in this plural and chaotic time that he started his own movement. There were the Pharisees, who were looked on as innovators because they introduced ideas like the resurrection of the body which scribal conservatives rejected. The latter belonged to the party of the Sadducees, who preserved the Torah, and had chief control of the Temple rituals. There were Jews who were Hellenizers, won over to the excitements and lifestyle of Greek civilization. There were Zealots, who were involved with plotting armed resistance to the Roman occupation. There were the Essenes and the Qumran community, who withdrew to a secluded life in the desert, in order to preserve the Torah intact and create a counterpoint to the Temple rites. There were in Alexandria the group known as the Therapeutai, who pursued the contemplative life in a spirit of asceticism. There were men like Philo of Alexandria, who took Greek learning seriously and sought to express the higher truths of Jewish belief and practice in Greek terms. These currents of belief flourished in Palestine and more widely in the Roman empire, for there was an extensive diaspora of Jews even before the fall of the Temple in 70 C.E.

## Jesus' Movement as a Jewish Sect

Yehoshu'a, or Jesus, (of Nazareth) lived at a stormy time, with political tensions high. The Jews had already shown themselves stubborn in the early years of the new Roman emperor cult, and this was to be a continued source of friction. Their exclusive monotheism may have been noble, but it also appeared, to the imperial administrators, to be strange. Jews were divided religiously, as we have seen, but these divisions also signified political ones. There was a stormy edge of revolt in Jewish society, and it was eventually such a revolt that led to the destruction of the Temple.

Yehoshu'a's movement ended up by being strikingly successful. He came from an obscure part even of the Jewish world, namely Galilee; he had a very brief and fairly turbulent public career of two or three years, after his baptism by his cousin Yohanan (John), another strong preacher, who like Yehoshu'a considered that the time was at hand when the kingdom of God would be ushered in. Yohanan was a wild man but a prophet, deliberately courting the empty places and the landscape beyond urban civilization. Yehoshu'a on the contrary mixed much with men and women of all walks of life, pure and impure, high and low, and worked in cities. He preached a message resting on the conviction that a new age had come with his coming, and that he had a specially intimate relation with God, whom he called Abba, Dad. He often referred to himself with the mysterious title "Son of Man," found in Daniel and elsewhere. But he also saw himself firmly embedded within the Jewish world. He would expound the Torah (or First Five Books of the Bible), the then scripture, which was to be expanded into the so-called Tanakh, or "Law, Prophets, and Writings," which make up the full Hebrew Bible (and which became, with slight variations, the Old Testament of the Christian community as it grew away from the Jewish mainstream). Yehoshu'a also frequented that important institution, the synagogue. Synagogue worship, congregational in style, was an important facet of orthodox Jewish life already, in cities such as Capernaum where Yehoshu'a himself taught.

He gathered about himself a group of men disciples and women followers, and began healing and teaching in a striking way: his parables and stories sometimes seemed esoteric but they were vivid. It was chiefly through such stories, and through colorful and lively epigrams and sayings, that he taught, judging from the style of what has come down to us. He may well have claimed to be *Mashiah* or Anointed One, and his family had some claim to be linked to the House of David. If he did use the idea, he used it in a novel way: not meaning a warrior king, come to restore Jewish rule, but as a Suffering Servant, a new sort of king with a crown of thorns. Many of his teachings used old concepts in new ways, and this maybe was a source of misunderstanding. At any rate he came into sharp collision with the ruling council or Sanhedrin, and was handed over to Pilate, the Roman administrator, for execution by crucifixion, with a notice on the cross to the effect that he was "King of the Jews." The transformation which overcame his group a few days later, according to the accounts in the New Testament, when they came to believe in his resurrection from the dead, was the source of the vigor with which they carried on the movement.

So, apart from all the other currents in Jewish religion of the time, we have the continuation of Yohanan's group and, more significantly in the Graeco-Roman world, the Yehoshu'a movement. This came to be transmitted by Paul, teaching especially in Greek and traveling to the various Jewish centers—that is, the main cities—of Greece and Asia Minor and then to Rome itself. And not only was there Paul but other vigorous disciples also. By not requiring circumcision of Gentile converts, Paul turned the movement into an easy access into some of the nobler features of the Jewish tradition, whose monotheism had an appeal to reflective Gentiles, and whose ethics were inspiring in many ways to people in the empire. This new offshoot of Jewish religion, full of verve and some apparent secrecy, had the appearance of a new mystery religion.

In the catacombs, the Roman piety toward the dead was formalized in niches such as these, where urns containing the ashes of the dead were stored.

Also around this period there grew up other religions with Jewish connections which are collectively known as Gnosticism. Precisely what form they took on the ground is obscure; but in content, though not in organization, they resembled Manichaeism. It was a Gnostic teacher, Marcion, whose doctrine was that the God of the Old Testament was evil, and who edited and in effect censored Paul's letters, who forced the growing Christian community, in the second century C.E., to set about the job of deciding which writings they used were canonical, or approved by the community as containing God's truth. The formation of the Christian Bible in the second and third centuries C.E. was one of the signs that the religion was crystallizing into that fully fledged form which we know as Christianity.

## Jews and Christians in the Hellenistic World

In all this rich interplay of religious movements, rituals, belief systems, and customs, and amid shifting allegiances within the overall stable framework of the empire, why did the Christians win out?

The new mystery religion had some inherent advantages. First, because of its Jewish monotheism it was universal in scope. Second, in looking to a God-human in Jesus it presented a theme very familiar to the Graeco-Roman world. Third, it was able, from the third century onwards in particular, to pick up themes from the Platonic tradition which would make the faith appealing to the educated person. Fourth, the nature of its "mystery," a sacred meal, was coupled to a scheme of initiation which meant much more in the way of commitment to beliefs than the other mystery cults. Fifth, periodic persecution, which Jews also experienced, reinforced the solidarity of the group. Sixth, the empty formalism of the emperor cult and the marked pluralism of belief among the imperial elite pointed to the lack of a coherent state ideology. It was the Christians' good fortune that Constantine I (d. 337)

The emperor Constantine, who symbolizes the triumph of Christianity over ancient paganism, is here portrayed as a Christian, bearing the cross in his hand.

saw in Christian teachings such an ideology, and reorganized the Empire with it as official teaching; it was at his command that the first great Council of the Church was called. Seventh, the new religion had consistent organization, with its system of overseers or bishops; it was only matched in this by the Manichaeans. Eighth, it was able to fight off its pessimistic Gnostic rivals and the Manichaeans with its relatively positive attitudes to the world.

### The Dimensions of Early Christian Religion

By the second century, Christianity was beginning to settle down. In *doctrine* it affirmed that there was but one God, who had created the world without any hindrance, so that it was basically good. Its *mythic* dimension affirmed, however, that the primordial humans had disobeyed God and had been driven from Paradise. Yet God wished to save the human race, and the people of Israel had been chosen as the instruments of this. By keeping faith in one God going, till the time when the Savior came to earth, they were crucial to the whole salvation-history. Christ on earth had died for human sins and had made available God's grace to the faithful. Those faithful basically were the churchly community; and the grace came in particular through the ritual participation in Christ through the thanksgiving service, held typically in wealthier members' houses.

In *ritual* there were the sacraments, like baptism, by which after a course of instruction a believer was admitted to the group. There was the eucharist, typically followed by a communal meal, in which the followers of Christ showed their mutual love and solidarity. Love was the root of the *ethical* dimension; and Christians got a good reputation for raising the status of women in marriage, for faithfulness, and for that general probity summed up in the Ten Commandments. The *institutional* dimension, with areas looked after by bishops and with a priest, as far as possible, for every community, was flexible in times of strife. Certain big bishops, those of Rome, Antioch,

---

### Christ the Creator: John's Gospel

In the beginning was the Word, and the Word was with God, and the Word was God. The same was in the beginning with God. All things were made by him, and without him was not any thing made that was made. In him was life, and the life was the light of men. And the light shineth in darkness; and the darkness comprehended it not.

There was a man sent from God whose name was John. The same came for a witness, to bear witness of the light, that all men through him might believe. He was not that light, but was sent to bear witness of that light. That was the true light, which lighteth every man that cometh into the world. He was in the world and the world was made by him, and the world knew him not. He came unto his own, and his own received him not. But as many as received him, to them gave he power to become the sons of God, even to them that believe on his name, which were born not of blood, nor of the will of the flesh, nor of the will of man, but of God. And the Word was made flesh, and dwelt among us (and we beheld his glory, the glory as of the only begotten of the Father), full of grace and truth.

242

*The breaking of the bread*, from the Catacomb of Priscilla, Rome, second century C.E.

and Alexandria, had special prestige; and so, later, had the bishop of the new imperial capital, Constantinople. They were also beginning experiments with monasticism, and this was later to be a vital stream of organized meditation and illumination in the Church. In religious *experience*, there was stress on the vision of Christ, in line with Gnostic practice; but also, and perhaps above all, the feeling of the Love of God which was manifested in the gatherings of Christians, inspired by the Spirit. It was early in the life of the community for there to be much *art*, especially in the context of Jewish imagelessness. But as a material object they did have the Greek text of the Hebrew Bible and of the new scriptures of the rising community.

The Christians had a human parallel to the Gospels and the other writings: they had the source of truth seen in the lives of the martyrs and the saints. It was the Christian holy men and women above all who showed the power of God and the grace of the new community—as they saw it—in the proliferating congregations of the empire.

### Roman Imperial Religion as a Total System

The Christians and Jews were of course somewhat hostile to the imperial religious milieu. What others saw as meaningful stories they saw as deceptions. They did not acknowledge that their own narratives might look like sacred myth to others. But they did exist for two or three centuries as a subtheme in that wider configuration which saw Zeus or Jupiter as supreme god from a popular point of view, but to be reinterpreted if you wished philosophically as the supreme Mind. The various deities represented so many powers and above all forces for the renewal of life. There was a strong air in the Empire of the need for propriety, so that the proper imperial and civic rites should be performed, to keep things going and to cement the good relations between

Among Christians cremation was replaced by burial awaiting the resurrection: the sarcophagus here depicts the death and final glory of Christ, in the center depicted by the Chi Rho symbols, being the first letters of the name Christos in Greek.

the Beyond and ourselves. Within the total loosely bound system there were alternative mysteries which pious folk might wish to take part in. Those which did not respect the emperor were subversive and deserving of persecution. The central gods of Rome were meanwhile being integrated with local deities throughout the Empire, from Britain to Cyrenaica, and this process helped to bring a sense of solemn loyalty to the far flung parts of the Empire. In its own way it was a satisfactory system, for it functioned to a great extent pluralistically.

## Judaism Defines Itself

Several crises assaulted the Jewish tradition. There was the tragic and tormenting sack of the Temple after an unsuccessful revolt against Rome in 70 C.E. There was the later razing of the city of Jerusalem itself and the building of a Roman city there, Aelia Capitolana, in 130 (occasioning the revolt, ending disastrously, of Shimon Bar-Kochba, hailed by the famed Rabbi Akiba as *Mashiah*). There was also the problem posed by the growing Christian movement, getting further and further as Jews saw it from the orthodox scriptural tradition. When Christian ideals triumphed and Judaism found itself having to adjust to the new reality, it had somehow to define itself. We can say that from the fourth century, when classical Christianity took its Roman and Greek forms, we see the formation too of Judaism as the religion which is still recognizable today. The long series of experiences leading through Israelite religion, its restoration by Ezra, the confusions of the Greek period, and the need to face up to the destruction of the heart of the ritual cult, now culminated in a fully formed Judaism. Like twins, Christianity and Judaism grew up together. It was not of course destined to be a happy relationship. The two religions differed markedly on how they saw the Hebrew Bible, and on most other things.

During the first centuries C.E. the position of rabbis in Jewish life was greatly strengthened: these were men of power and knowledge, charismatic leaders, but above all experts in the Torah. The reason for their prominence had in part to do with the fall of the Temple. There were to be no more

244

sacrifices to God. The glories of the renovated building were gone, and Jerusalem itself was devastated. The religious Jews who wished to perpetuate tradition had to find it in records: in books. Study came to replace sacrifice as the most central Jewish ritual, for it was by intensive study of the Torah that the whole of the rest of the ritual life of the Torah-following Jew was defined. Once life had been easier: you could go to Jerusalem. Also, the Jewish religion of the period was already heavily oriented towards the synagogue, and there scripture was preserved.

Christians could take what to Jews was an unkind line: Jesus had foreseen the destruction of the Temple. Jews had been disobedient because they had rejected the Messiah, and indeed had been caught up in the killing of him. A powerful anti-Jewish myth was brewing up in the mind of the Church. Also, Christianity was built on the assumption that the new king had already come. A new age had dawned; there was no great significance left in the Temple. So somehow Jews, by contrast, had to defend their Temple though it was gone. It was preserved in the memory of people, and the study of the rules and meaning of sacrifice became a substitute for sacrifice itself in the literal sense. There are, by the way, analogies here to the Upanishads, when sages asked for the meaning of the sacrifice and found it in an inner quest.

In certain respects the triumph of the new Judaism, in which the daily life of the Jew was in accord with the rules as minutely analyzed and interpreted for the changed conditions, was a victory for the Pharisee party. They already had begun to apply laws of purity, essentially devised for priests, to the community as a whole. It was also a victory for the notion of the dual Torah. There was the written Torah, the first part of the Hebrew Bible, but there was also the oral Torah, which flowed from Sinai (said the rabbis of the new age). This oral Torah, by an irony, became written down, as the Mishnah and its commentary the Tosefta. This collection already existed by about 200 C.E. The two versions of the Talmud—the Jerusalem or Yerushalmi and the Babylonian or Bavli—represent an extensive commentary upon these materials. The Babylonian Talmud was of course based on long experience in exile, in a foreign land, so authoritative expression could there be given to the oral Torah.

The development of a great mass of rabbinic interpretations in effect made rabbis the carriers on of revelation for the community. It brought them a central position, and learning became a central ideal of the Jewish way of life. So what we have emerging is a religion which is based, not just on the Hebrew Bible, but on the two legs of the written and oral Torah. It laid much responsibility on those with learning; and it centered on communities united in synagogue worship. The Jewish family unit was basic, and it was there that some of the most vital of ritual activities were performed in the unfolding cycle of Jewish feasts through the year, which enlivened and enriched the daily performance of all those duties related to ordinary living which the Law prescribed.

All this was very different from the interpretation of life in the Christian community. Christians had no oral Torah. In many ways, for them the Torah was abrogated. The Messiah had already come. The Jewish adherence to ritual observances and rules of purity from a bygone age seemed like perversity. For the Christian the right interpretation of the Bible was obvious, and those who did not see it were wilful. Thus was born an unfortunate epistemology which was to fuel later anti-Semitism.

## The End of Graeco-Roman Religion

Naturally the victory of Christianity was not absolute and immediate with the favor of Constantine and the subsequent Council in 325 C.E. Yet it was in many ways very rapid. In 391 the emperor Theodosius ordered the end of pagan sacrifices. In 399 the destruction or in some cases conversion of pagan sanctuaries was effected. Though the philosophical religions might hang on, they too were taken up into the emerging doctrinal synthesis achieved by the heirs of the Greek and Roman world, men such as St. Augustine (354–430) and the Eastern Fathers.

The result was a blend of two ways of life, for Christianity did weave into its fabric many of the values of the Hellenistic world and the Roman Empire. It was thus able to transmit across a rather chaotic period, from the fourth century onwards, a whole complex of Graeco-Roman values which were not entirely buried by Christian orthodoxy. But the Churches did get rather preoccupied henceforth with right doctrine. Christians saw themselves as the true believers, but Judaism had never put that much stress on belief *per se*.

# 11

# *Classical and Medieval Christianity and Judaism*

## The Trinity Doctrine

The Council of Nicaea was summoned by the emperor Constantine, as we have seen. It was the culmination of a process in which the Christians had been increasingly defining themselves in terms of what they believed. Doctrinal orthodoxy was important to establish from an imperial point of view, given that the faith was destined to become the ideology of the imperial state; but why was it so important too for the Christian leadership? In part at least the reason was that Christianity was not like Judaism, a mainly ethnic religion in the sense that you became a Jew by being born into the tradition. Yet it defined itself as a new Israel. How was that Israel to be defined in practice? To a greater and greater extent the definition had to be by belief.

Already in the years leading up to its dramatic success, in the hard days of martyrdom and underground proselytization, the Christian community had had to fight off reinterpretations of its message which were considered to be dangerously wrong. It had fought off in particular various Gnostic groups who had often, in their pessimism about the world and the flesh, seen Yahweh the Creator God of the Old Testament as being evil. Christians had insisted on the underlying goodness of the world despite the Fall of the primordial human beings, Adam and Eve. The Christians had had, too, to react to the synthesis offered by the Manichaeans, who saw the teachings of Jesus, the Buddha, and Zarathustra as converging in the worldview of Mani.

Also Christians had—while respecting Greek philosophy—resisted the seductions of Graeco-Roman paganism: they drew a line between Jewish or Christian stories and pagan ones. The latter were just stories, while Christian narratives, based on real facts, were indeed historical. It was from this negative appraisal of myth that the modern colloquial sense of myth being a false story has come.

The doctrinal dimension: at councils, such as the Council of Nicaea in 324, the more abstract doctrinal formulae of Christian orthodoxy were formulated and affirmed. Here, under the supervision of Constantine and Pope Sylvester, the heretical books of Arius, Victorinus and others are consigned to the flames. The clothing and other details are anachronistic and belong to the sixteenth century C.E.

Christians had already debated some of the issues concerning the relation between their faith and the glittering culture in which they found themselves, and through which they were making their way. The Latin-writing "Father" (a title Christians gave later to the most vital theological figures of the period), Tertullian (160?–?225) belonged to the literary circles of Carthage in North Africa, and used his literary and rhetorical training through many influential writings. But he was very rigorous in drawing the line between pagan ideas and practices and Christian ones. He is credited with the famous question, "What has Athens to do with Jerusalem?" Yet ultimately it was the synthesizers who won out. It became, if not necessary, at least helpful, to define some of the central doctrines of the community through Greek philosophical terminology. This essentially is what happened at Nicaea in regard to that most characteristic and yet also baffling teaching of Christianity, the Trinity doctrine.

Constantine in particular was worried by a serious rift in the Christian Church over the status of Christ. There was a group under the leadership of a priest called Arius (250?–?336), of Alexandria in Egypt, which made Christ

Christ the Pantocrator or Ruler of the Universe, from Dafni Monastery in Greece.

בעל הבית ונתן ביתו שאומרים יהודה

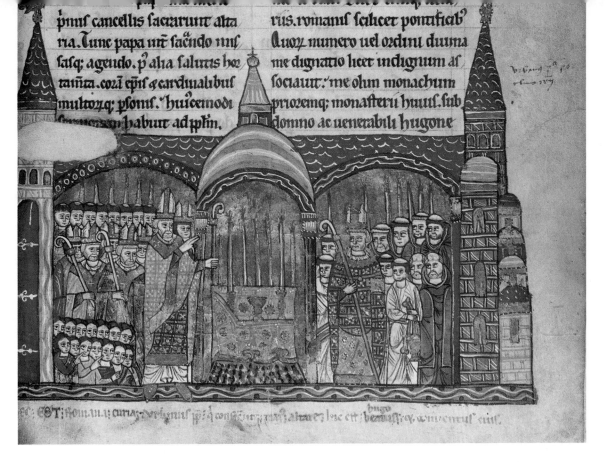

*Left* The ritual dimension: Jews, dressed in Moorish style, worship in a synagogue; while they had some disadvantages under Islam (and, on the whole, even more stringent ones in Christian countries), their ritual life was basically unimpeded.

*Above* The institutional dimension: the monastic center of Cluny in central France was a powerhouse of reform; here Pope Urban II (c. 1035–1099) consecrates the church. Until the rebuilding of St. Peter's in Rome it was the largest church in Western Christendom.

*Right* The narrative dimension: the Angel replenishes the four rivers in Eden, while Adam and Eve are cast out into the desert, from a twelfth-century manuscript.

Si tuit s'apruurent
que nir gent estoient
ens: et auoient leuee
la baniere au duc sour

les dont il y auoit plente.
Li dus mettoit afvrce ses
gens es tours a tous les.
en ces se hastuit d'enuru...

Bauduins de tour . Gas
ses d'wars . Gasses de brovers
Thomas de la fur . Guuts de

noneternal, being himself created by God; but on him the Father bestowed divinity. The slogan of the movement was "There was [a time] when he was not." Part of its motivation lay in the desire to preserve monotheism more clearly.

The Christian faith had found itself in a strange position in regard to Jesus. From both the practical and the theoretical point of view it wanted to affirm the divinity of Christ; but it was, after all, a movement which had come out of the Jewish tradition. It had suffered persecution because of its unwillingness to compromise with pagan polytheism. It was firmly committed to belief in one God.

From the practical angle, it was involved in a central ritual, the Eucharist, which involved the worship of Christ. It was blasphemous to worship anyone except God; so Christ must be God. This was the practical part of

*Opposite* The ethical dimension: it was considered a duty to fight to regain the holy places of the faith from the infidel Muslims. The taking of Jerusalem in 1099 is depicted here.

---

## Christianity some key terms

*Atonement* At-one-ment, that is, the bringing together of humankind and God through the death and resurrection of Christ.

*Baptism* The sacrament of immersion in water, or being sprinkled with water, whereby a person is initiated into the Christian Church.

*Bible* The collection of books which are treated by Christians as the record of God's revelation.

*Christ* The anointed one or Messiah who is the agent of salvation.

*Church* The community of Christians on earth and in heaven.

*Communion* Known also as the Eucharist in Anglicanism, the Mass in Roman Catholicism, and the Liturgy in Eastern Orthodoxy: the primary sacrament of sharing Christ's life by partaking of the bread and wine as his body and blood.

*Grace* The power of God entering into humans to empower them to good deeds and salvation.

*Ikon* A picture used in Orthodoxy as a window on heaven, and an object of devotion to the faithful.

*Love* Greek *agapē*, the reverential affection for other human beings which is the primary Christian virtue.

*Sin* The estrangement of humans from God, thought to be due to the actions of Adam and Eve in the first instance.

*Theosis* Process of becoming divinized or like God: the goal of Eastern Orthodox spiritual effort.

*Trinity* God as Three in One, as Father, Son and Holy Spirit: being three persons or centers of consciousness in one being.

and even there it retained its heartlands. On the other hand the West was badly overrun by barbarian peoples from the latter part of the fourth century onwards. The Goths had been mainly converted to Christianity before they broke into the imperial domains, but it was an Arian form of Christianity that had been preached by the great missionary Ulfilas. The destiny of Northern Christianity was in part determined by the baptism in 496 of Clovis, king of the Franks, who helped tame the Goths on behalf of orthodox Roman Christianity. It was to deal with the Arian heresy that the Western Church, at a Council at Toledo in Spain, inserted the clause *filioque* into the Creed. The implications of this we shall return to. Meanwhile the alliance between the Franks and the Church led to the ultimate foundation of the so-called Holy Roman Empire with the coronation of Charlemagne as emperor in 800 C.E. The bases of medieval Christianity, with its North-South axis in the West, were being laid.

The question of the small clause, *Filioque*, meaning "And from the Son", was more serious than at first sight might appear, and for two reasons. The purport of the insertion was that the Holy Spirit proceeded from the Father and *from the Son*. According to Orthodox theologians in the East this upsets the balance of the Trinity, which according to them consists in a perfect unity of Persons in which the Father eternally generates the Son and from whom the Holy Spirit eternally proceeds. The Father so to speak enhances a balanced unity. But secondly, and worse from the point of view of the Greeks, the formula was added by the West without consultation with the East and was indeed the usurpation of authority by the Bishop of Rome, that is to say, the Pope. He was arrogating to himself a role in the formation of new doctrines. Only a Council recognized by the whole Church could do this. These questions, first of doctrine and secondly of the authority of the Pope, have plagued relations between the two great wings of the Church ever since. They helped to confirm the mode in which these parts of Christendom were drifting apart.

As both parts were projected forward into the medieval world, the one as spiritual heir of an empire that effectively had broken up, and the other as the official religion of an empire which was also subjected to increasing external pressures, they differed somewhat in doctrine, organization and practice, and we can see something of these divergences by looking at the dimensions of the religions.

### The Dimensions of Christianity East and West

First, let us look at the *organizational* dimension of the two. In the West we have a gradually more centralized organization under the Bishop of Rome, the Pope. But it was a monarchy of a spiritual or religious nature, and the increasingly fragmented nature of Western Christendom maybe made it the more imperative that Rome should be seen as an authoritative center. In the East, so long as the empire lasted, there was a form of what came to be called "Caesaropapism," where the emperor considered himself one with the apostles and played an active role in the determination of Christian doctrine and discipline. In fact, however, the Patriarch of Constantinople and the other leading bishops of the Eastern Church often stood out against the emperor: so it was a dual system of rule by the secular and religious heads. But obviously the power of the emperor was great, and some emperors played a vital role in controversies, such as the debate about ikons. But from the seventh century great regions of Eastern Christianity came under Muslim rule, and in such conditions the Christians were considered a separate community and administered through the leading bishop or patriarch of each area, which gave the Church a limited secular function.

In the West the priesthood came to be secular; but in the East an ingenious relationship between monasticism and parish clergy was worked out. If, after training, a priest did not marry, he became a monk. It was from the ranks of the monks that bishops were elected.

As for the *material* dimension of the faith, the early Church had used decorations, for instance in the catacombs. With the coming of official recognition worship moved out of houses and villas which were used or donated for worship. Pagan shrines were suppressed, and their sites or buildings taken over. The basilica form became dominant in the West. This was originally a long building with high windows and aisles which was used for secular purposes. Now it was used religiously, with the end portion being screened off and used for the altar and the seating of the clergy, the central part for the faithful, and the forecourt for postulants (those who wanted to become Christians). Those who were undergoing instruction had to withdraw from the nave to the forecourt or the aisles during the Mass or liturgy proper. The Eastern tradition favored the domelike structure whether on the base of a Greek cross or on a longitudinal base in the manner of the basilica, as in the famous Hagia Sophia in Constantinople built under Justinian in the sixth century. Its great domes and vaults were covered with gold mosaic; its columns gleamed with polished marble and porphyry. It exuded golden light from within, seemingly weightless, a glorious example of the Byzantine style.

The tombs of rich Roman Christians had long displayed sculptures, but the East retained a ban on three-dimensional representations, as offending against the commandment forbidding graven images. But the ikon or picture of Christ or Mary or a saint became increasingly popular. It came to be customary to screen the wall between the nave and sanctuary with such holy pictures. But from 723 to 842 the Eastern Church was riven with a swaying struggle over ikons. The iconoclastic (ikon-smashing) party was dominant over much of this period. In the Western Church this notion that there was something heathen and heretical about the use of holy pictures and sculptures did not appear until the sixteenth-century Reformation. The excommunication by the Pope of the Easterners on this score deepened the rift, and had its expression in the crowning of the Frankish King, Charlemagne, as Holy Roman Emperor in Rome in 800, he taking the significant title of Augustus.

The experiential dimension: a sixteenth-century ikon of Christ seeks to combine the majesty of the numinous feeling of the worshiper and the sense of serenity arising in the contemplative life.

257

The ideologies of the Western empire and of Christianity were here fused. In the East the pro-ikon party won in due course, and since that time the reverence of ikons has been a central element in Eastern piety: much more important in fact than the corresponding use of pictures in the West.

As for *doctrine*, there were differences in emphasis, though not very great. The dominant theologian of the Western Church, until the medieval period, undoubtedly was St. Augustine of Hippo in North Africa. Converted from Manichaeanism under dramatic circumstances, he was a pioneer of different literary forms—of autobiography in his *Confessions* and of historical interpretation in his *The City of God*. In this latter book he contrasts the City of God with the City of Earth, of which Rome is the prototype. He does not strictly speaking identify the City of God with the Church, but he did come to accept that the earthly power might be used to ensure conformity of doctrine—a license for the state, under the Church's guidance, to persecute heretics. But more importantly, he laid great stress on original sin, the sin of Adam and Eve which was transmitted down the generations. It was God's incarnation, and his gift of grace, that overcame sin and brought salvation.

Augustine attacked the Celtic monk Pelagius (died 418) for affirming human free will. He laid the groundwork for the doctrine of predestination—that the individual from the beginning is chosen by God and predestined to salvation (or alternatively *not* chosen and predetermined to damnation). This somewhat negative emphasis was carried on in the Western Church, which tended to underline Christ's death as an atoning sacrifice for sin, thus putting us right with God. By contrast St. Athanasius emphasized how God became human in Christ so that humans might become divine; and the Eastern Church tended to stress this idea of *theosis* or divinization. These are only diversities of emphasis.

Doctrinally, also, the two sides split, as we have seen, over the *Filioque* clause. Eastern theologians have always stressed the important spiritual message of a correct view of the Trinity, more intensely than their Western colleagues.

As to the *narrative* of the New Testament and beyond, the Western Church put a great emphasis of course on the role of St. Peter, first Bishop of Rome. The commission to Peter by the risen Christ, "Feed my sheep," and other texts, were used to back up the Pope's primacy. Also Rome was seen as center of the world, after Jerusalem. The death of both Peter and Paul in Rome was an important ingredient in the whole story of the faith. But whereas in the West the secular Rome was decadent, in the East it had fused very easily with the Church, and the golden glories of Byzantine art added a new dimension to the Graeco-Roman experience.

Regarding the *ritual* dimension, a vital divergence was in language, since Latin was the Western vehicle of worship (so that later in the Middle Ages, as vernacular languages diverged from the Church's language, a certain alienation was bound to occur). In the East the liturgy was in Greek, and in a number of other languages that, like Greek itself, remained in secular use. More

The institutional dimension: here the decretals of Boniface VIII (1228–1303), seen in council, signify the increase in papal power, which grew throughout the Middle Ages, until the Reformation.

importantly, the atmosphere of the Eucharist in the two traditions began to pull apart, especially with the Eastern use of ikons, and the fact that the main ritual action was more concealed, since the altar area was thoroughly screened off by the wall holding the ikons, the iconostasis. The light is there behind the screen, and the priests make forays into the congregation, with the Little Entrance bringing the Gospel to be read, and with the Great Entrance bearing the bread and wine. The church is a representation of heaven, and the movement is from God to humans. The Roman churches, which were longer buildings, were more a movement up toward God.

The Western Church came to list seven sacraments as being recognized—the Eucharist, Baptism, Marriage, Confirmation, Absolution, Ordination to the Priesthood, Extreme Unction (for the dying). But the Orthodox had a wider view, including other rites such as blessing the house, burial, blessing water at Epiphany, etc. Both Churches celebrated Good Friday, when Christ died, and Easter, when he rose from the dead. But the Eastern celebrations of Easter are more dramatic, replete with the spreading light of candles in the early hours of Easter Day and the proclamation "Christ is risen."

As to *experience*, both East and West were committed to the monastic ideal, and within that the practice of contemplation and the notion of an inner, mystical union with the divine grew. Later, as we shall see, the Eastern Orthodox experimented with breathing techniques and the like, and the use of the Jesus Prayer, "Lord Jesus Christ have mercy on me a sinner," said in connection with breathing in and out. The importance of numinous visions of God and the Virgin remained in both wings of Christendom. These were expressed in diverse ways in the art of East and West. Especially striking is the deep and overwhelming majesty of the Eastern ikon of Christ Pantokrator or Ruler of All (p. 249).

The *ethical* injunctions of the two Churches were very similar. If anything the Western Church—in part because of St. Augustine—had the gloomier view of sexuality, which was the cause of the transmission of original sin. The increased spread of the ideal of priestly celibacy also had its effects on preaching. Celibacy and virginity were both held up as high ideals, the more so as the other great way of bearing testimony to faith, martyrdom, faded somewhat in the more relaxed days after Christianity became the official religion.

### Other Eastern Churches and Eastern Missions

We have so far been concentrating on the Greek Church of the Eastern part of the Roman Empire. But the Church from early days could be said to have an even more Eastern presence. There were the Aramaic-speaking Christians of Jerusalem, dispersed after the destruction of the Temple in 70 C.E. and the subsequent forcible expulsion of the Jews. Their successors were the Syriac Nestorian Church, based initially in Antioch, and spreading outwards. It was led by Nestorius (381?–?451), who was identified with the heresy known as Nestorianism, affirming that Christ has two natures, one human and one divine. The Nestorians came to control the diocese of Seleucia-Ctesiphon in Mesopotamia, and through that had an immense missionary activity to China, Central Asia, and India. Syriac Churches were an important part of the Eastern Christian world, even if formally in schism with the Orthodox.

In Armenia, Christianity became the official religion of the court even before it did in the Roman Empire, in 314 C.E. under Tiridates III. The country had previously been largely Zoroastrian. The Armenian Church, using an Eastern-type liturgy, accepted the first three Councils of the Church, namely those of Nicaea in 325, Constantinople in 381, and Ephesus in 431.

The ritual dimension: an Egyptian Coptic priest in his vestments, twelfth century C.E. Victoria and Albert Museum, London.

In Egypt and Ethiopia, Coptic Churches became established, so called from the language which they used, being an ancient Egyptian tongue written in a variation of the Greek alphabet. Ethiopia became especially important in later Africa because it symbolized an ancient black kind of Christian faith, important to remember in the colonial era when the dominant structures of Western religion were in the hands of Whites.

Meanwhile, Byzantine Christianity was reaching north toward the peoples of Eastern Europe and Russia. From early days it had made some inroads into what is now Romania; but it was not until the early Middle Ages that the great mission work of St. Cyril and St. Methodius was to be effective. But it is best for us first to see some of the work of the Latin missions which had a bearing on the area of Eastern Europe also.

### Outreaches of the Western Church

Probably the most important Church on the fringes of the West was that of the Celts in Britain and in Ireland. The British-born St. Patrick (390?–?460) was kidnapped and enslaved by the Irish in his youth, learned their language, and later returned to Ireland where he had a substantial role in the evangelization of the island. The Romano-British Church also played a part in the Christianization of Southwest Scotland through St. Ninian, who set up a center of study and monasticism in the Wigton peninsula. Later St. Columba from Ireland set up a monastery further north in the island of Iona.

The Celtic Church had a characteristic form of monasticism with monks and nuns together, and held to some customs not shared by the Roman Church, towards which it had some antipathy. But in 664 the Synod of Whitby led to a rapprochement between the Celtic Church and the Roman, dominated in Britain by the Anglo-Saxons who had been converted as a result of the mission of another St. Augustine to Canterbury in 597.

The British Church made its contribution later on to the task of converting the Germans and others in Northern Europe who had mostly lain outside the old Roman Empire. It was crucial for Christianity to move north, for in the seventh century it was hit by an obliterating storm from the south. The followers of Islam conquered the southern part of the Mediterranean and the Near East, thus slicing off a large part of both the Western and Byzantine Empires. They came into Spain and overran most of it and Portugal. Northern Europe was brought in to redress the balance.

The dynamism of Christianity in Britain and the strength of the Franks combined in the missionizing of Germany, most notably by St. Boniface (a native of Devon in the west of England) who worked in central Germany, in Hesse and Thuringia. In 716 he cut down the sacred oak at Geismar, a signal that paganism was being replaced by the Christian faith. In the tenth century two Norwegian kings brought the faith to Norway: Olaf Haraldsson, who became a martyr by dying in battle, and Olaf Tryggvesson who among other things pressured Iceland, bringing that country to vote for Christianity as its public (although not private) religion in the significant year of 1000 C.E. Poland, Hungary, and Bohemia were also proselytized from the West, as was Croatia.

And so by the eleventh century Europe from Sicily to northern Norway was effectively Christian. In the eastern part of Europe the Orthodox mission was also fairly successful. There were parts of the Baltic still to convert, but the main work was done.

It was sometimes done from the grassroots, by lonely missionaries, and, more importantly, by the planting of monasteries. These could train local vernacular clergy, provide learning, help with agricultural development, and supply a good example of Christian living. Sometimes, however, the acceptance of Christianity came from the top. Kings, emerging stronger in a period of chaos, could use Christianity as an ideology of rule: it supplied learning, which could be used in administration; it possessed a body of law; it was universal in its values; and it could be harnessed to a military worldview, despite the peaceful monks. It could promise greater consistency than the old pagan cults, which it was not afraid to attack, even physically.

*Eastern Mission—the Conversion of Russia*

The achievements of missionaries out of Byzantium were equally important, and especially those of the brothers St. Cyril (826?–869) and St. Methodius (815?–884). Both were in good positions, the one as professor at the imperial university and the other as a provincial governor. But they withdrew from these occupations and began mission work together, first among the Khazars, who lived northeast of the Black Sea, then in the Balkans. Their most lasting achievements were the devising of an alphabet (the so-called Cyrillic script) for the Slavic languages, and the encouragement of worship in the vernacular languages. Christianity infiltrated into Russia from various directions, and in 988 Vladimir, Prince of Kiev, was baptized. He was married to a sister of the Byzantine emperor, and it was Eastern Christianity that took root in Russia. Again, the Christian religion, losing ground in the south and east of the Byzantine empire, made substantial advances in the North.

So far we have extended the story of Christianity beyond its chief formative period, which was in the fourth and fifth centuries C.E. We have seen it evolve into its main classical forms. We shall later look at it in its greatest premodern period, that is to say, the so-called Middle Ages—both in East and West. This was a time of glory and achievement for a Christian-dominated civilization, faced, however, with a perhaps more glittering culture, that of Islam. Within its fabric it contained—as did Islam—another important faith, also emerging in its classical form in the fourth and fifth centuries C.E.; this was Judaism. We turn to see something of what happened to this religion in the early circumstances of its existence under official Christianity and then Islam.

## The New Life of Judaism

In the Roman Empire, before the conversion of Constantine, conversion to Judaism was not uncommon, but by edict Constantine made it punishable by death. Later, Islam made a similar provision regarding both Christians and Jews within the territory of Islam. This was a factor in the consolidation of Jewish identity. Nevertheless the Jewish people lived in remarkably diverse circumstances. There were the Jews in Yemen and among Khazars, both countries which for relatively short periods became officially Jewish; there was the great community of Babylon, so influential throughout the Jewish world; the Jews of Palestine, Egypt, North Africa; the Sephardic Jews of the Iberian peninsula, the Jews of Italy, France, Britain; the Ashkenazic Jews of Germany and Central Europe; and later those of Eastern Europe. There was no single circumstance of being Jewish. But there remained, even in these divisions, a reasonable amount of communications, facilitated by the fact that Jews played an important role in trade: because of the Christian and Muslim bans on usury, money business was largely left to them.

Amid the disadvantages of being Jewish, there were some bonuses. In Islamic countries there was a reasonable place for the Jewish community, and

Jews were able to benefit from the cultural and philosophical achievements of Arabic civilization, through which they had renewed access to the Greek classics. Especially in Spain there was a great period of Jewish culture, culminating in new forms of poetry, such as the *Crown of Royalty*, by Ibn Gabirol (1021–69), still recited by Sephardic Jews on the eve of Yom Kippur, new commentaries on the Torah, and the like. Yehuda Halevi (1086–1143), as well as writing poems about the love of God and Zion, composed a dialogue and polemic about why the Khazars had chosen Judaism over Christianity and Islam. The greatest philosopher in this creative milieu was undoubtedly Mosheh ibn Maimon, commonly known as Maimonides (1135–1204) who wrote a great commentarial work, the *Mishneh Torah*, and a famous philosophical treatise, *More Nevukim* or "Guide of the Perplexed." In this he employed the method of the negative way in theology—you can say what God is not, but not what he is. Maimonides thought, with Aristotle, that the notion that God created the world is compatible with the everlasting character of the world (a view much disputed by other philosophers). He had great influence also among Christian thinkers, including St. Thomas Aquinas. Maimonides also formulated the famous Thirteen Articles or principles of belief which have remained the most used summary of the Jewish creed since that time. They fall into three groups. The first concerns God—his existence, unity, incorporeality, and eternity. The second is about Torah—prophecy's validity, the uniqueness of Mosheh's message, the divine origin of the written and oral Torah, the eternity and changelessness of the law. The third group relates to reward and punishment—the omniscience of God, divine compensation for good and evil, the coming of the Messiah, and the resurrection of the dead.

*The Jewish Year*

It was during this early medieval period that the practice of the Jewish calendar reached its full form. Judaism had always emphasized the sacredness of certain times. Indeed with the taking away of the Temple and, effectively, of the land of Israel, Jews found their sacredness more in time than space.

The weekly rhythm underlined the holiness of the Shabbat (Sabbath) for practicing Jews. At sundown of a Friday—for Jews consider that the day begins with sunset rather than dawn—the woman of the house lights the special candles and says a prayer over them, and there follows a meal which is made holy by being the Shabbat meal. The day of course lasts till the following sunset, and is the occasion for prayers in the meetinghouse or synagogue. Jewish law prescribes the refraining from work on this day.

As well as the weekly rhythm there is also the yearly rhythm, beginning with the Jewish New Year, Rosh Hashanah, and followed ten days on with Yom Kippur, the Day of Atonement, the most holy day in the year. There is the family festival of Passover, and there are such other originally harvest festivals as Shavu'ot (Weeks) and Sukkot (Booths). In the winter there is Hanukkah, recalling the Maccabees' rededication of the Temple in 164 B.C.E.,

263

and there are various other less sacred days. This rhythm of the year helps Jews to reenact the vital points in their history and their relationship to God.

As well as the ritual year there were the 613 commandments which the pious Jew was supposed to observe, and the net of obligations and customs which the rabbis had woven to cast over life as a perpetual reminder of the Jews' special place in the world which God had made. By following the obligations of both written and oral Torah, the Jew not only followed an ethical path but in effect also a religious path. What counted above all was his or her inner realization of the meaning and dedication implied by the outer acts of conformity.

## Jewish Mysticism—the Qabbalah

The inner meaning of Jewish piety was no doubt reinforced by the outer problems of the community. The Crusades, beginning with the first in 1095, were occasions for pogroms against the Jews in many parts of Northern Europe. Such anti-Jewish hostility was in most countrysides not far below the surface. Both because they were religious nonconformists in an age when faith was increasingly enforced by a nervous yet powerful Church, and because they were much identified with commerce and lending money, the Jews attracted stereotypes which in turn stimulated oppression. They were expelled from England in 1290 and Spain in 1492, for instance.

It was in Provence and Spain, in the twelfth and thirteenth centuries, that there arose the movement known as the Qabbalah or Tradition, which revived the mystical strand in the Jewish tradition. This had been evident in the so-called Merkavah (Chariot) mysticism of a much earlier time, that of Rabbi Aqiba in the first and second centuries C.E. The "chariot" refers to the chariot of fire in which the prophet Eliyyahu (Elijah) ascended to heaven, and which is used as a symbol of the inner ascent of the mystic to the higher realms of experience.

Doctrinally the Qabbalists saw God as the Ein Sof, the endless, ineffable, somewhat like the Neoplatonic One; but from the Ein Sof there emanate ten powers or entities, referred to as the Sefirot. Symbolically they are arranged in a diagram which represents the human form, like a great person. Different lists use different names, but they are as follows: Crown or Thought; Wisdom; Understanding; Greatness or Mercy; Power or Judgment; Grandeur; Eternity; Splendor; Foundation; Kingdom. These emanations from God are supposed to have played a part in the creation of the world. Most importantly the Qabbalists explored the techniques of meditation and ecstasy, especially Avraham Abulafia (1240–?1291), who may have been influenced by Sufism or Islamic mysticism.

One strand in Qabbalistic thought was that human acts can have divine effects. It means that somehow God needs human beings as they in turn need God. This could give Jews a more profound way of looking at the process of keeping the commandments of the Torah: such acts had their reverberations on high.

Maybe such ideas were especially satisfying during a time of increasing oppression in Christian Europe. Eventually the norm in the Middle Ages was for the Jews to be heavily segregated, less so in Eastern Europe and Russia where they could begin to open up new agricultural lands; but especially in Germany and Central Europe, where existence in the ghetto became the norm.

## The Dimensions of Judaism

We can sum up Jewish life by looking at its dimensions in the medieval period. The *ritual* life was much more fully elaborated as a result of the victory, from the fourth and fifth centuries in particular, of the religion of the rabbis. The various injunctions of both written and oral Torah controlled the various acts of daily life, serving as a constant reminder of being God's special people. The ritual dimension was in part enacted in the meetinghouse or

---

**Judaism** some key terms

*Hasidim* (or *Chasidim*) A movement founded in Eastern Europe (Ukraine and Southern Poland) in the late 18th century, with an emphasis on mysticism.

*Haskalah* 19th century Jewish enlightenment, following on the opening up of Judaism to European thought and culture.

*Israel* The land which is the focus of Jewish aspiration.

*Kabbalah* The "received tradition" of Jewish mysticism expressed in such texts as the *Zohar* (13th century Spain).

*Kashrut* Jewish dietary requirements, i.e. what is "kosher" or unpolluted, pure.

*Mashiah* The "Anointed One" or future king who will establish a new age in Israel.

*Mitzvah* (plural *Mitzvot*) commandment: there are ten main ones and traditionally 613 in all.

*Rabbi* A teacher of the traditional Torah, and learned teacher and spiritual counselor of a community.

*Shabbat* The "rest" day, from Friday sundown to sundown on Saturday.

*Talmud* A major text of the Jewish tradition, in Aramaic, being in two forms, the Babylonian and Palestinian. The former is in principle binding, as to its legal and ethical or halakhic provisions, on all orthodox Jews.

*Torah* The teaching or law, handed down in both written and oral form to Moses on Sinai: identified in written form with the first five books of the Hebrew Bible.

*Yahweh* The chief name of God in Hebrew.

---

The ritual and the narrative dimensions: the Western or "Wailing" Wall of the Temple destroyed in 70 C.E. is the most sacred spot for Jews; praying there unites them with their ancient sufferings and dedication to God. The above scene was in 1867.

synagogue but also very substantially in the home. *Ethically*, Jews were expected to keep to the high standard of the Ten Commandments and other injunctions promulgated by rabbis (for instance in the early Middle Ages an edict from a rabbinical court forbade polygymy, being married to more than one woman, even though such a practice was well attested in the Hebrew Bible and had some currency among Jews within the Islamic civilization).

In *doctrine* the insistence on strict monotheism was vital and remained so: but Jews retained a different view of revelation from the surrounding Christian culture. They looked forward to the coming of the *Mashiah*, and their whole myth of history was different from that of Christians, for whom the Anointed One had already come. The sufferings of the Jewish people were still a necessary continuation of the special dedication of this community to God. The surrounding Christian culture did not take kindly to this *myth* of history: they thought that Jews were frustratingly willful in their refusal to see the true meaning of the Old Testament (which of course they did not even see as an *Old* Testament). The vast interpretations of the Talmud and the whole idea of Oral Torah were ill understood by Christians.

*Experientially* the Jews appreciated the experiences of light and fellowship in the round of the calendar year and the rhythms of the Shabbat. They also explored the whole experience of the mystical union with the Divine, through Qabbalistic techniques. *Organizationally* they were able to retain

266

some cohesion between parts of the Jewish world through travel in pursuit of trade. Rabbinical courts were not uniform in judgment, but the vast accumulation of interpretation of the Law gave a structural resemblance between diverse parts of Judaism. In the Islamic world there was greater opening to the lovely civilization about them, which gave them some room for maneuver. Christendom glittered less and was more oppressive, so that Ashkenazim (German and North European Jews) were more driven in on themselves and so more conservative and withdrawn than the Sephardim (Jews of Spain and Portugal) and other "southern" Jews.

*Artistically*, the chief places for ornamentation and the use of material forces for religious purposes lay in the decoration of synagogues and religious manuscripts. Early synagogues contained various mosaics, depicting the Ark of the Covenant; the *menorah* or seven-branched candlestick; branches of palm trees and lemons; even signs of the zodiac. The Ark containing the scrolls of the Torah was the chief liturgical focus in the Synagogue, and the containing material came to be increasingly decorated. In early synagogue buildings there seems to have been no special place for the women, but later they came to be segregated in galleries.

As Judaism entered the Middle Ages it had to live with what appeared to be a more and more monolithic Christianity in the West. It existed among Eastern Christians also; but much of its life was passed within the Islamic world. Yet any security that they had there was threatened by reconquest. The position of the Jews in Spain became problematic as the Catholics drove the Muslims from the peninsula, slowly during the centuries up to 1492,

An Hasidic Jew pictured in Jerusalem: his face reflects the desire to experience God, but through obedience to the Torah, which has a cosmic significance and provides the outer discipline for the inner quest.

when they were finally eliminated; and that was the signal too for the expulsion of the Jews.

# Medieval Christianity

## Eastern Christianity: Outer Retreat, Inner Advance

The Seljuk Turks took Jerusalem in 1071, and this heralded disturbing times for the Byzantine empire. Their advance into Asia Minor was marked by the capture of the emperor in the same year, and soon they were at the walls of Constantinople. Their victory at Manzikert, when the emperor was taken, was a decisive affair in European history. Henceforth Asia Minor or Anatolia would become the heartland of the Turks, and the boundary between Islamic East and Christian West would lie culturally between that region and the Greek islands. Constantinople held out.

The Turks also triggered the new movements known as the Crusades. The holy places of Palestine were now closed to Christian pilgrims; so the Papacy instigated the Crusades in 1095. The First was quite successful: Jerusalem was taken and remained in Christian hands for nearly a hundred years. But the Fourth Crusade was diverted, and Constantinople was sacked. A Latin kingdom was set up there; this trauma undoubtedly weakened a restored Byzantium. A new empire, that of the Ottomans, out of Anatolia, threatened the empire and made its way deep into the Balkans. So in many ways the Greek East was on the defensive during the medieval period. The ultimate fall of Constantinople in 1453 signaled a new great captivity for the Greeks, and the center of Eastern Orthodox power shifted to Moscow, perceived now as a Third Rome, the other two (Rome itself and Constantinople) having failed in their destinies.

But during this troubled period some remarkable developments took place in Eastern piety. Monasticism was renewed, especially on Mount Athos in northern Greece, which became in 1052 a kind of self-governing monastic republic, and which concentrated on the male celibate life of contemplation and the performance of the liturgy. One of its inhabitants for a time was St. Gregory of Sinai, a famous mystic, who had so strong a bent for the solitary life that he had judged the liturgy irrelevant, and had had to leave Sinai for a wandering life. He settled in Bulgaria, where he became the prototype of the later Russian *starets* or wandering holy man. More orthodox in his mysticism, and perhaps the greatest Eastern Orthodox theologian, was St. Gregory Palamas (1296–1359). Highly educated at the court in Constantinople, he became an ascetic at the age of twenty, residing on Mount Athos for a while, practicing the methods known as Hesychasm (literally Quietism). Here the adept used physical means, including control of the breathing, in order to gain higher states of consciousness, culminating in a vision of the divine light. One fierce critic castigated the Hesychasts as being *omphalopsychoi*—people with their souls in their navels. Gregory argued that though God in himself is inaccessible and indescribable, he possesses uncreated energies: the human

The material dimension: monks gather at what is supposed to be the oldest church in the monastic republic of Mount Athos in Greece. It is a replica of the original built by Constantine.

being can participate in the light which was displayed on Mount Tabor at the transfiguration of Christ. This uncreated light appears within the human being, and can be perceived if the human being can concentrate his intellect or *nous*, which is usually distracted, since the Fall, by the things of this world. The training in Hesychasm in effect is a method for ascending to the light within.

In attaining to God's uncreated light the human in effect becomes a god: he undergoes *theosis* (a great theme in the Orthodox tradition which we saw being expressed in the fourth century by St. Athanasius). St. Gregory

269

Monks painting ikons. The ikons serve as "windows on heaven," of which the most glorious was Christ himself.

Palamas, in setting forth this scheme of salvation, repeated and summed up some of the central motifs of the Orthodox tradition, while his defence of Hesychasm ensured the important place of the contemplative quest in the life of the Church.

Although the Church had to experience the rule of the Ottomans throughout Greece and the Balkans, from the fall of Constantinople in 1453, its renewed vigor in the preceding period made possible its survival. Also the religion was making headway in Russia, and the ideal of the Third Rome helped to give Russian Orthodoxy a messianic flavor.

### Western Medieval Culture—a New Civilization
In the West the Middle Ages saw the creation of a relatively homogeneous civilization, with its center of gravity in Northern Europe, where great monastic foundations had helped with the spread of agriculture and the creation of new wealth. Monastic reform, indeed, was one of the main bases of the medieval culture. Thus the Abbey of Cluny, founded in Burgundy in

910, provided a leading powerhouse of influence and reform. Under Abbot Hugh in the eleventh century, it underwent great expansion, and established many daughter houses. Many of these were well endowed, as rich lay folk saw a division of labor in society and paid the monks to pray intensely on their behalf. The monastery of Cîteaux, also in Burgundy, took reform further, and simplified the monks' life, going back to the rule of St. Benedict; and it too had enormous outreach. It was founded at the end of the eleventh century and fifty years later had over 300 daughter houses, partly because of the effective preaching of St. Bernard of Clairvaux (1115–53). There was also reform among the nonmonastic clergy, especially through the Augustinian canons who lived together in dormitories and thought of themselves as reviving the ideals for the clergy voiced by St. Augustine of Hippo. The hierarchical character of the Church was reinforced by the increase in bureaucratization and legalism at the Papal court, modeled after a lay court. The greater pretensions of the Papacy led to a bitter struggle between secular and ecclesiastical authorities, with the Church beginning to gain the status of a parallel power-system.

Two new orders in particular were to have profound influence. First, there were the Dominicans who were brought into being by St. Dominic (1170–1221), who wanted to get together a band of preachers who would live the good life of poverty. Initially he had in mind the conversion of the so-called Albigensian heretics in the South of France. But his order had a wider role in education, and then in the exercise of the Inquisition. Second, the Franciscans, created by St. Francis of Assisi (1181/2–1226), whose strict ideal of poverty later caused some dissension among his own followers, were an influence on ordinary people through their preaching and hearing confessions in the context of a modest way of life very different from that of the princes of the Church.

The Middle Ages also saw a new mobilization of the ideals of knighthood on behalf of the Church. The Crusades created a new channel for the energy of often violent and turbulent princes and warriors. The Orders of militant monks, above all the Templars and the Teutonic Knights, who pushed the bounds of Christendom northeastward along the Baltic coast, captured some of the ascetic values of Christianity on behalf of military action: very much on the assumption that battling on behalf of Christendom was a way of fulfilling the Gospel.

It was also an age of revived learning. Through the Arabic translations and then the Latin translations of Arabic, scholars had some access to Aristotle and other Greek writers. They proved to be a stimulus to new reflections, and above all to the synthesis achieved by the Dominican St. Thomas Aquinas (1224–74), whose many and magisterial writings, especially his *Summa Theologiae* and *Summa contra Gentiles*, left a lasting stamp on Catholic thought.

Aquinas' whole system was based on a distinction between what can be known naturally by reason and what has to be derived by revelation from

271

God. The former domain is extensive, for by Five Ways, as they were called, that is five main arguments, you could establish the existence of God. God also, by these proofs, was good, intelligent, incorporeal, and so on. So a pretty large edifice of philosophy was built by Aquinas on this essentially intellectual foundation. Supplemented by revelation, it provided a great system of ideas which defined the mental basis of the Christian life. Much of his work looked to Aristotle, but Aquinas made use of many other sources, such as St. Augustine and the writings attributed to Dionysius the Areopagite, the convert of St. Paul.

The distinction thus established between reason and faith gave a definite role to the philosopher, as governed hopefully by reason, in the illumination of the Christian faith. At first Aquinas' dependence on Aristotle, then not popular, made the authorities suspicious of his doctrines, but their rigor and clarity gave them great power in later thinking.

Popular piety was far removed from such speculations: it concentrated on relics, on hearing the Mass, on pilgrimage. Holy journeys to Canterbury, Rome, Compostela, and Jerusalem created much merit for the faithful and wiped away many sins. The whole system of Crusades also was a kind of pilgrimage: great enthusiasm was generated in a newly selfconscious Christendom ready to flex its muscles against the infidel. Alas, that included the infidel at home: Jews and heretics were often persecuted. Thus, in the thirteenth

The ritual dimension: Canterbury was a major pilgrimage center in the Middle Ages. This scene depicts a group from London arriving at Canterbury Cathedral.

272

century a full-scale Crusade was undertaken in southern France against the Albigensian heresy—so called after the city of Albi, a main center—which professed a kind of Manichaean doctrine, affirming the world evil and the Church corrupt. In 1233 the Dominicans were charged with the job of rooting out the heresy. Much cruelty was involved in putting down the movement, which had a threatening effect on the Church, partly because the ethical standards of the *perfecti,* or those committed to the higher life of Albigensian religion, were notably higher than those of many of the contemporary clergy.

Also important in medieval Christianity was a flowering of mysticism. In some ways the most powerful figure was that of Johannes Eckhart (1260?–?1327), whose philosophical account of the inner experience of God was daring and exciting. For him the creature gets his very being from God: God indeed is the only being, truly speaking. The mystical life consists then in striving to be conscious of the divine being within oneself. This chimes with what Bernard of Clairvaux had said—that to reduce yourself to nothing is a divine experience. But Eckhart's theology met opposition, and some of the propositions he affirmed were condemned.

A more personalistic way of expressing the ultimate experience of union with the divine was adopted by the Flemish priest Jan van Ruusbroec (1293–1381): "In this darkness . . . is born an incomprehensible light, which is the Son of God . . ." It was also an age of women mystics of great power, above all St. Catherine of Siena (1347–80), who saw God's being as consisting in truth and love, through which he reaches out to the human beings who have cut themselves off from him by the Fall.

There were tensions in this civilization, however, heralding the split which followed from the Reformation. There was the gap between the growing vernacular languages and the official Latin of the Church—hence the suspicion with which translations of the Bible were viewed by church officials. There was the persistent question of the supposed poverty of the clergy and its contrast with the magnificence of the Papacy and many of the princes of the Church. There was the cost of many of the huge and wonderful edifices that the Church was building across Europe. There were the political tensions between the kings and princes north of the Alps and the Papacy in Rome. There were the discomforts of ecclesiastical power in many spheres.

But the culture of Western Europe was nevertheless vigorous, as was seen by the way in which it was expanded northeast and southwest. The Muslims were being driven back out of Spain. New wealth was being created in Italy. The infidels were at bay in the Mediterranean. New techniques were being pioneered for exploration, and by the fifteenth century Portuguese ships were edging their way round Africa and making landfall in the East. In 1453 the fall of Constantinople brought classical learning flooding into Europe as scholars escaped the Turks.

How should we sum up Western Christendom at this time, during its medieval dominance? It was proud, conformist, increasingly confident against the infidel, complex in doctrine and philosophy, and catering to the masses in the richness of its kinds of piety. Masses, pilgrimages, the condemnation of heretics, beautiful frescoes on church walls, stained glass windows, statues of the saints, illuminated books, vast cathedrals, soaring spires, the pomp of prelates and the vestments of priests, candles, holy water, the veneration of relics, the hope of glory and horror of hell, the time-slices of purgatory, the feast days and fasts, the processions, the preachings of Crusades and other ventures, the lives of saints, the austerities of hermits, the composure of nuns, the great abbeys of monks, the grace of the Virgin, the prayers in Latin, the solemn chants—all these contributed to a mosaic of religious practices which channeled piety towards the sacred Trinity. For the intellectual, credible; for the pious, rich in devotion; for the mystic, deep in theology; for the woman, ideal in the Virgin; for the man, a vigorous and militant faith: the Church was involved in a memorable synthesis.

It was a synthesis which would split—partly because of the Renaissance, partly because of the great voyages and the new colonial ventures, and most of all because of the religious revolution known now as the Reformation.

## Worlds that Disappeared

### The Celts

The medieval Christian world submerged the paganisms of the north and west and east. The Celtic, Germanic and Slavic religions would become a romantic memory. Yet their spirit somehow lingered on. Let us end our account of medieval Europe by sampling these religions—so far, that is, as we can get at them from our somewhat varied and partly fragmentary sources.

Caesar remarked that the god the Celts worshiped more than anyone was Mercury: he was probably identifying that god with Lugh, who occurs across the Celtic world. He was the young one who vanquished the demons. As a David type, he killed with his slingshot the giant Balar. He was the deity of the harvest who associated with deep fertility goddesses. Above all he was a symbol of sacred kingship, and presided over the other world. Later he was to merge with one or two Christian saints. In all this we have echoes of other Indo-European ideas.

Likewise with the Druids, supposedly extirpated from Britain by the Roman general Paulinus in 62 C.E. Roman accounts of the Druids are melodramatic, yet there can be little doubt that such a priestly class existed— it was part of the deep structure of Indo-European societies. Their chief function was to preside over the sacrificial life of the people. A record of the twelfth century C.E. from Ulster tells of a horse sacrifice still being performed. The king had to mate with a white mare, and then bathe in the soup made of it, eat some of its meat and lap up some of the broth. There are echoes of the Indian horse-sacrifice here, from the other end of the Indo-European world. The priests had access to sacred knowledge and could exclude a person from the sacrificial cult, thus ostracizing him from society.

As for fertility cults, these no doubt lie behind the legend that St. Patrick drove the snakes from Ireland, serpents being above all symbols of fertility. And eventually no doubt the Irish, like other Celts, could find some solace and substitutions in the new Christian order. Christ, like Lugh, as a young man defeated the hosts of Satan. And Celtic saints could easily reincarnate the goddesses. The Irish goddess of learning, a figure like the Roman Minerva, who delighted in knowledge of nature and the fruits of the earth, and commanded poetry, in effect became Saint Brigid of Kildare, whose monastery of Cell Dara was on the site of a holy oak. She and her nuns, according to a later account, guarded a perpetual fire (like Vestal Virgins, no less) surrounded by a hedge, to which no male had access.

Celtic religion was close to the other world, so that there were many points of access: caves, streams, numinous places, sacred trees of varying kinds—oaks, beeches, and holly trees. The Christian world took over many of these sacred spots to build churches, and saints were associated with healing springs and the like. The magic of the Celtic world was transformed for the sober purposes of Christian living, and to win the hearts of those whose poetry was always bubbling to the surface.

## The Vikings

The Scandinavian seafarers were remarkably effective, and sometimes destructive, in their foraging into foreign lands to settle. They dominated the east coast of Ireland and the Isle of Man, southern and western Scotland, England, Normandy, the Baltic coasts, the rivers of Russia, Iceland, and parts of Greenland. Their impact upon monasteries in the Christian West was often severe. But eventually they too succumbed to the seductions of Christian ideology. In this they were helped by some of the figures of the Scandinavian pantheon.

In the great religious center at Uppsala there were images of the three great deities Odin, Thor, and Frey. Odin is the father of all, master magician, knower of great runes (or *mantras* as we might say, looking to India), dealer in law, ruler of the underworld. Thor is lord of the air and thunder, and is a great warrior deity, given to taking great drafts of intoxicating drinks, and so somewhat like Indra. If Odin is master of the priestly power, Thor incarnates the warrior power; while Frey deals in fertility. His mount is a swift boar, which was in this ancient world a fine edible creature. His sister Freya is the most powerful of the female divinities, very promiscuous, who has sex with all the gods, thus giving them vital power.

This quartet is far removed in spirit from the Trinity and the Virgin. But the hero Balder, son of Odin, is of a different cast: young and beautiful, he has nightmares. His mother Frigg makes all things swear never to harm her son, but forgets the mistletoe. One of the gods, blind Loki, throws a branch of it at him; it pierces him, and he dies. He is buried with his grieving and dying wife in a ship. The goddess of the nether world will not release him unless all things weep for him—and they all do, save one giantess. He will not return till after history finishes in the great storm of Ragnarök. This end-of-the-world motif is very vivid, and came to be reinforced in Christian times. It is the twilight of the gods, *Götterdämmerung*.

Some scholars think that the myth of Balder owes something to Christian influence. It may be so; but in the form I have just set forth it is of course thoroughly "paganized," and the new Christian message coming from missionaries would still sound fresh and call forth echoes. But in the dark and stormy world of Germanic myth the atmosphere is very different from the medieval Christian myth, wrapped in its clothing of learning and reason which lay far beyond what counted for knowledge on old runic shores.

## Slavic Themes

Again in the Slavic lands we find the dominating force of the Indo-European gods. And yet below them we can also see the lineaments of an ancient pre-Indo-European goddess, who deals in death and fertility, who is both a hag and a virgin, a sign of matrilineal society, a moist Earth Mother, pregnant before the spring. The white god Belobog is ruler of the day and year, and contends against darkness and death. In the Slavic world the bipolar oppositions are powerful: light and dark, day and night, life and death. There is almost a Zoroastrian feel to pre-Christian Slav religion. Among the gods Perun, god of thunder and associated with the oak, was powerful in dispensing justice and in fighting against enemies. And as elsewhere the ancestors were strong to protect folk. When a rich person died he was dressed up in his finery and seated in a boat, to take him to the other shore. His weapons were placed around him. His wife was stabbed and seated beside him, to share in his life beyond life. The boat and all the finery and goods were burnt in a great blaze, and feasting would continue for days; and then people would be careful in maintaining the cult of the dead for the days and months and years to come.

The round Slav temples on hilltops, with images of the gods within (images which have virtually all perished), might give kings and chiefs power here and there. But with the building up of Kiev as a city, new knowledge and new values had to be taken up. Islam had its advantages as an ideology; and Judaism had been taken up by the Khazars. But as it happened it was the Orthodoxy of the Byzantine empire which had the greatest appeal, and so Christ had to be identified with the god of light, and Satan with death and darkness. The light had to be found within, in the mysticism of the Church.

It was these and other forms of culture across the North European plain which were absorbed and submerged in the new Christianity. It turned out that the poetry of the Celts, the story-telling of the Scandinavians, and the religious intuitions of the Slavic peoples, took new forms in Christian civilization. The Cross was pictured like a world-tree, Yggdrasil, with the judgment seat of the new God beneath it, and Christ not Odin hanging from it. Thus the fusion of North and Christian South sets the seal on European medieval civilization.

# 12

# *Classical and Medieval Islam*

## Islam—an Overview of its Spread

Islam, the religion of Submission (as its name indicates) to the one God, took off from the northwest part of Arabia in the seventh century and rapidly spread north and west. It went north into Palestine and Syria, Iraq and Iran, and into Central Asia. It went west into Egypt, Libya, Tunisia, Algeria, Morocco, Spain, and Portugal. Beginning with Muhammad's migration from Mecca to Medina in 622, the political rule of Islam expanded with amazing rapidity. By 664 the new empire had taken Kabul in Afghanistan and by 670 Kairouan in Tunisia. By 732 it was beyond Bukhara and Samarkand in Central Asia, and fighting at Poitiers in France (where however it was defeated). This first phase, till the establishment of the Abbasid dynasty and the shift of the capital to Mesopotamia, may be called the early period. From 750 to 1258, the time of the Abbasid rule over all or part of Islamic territories, was what may be termed the classical period. Then from the mid-thirteenth century C.E. until the impact of Western powers in the colonial experience—until roughly the eighteenth century—we have what may be called the medieval or premodern period.

Altogether Islam became the dominant religion over the whole of the Arab Middle East, along the shores of North Africa, across the Sahara in northern West Africa, through much of East Africa down to Kenya, through Iran, Afghanistan, and what is now Soviet Central Asia, in north and northeast India, in Malaysia and Indonesia, in Turkey and a part of the Balkans. It is a significant minority religion in the Indian subcontinent as a whole, and in Thailand, the Philippines, China, Madagascar, Yugoslavia, and Tanzania. Broadly, it stretches in a crescent from the eastern tip of Indonesia to West Africa. Though the religion has strong Arab cultural ingredients, above all in

Map 9 Islam from
Africa to India

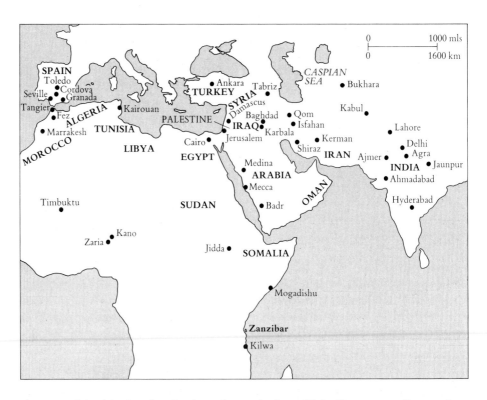

the use of Arabic for the Qur'an, the majority of Muslims come from other
cultures. The most populous Islamic countries are in South and Southeast
Asia: Indonesia, Pakistan, Bangladesh, and the Republic of India.

Islam established its main outline very rapidly, partly because it had a single
founder, namely Muhammad, partly because it had a foundation document,
namely the Qur'an, and partly because in having a political aspect it had to
take rapid decisions on organization in view of its great success. The story of
the religion turns of course very considerably on the life of the Prophet, and
with that we begin.

## The Life of the Messenger of Allah

The Prophet Muhammad was born in Mecca, which at that time, probably in
570 C.E., was a highly prosperous place. This was because of its strategic
position across the routes from the eastern Mediterranean, and from such rich
cities as Damascus, to the ports which served the trade to India and Sri Lanka.
It was also even then a sacred city, for it contained the sacred building, the
Ka'bah. Accordingly it was the scene of annual pilgrimage from the tribes
round about; and the area round the Ka'bah was a sanctuary during certain
months, thus moderating the impact of tribal warfare. The dominant tribe in
Mecca, to which Muhammad belonged, was the Quraysh. His father and
mother died when he was young, and he was raised by relatives. As a young

man he found himself without the capital necessary to engage in trading; but a wealthy widow, Khadijah, employed him and subsequently married him. Though he became active in trade, he had had opportunities for reflection: he is said to have spent a month each year meditating in a cave near Mecca.

It was in 610 that he began to have some striking religious experiences which set him off in his career as a messenger of Allah. To begin with he mentioned his revelations only to his family and close associates; but after about three years he began his public career. His message was not altogether welcome for at least two reasons. First, in attacking polytheism, which he came to do with increasing clarity, he threatened the livelihood of those who depended on Meccan shrines: and in any case in such matters people tend to be conservative. Second, the ethic he pronounced was not fully in accord with the money-making policy of the rich merchants of the city: everyone would have to appear in the end before the judgment seat of the mighty God. Later, too, Muhammad would be involved in conveying revelations which altered the legal shape of society, especially in regard to marriage.

His message made little headway at first in Mecca, though he accumulated some fifty loyal followers. In 620 and 621 he received feelers from the city of Medina to the north, and in due course, in 622, he was invited to migrate there and take up the leadership. The city and area had been in a state of faction for a number of years, and the hope was that Muhammad with his diplomatic skills and unifying message would be able to bring harmony to Medina. This he did and came to control its political affairs. Then began an armed struggle against the Quraysh and the people of Mecca; and in 624 he defeated them in battle at Badr. After a few years of intermittent struggle Muhammad entered Mecca and became its leader. A battle shortly thereafter, at Hunayn, disposed of some of the outlying tribes, and Muhammad was master of a large slice of Arabia. Already he had plans for conquests in Syria and Iraq. But in June 632 he died.

He was a considerable military and political leader, magnanimous and decisive, and had behind him the assurance of faith, as a result of his prophetic experiences. To Muslims he is an ideal figure, someone to be admired and followed, and seen as virtually perfect—the finest of human beings, to whom Allah entrusted his final revelation. Though Muslims are of course much opposed to any attempt to deify Muhammad—for that would be to set up another god beside God, which is the deadliest sin—in practice he is the supreme ethical ideal and more closely followed than Christ, partly because of the accumulation of biographical stories about him. These traditions, or *hadith*, are carefully sifted according to traditional methods, and constitute in effect a secondary source of revelation to that which is contained in the holy Qur'an.

## The Prophet and His Experiences of Revelation

Muhammad seems to have started his religious career as Prophet in part because of his first experiences, which were of a numinous character. There

279

*Opposite* The narrative dimension: Muslims swearing allegiance to the Imam 'Alī at Kufa after the murder of 'Uthman the Khalif— this is a vital part of the narrative of the beginnings of the Shi'a.

There is only the One, and all subject-object consciousness disappears. When he returns to the world the mystic experiences *baqa'* or "survival," in which he sees the Many in the light of the One. The One manifests itself as a determinate God and as the world of creation. There are resemblances between Ibn al-'Arabi's system and that of Advaita Vedānta in the Indian tradition, and he was to have an influence on Dante Alighieri.

As well as the poetical, philosophical, legal, and other riches of the Spanish Muslim tradition, there were great architectural achievements, such as the Great Mosque in Córdoba and the wonderful Alhambra palace in Granada.

### Developments after the Mongol Incursion

The thirteenth century was a terrible era of devastation, because of the irruption of the Mongols, initially under the leadership of Genghis Khan. In the first years of the century the Muslim centers of Central Asia were destroyed, along with much of the Persian empire. In 1256 Hülegü Khan, Genghis's grandson, sacked Baghdad and slaughtered large numbers of Muslims. The Mongol successor state in Persia, the Il-Khan principality, was eventually won over to Islam, so that the Mongol rulers began to favor the faith. Later, Turkish power under Timur caused devastation across Central Asia and into India, where the Muslim capital of Delhi was sacked. But a descendant of Timur, Babur, established his rule in Delhi and founded the Mughal Empire, which turned out to be a great patron of both Islam and the arts.

Meanwhile, though the Mongols had struck at the rising Ottoman regime, the latter was to make its way in Asia Minor. Turkish in texture, it ultimately conquered the Byzantine empire and established rule over most of the territories formerly ruled by it, in a kind of alliance between Muslims and Christians. In the fifteenth century, although Islam was driven out of Spain, in much of the rest of the world it underwent a renaissance. It was penetrating deeply into Indonesia and Malaya. It made its way through the patronage of the Mughals in India. It was busy crossing the Sahara and moving into Black Africa. Though the Middle Ages of Islam brought it into conflict with rising European power, it was nevertheless a constructive period. In Central Asia, in India and in Ottoman territories, rich varieties of architectural style, calligraphy and painting flourished.

### Islam in Central and South Asia

During the reign of Timur, who was a pious Muslim, virtually all non-Muslim practice in Central Asia was wiped out. But a great part of the consolidation of Islam in the region was due to the work of the Sufi orders. As elsewhere in the Muslim world, the tombs of mystics became more potent often than mosques in the popular imagination, and the houses where adepts met and were to be seen in prayer became symbols of the new piety. It was in Bukhara that the influential Naqshbandi order was founded in the fourteenth century; it penetrated both intellectual and unlettered circles. The tomb of its

founder, outside of the city of Bukhara, became a famous place of pilgrimage in the region. Other orders, by introducing shamanistic practices, also helped to bridge the worlds of Islam and indigenous religion.

The Mughals in India created a fine syncretic civilization, incorporating Central Asian and Indian motifs. Admittedly the emperor Akbar failed in his attempt to found a pluralistic ideology for his rule, and there were also severe Hindu-Islamic tensions, especially during the reign of his successor Aurungzeb. Perhaps the most creative of all the Mughals was Shah Jahan, who came to the throne in 1627, and was the ultimate creator of the Red Fort and the Taj Mahal, blending Persian and Indian themes in a great new architectural synthesis. Also wonderful was Akbar's city of Fatehpur Sikri, which was eventually left empty because it had no assured water supply.

In India, as in Central Asia, a great part of the missionary activity on behalf of the faith was done by Sufi orders. The figure of the Sufi master was a familiar one, with echoes of guru, *sadhu* and yogin. The Sufi orders were willing to move away into peripheral places, and not stick to the centers of power. They made use of vernacular languages, from Bengali to Tamil, and they also participated in the widespread *bhakti* style of religion of the period. They involved themselves in social rites to provide a counterpoint to Hindu society. Sometimes the Muslim wandering ascetics looked very much like Hindu ones, and were scarcely respectable by ordinary Muslim standards, e.g. in their relative nakedness, use of smeared ashes, and so forth. For some, becoming Muslim was socially advantageous, and the Hindu world had to pay penalties for untouchability.

At a more intellectual level, the influence of Ibn al-'Arabi was great, since he presented a point of view congenial to the Hindu mystical tradition. Also important later on, from the time of Aurungzeb, was the spread of well-endowed teaching institutions or *madrasahs* which could create a class of indigenous scholars of Islamic teaching and law.

*Opposite* The material dimension: the great glory of Islamic civilization is revealed in its wonderful and graceful architecture — seen here in a mosque in Isfahan in Iran.

## Dimensions of Medieval Islam

In reflecting upon the achievements of medieval Islam, we can see something of its varieties in the different dimensions of religion.

*Ritually*, it had its unity because of the *hajj* and the patterns of daily prayer, virtually universal throughout the length and breadth of Islam, from Indonesia to West Africa and from Bukhara to Zanzibar. But in many areas folk religion had gradually decreed the sacredness of the tombs of saints, thus blending popular piety and the inner pursuit of union with Allah. The cycles of the Muslim year were not the same for Sunnis and Shi'a, especially because of the mourning of the death of Husayn.

*Experientially* there remained tensions between those who saw Islam in terms of orthodox prayer, and the sense of the numinous majesty of Allah, and those who saw the central experience as lying in and beyond *fana'*. Such tensions also involved diverse ways of interpreting texts and the role of the Prophet.

Legally and *ethically*, Islam had its medieval variations, and the need to adapt to very different societies had its effects. But the world of the *madrasahs* was relatively uniform, and prestige was attached to great centers of learning and law such as al-Azhar. There were similar centers in the Shi'i world, for instance the holy city of Qum in Iran, with its academies and leading scholars. At the edge of Islam there were sects with a reputation for flouting the law, such as the Isma'ilis.

In *doctrine*, we have great riches of philosophical diversity, from the somewhat assertive positivism of al-'Ashari to the problematic ideas of the Aristotelian, Ibn Rushd (who as Averroes was so influential in the discussions of the Latin-speaking world), and from the rationalistic (but fading) Mu'tazilah to the luxuriant thought of Ibn al-'Arabi. In *myth*, the chief divergences were about the Imams and the nature of the hidden Imam. Ibn Khaldun (1332–1406), the famous Islamic historian, could give a balanced view on the nature of the Caliphate and the question of the end of the world, both recurrent themes in political and popular speculation.

*Institutionally*, Islam had no priesthood and no central hierarchy: even political power was thoroughly fragmented by the medieval period, though the Ottomans could claim a wide sway over many of the heartlands of the faith and so could have claims to the Caliphate. Establishments were informal and depended much on reputation. There were scarcely any controls, other than consensus, on Islam as a system: and the surprising thing is not its diversity—which was great—but its degree of homogeneity.

In the arts and the *material* side of religion, medieval Islam saw a vast flowering of the poetical heritages, the architectural achievements, the literary creations, the calligraphic varieties and painting schools of the diverse empires, from the Ottomans to the Mughals, and from Morocco to Indonesia. But it was an uncertain civilization, for it was already coming into conflict and contact with new forces from the West which heralded catastrophes and unexpected conquests. Why should it be that the great faith which the Prophet had conveyed to the Arabs, and the Arabs to the world, was destined for trouble, worse than that brought by Genghis Khan?

CHAPTER

# *Classical African Religions*

## The Configurations of Africa

The traditional religions of Africa before the colonial period divide roughly into four groups. Firstly, there is old Christianity, which in its Coptic form is present in Ethiopia and has had a long history, from at least the fourth century C.E. There has also, secondly, been a community of Jews there. Thirdly, there is Islam, which occupies most of North Africa, though traditionally there are some Christians, including the Coptic Church in Egypt, scattered in among the Muslim majority. Islam has also come south, across the Sahara to much of West Africa, and into the Horn of Africa, the Sudan, and beyond. Then, finally, there are what may be called the classical (traditional) religions of black Africa. It is with these latter that we are concerned in this chapter.

During the period up to 1500 C.E., Trans-Saharan trade from the Muslim countries of North Africa stimulated the creation of larger kingdoms to the south—for instance the empire of Ghana in the interior of West Africa, from the eighth to the eleventh centuries, and its successor Mali, at its peak in the fourteenth century. There was also the state of Songhay and important Hausa trading cities in what is now northern Nigeria. In Nigeria and to the west were the forest kingdoms of Oyo, Benin, and Akan. Further east, in the fifteenth century, there was the Funj empire in the Sudan. Various nomadic peoples were filtering south through Africa, among them Bantu-speaking groups. In Zimbabwe, between 1200 and 1500, and in the lower Zaire, in the region of Kongo, were other concentrations of culture and power. Some of these developments were affected by the incoming European influence which had become more marked with Portuguese settlements and expeditions from the fifteenth century. But the dearth of written records means that it is hard to penetrate clearly into the early period.

Map 10 Africa

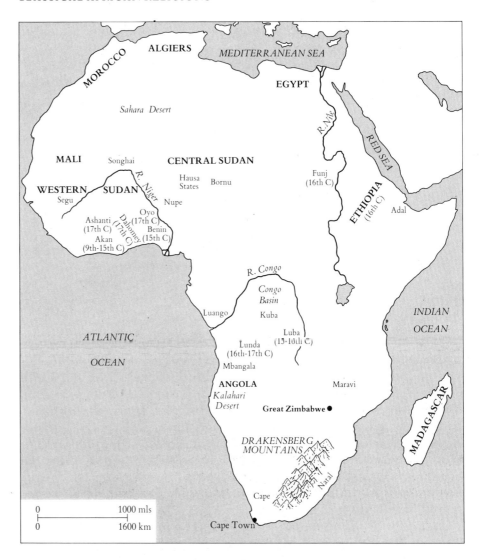

It is also, of course, hard to say that there is anything precisely common which we can label as African religion: it is only in recent times that African self-consciousness has arisen. Yet there are themes which recur. What we shall do is survey what we can know about religion as it existed when European contacts began. Classical religion of course was to be deeply affected by the colonial experience, and that is the theme of later discussion. So also is the emergence of Afro-American religions in the Caribbean, Brazil and North America as a consequence of the slave trade.

The creation of kingdoms in the medieval period involved the formation of an ideology of divine kingship, which can still be found in the classical religions of West Africa in particular. This was a natural change, but not of course without conflict, and so we find some traces in ritual of the fight which local cults put up in face of imperial pretensions. As elsewhere in human culture, kings were often associated with the fertility of the land. Generally speaking we are looking at a period after the introduction of settled agricultural practice (often necessary to create the wealth to sustain a widespread monarchy), and this itself tended to breed cults related to the production of riches from the land. These could be grafted on to the kingly ideology. It seems to be the case that the ideal of the sacred king was arrived at in several places in Africa independently, a testimony to the human force of certain ideas with new economic and political developments.

Changes in the practice of agriculture spread south from the Sahara from about 1500 C.E. onwards, with shrines emerging related to the promotion of the fertility of crops. Other changes occurred with the introduction of new technology, notably ironworking. It is therefore worth bearing in mind that much of our evidence relates to a period which is the result of a variety of changes in religious as well as social organization and ideas.

## Dimensions of African Religion

### Some Doctrinal Themes

Mostly, the *doctrinal* content of African religion is anthropomorphic: that is, gods and spirits, those unseen forces which explain and affect human life, are

A Bushman or San woman, belonging to the diminishing group of hunters and gatherers around the Kalahari desert, who represent an ancient non-Bantu population of small, yellow-skinned peoples; her face-paint is designed to ward off threatening spirits.

stories tell of a founder, Oduduwa, and this probably reflects some historic memory of the usurpation of power and the foundation of the people. One of the most vital feasts of the sacred year is the annual celebration of male ancestors, which takes the form of a stately procession and masquerade in which the participants are clothed in swathes of material which whirl outward in constantly changing forms, making the ancestors manifest. Another festival, the feast of the mothers, celebrates female power. Other celebrations deal with the founders of towns, and with the dialectical relations between chief and priest, king and sacred expert.

At the head of the extensive pantheon of *oriṣa* (gods, conceived of typically as having originally been humans, who through their great achievements attain high status in the afterlife) is Olorun. The other gods are thought of as his children. They are reckoned to be 401 in number. Olorun is not worshiped directly, though in recent times some shrines dedicated to him have been founded: the assumption is made that offerings to the lesser gods make their way to Olorun, so that many rituals end with the formula: "May Olorun accept it." Again, he did not create the world directly but deputed this task to Obatala, though it was Oduduwa who actually finished off the job. There was a great battle between him and Obatala, which is ritually reenacted. The banishment of Obatala is followed by his being invited back again amid great rejoicing.

The many gods in fact represent the greatly fragmented character of Yoruba society, and so the various gods are favorites in different places. To some extent the breaking up of Yoruba society is a modern phenomenon, dating primarily from nineteenth-century struggles for power. Olorun therefore also expresses a sense of ultimate unity. Moreover, he is the determiner of individual destinies. Before birth a person's guardian soul kneels before the great God and a destiny and time of life is fixed. Some variations may be possible later, but the span of life remains inflexibly destined. If you have followed a good life, Olorun will judge you worthy after death, and after a short while you will be reincarnated. Those who lead a bad life are consigned to a hot place of destruction and punishment.

Of all the gods of Yoruba religion the most widely found and effective is Ogun, deity of iron and war and hunters, a kind of celestial Bismarck. To him is sacrificed the dog, who can help in hunting and war. His fierce character betrays the human fact that we live off the destruction of others, and a people safeguards its identity by making war on others: for otherwise they would swallow your people up. And eating necessitates such activities as the hunt, the primordial activity of the human race before even the plants were tamed, still less the animals.

The rituals of sacrifice have power to bring the spirits into the presence of the worshiper, and to channel the numinous power which pervades the cosmos. Despite the many spirits in the Yoruba pantheon, the conception of the world both seen and unseen is a unified one.

A shrine to Ogun, God of Iron and War, at Ije in Nigeria: characteristically this spirit has no covered shrine, but lives by the roadside.

## Nuer Religion

The Nuer, like their close relations the Dinka, herd cattle amid the great savannas and marshes of the southern Sudan. Their life centers on cattle, so that alliances and rifts reflect themselves in gifts and thefts of beasts. They traditionally looked upon themselves as the only true humans, assigning to other groups only a shadowy existence. So their world was sky and grassland and cattle and constant wandering migrations—in many ways a beautiful and easy life, yet marred by human strife from time to time. The great spiritual being or force is Kwoth, who dwells in the sky but also pervades life, either through his own energy or in the form of lesser spirits of the sky and of the earth. These beings are sometimes threatening and difficult, bringing sickness and misfortunes; but Kwoth himself is benevolent. Sometimes the problems besetting people are caused by sins they have committed, and sacrifices will restore the situation.

We see here something of a simplified pattern of relation between the many gods and the one Spirit. It reflects a comparatively simple society, which has priests but no elaboration of kingship and the like. It was the British anthropologist E. E. Evans-Pritchard whose *Nuer Religion*, published in 1956, helped to change many attitudes to African religion: first, because he took religion seriously as an independent variable at a time when others often saw it as a mere side effect of social relationships; and second, more importantly, because his account of Kwoth made the deity sound much closer in idea and feeling to God as understood in the known theistic traditions than had other accounts of African divinity. And rightly so: though Kwoth is especially associated with the sky, and the rainbow is imagined as the necklace of God, so it was too with Yahweh, and Jesus' prayer does start "Our Father who art in heaven . . ."

## Mbuti Religion

If we now move southwest from the Sudan into the rain forest of the Ituri in Central Zaire, we come upon one of the Pygmy peoples who live their lives in a difficult environment in which every expedition for game is fraught with danger. For most of their history, such Pygmies have lived in their own secluded way, and it is only recently that they have been in communication with the wider world. Theirs is no doubt a vanishing mode of life.

Their world is a dense tropical rain forest, full of haunting calls and the screeches of birds, and the chatter of wild animals. Their life is hunting and gathering, and hunting is a vital part of their fight for existence. There is in their religion the sense that the world was created by a God who retired to the sky: a *deus otiosus*. More important is the divine culture hero, Tore, who is responsible for endowing the Mbuti with fire and other arts, for instance skills in hunting and the collection of honey, an important part of their diet. The forest itself is replete with divine forces, which must be dealt with, and the dead are merged into the forest to take their place among such spirits.

The Mbuti have fairly extensive initiations, for instance for girls. The ceremonial known as Elima occurs when a girl first menstruates. She and others in similar condition are secluded in a special hut in the forest for several weeks and receive instructions from the older women about what they need to know. This includes the music which women sing. Indeed, music forms an important ingredient in the invocations of the forest spirits, and in order to revive the life of the forest after some calamity, such as the death of a member of the village. Ceremonials here are postulated on the thought that the divinity behind the forest has caused it to sleep and not to look after human beings, and it is for such a reason that death has come into the life of the group: the forest needs to be roused if it is to resume its beneficent aspect. Pygmy groups also celebrate a ritual of apology to the spirit of the animals

that they have killed—something which is reminiscent of bear rituals in Northern Siberia. One cannot fail to be impressed by the echoes sounding from one hunting society to another.

*Mbuti pygmy women of the Ituri rain forest in Zaire. They are hunter-gatherers without much degree of internal social differentiation and live in symbiosis with the Divinity surrounding them and permeating the forest.*

### Zulu Religion

It is only a little over 150 years since the Zulu were welded together as a people, in the beautiful rolling hills of Natal, beneath the great ranges of the Drakensberg Mountains. Since then great changes have occurred, including the conversion of most Zulus to various forms of Christianity, including Zulu Zionism. That is something we shall have to look at in Part II.

Zulu religion as such blends together some old themes, including the story of death recounted earlier, in this case how the lizard outstripped the chameleon, both of these creatures being despatched by uMvelinqangi, the first being to come into existence. He is also credited with bestowing on humanity their ancestors and the customs for dealing with them. These ancestors, known as *amadlozi*, are important in Zulu thought, which sees the world as having a large invisible community stretching beyond the human. Ancestors more than three generations back are settled and not threatening, but later than that they need to be appeased—so that they may settle—with the offering of sacrifices such as goats. After death rituals are performed to bring the shade of the departed into the community of the ancestors. The senior males are involved in managing such rituals, which gives them authority in settling disputes, since the *amadlozi* are involved in the processes of harmonizing the community. The king's ancestors are traditionally called on before battle, and were important for the welfare of the whole nation.

An important deity is a great fertility deity, iNkosazana, the Princess of Heaven, who is invoked before agricultural activities, many undertaken by women. They may plant a special small field for her beside a river if possible, and such an offering may generate fertility. She also plays a vital role in the initiatory ceremonies for girls as they enter upon puberty. The role of women is ambiguous in Zulu society, since they form a bridge between different patrilineages, and have an outsider status in their husband's group, but nevertheless form a vital part of the transmission of lineages. The diviners are predominantly women and have central roles in the cure of sicknesses and othe disharmonies. Women are specially subject to possession by spirits, and when this occurs it gives them shamanic powers.

But the traditional cosmology is fading under the impact of wars, land seizure, and other ills which have befallen the Zulu people in the last hundred years or more. That, as I have said, is a later story.

## Reflections on African Religion

We have had glimpses of diverse societies — the urban kingship of the Yoruba, the pastoral simplicity of life among the Nuer, the green menace of Pygmy forest life, the great cattle-rearing society of the Zulu — which provide a sample of thousands of societies and religions. We have noted some themes from the dimensions of classical religion. Though there is some talk of revival of these ancient ways today, it is likely that their future lies within some larger synthesis, not only between differing African societies and conceptions, but also between them and the forces which have been crowding into Africa from outside. African religion is a deeply important facet of human history up to the modern period. It will remain a resource for Black Africans, and more widely for humans. But it has never been a single system, or even approximated to the sense of a single tradition which has marked some of the historical world religions.

If there is now a sense of African unity, it is due to the reaction against a threatening colonialism. It is to the history of this colonialist epoch in the world's affairs that we now turn.

*Above* The social dimension: in a number of West African contexts kingship is integral to social organization, and the king may play a role as intermediary between heaven and earth; shown here is a beautiful burial mask from the Ashante in Ghana.

*Right* A fine Yoruba sculpture of the fourteenth or fifteenth century C.E. Yoruba culture survived, though in somewhat fragmented form, in some of the Afro-American groups whom slavery transported to the Western hemisphere.

*Overleaf, top* The ritual dimension: masked dancers among the Dogon, whose subtle and complex cosmological doctrines are reflected both in the material layout of their villages and in the organization of ceremonial life.

*Overleaf, bottom* The ritual dimension: among the Dinka of the Sudan the leadership role is played by priestly persons known as Spearmasters. Here a funeral ritual is followed by relatives crawling over and around the grave. In the background is an ox that has been sacrificed.

PART

2

*Opposite* Martin Luther and his friends. At the center is John Frederick, Elector of Saxony, with Luther to the left and the famous theologian Ulrich Zwingli to the right; on the extreme right is Philipp Melanchthon.

sometimes welcoming, often hostile. The religious possibilities were limited, and they were all realized in the ensuing drama of the way Judaism and Jewishness figured in the modern world. In nationalism, it turned out there lay a deadly enemy: for it was a form of nationalism that fueled the Nazi party, and with it the Holocaust.

## Russia and the New Learning; the Drive East

Because the Muslims in the shape of the Ottoman empire had more or less occupied the territories of the old Byzantine empire, this whole swath of Eastern Orthodoxy was cramped for living and breathing space. It continued to survive under the Ottomans, but its possibilities as part of the so-called Millet system (which allowed for subcommunities such as Christians and Jews to follow their own laws and to be administered through their own leaders) were limited. But Russia, already vast and destined to acquire an even vaster empire to the east, was there to represent the Faith. Moscow was to be the Third Rome, destined in hope to lead the forces of the faith in the restoration of a purified and true Christianity, now that the second Rome was conquered and the first Rome was corrupted and weakened by Protestantism. Although Christianity was established first at Kiev, this center of power was shattered by the Mongols, and though there were important other Christian centers at Novgorod and Pskov these fought a hard battle for self-preservation against the Teutonic Knights pushing forwards from Prussia. It was Moscow, therefore, which succeeded in becoming the new capital, and in the late sixteenth century its archbishop was dignified with the title of Patriarch and became the major Orthodox religious leader outside of Islamic captivity.

After the defeat of the Mongols of the Khanate of Kazan in eastern Russia in 1552, the way was open for the annexation of lands to the east. By 1689 virtually all of Siberia was taken over, mainly because of the lucrative fur trade. Under Peter the Great (reigned 1682–1725) and Catherine the Great (reigned 1762–96), Russia conquered areas of the northwest and of the Black Sea coastal region which enabled it to open up new seaports at St. Petersburg and Odessa, greatly enhancing trade. But Peter's modernization also involved controlling the Church: the Patriarchate was abolished, not to be restored till 1918, and the Church was ruled by a synod. Already there had been schism: in the seventeenth century Patriarch Nikon (1605–81) had tried to bring in reforms of the ritual, including the use of three fingers rather than two for making the sign of the Cross, and this was seen as impugning the special calling of Moscow to be the Third Rome. What Nikon was trying to do was to bring Russian practice in line with that of Byzantium. A large breakaway group known as Old Ritualists or Old Believers continued in the old ways, despite persecution. The majority of Ukrainians, for separate—largely nationalist—reasons, constituted themselves the Uniate Ukrainian Church, in communion with Rome but using Eastern rituals and customs.

The new lands to the east, which extended into Alaska in North America,

Map 12 *Overleaf* European Colonial Empires 1914

ALASKA

DOMINION OF CANADA

UNITED STATES OF AMERICA

MEXICO

CUBA

JAMAICA

BRITISH HONDURAS

PANAMA

BRITISH GUIANA
DUTCH GUIANA
FRENCH GUIANA

SOUTH AMERICA

NETHERLANDS
GREAT
BRITAIN

BELGIUM

PORTUGAL

SPAIN

FRANCE

ITAL

MOROCCO

RIO DE ORO

FRENCH WES
AFRICA

GAMBIA
PORTUGUESE GUINEA

SENEGAL

SIERRA
LEONE
LIBERIA

NIGE

CAMEROONS
FRENCH CONGO

GERMAN WEST –
SOUTH AFRICA

Colonial powers in 1914

British

French

German

Portuguese

Ottoman

Dutch

Italian

Spanish

Belgian

Russian

0                    2000 mls

0

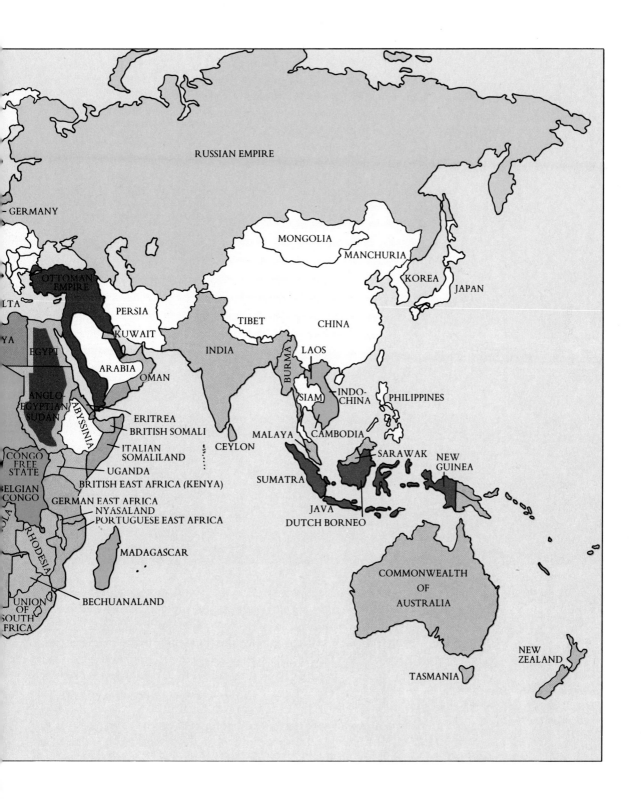

RUSSIAN EMPIRE

GERMANY

OTTOMAN
EMPIRE

MONGOLIA

MANCHURIA

KOREA

JAPAN

LTA

PERSIA

KUWAIT

TIBET

CHINA

YA

EGYPT

ARABIA

OMAN

INDIA

BURMA

LAOS

ANGLO
EGYPTIAN
SUDAN

ABYSSINIA

ERITREA
BRITISH SOMALI

SIAM

INDO-
CHINA

PHILIPPINES

CONGO
FREE
STATE

ITALIAN
SOMALILAND

UGANDA

MALAYA

CAMBODIA

CEYLON

BELGIAN
CONGO

BRITISH EAST AFRICA (KENYA)

SARAWAK

NEW
GUINEA

GERMAN EAST AFRICA
NYASALAND
PORTUGUESE EAST AFRICA

SUMATRA

RHODESIA

MADAGASCAR

JAVA
DUTCH BORNEO

UNION
OF
SOUTH
FRICA

BECHUANALAND

COMMONWEALTH
OF
AUSTRALIA

NEW
ZEALAND

TASMANIA

In contrast to the Reformation simplicity a new ornateness pervaded the revived Roman Catholic Church. This Jesuit church in Antwerp signified the vigor of the new Order which was a powerful instrument of the papacy in the struggle for converts.

were subject to considerable missionary activity in the eighteenth and nineteenth centuries. This was also a time of revived spiritual life. The practice of Hesychasm was brought in from Mount Athos, and texts of Greek spirituality were translated. The figure of the holy elder (the *starets*) became a regular feature of Church life: a person who by his charismatic personality and saintliness was reckoned to have treasures to teach—somewhat like the Hindu guru, but in the very different religious and cultural milieu of Russia. The most famous of all such holy men was St. Serafim of Sarov (1759–1833), who entered the monastery of Sarov as a young man on the advice of a *starets*. From 1793 till 1815 he lived as a hermit near the monastery; in the years 1815–25, retiring to a cell, he was inspired by divine revelation to counsel

340

people and speak with them. For him the heart of the Christian life was experiencing the grace of the Holy Spirit; and the light of the Spirit reportedly shone from his countenance for those who approached him for healing, advice, and prophecy.

Such figures had profound influence on some of the great writers of Russia, including Fyodor Dostoyevsky (1821–81) and Leo Tolstoy (1828–1910). They in turn formulated profound religious ideas in their writings. Dostoyevsky, in his famous novel *The Brothers Karamazov*, portrayed a *starets*, Father Zosima, who presented anew the ancient Christian faith, but purified in a way by the scarifying critique of God produced by Ivan in the novel, and his story of the Grand Inquisitor of Spain who gives short shrift to a returning Jesus. Tolstoy in his later years preached a simple love and pacifism which were to earn him excommunication from Orthodoxy but the gratitude of M. K. Gandhi, whose mind he helped to form.

But despite the Orthodox Church's strength, clouds around it were forming. The Russia of the late nineteenth century was divided between modernizing Westerners—often armed with strange new revolutionary theories, from liberalism to anarchism—and Russophiles who put their faith in the old Russia, the wisdom of the peasant, the holy mission of Russia in a suffering world, and so forth. In 1861 the serfs were liberated, and Russia embarked on a new wave of modernization. But its effects were vitiated by poor leadership. In 1905 Russia was humiliated by the Japanese at the land battle of Mukden and the sea battle of Tsushima. Unrest gave a foretaste of revolution, as workers demonstrated in the streets and troops shot them down. The doom of the monarchy and of the old order was sealed by defeat in World War I: with that collapse there came revolution.

Meanwhile it should be noted that Tsarist expansion had continued as the frontier of the Empire was driven south through Central Asia, so that now it contained a substantial Muslim population on the borders of Afghanistan and Iran.

# Modern Europe

## Developments in Christianity in Western Europe

The new knowledge and the new methods of enquiry stimulated by the Enlightenment involved elements which were to prove a threat to Biblically based Christianity. The use of history in a modern manner to probe the past rather than just to tell a story inevitably began to raise questions about the historicity of the Bible; while the formation of Evolutionary Theory was among the factors in greatly shaking confidence in traditional cosmology (which already had had to be modified in view of Newtonian physics).

The first of these strands in the intellectual challenge to tradition was in part sparked by the highly influential philosophy of Georg Wilhelm Friedrich Hegel (1770–1831). In his view the processes of existence are manifestations of one Absolute Spirit (*Geist*). One of his reasons for this was the breakdown of Kant's compromise. Kant thought that we project categories on the world of experience, but that experience itself is the product, in some sense, of "things in themselves" beyond the phenomena. Critics saw this as a weak point: in Kant's own view categories could not be applied to that which lies beyond experience, and so one should use neither singular nor plural nor the notion of cause or existence in speaking of the "things in themselves." So Idealists like Hegel, having scraped away objective reality from behind the world of experience, saw the world as experience.

Hegel's originality lay in seeing the Absolute as dynamic—as working, for instance, through the processes of history. And he saw these as following a logic, which he called the dialectic: a notion of profound influence on Karl Marx and so on the world. In history, according to Hegel's view, one movement (the thesis) is faced with its opposite (the antithesis); in the conflict between the two a synthesis is formed. This synthesis then becomes the thesis, which stimulates its own antithesis and a new synthesis; and so on.

Different religions are popular, imaginative, and intuitive ways in which human beings have tried to grasp the Absolute; in Christianity the Absolute is thought of as achieving self-consciousness. Ferdinand Baur (1792–1860) took up Hegel's dialectical view and saw Jesus as thesis, Paul as antithesis and Catholicism as synthesis. All this was a speculative trend, but stimulated much historical enquiry into the actualities of what we could know about Jesus. From this arose the great industry of modern critical scholarship directed at the New Testament and at the earliest Christianity. Such an industry flourished especially in the nineteenth century, in the Protestant faculties in German universities, and from there spread to Britain, the United States, and elsewhere.

Once the Bible was treated not as authority but as evidence, not as holy writ but as historical material, not as evidently true but as often woven together from theological desires and oral traditions, it lost its old authoritative force. This presented a clear crisis for the Churches.

This crisis was deepened by the publication of the Evolutionary Theory of Charles Darwin (1809–82), published in 1859 in his book *The Origin of Species*. If Christians had before accepted physics, it was only because a sharp line was drawn between it and the study of living things. It seemed a great shock to Victorians (both to many scientists and to many but by no means all Church people) to think of humanity as descending from apes, as being so closely kin to the animals—which were often seen in a poor moral light, as witness the use of such words as "brutish," "beastly," and so on. Besides, Holy Scripture spoke of the direct creation by God of the species, not their slow and hungry evolution as Darwin proposed. Moreover it seemed that some of the strongest arguments people had had for belief in a good Creator—such things as the cunning anatomy of the eye, the beautiful design of an eagle's wings, the delicate artistry of the lyre bird and the spider—were undercut by the theory that these wonders had arisen as a result of the survival of the fittest.

The doctrinal dimension: *Punch* here laughs at Darwin's evolutionary theory, often seen to be in conflict with Christian and Biblical orthodoxy.

A preacher in a
workhouse reading the
Bible to the homeless.

History and Evolution—these ideas and much else besides called in
question the literal accuracy and truth of the Bible. Adam and Eve would
disappear among the monkeys. Jesus' sharp outline would melt behind the
hot uncertainties of historical scholarship. Little could be depended upon
absolutely, and much of what was orthodox belief might have to be hedged
with maybes. Was science becoming a cuckoo in the nest of theism? Was
scholarship taking the backbones out of believers?

Another, quite different, challenge was the uprooting of society which the
new industrial revolution presented. Men and women flocked into sordid
cities, where they were enslaved to great machines and tyrannized by clocks.
If some turned to gin and prostitution it was not surprising. Meanwhile the
country parish system crumbled, designed for a different age and another
kind of life. So the established Churches everywhere felt themselves weakened,
even though in England, for instance, Methodism was very active in the
industrial era and there were gallant attempts to reshape religious organization
towards the needs of the new society.

These three examples stand for all those forces of scholarship and philosophy, of scientific enquiry, and of social challenge that met Christianity in
the Europe of the nineteenth century.

One response to all this was to embrace it. The quest for the historical Jesus
and the new discoveries of science might weaken confidence in the literal

truth of the Bible: but so what? It did not need to be either a textbook of history or a manual of biology. Science has to do with this world: religion deals with this world seen in the light of the next world. Religion sees tigers and planets lit by the light of God and seen in the eye of faith. And the Bible is about the actions of God but is not itself a guaranteed recording of them. Moreover, Evolution is good news: it hints at how we have risen from earlier stalkings and screams in the undergrowth to our present moral stature: and in that elevation of humankind religion—above all, so the argument goes, the Christian religion—has played a crucial part. As for the sorrows of capitalism, yes, they should be mitigated: but human invention and energy are already fashioning a brighter world. We should be optimistic at rising towards the Kingdom.

In many ways the greatest of all exponents of this nineteenth-century liberal Protestantism was Adolf von Harnack (1851–1930), who saw Luther as having only partially reformed Christianity, freeing it of ritualism, hierarchy, and so on, but keeping the dogma uncritically in place. We need, in Harnack's view, a historically anchored faith which looks to the Gospel of Christ, which stresses the love of God the Father, which we can experience, and the love of one's neighbor by the help of God's grace, but which takes a critical view of Christian tradition.

Another response, which I shall describe more in detail when dealing with North American religion, is to deny the force of liberalism and to go on affirming the literal truth of the Bible in the teeth of scientific skepticism. This fundamentalism often combined with a fervent evangelical zeal, and remained a dynamic force in the Christian tradition. Yet another response was to bolster the strength of faith by emphasizing the importance of the organization of the Church. Within Protestantism this kind of move occurred in effect as the Oxford Movement, which underlined the vitality of Catholic ritual within the Church of England, and revived high theories of the sacred authority of the Church—but some of its adherents, most notably John Henry Newman (1801–90), crossed over into the Church of Rome. This revival had its effects very much in the ritual dimension and material aspect of Anglicanism, being a stimulus to the revival of Gothic architecture in the large church building and rebuilding program undertaken for the expanding population of Victorian England. The Pre-Raphaelite movement in art helped, too, to present a revitalized late medieval style of religious painting.

But more important than all this was the reaffirmation of Roman Catholic Church authority, partly through the Council known as Vatican I, held in Rome in 1870, which asserted the doctrine of the infallibility of the Pope in matters of doctrine and ethics when he speaks *ex cathedra*, literally "from the throne," that is, in his sacred and official capacity. It was also reaffirmed through the crackdown in 1907 on what was called Catholic Modernism: a number of writers and theologians were exploring the liberal approaches which had had such impact in Protestantism. Biblical scholarship in the Catholic tradition, and certain philosophical lines of reasoning, were greatly restricted. This attempt to trammel the members of the Church was in the long run bound to end in failure, but it held the line until the Council known as Vatican II (1962–65), summoned by Pope John XXIII (1881–1963).

As to the challenge of the new social world, some Christians in Europe responded by adopting a version of Christian Socialism. In Britain the Labour movement, with its trade union affiliations and leanings towards a Socialist solution to economic problems, was greatly permeated by the spirit of the nonconformist Protestant denominations, such as Methodists and Baptists. Indeed, Methodism had been in the vanguard of social action from the early part of the nineteenth century. In the United States the movement known as the Social Gospel was important, and we shall come to that later (p. 363).

## New Ideologies as Alternatives to Religion

Of all the new thoughts which were produced in the nineteenth century the set which had the greatest impact on the world was Marxism. It became the ideology of revolutionary groups who identified the troubles of the world with the capitalist system itself. Karl Marx (1818–83) had early in his career fallen under the influence of Hegel, but he took key Hegelian categories in very different directions. He edited radical journals in Germany and Paris; eventually in a year of great revolutionary activity in Europe, 1848, he settled in the more tolerant atmosphere of London. There in great poverty he wrote prolifically, helped financially by his rich friend Friedrich Engels (1820–95), and engaged in revolutionary organization.

His, and Engels', philosophy was materialist, as distinguished from the idealism of Hegel. The dialectic of history was to be seen in differing economic systems in collision and contradiction. Capitalism itself contained

The iconography of the Russian Revolution and its aftermath: Marx, Engels, Lenin, and Stalin.

contradictions, because the interests of the bourgeoisie who owned the means of production demanded that they exploit the workers: their profits came out of the extra value imparted to materials by labor. Class conflict was bound to intensify, held Marx, and would lead to a revolution, then to the so-called dictatorship of the proletariat, and then to the establishment of a classless society. It was a fine vision; it was backed with impressive economic evidence and theory; it gave confidence, since revolutionaries were on the side of history; it was itself a secular eschatology, having some of the flavor of Messianism.

As to religion, that, to Marx, was a byproduct of the socioeconomic situation and a symptom of alienation. It was the cry of the oppressed and the opium of the people. The exposure of religion was the first intellectual task of all, and in his famous *Theses on Feuerbach* Marx showed his indebtedness to Ludwig Feuerbach (1804–72), another follower and critic of Hegel. Feuerbach saw God as being a projection, by us, of essential human attributes such as reason and love. Marx took this "projectionist" strand and gave it an economic interpretation. It may be noted that projectionism—that is the theory that God and other supernatural entities are projected onto reality by human beings—is a powerful ingredient in modern thought, appearing in a different form for instance in the thought of Sigmund Freud (1856–1939).

In many ways, Marxism itself was a worldview with a religious flavor, not directed towards a higher world but towards the transformation of this. For *doctrines* it had the writings of Marx, Engels, V. I. Lenin (1870–1924), and others. For *myth* it had the pulsating rhythm of history culminating in the earthly paradise of a classless society. For *ethics* it had the ceaseless pursuit of social justice and the maintenance of class struggle. For *practice* it had the need to realize theories concretely, in revolutionary activity. For *experience* it had the nurturing of ardor and of hatred towards class enemies. For *organization* it had the various Communist parties. When it became the official doctrine of various countries, these religious features were to be much accentuated.

Not all Marxists were Communists: there was also a more moderate strand of Marxian Socialism which became important in Europe and elsewhere, and tried to combine Marxism with a liberal-democratic idea of the State. For Marx himself had been skeptical of the importance of law and other means of preserving political rights. He despised some of the creations of the bourgeoisie as shams, and so the ideal of individual freedom did not, in a political sense at least, figure largely in his thinking, and as it turned out virtually all the Communist parties turned out to be totalitarian in outlook. Democratic Socialism with Marxist ingredients was, however, an alternative option.

The rise of Marxism in the late nineteenth century stimulated some responses from Christians, probably the most notable being the Encyclical letter to the Church entitled *Rerum novarum* ("Of new things"), issued by Pope Leo XIII (1810–1903) in 1891. Leo had earlier condemned Socialism as a plague, but he recognized that in the industrial age new forms of organization were necessary, and in the Encyclical he laid the theoretical basis for the formation of Catholic labor unions and ultimately of Catholic political parties committed to democratic forms. He had also been prominent in the reform of Catholic education, and in his *Aeterni Patris* (1879) had made a revived form of Aquinas' thought, called Neo-Thomism, virtually mandatory for Catholic thinkers. As it happened, this was not a strong enough system to challenge easily the growing power of Marxist and secular thought on European intellectuals. Indeed, among European intellectuals in the early twentieth century, Christianity was no longer a predominant belief.

Various forms of secular ideology were influential. For those who thought that Marxism was not based enough in realities and was too speculative, and who favored a more liberal and democratic way of thinking, a kind of empiricism with humanist ethical values was attractive, such as the thought of Bertrand Russell (1872–1970). He was a notable representative of scientific humanism, which sees humanity as the highest value, love of fellow humans as the highest ethic, and science as the best way of relating to the cosmos. Humanism was an alternative to religion in the West: it was and is atheistic, though some humanists prefer to use the word "agnosticism" to characterize their position, meaning the lack of knowledge and evidence one way or another to assert or deny the existence of God (the word was invented in 1869 by the biologist and philosopher T. H. Huxley (1825–95). Later, humanism was given a more personalist tone and a grounding in dramatic human choice in the atheistic Existentialism of Jean-Paul Sartre (1905–80) and others. A form of scientific humanism came to dominate English-speaking philosophy under the influence of scientific empiricism and language analysis.

Partly under the influence of Hegel, who saw the State as a kind of incarnation of the Absolute Mind, right-wing ideologies appeared, which were hostile both to the liberal ideals of the Center and the revolutionary impulses of the Left. In Italy there was Fascism, espousing a corporate State which organized professional, union, and industrial life in the service of nationalist expansion and a return to the glories of the Roman empire, under Benito Mussolini (1883–1945). More serious and more devastating still was the Nazi ideology, which presented a hypernationalist ethos, an assertion of German and "Aryan" superiority, and a program for conquest and the elimination of inferiors, notably Jews. Though Fascism in Italy could live on reasonable terms with Catholicism, in Germany the Nazi ideology had a religious (and anti-Christian) character of its own. The parades, the Hitler salute, the uniforms, the flags, all gave it a strong *ritual* element. The *emotions* of being saved through the Leader in the restoration of a fallen Germany were strong. Though its *doctrinal* and theoretical bases were weak, the *myth* of Aryan Germany was a powerful one. And the idea of the Thousand-Year Reich was a beguiling eschatology. The role of the Führer was religious too: the plain German who had fought in World War I, now ready to transcend aristocrats and generals and lead the nation on the warpath (never mind that he was an Austrian!) Though Fascism and Nazism scarcely survived the death

347

of their leaders, much the same tendencies can coalesce into the modern right-wing dictatorship, often military, and sometimes in alliance with and sometimes in conflict with the churches.

### Imperial Expansion and Missions Outside Europe

Nineteenth-century European history is greatly incomplete without the story of European expansion (see Map 12, p. 338–9). Apart from Russia's vast land empire, there was the formation of formidable empires by Britain, France, Holland, and Germany, and lesser empires by Belgium, Italy, and Denmark. By contrast, the older empires of Spain and Portugal were substantially diminished through the independence movements in Central and South America, and at the end of the century by the detachment of Cuba and the Philippines from Spanish rule by the United States. But Britain consolidated its rule over nearly all the subcontinent of India and was probing north and northwest into Afghanistan and Tibet. It held part of Southeast Asia and great parts of the Pacific. It controlled the Cape and was poised to take part in the scramble for Africa. It was dominant culturally in Canada and the Caribbean. France had much of Indochina and was moving into North Africa. Holland held Indonesia and some other island possessions. Germany took part in the African carve-up, acquiring large tracts of Southwest and Southeast Africa and parts of the West. Britain dominated in East Africa and Southern Africa, but also was substantially present in the West. France had huge swathes of West and North and Central Africa. Belgium took the Congo, later Zaire; Italy was later to move into Libya, Somalia, and eventually Ethiopia.

All this gave great opportunities for mission work. The Christian Churches moved in under the aegis of the empires. Protestant missions predominated in Protestant empires, and Catholics in Catholic ones; but over much of the globe rival missions, either from differing denominations or differing nations, were in competition. The scandal of this from a Christian point of view led to one of the first major events in the so-called Ecumenical Movement or movement for Christian unity, namely a mission conference in Edinburgh to promote Christian cooperation. The results of the missions we shall see in other chapters: but their existence reinforced the European idea that the British (or French, or whoever) represented a Christian civilization which would bring both rational and spiritual enlightenment to the unfortunate masses of the non-European world. But Christian missionaries also became involved in nationalist movements which sought the same liberty and rights for the conquered as were enjoyed by the conquering nation.

### Christianity and Judaism in Twentieth-Century Europe

The destiny of the religions was considerably affected by the secular ideologies which functioned as alternatives. In Russia, the Revolution brought the Church into a new captivity. World War I, with its devastating power to kill mass armies, saw the collapse of that optimism which had been one ingredient of liberal Protestantism. The rise of Fascism in Italy in due course tempted the Catholic Church into a new deal or concordat with the Italian State in 1929 which gave the Catholics certain rights over education and marriage law and the like. The rise of Nazism posed dilemmas for the German Churches, and brought agony to the Jews. Secular humanism came to be the prevailing ethos in most parts of Scandinavia and was strong in Britain. World War II, often thought of by the Western Allies as a struggle between good and evil, mobilized Christians on both sides, as usual, and ended with the extension of Stalin's Communist empire into Central Europe. The Spanish Civil War of 1936–39 saw bitter anticlericalism at work. Altogether the period up to and indeed beyond World War II was an unhappy one for the major religions, and for Judaism it was catastrophic.

Two significant books were published in 1917 and left their imprint on the European religious scene. One was by Karl Barth (1886–1968), and was his commentary on the Epistle of Paul to the Romans. It heralded the production of his major work, *Church Dogmatics*. It was a statement of Protestant theology which cut against the optimistic liberalism dying along the Western Front. It kept to modern canons of scholarship but from a conservative angle. For him the "Christ-event," rather than the words of scripture as such, constituted the revelation. But he kept strongly to Paul's notion of grace, and restated this in a way which rejected all forms of natural theology. Only by revelation do we know anything of God. It was a hard-line position which made Christian revelation discontinuous with all other religious ideas and teachings. These were, just as Feuerbach had said, a mere projection of human concerns. Christianity has value only as the response of people to the revelation in Christ. This dogmatic position, narrow and nonrational, had great influence between the Wars both among Christians of the liberal wing and in the mission field. Its prestige was enhanced because Barth stood up against the Nazis and, with other members of the so-called Confessing Church which resisted Hitler, signed the so-called Barmen Declaration of 1934.

The other book was Rudolf Otto's *The Idea of the Holy*. Otto (1869–1937) saw in the Holy the key category of religion and analyzed the experience of the Holy as numinous, a mystery that both awes and fascinates. In thus basing his philosophy of religion on a kind of experience, Otto revitalized an older tradition, but he did so very much in the context of the comparative study of religions. By the 1970s and 1980s, Christian theologians had at last begun to see with clarity that other religious traditions in the world represent a genuine challenge to old-fashioned theology and need to be taken seriously. The imperial age had not been without its fine Christian scholars who studied other religions, but the main tenor was of European and Christian cultural superiority. Otto as one of the revitalizers of the comparative study of religion was an important figure. It turns out that his emphasis on the numinous is good in characterizing the feel of various kinds of theism, where God is the Other; but it does not work so well in characterizing non-theistic mystical experience, especially Buddhist. So we need to think of more than one basic type of religious experience. But that does not invalidate the approach which Otto was pioneering.

In Europe, over much of the twentieth century, the huge questions have been very immediate because of the rise of dictatorships. Neither Protestantism nor Catholicism had an altogether honorable encounter with Hitler, but there were martyrs to the faith, notably Dietrich Bonhoeffer (1906–45). The largest question has been reaction to the Holocaust or *Sho'ah*—the killing of about six million Jews in Europe in the concentration camps and gas ovens of the Nazis. Other groups were also terribly treated, such as Gypsies, Russian prisoners, and many others: but anti-Semitism was a vital ingredient in Hitler's thinking, and a central part of the Nazi ideology, which was drenched in thoughts of pure Aryan blood and so forth. Christianity had a role in the creation of anti-Semitism: partly because of old charges, from the New Testament time onwards, that the Jews "killed God"; partly because of a naïve epistemology which held that the Jews culpably failed to recognize that the Old Testament foretold Christ; partly because of the xenophobic Crusading spirit; and in various other ways. Christianity is only now coming to terms with this past.

But the Holocaust has been of course even more of a trauma for Jews. Many a German Jew was proud to be German until Hitler, and so in a number of other countries. So there was the initial shock of rejection. But when the full awfulness of the Holocaust unfolded, there was a deep question shockingly posed to believing Jews: How could a good God have produced such a calamity? Some have turned away from the faith. Others have seen it as just an extreme case of the free will with which the Creator has endowed people. Others have seen it as opening up a new period of Jewish history, when faith in God and adherence to the Covenant become absolutely voluntary, since the monstrous event of the Holocaust releases Jews from their obligations (this position is found in the writings of Irving Greenberg). Some Orthodox Jews have seen it as a punishment for sins, maybe for Zionism. But such an interpretation scarcely rings true: for so devastating a punishment the sin would have to be disproportionately monstrous. Meanwhile hope continues, for it was partly out of the ashes of Europe's madness that the State of Israel was built, achieving independence in 1948 and surviving miraculously through several wars.

The effect on the Jewish people of the Holocaust and the founding of Israel was to concentrate them densely in North America and in Israel—for many Jews from Arab and Muslim countries also migrated there. There are of course other centers of Jewish life, such as South Africa and Britain, but the center of gravity has shifted to the United States, while modern Israel has come to occupy a more vital place in the thinking of most Jews than even the old Zion had. "Next year in Jerusalem" has a concrete meaning now.

*The Updating of Catholicism*
Among the Christian Churches of Europe probably the most vital events

since World War II have been those connected with the Ecumenical Movement—the founding of the World Council of Churches in 1948—and the reforming Council, Vatican II (1962–5), which led to radical changes in Roman Catholic thinking and practice.

In *doctrine*, Vatican II saw the melting away of Neo-Thomism. In matters of *narrative* the winds of Protestant scholarship were allowed to riffle the pages of the Bible. In *ritual* the Latin tradition was abandoned and the Mass was simplified and translated into the vernacular languages of the world. In *ethics* a more open attitude prevailed, and renewed concern for the poor. In *experience* new experiments with devotion and charismatic ecstasies were initiated. In *organization* the Church was somewhat democratized. In architecture and the *arts* new forces of modernity were released. Ecumenically, the Roman Catholics became much less reserved, and now play a vital role in initiatives of Christian cooperation.

In short, Vatican II represented a vast source of change. For John XXIII it was an act of *aggiornamento* or "updating" the Church. Large numbers of priests and monks and nuns, however, about this time began to leave their vocations, though most remained loyal Catholics. New forces of rebellion were released in the Church, which consequently became highly dynamic and not always obedient to the dictates from the Vatican (notably in matters such as birth control, where many Catholics simply disregarded papal pronouncements against the use of artificial methods).

In postwar Europe there has been another force affecting the practice of Christianity. The fact that Church authority is largely unenforceable in pluralistic communities has led to a wide proliferation of new religious movements, while Christianity and Judaism have come face to face with other world religions on what they had come to regard as home territory. Many adherents of Islam, for instance, have come to work in Western countries, so that it is the third largest denomination in Britain; and young people have found much in Buddhism, in Hindu movements, and in new experiments in living. With the added fact that the majority in virtually all Western European countries are non-practicing and many of them reject traditional Christianity, there now exists a much more fluid picture of belief in Europe. Things are not quite the same in the Communist East.

## Reflections on Modern Europe

It may be noted that in Europe, more or less continuously from the reign of Constantine the Great until this modern period, Christianity in one form or another has had official status. It is now, for the European populations, more or less a voluntary matter. There is thus a new weakness and a new vitality in religion. The weakness is that the Churches appear statistically in decline; the strength is that voluntary religion is deeper than conforming religion. Further, we note that since the various postwar economic revivals—German, Italian, British, and so on—Western Europe is a consumerist entity. Choices have rarely been so abundant. And something similar is beginning to happen in religion; a kind of consumerism, with many new varieties being added as cultures cross and merge. Poverty remains, but more at the margin in the West. Hence Christianity looks increasingly to the global village to fulfill its role of serving the poor.

Oddly, though, despite the multiplications of new sects and religious movements, the currents of mainstream Christianity have greatly converged. The differences of *ritual*, for instance, have been greatly moderated since Vatican II and among the Protestant denominations. Nor are there quite such acute divergences of *doctrine*. Only perhaps on the *mythic* side is there acute division: those who take the Bible more or less literally form a conservative movement cutting across denominations; and there is a corresponding movement of more liberal Christians who likewise have similar interpretations of the Bible. There are differences in *ethical* stance, e.g. over abortion; but somewhat at the margin. Martin Luther King, John Paul II, Mother Teresa, Allan Boesak, Archbishop Robert Runcie of Canterbury, although of quite different historic pasts, gain wide Christian recognition in this ecumenical age. But the center of Christianity has already moved southward from Europe, into Africa and Latin America and in general the so-called Third World. No doubt Europe will be open to new influences.

# 15

# *North America*

## A New Pluralism

The Christianities and Judaisms of North America, and particularly of the United States, have pioneered a number of new forms and circumstances. For instance, the division of Church and State in the American constitution was a novelty in its day, largely unprecedented at least among European nations. Again, it was in North America that some of the most vigorous revivalist movements of modern Christianity occurred. There are also religions born in North America, like the Mormons and Christian Science. Roman Catholicism and Eastern Orthodox Christianity had to take on rather a different flavor in the New World. And it was in America that the modern forms of Judaism were most extensively developed and in some cases created. Side by side with all this, there is the fate of the Native Americans to contemplate, their populations greatly diminished by European diseases and bullets, their cultures greatly subverted, and developing new varieties of religion to cope with such disasters.

North America is also vital for the history of modern religion because it demonstrates the ways in which great immigrations and a melting-pot of cultures affect traditions. All these facets of American religion give it great vigor. Very often the migrants became much more committed to their faith than they would have been had they stayed at home, and this sometimes makes it difficult for Americans to appreciate the degree of religious secularization which has occurred in parts of Europe, especially the North.

In the twentieth century, too, North America has seen experiments in living, mainly from the late 1960s on, which have multiplied options and incorporated some Eastern religions into Western patterns of life. It has also had the vigor of Black religion to vivify it, and this has incorporated Islamic elements, as well as the strongly emotional faith of evangelical Protestantism. In addition there has been migration, especially from the Far East, which has brought Chinese and Japanese, later Korean and Vietnamese, Buddhism (and other concomitant religious forms such as Taoism and Confucianism) into the North American picture, especially in California.

There are differing periods for us to look at. First there is the colonial period up to Independence; then there is the initial period of United States religion up to the mid part of the nineteenth century; then the period of rapid immigration, the opening up of the frontier and the Civil War; then there is the twentieth century. In Canada, roughly the same framework will work, since similar conditions prevailed, though without slavery.

## The Religious Affairs of the Colonies

In the settlement of North America, Britain predominated along the eastern seaboard, especially after the fall of New Amsterdam to Britain, as New York, in 1664. The more southern colonies, Virginia, Maryland, the Carolinas, were settled in principle by members of the Church of England; while the more northern colonies, Massachusetts, Connecticut, Rhode Island, Pennsylvania, and west New Jersey, had a predominantly dissenting character.

The most famous landfall was that of the *Mayflower* at Plymouth Rock in Massachusetts in 1620. The New England colonies provided a refuge from persecution and social disadvantage in England and a focus for new religious aspirations to found a "City upon a Hill," a new Zion. The Puritans of New England did not necessarily extend to their members the rights of religious toleration: a new conformism became apparent in the colonies, which were substantially self-governing. New theocracies were built. However, some notable exceptions to this were not long in appearing.

One was the Rhode Island colony founded primarily by Roger Williams (1603–83). He was in his beliefs a Calvinist; but he was most vigorous for the separation of Church and State. He joined the Baptists, as conforming best to what he expected of a Christian group, and founded the first Baptist church in America, in Providence. He secured eventually a permanent charter for the new colony, of which he was president for three years, and there freedom of religion was assured. In retrospect he has been seen as a great pioneer of separatism and a forerunner of the later First Amendment of the United States Constitution, passed in 1791: "Congress shall make no law respecting an establishment of religion or prohibiting the free exercise thereof."

The Quaker colonies of west New Jersey and Pennsylvania also incorporated religious toleration. William Penn (1644–1718) played a leading part in efforts to secure the passing of the English Act of Toleration Act after the so-called Glorious Revolution of 1688. In Pennsylvania there were ethical restrictions imposed, such as the rejection of forts and armaments, since the Quakers were pacifists, and the outlawing of slavery. Incidentally, full rights were accorded the Delaware Indians. So religious dissent had an important political message. This stemmed from the thinking of George Fox (1624–91). The movement which he founded, the Society of Friends, nicknamed Quakers, looked to inner experience and the "light that lights every person" as the source of true religion, and conscience as the source of true morality. They simplified worship to the meeting in which people awaited inspiration before speaking or leading the group in prayers. Their meetinghouses were of the simplest. They were pacifists, and accorded each person equal dignity. It was the recognition of Christ in every person that took them on the path to a fine egalitarianism, which of course extended to slaves and Native Americans. They became an important strand in Puritan thinking in America, but only in the very earliest days of the Pennsylvania colony did they have a majority role, and for the most part they have been a relatively minor group, though influential beyond their numbers. Both Quakers and Roger Williams made a point of friendship with the "Indians," in often bleak contrast to other White-Native American relationships.

Many of the New England Puritans were Congregationalists in their organization. Someone has referred to Congregationalists as decentralized Calvinists. Their government was through independent congregations, as the name implies, and they rejected the more complex and centralized Presbyterian system, for the most part (Presbyterianism was stronger to the south in the Middle Atlantic States). In their thinking they were often millenarian, and they saw a special destiny in the New England dream of a purified faith. Thus, Cotton Mather (1663–1728), famous son of Harvard and Boston preacher, defended the fusion of Church and State because he saw a redemptive role for society in New England. In this he followed his father

The narrative dimension: the Puritan migration to New England has entered powerfully into the story of America's history. Puritans are seen here illustrating a ballad celebrating the Independents' voyage to New England, a journey from persecution, shown on the left, to a new life, shown on the right.

Increase (1629–1723)—wonderful, these Puritan names!—who thought of New England as a place for the final consummation of the work of the Reformation. Cotton Mather thought that the Second Coming of Christ might take place in his time and in New England. Such shining hope and the feeling of a special destiny for the American colonies was to carry over into the optimism and sense of chosenness in the Republic.

Early on, the Congregationalists had paid good attention to education, founding Harvard in 1637 and Yale and other colleges a bit later. As a result America had much more investment in higher education than England, which till the early nineteenth century had only the two universities of Oxford and Cambridge. But though intellect was important in colonial American religion, the heart was too.

The Great Awakening of the eighteenth century was a formidable revival, the first in a cycle to influence and stimulate American piety. Its onset in 1734 was experienced in the church of Jonathan Edwards (1703–58), perhaps America's greatest theologian, in Northampton, Massachusetts. The movement was passionate and charismatic, and was further spurred by the preaching of George Whitefield (1714–70), English preacher and itinerant revivalist. His sermons were marked by great enthusiasm up and down the Atlantic Coast. He was looked at askance by the Anglican Establishment, though ordained a priest, but got a good reception from Congregationalists, Presbyterians, Reformed, and Baptists. Among other causes which he espoused was the opening of Dartmouth College in New Hampshire to Native Americans.

The Baptists benefited from the Great Awakening, for it made some of their doctrines and practices more relevant. Their separatism (that is, their rejection of an established Church) was meaningful in an enthusiasm which saw true Christianity in the fruits of religious experience rather than conformity to orthodoxy; and their itinerant mode of preaching was something which now became normal. They began to make great advances, and from that base were to be very effective as the frontier moved over the Alleghenies and into the wide beyond. More complex, established Churches found it hard to follow the shifting populations.

Moreover, the Baptists, with their warm and charismatic appeal and favoring of conversion-experiences, had a special appeal to the Blacks. For by the mid-eighteenth century there were already over 100,000 slaves in the South. The Baptists were on their way to becoming the largest religious denomination in America. In advocating adult baptism they followed the Anabaptist principle.

Another important strand in American Protestantism was beginning to grow just before and during the period of the Revolution. It was Methodism, so called from the notion that one should live according to a "method" laid down in the Bible. This movement had started, through the work of John Wesley (1703–91), as a means of revitalizing the Church of England. But Wesley was much influenced by the Moravians, a mainly German group

A Mennonite assembly in America: note the simplicity of the meeting house and the prominence of the pulpit.

stemming both from the work of John Hus (1369?–1415), the Czech reformer before the Reformation, and from eighteenth century Pietism, a warm devotionalism associated with the leader Count Zinzendorf (1700–60). Their warm feeling for Christ and devotion to him was appealing to Wesley. The Methodist movement was enhanced by the great hymns composed by Charles Wesley (1708–88), and was to make important strides in postcolonial America.

Mingled with emotionally oriented religion and the Puritan ethos were ideas derived from the Enlightenment—anticlerical Freemasonry, deism, feeling for the rights of man, commitment to toleration—and all these found their fulfillment, as far as religious organization went, in the First Amendment, which made a vital statement about the meaning of the American Revolution. So it was that Anglicanism reformed itself, no longer as an Established Church, but as the Protestant Episcopal Church of the United States. In Virginia its endowments were lost, and many clergy left for Canada.

357

Nevertheless a vigorous Anglican tradition survived. The first American bishop, Samuel Seabury of Connecticut (1729–97) was consecrated by Scottish Episcopal bishops, who had no established status and indeed were regarded at the time as being in schism with the Church of England.

### Roman Catholics in Colonial North America

The most important area for Catholicism was not in the British colonies but in Quebec. There the Church became in part a sign of ethnic identity, especially after the fall of Quebec to the British in 1759 during the Seven Years' War, a disaster for the French. The Quebec Act of 1774 however granted full citizenship to Catholics and allowed the Church to maintain its tithing system. The Province was brought into the colony of Canada.

The position of Catholics in the British colonies to the south was much less favorable. Maryland had in principle been a colony for English Catholics, but a Puritan majority in the colony repealed the Act of Toleration in 1664, and Catholics were deprived of voting rights.

It was during the nineteenth century that American Catholicism made vast progress, because of the large numbers of migrants from Ireland, Italy, Poland, and other European countries with strong Catholic populations. We shall come to that shortly.

## From the American Revolution to the Middle of the Nineteenth Century

The opening up of the frontier into Kentucky, Ohio, and elsewhere beyond the Alleghenies had begun in earnest, and in the new optimism of the young Republic a Second Great Awakening occurred at the turn of the century, with revival meetings in tents along the areas of new occupation. The mobile folk who were opening up American farmland were susceptible to evangelical fervor—and so it was that the warmest type of preaching and religion— Baptists, Methodists, Congregationalists—made the greatest impression.

Meanwhile, in New England, there was a shift among many Congregationalists towards Unitarianism, which took over many of the beautiful churches of the area. This move into the Unitarian persuasion was in no small part due to the influence of William Ellery Channing (1780–1842), of Boston, whose sermon on Unitarian Christianity in 1819 summed up what many already thought—that Christ, though morally perfect, was nevertheless subordinate to God. It was like the old Arian position (see p. 248), which made Christ noneternal, being himself created by God. It rejected the full-blown version of the Trinity doctrine which had been the hallmark of Christian orthodoxy. Unitarianism was to make strong advances among the educated elite of the period and the area.

It also had a frontier with the movement known as Transcendentalism, associated above all with Ralph Waldo Emerson (1803–82) and Henry David Thoreau (1817–62). Transcendentalism as a view emphasizes the presence of the divine in Nature, and the need of the individual to be true to himself and to work in harmony with Nature. It has affinities to Taoism and some aspects of the Hindu tradition, by which Emerson was somewhat influenced. Transcendentalism helped to stimulate interest in the comparative study of religions, and was one of the factors lying behind the famous World's Parliament of Religions in Chicago, 1893. It also had an influence on Christian Science.

It was in the first part of the nineteenth century that the first important homegrown American religion was created, by the prophet Joseph Smith II (1805–44), from upper New York State. Stimulated by visionary experiences and guided, he said, by an angel, he discovered at the Hill Cumorah some gold plates which he translated as *The Book of Mormon*. This claims to give the story of some of the peoples of North America before Columbus, some of whom were ancestors of the Native Americans, and who were migrants from the Lost Tribes of Israel. In 1830 the Church of Jesus Christ of the Latter-Day Saints was formed (the full name dates from 1838). The story of this new movement was tremendous. Smith and his followers moved to Kirtland, Ohio, and then further west, eventually setting up a fine city with its own temple in Nauvoo, Illinois. Near there, at Carthage, Joseph Smith

Brigham Young, the great
Mormon leader.

and his brother Hiram were murdered in 1844. Their new theocracy was becoming too powerful, and some of the new teachings and practices (including polygamy) were scandalous to outsiders. Brigham Young (1801–77) led the main body of the Mormons, as they were nicknamed, to Salt Lake City in Utah. He set about establishing an empire there, the State of Deseret; but Congressional unease and pressure led eventually to the incorporation of Utah into the United States, with theocracy and polygamy abandoned. Many converts, especially from Britain, went out on the hard trail to Utah. Mormon cohesiveness, puritanism, and family values had a strong appeal. Some of the doctrines—that God is material, that there are many Gods, and that human beings may become Gods—have been modified, and in many ways Mormonism is now a conforming evangelical kind of Protestantism, with the colorful additions of the *Book of Mormon* and the charismatic memory of the genial and masterful Joseph Smith.

## The Effects of Mass Immigration

In the second half of the nineteenth century the processes of settlement and industrialization speeded up. This sucked into America large numbers of immigrants, many of whom were Catholic and Jewish, foreign to the prevailing Protestant ethos. Both groups were regarded with some suspicion. But up to the period of World War I these groups made their fundamental adjustments to the New World.

For Catholics the question was a double one of integration. On the one hand, how were the masses of immigrants of different nations to live together in one Church? There were Irish and Poles, Hungarians and Italians, Germans and Mexicans, to be blended together. On the other hand, how was Catholicism to be woven into the fabric of American life? The key to both of these operations was education, and Catholicism paid a great deal of attention to it. There evolved a system of parish schools and Catholic colleges and universities which made the transition into American life feasible without the loss of religious tradition. Part of the task, too, was showing others that Catholicism was in no way disloyal to the American heritage: by prominence in games, such as American football, in cultural life, and appropriately in politics, Catholics could demonstrate their all-American character. The Church devoted most of its energies to social affairs, to building (most extensively and floridly), and to education. Catholic Orders were prominent, many engaged in these social and educational tasks.

For Protestantism the immigration brought North Europeans, especially Swedes, other Scandinavians, and Germans. All this added up to Lutheranism, which became especially strong in the Midwest and often provided a bridge between the national culture and the New World. In Canada a similar process of migration brought in many Scots and Northern Irish Protestants, as well as Germans and others, and this gave its own flavor to the Protestant heritage in Canada, which became very strongly Presbyterian.

The period saw new chances for Black religion to flourish, for the Civil War ensured that Blacks would gain emancipation, and Churches which had existed before now blossomed out. Already in 1816 there had been formed an African Methodist Episcopal Church, following the lead of Richard Allen (1760–1831), who had formed the first Black Methodist congregation. With emancipation there was a great exodus of Blacks from White-controlled denominations to create new organizations for Black Baptists and so on. The Reconstruction period saw the foundation of various important Black colleges and universities. But it was followed in turn by a darker period of renewed oppression.

One option was to look to migration back to Africa. Freed slaves were settled in Liberia, which became independent in 1847. Africa remained a symbol for Black Americans. Bishop Turner (1834–1915), a Methodist, said that it was necessary for Black people to have a Black God, and that only in Africa could Black people exercise their full powers. The ideal of a restoration of Africa's past glories by the action of those who had gone through the suffering of slavery was a not uncommon theme. In fact rather few Blacks actually returned to Africa. But there was much dynamism in Black Christianity, and even more from the time of World War I onwards.

The spread of White settlement across the Plains to the far West was an unmitigated calamity for the Native Americans. From early on, the Native American experience of the Whites had not been happy. Thus, in 1622 the Pamunkey Algonquians rebelled against their treatment at the hands of the Jamestown settlers in Virginia, and were defeated. With the coming of the Whites across the plains and the diminishment of the buffalo, various new religious movements emerged, which tried to deal with the problems of the Indians. The Ghost Dance religion of Wodziwob foresaw a time, imminently, when dead Indians would be raised up, the Whites would go away, and a new life would begin again. A second wave in 1889 started from Nevada, under Wovoka, and spread across the Plains, sadly culminating in the massacre of Wounded Knee, when Sioux had thought their sacred shirts would render them immune to bullets (a belief found in various parts of the world during the period of colonialism). The Native Americans were shifted, put into reservations, and reduced to a miserable condition, ravaged by loss of morale, alcohol, and impotence in the face of White control. Nevertheless revival was on its way, during the twentieth century, with a reassertion of Native American values. To this we shall return.

### Varieties of Judaism in the Formative Period

The destiny of Judaism and of the Jewish people was bright in America. But it was not without pain that the solutions to living in the modern world were worked out there. The price of toleration was that religion had to become substantially a private matter, and though Jews could assemble in living areas in the big cities, they did not have the relative legal independence that they had sometimes achieved in Europe and the Middle East.

The first main wave of migrants to America, often German in origin, were ready for modernization. By the end of the Civil War a reasonable affluence had been achieved in the community, and the formal organization of American Reform Judaism was appropriate. In 1869 a group of rabbis formulated a statement of belief which rejected the notion of a personal *Mashiah* and of the restoration of Zion, in any literal sense. In brief, Jewish expectations were demythologized. A few years later Rabbi Isaac Wise (1819–1900) formed the Union of American Hebrew Congregations and through that organization started Hebrew Union College in Cincinnati, which remains the premier instructional center for Reform Judaism. Reform Judaism was supreme in America: it sought to present Judaism as a universal religion, working for the establishment of God's kingdom in which human beings would be united and sanctified, and not as the structure of a divisive community. Worship was remodeled, anglicized and (from the Reform perspective) purified. It corresponded much more to Protestant norms, and the buildings tended to be called temples rather than synagogues. It was liberal and modernist in theology and combined up-to-date literary and historical scholarship with traditional Jewish learning.

At the time when Reform Judaism was taking shape there were new waves of migrants from Eastern Europe—many of them Hasidim, and most of them concerned not with German-style Reform but with Polish- or Ukrainian-style Orthodoxy. The Orthodox became self-conscious in this Orthodoxy as a reaction to the shape of Reform. The first attempts to deal with the problem of new immigrants (half a million up to 1900, and more than a million more between 1900 and 1914) were not successful, for instance the founding of the Jewish Theological Seminary of America in 1885; but after a second try the new form of organization proved more effective. The Jewish Theological Synagogue was reshaped in 1901, and Solomon Schechter (1847?–1915) was brought over to head it up. But the direction in which it developed was towards a third force in Judaism, namely Conservative Judaism, which combined a high degree of liberal scholarship with a conservative view of the practice of Judaism.

Orthodox Judaism created the Yeshiva University for the training of rabbis and others. Since this included secular studies it was fairly adaptive. Indeed, American Orthodoxy has tended to live successfully within the economic and social institutions of the United States, while keeping to the practice of the Torah. The beliefs of the Orthodox tend to be conservative, considering the Torah as Pentateuch to have been revealed by God at Sinai, and conforming closely to traditional laws or *halakhah*. For the Orthodox the Conservatives have moved too far and the Reform Jews have abandoned the substance of the faith. But after World War I times there were further developments, with the increased influence of Hasidism and the variation on Conservatism known as Reconstructionism.

Meanwhile in all this was the complication of Zionism. Generally speaking, the Orthodox and many Conservatives were anti-Zionist. The secular aspirations of the Zionists were unacceptable. Even so, there were some religious Zionists, who later were to become more important in the state of Israel itself.

There was also a fifth movement in regard to Judaism—away from it: Jews who left the Jewish religion and sought their destiny in the wider delights and challenges of American society.

## Christianity and the Social Gospel

In looking at the latter part of the nineteenth century and the early twentieth, we need to take account of the movement often labeled the Social Gospel. This was one of the major ways in which Protestantism addressed itself to the consequences of capitalism and the problems of modern urban life. It was stimulated chiefly by the work and thought of Walter Rauschenbusch (1861–1918), who worked in the Second German Baptist Church in New York for over a decade and was able to experience the sufferings of those who toiled at the bottom of the urban heap. The Churches were less fitted for the large modern city than for the easier integration of small town life.

## More New Religions

In the latter half of the nineteenth century the creation of new forms of religion continued. Three characteristic and important ones are the Seventh-Day Adventists, the Jehovah's Witnesses, and Christian Science: in the first and last of these, women played a crucial role. The Adventists were built up by Ellen Gould White (1826–1915) and her husband James. They arose from the disappointment of a prediction made by the Adventist group founded by William Miller (1781–1849), that Christ would come on October 22, 1844. Some time later, Ellen White, who had been injured by a rock thrown at her head when a child, and had been unconscious for weeks—so that by consequence she was subject to much sickness during her long life—had a vision. This taught her that the Sabbath, as the Bible says, is on the seventh day, namely Saturday; and that indeed a new era of judgment had started on October 22, 1844. As a result, she and her husband became the central figures in the creation of the Seventh-Day Adventist Church, which steadily grew. It also adopted health methods dictated by Ellen White's visions. After his death she became matriarch of the group, and her theology shifted more towards an emphasis on grace, thus bringing the Adventists closer to mainstream evangelical Christianity. Her life, with its initiatory vision and its near-death experience, exhibited, in very modern form, themes of shamanism.

The Jehovah's Witnesses stem from the teachings of Charles Taze Russell (1852–1916) and of his dynamic successor Joseph Franklin Rutherford (1870–1942). Their name springs from the conviction that Jehovah is the proper Biblical name for God. They look forward to a wondrous restoration of the earth and the salvation of 144,000 souls who will reign with Christ in heaven. They pray to Jehovah through Christ; but their chief activity is publication and preaching. They consider that since 1914 Satan has been ruling over the world, and so they should not take part in State activities or fighting, and for this reason are much persecuted for pacifism and insubordination. They forbid priesthood and the like, and refuse blood transfusions, being contrary to Jehovah's laws (Leviticus 17). They have remained very energetic in mission work, and there is scarcely anyone in the West who has not been approached by them.

Mary Baker Eddy (1821–1900) was a product of New England Puritanism, but rebelled against Calvinist predestinationism. In her search for the truth the most decisive experience occurred to her in 1866 when she miraculously recovered from the consequences of a severe accident while reading an account of one of Christ's healings. She then set about trying to understand the world and the New Testament in the light of this, and nine years later she brought out her *Science and Health with Key to the Scriptures*. For her God is All, and so matter, considered in itself, is unreal: we can be healed first of sin and then secondarily of sickness by yielding to God's grace or influence, and by seeing the all-pervasiveness of Mind or Spirit. There are echoes of Transcendentalism in her thought. But when she came to preach this message she found a lot of hostility from orthodox Christians. In due course she founded her own Church, and later recognized it as the First Church of Christ Scientist in Boston, in 1892, which serves organizationally as the mother church to all the churches round the world. Again, as with Ellen White, we meet the confluence of healing and the Gospel: in many ways it is a religion which has rediscovered a major aspect of original Christianity. In 1908 she founded *The Christian Science Monitor*, indicating her commitment to education.

These three are, with Mormonism, samples of the new American religions. They reverberate with differing parts of American religious dreams. Mormonism has the sense of moving west to the chosen land, the sense too of being the instruments of God's will, and seeking for a theocracy, alas in a land committed to the First Amendment. The Jehovah's Witnesses testify to the dream that Satan rules—there has often been a feeling of the great struggle between good and evil in the American heart. The Seventh-Day Adventists seek to figure out the end of history. The Christian Scientists look to salvation here and now.

## Evangelicals and Fundamentalists

### The Rise of Fundamentalism

We have noted already how liberal Protestantism played a dominant role in Europe. Such liberalism of scholarship could not be far away from the American scene, with its high commitment to education. And yet so much of American religion was tied to the Bible. It was in America, therefore, above all, that the conservative reaction to liberalism took place. This was to be known as fundamentalism, a term derived from a series of pamphlets called

*The Fundamentals: A Testimony to the Truth* which appeared before World War I, attacking modernist or liberal views of the Bible and defending "fundamental" doctrines, namely the literal infallibility of the Bible, the Virgin Birth of Christ, the Substitutionary Atonement (Christ's death atones by way of substituting for sinful human beings), the Resurrection of the Body, and the Second Coming. More loosely, fundamentalism means taking the Bible as literally inerrant or as "literal where possible" (for obviously the Bible itself contains metaphors). More loosely still, the term is applied to a strong antimodernist reaffirmation of any faith, for instance Islam. In the Christian context it is associated with evangelicalism—that is, the belief in the authority of the Bible, the claim that salvation can only come through close personal faith in Christ, the regeneration of spiritual life, typically through some conversion experience, and a transformation of moral life, including typically Bible-reading, prayer, abstention from specified wickedness (such as smoking, drinking, and promiscuity). Fundamentalism tends to be a branch of

The feast of Thanksgiving became a vital expression of American feelings about the hope of a new world, and the founding of a Christian society.

evangelicalism: not all evangelicals are fundamentalists. But since they all tend towards an authoritative and inerrant Bible, the lines are hard to draw.

*Opposite* The Crystal Cathedral, Anaheim.

In the nineteenth century the emphasis of fundamentalism in America became oriented towards a gloomier view of human nature and destiny through the doctrine of premillennialism. This is the view that Christ will come again after a dark period of strife and war in order to institute the millennium. The alternative, postmillennialism, is more optimistic: human affairs are improving, and we shall establish the millennium on earth before the Second Coming. A powerful figure in the premillennial movement was the great revivalist Dwight L. Moody (1837–99). Most fundamentalist and evangelical revival was involved in promoting personal, individual holiness, but not all. The Salvation Army, founded in 1865, was at the forefront of social work in the big cities of Britain and the United States, organized as a military group, and hoping to save the derelict by setting a caring example to induce them to reform.

The evangelical movement comprised large denominations or parts thereof, such as the Southern Baptists and Missouri Synod Lutheranism, and much Black Protestantism. So there were wide sympathies for the more strident affirmations of Biblical inerrancy by tough-minded fundamentalists.

The latter were also influenced by the method of interpreting the Bible called dispensationalism, associated with Dwight L. Moody, and expressed in a relatively scholarly way by C. I. Scofield (1843–1921), who published his *Scofield Reference Bible* in 1909. According to this way of reading the Bible, it refers to a succession of different eras or dispensations—e.g. the age of innocence at the start of the human story in the Garden of Eden, the dispensation of the Law from Moses to Christ, and so on. Human history nears its end, which will be marked by the Second Coming of Christ, the "rapture" of believers who will be taken up into the sky to meet him, a vast war, the conversion of the Jews, a thousand-year kingdom ruled over by Jesus from Jerusalem, and finally the Last Judgment. This theme is a powerful one for modern fundamentalists.

### Twentieth-Century Evangelicalism

For many evangelicals in America, the aftermath of World War I was disturbing. Already there was a sense that the older evangelical values which they thought were intrinsic to American nationhood were being submerged or swamped. Already the immigration before the War had deeply marked America with the Catholic (not to mention the Jewish) influx. Old bastions of New England Protestantism, such as Massachusetts and Connecticut, now found Catholic majorities in the major cities. The same went for some sizable Midwest towns, notably Chicago. Then, the immediate ethos of the 1920s was culturally frivolous, or so it seemed. A new pluralism seemed to undermine mainstream values. It was partly in this mood that the nation had decreed Prohibition in 1919. As it turned out, this produced the speakeasy and the Mafia, and it was done away with by President Franklin D. Roosevelt

(1882–1945) after he came to power in 1933. But it was a powerful expression of evangelical values in American society.

Less effective, however, was the challenge to science mounted by the politician William Jennings Bryan (1860–1925), who acted as prosecutor in the famous Scopes trial in Dayton, Tennessee, when a teacher of that name was indicted for teaching Evolutionary Theory. Bryan's position attracted much ridicule in the world press, and shortly after the trial, as it happened, he died. Periodically, to this day, there are similar legal challenges to the teaching of biology and of pluralist values in the public schools. Part of the problem lies in the dogmatic epistemology (or theory of knowledge) of the fundamentalists, who cannot think that there might be legitimate alternatives to the interpretations that they place on the Bible; or indeed genuine alternatives to the Bible itself. This leaves a tension between their Christianity and the essentially pluralistic character of the American Constitution and way of doing things.

Fundamentalism withdrew into a period of regroupment in the 1930s. But evangelical religion remained a great dynamic, especially among Blacks. It was out of this milieu that there came the most important Christian leader in the United States in the twentieth century. This was Martin Luther King (1929–68). Raised in Atlanta, and educated at Morehouse College and Boston University, he was influenced by Walter Rauschenbusch and sociological reading, by Thoreau and his line on civil disobedience, and by Gandhi. In Montgomery, Alabama, he led a bus boycott and in other ways campaigned nonviolently for civil rights, helping to alleviate the condition of Southern Blacks, especially in education. He was assassinated in 1968. His was a liberal evangelical position, influenced by a touch of the Hindu tradition.

The more ecumenical wing of evangelical revivalism was represented by Billy Graham, a highly successful preacher and crusader, who opened out his campaigns to cooperation with all the mainstream Churches. But it was to be the arrival of television which created the most prominent type of preaching —the TV evangelism of such as Jerry Falwell, Oral Roberts, and Robert Schuller of the Crystal Cathedral in Anaheim. The last of these is really rather removed from mainstream evangelical preaching, stressing the credo of the power of positive thinking in a vaguely Presbyterian setting. The others, though, have a fundamentalist background, and it was in part the resources of TV ministry which powered the revival of the religious Right in the late 1970s. It was in 1979 that Falwell formed the movement known as the Moral Majority, and in this and other ways evangelicals entered strongly into the political process. President Jimmy Carter helped give evangelicalism in general fashionability. But whereas he and other liberal evangelicals were not opposed to some fundamentalist legislation in the 1970s, the Moral Majority saw the times as decadent. Old American values were being attacked. There were Equal Rights, whittling away at the traditional family role of women; legalization of homosexuality; legalized abortion; new religious movements and cults; defeat in the Vietnam War (1965–73 for the

United States); and Watergate. Since the new campaigning appealed to conservative ethical values, it combined easily with patriotism and attracted alliances with the Roman Catholics—which would have been anathema in the 1920s.

The ritual dimension: an important ingredient in the proselytizing of the frontier was the evangelical meeting, here seen in modern form.

## Dimensions of Evangelical and Fundamentalist Christianity

It is useful to look back on the evangelical experience and its fundamentalist variant to reflect on its dimensions. As to the *narrative* dimension, the stress is of course on the Bible—the story of Eden, Israel, Christ, and the coming of the Spirit. This vivid narrative can be arranged for interpretive purposes as a series of dispensations. There is division about the future story between those who look to Christ's coming as before or after the great harmonious and victorious period, the thousand years or millenium. The threat to their story posed by liberal or modernist readings of the Bible, and by such theories as Evolution, leads them to take a strong stance on revelation.

The *doctrinal* dimension affirms unequivocally the existence of God and the Trinity; and it also seeks a philosophical position which will allow a literal interpretation of the Bible to live with most of science. The Evolutionary thesis is attacked (often not without some reason) as itself being overdogmatic and having difficulty over the methods of evolution (random gene shuffling plus natural selection do not seem adequately to account for quantum leaps in animal evolution). The fundamentalist wing of evangelical Christianity has lately espoused a seemingly scientific alternative theory (that is, one using the jargon of science), known as Creationism.

The *experiential* dimension is of great importance, not only because of the general evangelical espousal of conversion and being "born again," as the modern fashion has it, but also because there have been fed into evangelical Christianity streams of Pentecostalism, both among Blacks and Whites. This encourages speaking with tongues and ecstatic experiences of the Spirit, in line with the accounts of Pentecost and the coming of the Spirit in the early Church. There was, for instance, the Azusa Street revival started in 1906 in Los Angeles by William J. Seymour, a Black preacher. At first the various forms of Pentecostalism tended to be rejected by mainstream Christianity, but they gradually made their way in. Some of these motifs combined with faith-healing, which also was used in television religion in the 1960s and on. In any event, one way or another both White and Black evangelicalism is fervid in its emphasis on personal experience of Christ.

As to the *ritual* dimension, there is a strong emphasis on personal prayer, and preaching is probably the prime form of rite, with hymn singing and Bible readings. The revivalists did much to stimulate hymn-writing, usually to Victorian tunes. The pastor or preacher has to develop his skills as a rhetorician, and this gives evangelical Protestantism a very fluid nature. People switch congregations because A is a superior preacher to B, and gathering a congregation is a vital task: its size being an index of evangelical success.

As to the *social* and institutional dimension, there is a tendency for the hardline fundamentalists to separate themselves off from evangelicals who are in their view too soft, or who cooperate with the wrong people, such as liberal Christians, Roman Catholics, and Jews. So there are networks of fundamentalist congregations. But, as we have seen, there is a wider cooperation on the political front, through the so-called Moral Majority. Evangelicalism is heavily entrenched and possesses some notable seminaries, such as Fuller Theological Seminary in Pasadena, California.

As to *ethics*, there is a strong affirmation of what may be called conservative individualism. Society is made up of individuals, and its quality will reflect the life of individuals—who should be sober, hardworking, sexually faithful, patriotic, keeping the Sabbath, and so on. Some fundamentalists particularly dislike certain fashions which they identify with permissiveness—long hair, beards, and women's slacks, for instance. They are unsympathetic to liberal political causes, on the whole; though among evangelicals there are widespread social concerns.

Finally, in *material* terms, evangelicals are not much committed to the visual side of religion, being somewhat heirs to the old iconoclastic tradition. But it is characteristic for them to be keen on up-to-date methods of disseminating their message. The new-style television preachers are a case in point: all the most recent technology is used. It was reported for instance in the Los Angeles Times of March 11, 1978, that the Christian Broadcasting Network in Virginia Beach, Va., had acquired the use of the RCA Satcom II satellite and had ordered 12 million dollars' worth of earth stations. In an earlier age, Aimee Semple McPherson (1890–1944), the Pentecostalist evangelist and founder of the Foursquare Gospel Temples, had used radio dramatically (not to mention great choirs and theatrical techniques). This modernity of means is summed up too in the fact that Robert Schuller began his successful preaching career in southern California by holding meetings in parking lots (he considered most churches limited their membership in an automobile age by not having extensive enough parking lots).

In many ways, then, evangelical Christianity can be nontraditional, but at the same time it claims to stand for older values that it feels may have been betrayed by the liberals. It represents one way of coping with the crisis in authority posed by the relation of modern knowledge to the Bible. But it flourishes because it represents a concrete way of life that it can identify as Christian and involves great intensity of experience and ritual.

## Developments Since World War II

### The Religious Revolution of the 1960s and 1970s

After World War II there was a variant on the loss of satisfaction experienced by many Americans after World War I. This time the threat to the American way of life was perceived externally as the Communist menace. A somewhat Zoroastrian myth underlay foreign policy, of a cosmic struggle between good and evil. McCarthyism came in as an internal force to root out dissent. By the 1950s, during the Eisenhower years, America was comfortable and conformist. This was the heyday of the mainstream liberal Protestant Churches and of unreconstructed Roman Catholicism. It was followed by the hopeful Kennedy administration, which itself betokened a new living together between Protestants and Catholics. It was also the period when the United States was concerned most with supporting the new state of Israel, and a genuine confluence of what were perceived as Christian and Jewish interests emerged. The new religious establishment was Protestant, Catholic, and Jew. But it was a period of relative harmony due for a big shake-up. The late 1960s saw the rebellion of many young people and the birth of the Counterculture. It was a rich and fruitful period, but a disturbing one. Ominous events were at hand: the assassination of President John F. Kennedy (1917–63) and the opening of the Vietnam War (1965); while for Catholics there was the exhilarating but disturbing second Vatican Council (1962–65). For Blacks the 1960s were a period of new opportunities, though the killing of Martin Luther King in 1968 was a reminder of the violence and prejudice still there in American society.

The revolt, partly against mainstream American religion, took various forms. One was a search beyond Western religion—a complex voyage into Eastern religions. Above all, this search concerned inner consciousness and the pursuit of mysticism. These features of religion of course existed within the Catholic and Orthodox traditions, but the latter was little known, while American Catholicism tended to be activist and in that epoch was in any case digesting the reforms of Vatican II. Monks and nuns were leaving orders, while the young sought mysticism in foreign traditions. It was an irony. Under the guidance of gurus such as Alan W. Watts (1915–73), who expounded Zen, and of writings such as those of Aldous Huxley (1894–1963), whose *The Perennial Philosophy* put mysticism at the heart of universal religion, and whose *The Doors of Perception* commended depth experiences created by mind-altering drugs, young folk took off into Eastern religious experiences. The Beatles sat at the feet of the Maharishi Mahesh Yogi in Rishikesh, India; and others experimented with LSD and other substances. The ethos was against the Protestant ethic and in some measure against the capitalist and technological world. Paradoxically the young sometimes used the technology of drugs to overcome the technology of the outer world.

The Counterculture also had its violent strand, especially in those circles where Marxist-style revolution was adopted as the ideal. That Marxism could ever be fashionable in America after the McCarthy era was surprising. But the writings especially of Herbert Marcuse (1898–1979) became fashionable. Some of this revolutionary feeling was triggered by the Vietnam War, with its inequities and burnings. The pacifists increased, partly under Eastern influence: hippies came to be seen as against war, holding up flowers and chanting the slogan "Make love not war." A new antiwar activism stirred the mainstream churches. Mingled into these movements was a new concern for the environment. There was a large move towards sexual liberation too, and from that epoch stemmed the now customary cohabitation of people without marriage and the "coming out" of homosexuals. All this remains shocking still to many Americans, but it became widespread social fact.

Of the more permanent consequences of that era we can point to the rooting of Eastern religions, especially Buddhism, from Tibetan to Zen and from Mahāyāna to Theravāda, on American soil; the stronger presence of the Hindu tradition, partly through the Hare Krishna movement; the survival of smaller so-called cults, such as the Unification Church of the Reverend Sun Myung Moon and the Children of God movement; the wider use of yogic and other meditation techniques among the wider population; the increased recognition by Christian and other mainstream religious groups that they need to take the challenging existence of world religions more seriously; the environmental movement, and increased interest in vegetarianism and animal liberation; and greater sexual permissiveness. Also given a boost during this period, because of the advent of Black Power, was Islam among Blacks, as we shall see.

The perhaps inevitable backlash against many of these movements and ideas came in the late 1970s and early 1980s. The Moral Majority was a symptom of this. But the trends listed are here to stay. The Eastern emphasis among Whites was reinforced by immigration from East Asia especially, so that in California, for instance, Anglo Buddhists mingle with Asians of various nationalities, who enrich their experience of Buddhism. All this has brought into relief the great extent of American pluralism, and this makes it hard for those who wish to put the clock back to a more monistic Protestant era.

Meanwhile the radicalism of the 1960s and early 1970s encouraged new patterns of identity among Blacks, Native Americans, those of Mexican descent, and others; and helped to give great vigor to the women's movement, which had some strong effects in relation to religion.

### Women in Christianity and Judaism

It was in the 1960s and 1970s that women most prominently began to conduct a critique of the Christian—and to some degree the Jewish—traditions. An example is Mary Daly's *Beyond God the Father*, which drew attention to the persistent gender discrimination in the Christian tradition, and the assumption that the male gender is primary. The language of the Bible is largely sexist. It does not take much reflection for us to see that gender as applied to God cannot be literal, except on some very strange assumptions about the material character of the Divine Being, which virtually all religions reject (for God is held to be a spiritual Being). God does not literally have hair on his (or her) chest, so any literal ascription of gender is nonsense. But when we see that gender is metaphorical, then it becomes important to use "she" of God as well as "he." Strictly God is neither male nor female, nor both, nor neither. The women's protest movement in Christianity drew attention to male supremacy as expressed not only in so much of the language of religion but—perhaps more importantly, and certainly more concretely—in the organizations of religion. Maleness has been largely entrenched in the hierarchies of episcopal religions, from the Orthodox to the Anglicans, and has been there too in the other denominations. The struggle for greater women's rights in these matters is far from over. In her *In Memory of Her* (1983), the writer and Biblical interpreter, Elizabeth Schüssler-Fiorenza, draws attention to the centrality of women's experience in the founding of Christianity; and here and elsewhere, the new discipline of women's studies gives a new and stirring perspective on the development of religions. Similar critiques and new slants have emerged in the Jewish tradition, and while the women's movement is strongest among liberal Protestants it has a sizable presence in Roman Catholicism.

### Black Experience: Turning One's Back on Christianity

Black Christianity had been powerful in the 1960s and it achieved much. But at the same time there were attractions in seeking identity by an alternative route, and the chief of these was Islam. The story of Black Islam is a

373

fascinating one, as we shall see, because of its move from unorthodoxy to orthodoxy. Blacks in America, generally speaking, did not have much contact with worldwide Islam, though of course quite a number of slaves had originally been Muslim. In the 1920s some Ahmadiyah missionaries from India came to America, and a number of black converts were made. But much more significant in the next forty years was the so-called Nation of Islam.

A peddler called Wallace D. Fard came to Detroit in 1930 and began preaching and organizing, but disappeared in 1934. His chief minister was Elijah Poole (1897–1975), renamed Elijah Muhammad. He declared that Wallace D. Fard was Allah, and that he was his messenger. He taught that human beings were originally black, but a bad scientist created an evil race of Whites who were allowed by Allah to rule for six thousand years, after which civilization would collapse in chaos, to be replaced by a new world ruled over by Blacks. The moral was that Blacks should segregate themselves. Purity of life was to be followed—no alcohol, no smoking, no drugs, no pork, no movies, no cosmetics.

Eventually the most articulate spokesperson for the movement came to be Malcolm X (1925–65), who rejected Martin Luther King's nonviolent approach. However, he went on a pilgrimage to Mecca in 1964 and saw that in fact the teachings of Elijah Muhammad were incompatible with those of true Islam. When he returned, he broke with his erstwhile mentor. He was killed in 1965; and ten years later Wraithuddin Muhammad, son of Elijah Muhammad, took over the movement on his father's death and moved in the

A crowd raises its hands in response to the preaching of Malcolm X, a major leader of Black Islam in America.

374

direction prefigured by Malcolm X. He became Orthodox, opened the community to Whites, changed the name to the American Muslim Mission, and stimulated the membership to take part in political life and social action and not cut themselves off from the mainstream of American life. Some of the Nation of Islam predictably stayed faithful to the older vision, under the militant leadership of Louis Farrakhan. Meanwhile Muslim communities from other parts of the world have settled in the States and have been joined by American Blacks. The Muslim population of greater Los Angeles is rapidly overtaking the Jewish population, for instance. It is obvious that Black experience of Christianity has often been negative, in times of slavery and segregation and persisting racial prejudice, and this constitutes a main reason for seeking brotherhood in Islam.

## The Revival of Native American Religion

Meanwhile the twentieth century has seen some success in the Native Americans' struggle for recognition of their rights. In some degree this has furthered and been furthered by a pan-Indian ideology. To start with there has been the spread of practices and ideas across cultural and national boundaries. Notable among such is the peyote cult, focusing on the sacramental use of the peyote cactus. This had been in use in Mexico before the present century, but it gathered force in the 1890s, spreading through the Plains. The rituals are conducted under the loose canopy of the Native American Church, which has had a powerful struggle to gain recognition (the combination of missionary prejudice and the fact that they used a mind-altering drug placed special obstacles in their path). The central ceremonial, to commemorate birthdays, for funerals, at prayer meetings and so on, takes place in a *tipi*, and is conducted according to a fairly complex pattern culminating in singing under the influence of the peyote, which brings a feeling of nearness to God (often conceived in Christian terms, with the Virgin and so forth: some adherents of the tradition use the Bible in the ceremonial, so it is in a sense a partly Christian movement, but with strong Native American grounding). All this has helped to give a sense of—if not pan-Indian—at least cross-Indian solidarity.

Further in this direction of Native American unity is the use of a combination of traditional rituals, from peyote to the sweat lodge and from the Sun Dance to the Ghost Dance, in order to promote health and well being; and this loose pan-Indian religiousness is fast becoming a primary underpinning of struggles to regain sacred places. In this the activist American Indian Movement has been a major force. At the same time, in higher education, increasing attention has been paid to Native American religions, a consequence of the great growth of Religious Studies as part of the new flow of ideas in the 1960s and the 1970s. To some extent this revival links with the struggle of Americans of Mexican descent to establish their rights and dignity, since there is a like concern with some of the ancient religious traditions of Mexico and Central America.

*Eastern Christianity in the United States*
Although a much lesser group than the dominating Protestants and Catholics in America, the Eastern Orthodox Churches have a presence through the migration from countries such as Greece, Romania, Bulgaria, Yugoslavia, and Russia, as well as from the Arab Christian Levant. While Greek Churches depend upon the Greek Ecumenical Patriarch, the trend in other nationally organized groups in North America is to join the so-called Orthodox Church in America, which was constituted under that name in 1970. There is also an independent Russian Church known as the Orthodox Church Outside Russia, which is based in New York. Arab Orthodox Christians look to the Patriarchate of Antioch. The swing toward cooperation and unity is assisted by the replacement of the vernacular languages by English. Orthodoxy has a significant if numerically small role to play in the total life of American religion.

# Liberal Christian Theology in the Twentieth Century

Meanwhile amid the complexities of some of the developments we have noted, the dominant Protestant thought remained in essence liberal—in the scholarly though not always the political sense. The most important figure during the 1930s and on into the early 1950s was Reinhold Niebuhr (1892–1971), who served for a short time in a parish amid the car workers of Detroit and taught at Union Theological Seminary in New York, which was the most vital center of Protestant theology until the 1970s. Niebuhr's Detroit experience engaged him with political and moral issues. His stance was somewhat like Barth's, and he was often called neo-orthodox, although he disliked the term. In politics, for long, he was thought left-wing and for a time was a socialist. But with his Old Testament emphasis on linear history, his strong sense of the sin and frailty of human beings, and his emphasis on God's grace and love, he was far from holding any utopian views; and he was far from thinking that there were easy solutions to human social problems, as the title of his most famous book indicated: *Moral Man in Immoral Society* (1932).

Another Union teacher was the second overshadowing figure in Protestant theology, Paul Tillich (1886–1965). He was removed from a teaching position in Frankfurt am Main, Germany, in 1933, and was at Union from then until 1955. His position was a twentieth-century reshaping of natural theology, but in the mould of Existentialism, that is a philosophy which takes seriously human experiences of the world. For him, religion was a pervasive aspect of all life: it was humanity's ultimate concern, that of the individual. We have to interpret religious symbols in this light. For instance, the story of Adam and Eve is ultimately about human finitude (and so about our sense of the infinite—which is symbolized as God). A person grasps the inner meaning of the story through her own experience of facing up to finitude and living in the presence of death. By his symbolic, emotionally anchored account of the

Christian faith, Tillich managed to present it in a form which many found refreshingly modern and credible, especially in his *Systematic Theology* (1951–63). In his last days, part of which were spent in Japan and in California at Santa Barbara, he came to appreciate the vital importance of Christian dialogue with other religions.

But if Tillich was popular in the 1960s, new skeptical forces left him somewhat behind. New secularist emphases took a grip of much Protestant theology, in the thought of writers such as Paul van Buren and T. J. J. Altizer, known as the "death of God" school. In many ways the most influential of these writings was *The Secular City* (1965), by Harvey Cox (who later much changed his position at least twice). The death of Jesus was seen as a negation of the very notion of the transcendent God "out there," and these thinkers experimented with a kind of Christian atheism. This was the ultimate in the liberal attempt to keep Christian faith believable in an age of empiricism and science: it abandoned belief in favor of feeling and action.

This phase of theology did not—could not—last long, for now the tide of the 1960s, romantic, credulous, pluralistic, religious, washed across the nation. Partly because it was a revolt against the Vietnam War, it was transmitted rapidly into Canada where many young people migrated in order to avoid the draft. This development did not at first affect Christian theology much, though methods of Yoga and Eastern spirituality were often incorporated into Christian and especially into Roman Catholic faith. But both the work of Martin Luther King and the antiwar struggle by many Christians, including the Catholic Daniel Berrigan and the Protestant William Sloane Coffin, revitalized Christian pacifism.

By the 1970s the women's movement and other growing concerns stimulated a new view of the Christian and Jewish traditions; and there were influential attempts at minority theologies—Black and Red, for instance. Towards the end of the decade there was greater interest and concern with so-called Liberation Theology from Latin America, which combined Marxist and Catholic (plus a few Protestant) motifs. To that we shall return in looking at the Hispanic American situation in Chapter 24.

Among Roman Catholics, probably the most influential figure in these times was the Jesuit Karl Rahner (1904–84) who combined traditional and existential strands in his thinking, somewhat like Tillich. Also widely received in the United States was the Tübingen dissident Catholic theologian Hans Küng, whose questioning of Papal doctrines and willingness to translate tradition into modern forms has a wide appeal. Increasingly Roman Catholics in the United States since Vatican II have converged in their style and substance of thought with Protestants. So there is a broad stem of relatively liberal theology which has maintained its vigor, though probably it reached its greatest solidity during the 1950s and 1960s.

*Some Secular Forces*

Meanwhile the context of religion in the United States was of a pluralism in

vigorous by the 1980s, despite a decline in the overall number of practising, especially Orthodox, Jews. This decline is in part because of legal requirements for marriage; for throughout the modern period intermarriage between Jews and Gentiles has been widespread, and it has favored groups like the Unitarians rather than the Jewish community.

## Reflections on American Religion

Several patterns emerge from the foregoing account. First, liberalism, industrialization, capitalism, pluralistic democracy, individualism, and modern science and technology have arisen from within Western civilization, and indeed partly under the stimulus of Christianity and especially Protestantism itself; but Christianity has still had to cope with them as if they were external forces. The question has been: How much of beloved tradition could one persist in maintaining? How far was a revolution forced on the various denominations?

Second, the dominant Protestant ethos in America, while of course favorable to democracy, was eventually faced with the dilemma that pluralism was in conflict with its civil religion of trust in God, manifest destiny, and a working ethos. The 1960s and 1970s underlined the pluralism both moral and religious—within American society. The contradiction was not so evident in slower-moving Canada, with its establishmentarian leanings. But the United States Constitution built into itself a pluralism which was at odds with maintaining the traditional Protestant dominance, at least ideologically.

Third, the reaction against the attempt to synthesize liberalism and science on the one hand and Christian belief on the other—an attempt that was characteristic of mainstream Protestant Churches—became hard-edged in the fundamentalist movements, which in some respect were actually more revolutionary and radical than the mainstream synthesis. The mainstream made adjustments to doctrine and reshaped myth, but left much of the ritual and organization in place. Increasingly, revivalist Christianity took individualism, capitalism, and technology seriously: the preaching was and is set squarely in the marketplace, and it uses up-to-date technological methods, it often discards established Churches and denominations, and it concentrates on the experience of the individual. Instead of rooting faith in a Bible that most Christians could agree was revelation, the fundamentalists turned the very ground of faith itself into an article of faith. Commitment had to be to both Jesus and Bible, often more to the Bible, and interpreted as literally as feasible. The cost lay with the doctrinal dimension, for the question of whether you did not really have to sacrifice science and humanistic history in all this could be acute. Also, the epistemology or model of knowledge, based in faith and authoritarian in tone, was at odds with pluralism; so that fundamentalism tended to cling to a form of civil religion and patriotism, especially after the traumatic blow to national pride consequent on the Vietnam War.

Fundamentalism is usually called conservative, which it may be politically; but in fact it takes the Bible out of its ancient milieu and uses it today as if it were a contemporary newspaper. It is what may be called neofoundationalist, taking the foundation epoch of Christianity (its own version of Biblical Christianity) and using that as the exclusive norm.

Meanwhile, and fourthly, the Catholics have undergone their overdue attempt to update the faith, which means to synthesize with modern historical and scientific knowledge, to make the liturgy more immediate and simple, and so on. The Roman Catholics have changed through all the dimensions, but have retained the basic characteristics of organization. For it is through the framework of the *organization*, relatively stable, that they have been able to achieve great experimentation. In *experience* there have been experiments with pentecostalism and a revival of the mystical tradition. In *ritual* there has been the move into the vernacular language. This has welded together Catholics with differing ethnic identities. In *ethics* there have been divisions, with generally speaking a loosening up: in fact most American Catholics do not heed Papal pronouncements on birth control, though on the other hand anti-abortion sentiment has led to an alliance on this and some other issues with conservative Protestants. In *doctrine* there have been new attempts at updating, especially through the lowering of resistance to Evolutionary thought. In the *narrative* dimension the Bible has come fully under modern scrutiny among Catholic scholars, since modernism is no longer condemned as it was at the beginning of the century. In *organization* there has been stability as I have said; but house meetings and other ways of intensifying study and devotion are not without significance.

Meanwhile Black Christianity has greatly come in from the cold. Women's rights have made their impact on many religious groups. Native Americans are synthesizing a pan-Indian religion with which to deal with the oppressions and incursions of the beefier civilization.

Altogether, with analogous Jewish reactions playing their part, modern America has a much more pluralistic and diverse aspect today than heretofore. It foreshadows a world situation of intermingling and experimentation, of consumerism and searching in religion, of individual choice. It is an exciting and creative period, doubtless, but one which leaves many people naturally perplexed. Maybe this is why the appearance of certainty in preaching and in tradition is attractive.

Are there discernible patterns in American moves into modernity? Surely. Where the social and organizational dimension was strong enough, as in the Catholic tradition, it was possible to resist liberalism, to moderate individualism, to mount social programs to cope with industrialization, and to make necessary but perhaps not excessive concessions to nationalism. But in the long run most groups have made powerful accommodation to modern life.

# South Asia and Reactions to Colonial Intervention

## The Varieties of Indian Life

Our concern in this chapter is with the South Asian scene, and with the consequences of the conquest by Britain of the subcontinent (including what is now the Republic of India, Pakistan, Bangladesh, and Sri Lanka, with operational control of Nepal, and a political interest in Tibet). This major conquest was foreshadowed by earlier operations of the Portuguese, Dutch, and French. It was the aftermath of the Seven Years' War (1756–63) — when the British, largely by their superior naval power, defeated France — that brought British domination of Ceylon (Sri Lanka: since "Ceylon" was the name most used during the colonial period, and until 1972, I shall use it in discussing the developments of this period) and India (again, at this time the term covered the whole subcontinent, and this is how we shall use it for events up to 1947). It was a novel experience, historically speaking, for India, which had hitherto always been invaded from the northwest. It was also novel because the nation that came to conquer was already undergoing various industrial, social, and political changes which were to have their echoes in India and Ceylon. How could these old civilizations respond to the challenges of an emerging modern world? The matter was complicated by the very heterogeneous character of India and Ceylon themselves at this time.

The Islamic impact on India had been great, but by the time of the major British advances it was in severe decline. It was said that the power of the great Mughal, whose seat was in Delhi, only reached as far as Palam, where Delhi airport now stands. In the latter part of the eighteenth century there were various powers in India — the Maratha Confederacy dominating central India, the state of Mysore and a number of smaller kingdoms in the south, the remains of the Mughal Empire, the rising Sikhs in the Punjab, and many

*Opposite* The material dimension: the ritual center of Sikhism is the Golden Temple in Amritsar, which is also a beautiful material expression of the Sikh religion.

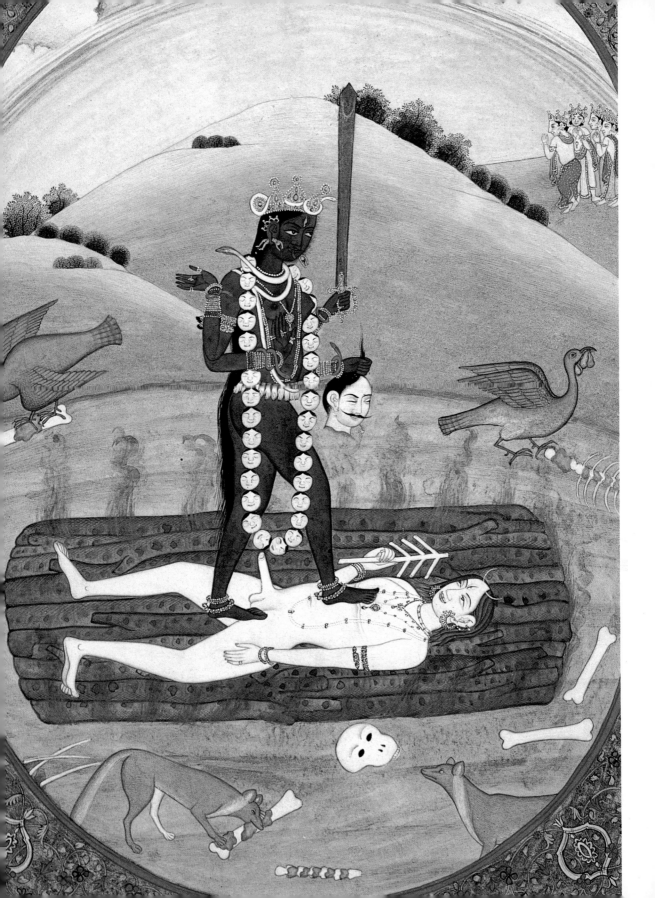

other principalities. It was not yet a unified land. Differences of language, religion, and interest left it largely divided as the British extended their control. By 1805 the Mughal emperor had come formally under the control and protection of the conquering power. Much of the Ganges river area was under the British, who ruled out of Calcutta. The east coast was conquered, and so was a large part of the south. The British had taken the island of Ceylon from the Dutch, except for the kingdom of Kandy in the central mountains (it fell in 1815). The various pieces of the area controlled, however, still displayed great variety. In many areas Islam was the dominant religion; in most of the rest, that undeveloped federation of rituals and beliefs which we now know as Hinduism, and in Ceylon Buddhism predominated. Christianity was beginning to capitalize on colonial rule. The Sikhs were breaking away to form a new political power and, in effect, a separate religion.

*Opposite* The great Goddess, Kali, showing her power.

### The Formation of Sikhism

As a preliminary to the story of the interaction of the British and the traditions of India, it is useful to trace the story of Sikhism, which represents the result of the collision of Hindu and Islamic power. We have already seen some of the first developments: but these belong to the early times, before the Sikh clash with Mughal dominance led to the fashioning of a new community cemented together by the turban and other external marks of male belongingness, and by loyalty to the religion of the Guru Granth. This community was fashioned, too, by an alliance of different Punjabi castes, notably the cultivators known as the *jāts* and the merchants who were strong patrons of *bhakti* or devotional religion, which the Sikh tradition embodied. The evolution of Sikhism from a syncretic and peaceful way of combining Hindu and Muslim motifs—the religion of Kabir and Nanak—to the militant organization which was finally fashioned by the Tenth Guru, Gobind Singh (1666–1708), has puzzled observers. But it is only the tendency of religions to represent themselves as unchanging, as though the religion of Kabir were the religion of Gobind Singh, which causes this puzzlement. It was basically in the time of Gobind Singh that Sikhism as we know it was formed. It makes use of a past tradition and leadership, of course, going back to Nanak.

Already before the time of Gobind Singh the community was in process of forming itself into a military organization: but it was his reforms which set Sikhism on the path of becoming both a military and a religious power. He is represented as being the very ideal of chivalry and loyalty and is an example held up to the male Sikh. This quality of chivalry combines both martial and spiritual dedication.

His father Tegh Bahadur, the Ninth Guru, was executed on the orders of the Mughal emperor in 1675, and before his death proclaimed Gobind as his successor. After some successful warfare against both the Hindu Rajputs and the Mughals, Gobind established his capital at Anandpur, and summoned his followers there for a ceremony on April 13, 1699. After the morning

A nineteenth-century lithograph from Amritsar, showing Nanak reciting poems to various Sikhs, ascetics and others.

devotions he called for five men to offer their lives in sacrifice, and took them behind a tent, to reappear with a sword dripping with blood. However, he had killed five goats, and the men reappeared, to be nominated by him as founding members of the new community or *Khalsa* (literally "Community of the Pure"). He caused them to drink out of a common bowl, from a drink he had made called *amrit* or nectar, conferring immortality. Importantly, this sacramental act was designed to break down caste barriers within the new community. They were to change their names to Singh or Lion. So in theory every Sikh is called Singh. In practice, as we shall see, there are complications to the story.

Each Sikh man has to wear five badges of his belonging, the five K's as they are called: to keep his hair and beard uncut (*kais*); to carry a comb (*kangha*) to keep his hair tidy; to wear *kacchā* or knee-length breeches, then used by soldiers; to wear a bangle (*karā*) on his wrist as a sign of loyalty to the Guru; and to carry a short sword (*kirpan*). Sikhs are forbidden alcohol, tobacco (then being introduced into India), and meat slaughtered in the Muslim manner, that is, by being bled to death.

The final great reform of Gobind was to proclaim that after his death they were to have the Adi Granth, or sacred book, as their Guru. It is therefore referred to as the Guru Granth (Teacher Book), and is a central object of veneration in the typical Sikh temple or "Guru House," *gurudvāra* or Gurdwara. The Granth is a collection of writings going back in part to Nanak, including saints from before him, such as Namdev, Kabir, and

386

Ravidas. Its final recension was done by Gobind Singh. The original collection in this form was put into the Golden Temple at Amritsar in the Punjab, which became the spiritual center and focus of pilgrimage for the Sikhs.

With its great variety of languages from north India and its styles of poetry, the Granth gives a broad sense of the devotional life of the region. At the social level it has a lot of emphasis on the irrelevance of caste and race. It condemns distinctions. It also underlines the vital role of purity of motives. One does not win God's grace by the performance of external acts but through the devotion of the heart. It emphasizes the performance of truth, sincerity, and the attainment of equipoise (*sahj*) and knowledge of the Divine.

Despite these teachings, Sikhism developed, as we have seen, its own battery of external practices. Maybe this was inevitable. But it creates a lively dialectic between loyalty to a particular, transcaste community and the realization of universal humanity.

The new community eventually established dominance in the Punjab under the leadership of Ranjit Singh (1780–1839), but shortly after were defeated by the British and incorporated into British India. The British harnessed the military expertise and spirit of the Sikhs by using them prominently in the Indian Army which they created. But not all Sikhs were actually oriented towards full incorporation in the Sikh community. As well as the "unshorn" ones who carry on the externals, there are many other followers known as *sahajdhāris*, who are regarded as taking longer to attain full membership. After all, the tradition of Nanak was a general *bhakti* form of religion, and so a cloud of devotional Hindus form a penumbra of the Sikh movement.

There are also other movements which have relationships to Sikhism. On the one side are the followers of Kabir, known as Kabirpanthis (those who follow the path of Kabir); on the other hand, more directly indebted to Sikhism through the Adi Granth, are the Radhasoamis, founded in Agra by a banker, Shiv Dayal (1818–78), who carry on the Guru tradition and stress the vital importance in God's communication to the world of the essence of sound, *shabd*, the Word. In this form of faith, which itself is split into differing groups, there is stress on the union of the disciple with the Teacher and the unity of the Teacher with the Divine. It is a kind of incarnational Hinduism, but it owes a lot to the Sikh connection. The name signifies the unity between the soul, symbolized by Rādhā the lover of Krishna, and the Master or *somai*. The Khalsa idea (see above) has remained strong, and in fact during the latter days of the British became more militant in a blend of Punjabi and all-Indian nationalism. Later still, in the 1980s, Sikh militants have gone further, agitating for an independent state which would be predominantly Sikh, in the Indian Punjab.

In a way the history of the Sikhs illustrates in sharp form a general point, that when religion A meets religion B it may turn out that a blend, AB, occurs, which becomes by the force of circumstances a third force—in effect a new religion. In the Sikh case this move also led to a marked transformation, of a sharp kind. In the circumstances Sikhism could easily have been counted just as a variant on Hinduism, as the Kabir movement was; for Hindu religions have fluid boundaries. It could simply have learned from Islam and incorporated Islamic elements into its fabric. But by forming a political community its role has become less ambiguous. By and large, Sikhs now feel themselves as belonging to a separate religion: and a modern complaint about the Indian Constitution is that it does not recognize separate status for the Sikhs in terms of the law and the like.

## The Rāj: Challenge and Response

### British Influences

With the defeat of the Sikhs in 1849 and the occupation of Sind, the mosaic of British rule in India was complete. However, in 1857 a rebellion by Indian soldiers, disturbed at rumors that the grease used for gun cartridges contained beef and pork fat, offending religious susceptibilities, spread into a wider revolt. This in a sense was an early war of liberation, though rather blind, since there were no clear ideological goals. It was fiercely crushed, and in 1858 the old administration by the East India Company—originally a purely commercial enterprise—ended. In 1871 the empire of India, with the Queen as Empress, was instituted. This British rule, or Rāj, was complex, since many states, some quite large such as Hyderabad in the center south, were left, in a kind of internal patchwork embedded within the areas of direct rule. The princes recognized the supremacy of the Queen, but had a fair amount of leeway as to how they might rule, under the advice in each case of a British Resident.

But the system was a kind of unity, and it brought the whole of India under one aegis, and one moreover that was interested in modernizing and unifying the country. Under the East India Company, missionaries were long excluded from Company territory, since commercial interests did not like the prospect of upsetting the inhabitants. But from 1820 onwards mission activity in British territories began. Before that—apart from the old Catholic missions under such workers as the highly original Roberto de Nobili (1606–56 in India), who adopted Brahmin ways and Indian philosophical concepts in expounding the Christian religion—there had been the highly successful work of establishing a college and missionary center in Serampore, which was a Danish enclave, and in one or two other places.

In the early British mission period the evangelical Christian critique of Hindu customs was strong, and led to the government's suppressing suttee, namely the practice wherein a widow followed her husband on the funeral pyre. It was partly because of such incursions on tradition, and out of a desire to restore the old order, that the Indian Mutiny, so-called by the British, occurred. But after 1858 there were plenty of modernizations and critiques of tradition—railways, a whole system of higher education, new commerce, agricultural changes, English as the language of government, and so on. It was these changes which led to various responses on the part of the Indian religious traditions; the same could be said of Ceylon also.

The forces which the British Rāj brought with it can be systematized as follows, particularly as they bore upon the developing Indian middle class which was at the interface between the cultures.

First, there was mainly evangelical Christianity, confident in the superiority of Western culture, and often believing that modernization and Christianity would go together. It was critical of Islam's social backwardness (in the eyes of Christians from abroad) and of Hindu idolatry and harmful customs (e.g. child marriage, caste, and temple prostitution).

Second, there was the more secular ethos of imperial administrators, heavily influenced by the utilitarianism of Jeremy Bentham (1748–1832) and John Stuart Mill (1806–73), which held that the rational basis of ethics and law is the maximizing of happiness and the minimizing of suffering. Such administrators did not shrink from social and administrative reform.

Third, there was the force of capitalism, which demanded a railway network (a major creation), but also ruined indigenous industries such as cloth-making in favor of the cotton mills of Lancashire: but it was a force which, with imperialism, was creating a global system of economics, and from that no country could escape.

Fourth, there was the force of nationalism, which in Britain's case held to the superiority of Western Christian civilization and in particular that of Britain: it was self-righteous and confident, and epitomized in the attitude of the historian Lord Macaulay (1800–59), who advised higher education for India because then the follies of Asian thinking would be left behind. But of course nationalism spreads by generating its opposing nationalism, and for the first time, in the 1860s onwards, India began to experience a sense of India as a people.

Fifth, there was the force through which many of these others were to be conveyed and implemented: education and in particular higher education, whereby a new English-speaking elite was fashioned which was to be the main impetus towards change. Colleges and universities were set up in various centers: Bombay, Madras, Calcutta, Delhi, and the princely states. Education was encouraged by missionaries, many of whom devoted their lives to it feeling that by some osmosis Christianity would rub off on the new elite.

Sixth, lying behind education was the force and prestige of science. It could be seen that a new scientific worldview had contributed to the technical powers of British and Western civilization, which had such important economic and military effects.

*First Stirrings of Hindu Response: the Brahmo Samāj*
Bengal was the center of the East India Company's power, and it was there that the first consciously reforming movement within the Hindu framework started, led by Ram Mohan Roy (1772–1833). He had been educated in the

Muslim center at Patna on the Ganges, and had then undertaken Sanskrit studies. His linguistic aptitude led to his learning English, and he gained a job with the Company in 1803. He published in 1804 a book in Persian, which criticized the polytheistic aspects of the Hindu tradition. His exposure to Islam here allied itself to his attraction to eighteenth-century rationalism. His translations of five main Upanishads into English were designed to show that the Hindu tradition had as its true focus the one Reality, Brahman. He published, too, in 1820 a book called *The Precepts of Jesus* which argued that Jesus taught a vigorous ethical way of life, which need not be overlaid by the complexities of myth and doctrine which the Christians had added to the original message. In brief, he expounded a Hindu unitarianism, espousing belief in one God, and was iconoclastic about the many images and rites presided over by the priesthood.

Roy founded the Brahmo Samāj or Divine Society, which carried forward, through other leaders such as Debendranath Tagore (1817–1905) and Keshab Chandra Sen (1838–84), the message of social reform from a Hindu perspective. Roy was also influential in the agitation which led to the abolition of suttee in 1829. He was influenced by unitarian missionaries in Calcutta, but was keen to express what he himself could take to be an essentially Hindu worldview. This he found in his unitarian interpretation of the Upanishads. Smitten by a disease when visiting England, he died in Bristol in 1833.

His movement was of profound importance in pioneering a new view of the Hindu tradition from the perspective of a class of upwardly mobile caste Hindus. These were not of the upper echelons of the Brahmins, whose concern was too much with ritual purity, but lower-class Brahmins, merchants, landowners and others, who stood to benefit by the replacement of Muslim power and culture by British. The ultimate problem for the Brahmo Samāj was that its "rationality" and purism in belief would cut it off from the mass of Hindus.

There is of course more than a hint in Ram Mohan Roy of the transcendent unity of universalist traditions (Muslim, Hindu, and Christian), and this cross-religious unity was ultimately destined to be a most vital factor in the formation of a modern Hindu ideology. As far as the forces sketched above are concerned, the Brahmo worldview could cope well. It was able to make a reply to evangelical Christianity of its purity and even faithfulness to the original message of Jesus (naturally such a "reduction" of Christianity greatly infuriated the missionaries in Calcutta). It was adapted to social reform and a new economics. It was compatible with the new English education. It had not yet developed a nationalism, which was yet to come: it was early days for Indians to think of themselves as unified. But it appealed to Bengalis, who had their own national sentiments.

*Dayānanda Sarasvatī and Hindu Fundamentalism*
Brahmo Samāj also had some influence on a Gujerati guru whose movement was to have wider influence; Dayānanda Sarasvatī (1824–83), founder of the

Arya Samāj ("The Noble Society" or "Aryan Society"). His reform ideas went even further back than the Upanishads, to the rishis (*ṛṣis*) of the Vedic hymns.

Born in Kathiawar in western India, Dayānanda left home to become a wandering recluse: into this mode of life as a *sannyāsin* he was ordained in 1847. For a while he studied with a famous grammarian of the old style in Mathura in north India. The pundit held that the only true texts were the ancient ones of the seers, and that much later Hindu philosophy and theology was false and sectarian. Dayānanda came to attack Hindu image worship: but it was not until he visited the Brahmo Samāj that he saw the value of modern methods of propagating his message. Debating in Sanskrit was not the way.

In 1875 he founded the Ārya Samāj, and two years later the movement took off when he gained the support of merchants and others who wanted arguments to stave off Christian attacks on the Hindu tradition. The message was radical, in that so much of the Hindu tradition, including the rights of Brahmins, was renounced. Dayānanda held that the only true scriptures were the Vedic hymns: even the Brahmanas and Upanishads were to be abandoned as later accretions. The germ of modern science was to be found in the Vedic hymns (such items as atomic theory), and their main teaching was pure monotheism.

The rituals of the Ārya Samāj—their worship of the one God—were open to all, and could be conducted by anyone; women and outcastes could study the scriptures. It was thus a radically egalitarian movement, with some feeling of nationalism, not yet however fully developed. It happens that the Ārya Samāj made great headway among overseas Hindus of the Indian diaspora, in such places as South Africa, or Fiji, whither Indian laborers had been transported on contracts known as indentures, so that they were called "indentured laborers," after the abolition of the slave trade, to work in the plantations of (mainly) sugar.

But because the Ārya Samāj is so strong a reforming movement it has become rather cut off from the mainstream of the Hindu tradition. It has become, if you like, a sect within the wider confederacy of Hindu religions. In response to Christianity and to the dominance of Western civilization, something more forceful was needed, which would mobilize and reform the Hindu way of life. It would have to make sense of the mass of Hindu practice and at the same time provide new growing points in the intellectual and nationalistic life. For one thing, the Ārya Samāj's extreme scriptural fundamentalism excised too much of Hindu learning; for another its iconoclasm was unacceptable to many, many Hindus, fond of their myths and festivals, and less in revolt against the Brahmins than against too much foreign influence.

It may, however, be useful to pause here to consider the strategies of response to foreign criticism and reform. If you want to remain somehow true to your tradition, and yet you wish to or need to effect reforms within it, you can base your reform on some element in the past, for instance you can reach back right to what you conceive the very beginning of your tradition. Such a reaching back to foundations is better called "neofoundationalism" than "fundamentalism," and can, while appearing to be very conservative, be remarkably radical. In the case of the Ārya Samāj, virtually everything was changed—ritual, ethics, doctrine, myth, social organization, material focus.

There can, though, be other models. You may wish to repudiate some features of your tradition in the name of establishing some golden past that may be later than the scriptures. If it be the classical age of your culture, you could call such a reforming move "neoclassicism." It was this reaching into the classical past, and then interpreting it in modern terms, that turned out to be the most successful way of coping with the challenge of the West, both in India and Sri Lanka. In these various ways to hold on to tradition while making the adaptations necessary to survive vigorously in the modern world, part of the question was as to how much of the existing tradition it is necessary to sacrifice. The more one can retain the more satisfactory the adjustment will seem.

In fact the Ārya Samāj, though using more up-to-date methods of missionizing, still did not come to terms fully with modern science and education. Modern scholarship had already turned its attention, of course, to India's past, including its scriptures. The neofoundationalist appeal of the Ārya Samāj had less appeal to those who knew something of liberal scholarship. Its position about the Vedic hymns was not easy to sustain. Moreover, Dayānanda Sarasvatī, through no fault of his own, did not understand well the nature of modern scientific method. To hold that the scriptures contain the gist of modern scientific knowledge is to miss the point of the dialectical, critical character of the development of science. Nevertheless, his movement was able to continue and to expand because he devolved responsibility to branches, and gave expression to practical democracy.

There was another factor at work, which militated rather against the hard line of the Ārya Samāj. That factor was the coexistence of different religions in India. From the perspective of Indian nationalism, now growing with greater self-consciousness, some view of Hinduism which could make sense of the other religious traditions could be important and attractive.

### Ramakrishna, Vivekānanda, and the Modern Hindu Ideology

It was indeed such a pluralist perspective which made itself felt through the life of Ramakrishna (1834–86) and the missionizing work of Swami Vivekānanda (1863–1902). Vivekānanda can be said to be the chief spokesperson for the modern Hindu ideology. This drew on the resources of the classical age in the shape of the Vedāntin philosopher and religious reformer Śankara, and through a modern interpretation of his thought presented a picture of the Hindu tradition that seemed to make marvelous sense of it, but also of the other religions too. It also made wonderful sense of the great sweep of Indian culture, and could become a framework for expressing Indian nationalism. It was, moreover, an ideology well able to cope with the

A statue of Ramakrishna in a Ramakrishna Vedānta temple.

various forces mentioned earlier. It could also help to resolve a question of the times: whether the only way forward was violent revolution, as some held; or whether there could be some evolution which would allow India to develop its own form of democracy. The issue of violence was taken up, of course, by Gandhi, and the democratic impulse was developed further by his great political ally, Jawaharlal Nehru. To these figures we shall of course return.

The alliance between the sainthood of Ramakrishna and the sophisticated teachings of Vivekānanda gave a kind of dual status to the new ideology—it could appeal both to the masses, for whom the figure of the Kālī-worshipping guru was familiar, and to the middle classes, to whom the English-educated Vivekānanda could write appealingly. It paralleled the later alliance of the archetypal Gandhi and the sophisticated Nehru.

Ramakrishna (his religious name: he was born Gadadhar Chatterji) came from a Brahmin Vaiṣṇava family in rural Bengal. After the death of his father, he went to Calcutta to assist his brother who was running a new temple to Kālī, which also had shrines to Śiva and to Rādhā and Kṛṣṇa: it thus effectively contained the main strands of Bengali and Indian *bhakti*. After his brother's death, Ramakrishna became priest of the Mother (Kālī) and became absorbed in ecstasies relating to her. He felt himself mad with Kālī, but a wandering ascetic woman, skilled in Tantra, came to the temple and put him through a long course of Tantra which moderated his *bhakti* and turned his ecstatic experiences into more playful and manageable forms. Still later an Advaita Vedāntin ascetic came there, one Totapuri. Ramakrishna took up the practice of nondual meditation and achieved the highest state, regarded as liberating, in which even the Mother and God as personal entities disappeared.

Ramakrishna also experimented with meditating on Allah and Christ, and claimed that his intense visions of God in following these paths were of like character to his Hindu experiences. This convinced him of the ultimate unity of all religions.

Despite all this inwardness, Ramakrishna was a teacher of some popular appeal, speaking in vivid images and stories and parables. He attracted attention among the middle classes of Calcutta too, and among those who were toying with Western religion in order to "modernize." Ramakrishna recalled some of the strength of the Hindu heritage, especially its experiential dimension. Among these folk coming to the half-mad religious genius of the Kālī temple in Dakshineshvar was young Narendranath Datta, of the *kāyastha* caste (originally *sudra*, but upwardly mobile and part of the gentle-folk, or *bhadraloka*, of Bengal). This young man was impressed enough himself to become a renunciant, under the name of Vivekānanda, but only after completing college and after his father's death. Ramakrishna saw in him a person of great power and destiny.

It happened that Vivekananda was a member of the Brahmo Samāj, and he found Ramakrishna's image-laden earthiness a problem, but he held him as his guru and prepared himself spiritually up to the time of Ramakrishna's death, after which he helped to continue Ramakrishna's message. During an extensive pilgrimage which he made through the length and breadth of India he came to evolve the main tenor of his philosophy. This was to have profound impact because he was able to visit Chicago for the World Parliament of Religions in 1893, where he made his reputation and eventually returned to India a famous man. In 1895 he founded the Vedānta Society in New York, now seeing his mission as worldwide, and in India in 1897 he started the Ramakrishna Mission, with an order of monks as a modern group to teach social reform, perform works of education and social service, and preach a universal Hinduism.

Basically Vivekānanda's views were as follows. The Divine exists at two levels. At the higher level it is without qualities; it is not to be described. But in the nondual meditative experience it can be known: indeed, one knows the Divine from within, for one is divine. This realization dispels any illusions we may have about the world. But at a lower level God has qualities and takes on form: she is Kālī or he is Śiva or Viṣṇu . . . or Ramakrishna. Humans experience God in these various images, and she or he becomes the recipient of devotion or *bhakti*. All the religions have the divine at the core, but they image God in differing ways. The Hindu heritage is the one which has seen most clearly that the various names of the Real are just that, different labels. World religions could work together if only they took this positive path of seeing the different myths and doctrines as providing the guidelines for paths which all lead to the One. Within each one of us there resides the divine, since we can achieve nondual union with it. So humanity is itself divine. Once we see the divine in one another, it will promote an ethic of love and social concern.

This ideology presented Hinduism not as a backward religion but at the forefront. It was the rather benighted Christians who tended to ascribe absolute truth to their own faith and complete error to alternatives. It was the forward-looking Hindu who saw his own pluralistic faith as a foreshadowing of the emerging World Religion. Vivekānanda's Neo-Vedānta also made sense of Hinduism for perhaps the first time. Now Hindus could explain the unity of their own baffling, diverse religion or religions. It could be said that now Hinduism truly came into existence, or at least into self-conscious integrity. This was why Vivekānanda's message became so immediately popular with the English-speaking elite. And it did so without taking a superior line about the imagery and ikons of village and popular Hinduism. It might be that the person who venerates a snake has a rather limited view of the divine, but he is on his way, and may in due course rise to the heights of nondual awareness where all differences are put on one side. So Vivekānanda first of all dealt effectively with the Christian challenge.

Next, as to utilitarianism and social reform, he could claim, too, to be a humanist concerned about human happiness: but happiness has to be seen in depth. It is not enough to equate it with fun and pleasure. You must be true to human nature, and human nature is divine. And of course we need to take seriously the needs of individuals, and it is for this reason that the Ramakrishna Mission engaged itself on social action. As for the new global awareness brought on by the capitalist system, he, Vivekānanda, was living testimony to this by going to the World Fair in Chicago; and what he there preached was a religion for the whole of humanity, a new global religion but at the same time a very ancient one. From the gleaming insights of the rishis you could draw light for the modern and future world. As for nationalism, Vivekānanda's ideology was perfect for India: it could unite all Indians, Muslims, Jains, Parsees, Christians, as well as Hindus. It expressed pride in India, for its vast cultural achievements, and it could do all this in ways that were not necessarily chauvinist. With Vivekānanda, Indian national self-consciousness came of age.

The ideology also fitted higher education. The philosophy which was taught in colleges in his day was neo-Hegelianism, following some of the British developments of Hegel's ideas. It was very similar to the philosophy of Śankara, and so it was easy to combine the two. The Logical Positivist and empiricist revolution was yet to come. So it was not difficult to harmonize the thought of East and West. Moreover it was clear to those who went into these matters that Indian philosophy itself was highly sophisticated, and had much to offer those who wished to have greater understanding of the relation of science and religion. As for science: the scientifically educated person should have no great problem with Vivekānanda's philosophy. There could not be any clash between physics and biology on the one hand and belief in God on the other, since the Divine in itself was inexpressible, utterly transcending thought but not experience. As experienced, too, religion was empirical. It was not just uncritically accepted dogma. Moreover, the Hindu tradition was not plagued, as was Biblical Christianity, with the problem of Evolution: in Sāṃkhya philosophy (p. 74) it indeed laid out an evolutionary scheme. Not only this, but historical enquiries into the sacred texts did not invalidate their central meaning. They were like fingers pointing to the moon, and the moon is the nondual experience of the Divine Being.

Though Śankara's philosophy provided the underpinning, it was in fact adapted by Vivekānanda, and also by later exponents of the modern Hindu ideology. The main problem with the original Advaita Vedānta philosophy was that it stated that this world—indeed everything other than Brahman, the indescribable Absolute—is an illusion (māyā). This doctrine was scarcely designed to stimulate social and political action. The teaching about māyā was therefore played down—with some justification, in the sense that Śankara's reason for taking this world as illusion was that it was noneternal. Nothing which is not eternal is fully real, from a spiritual point of view. But it is not of course literally the case that what is impermanent is unreal. Anyway, the new prophets of Indian nationalism and of the unity of religions took a positive view of this world. For this they could indeed turn to the teachings of the Gītā, and the notion that one should serve the divine through the path or discipline of works or action (karmayoga). This stress on karmayoga was something which Gandhi would also draw from his beloved scripture.

Although Vivekānanda's own message and mission were channeled through the Ramakrishna movement which he founded, his appeal was much wider, and the general kind of position which he expressed became the regular middle-class view about Hinduism and religions. The dividing line between piety and patriotism could easily be blurred. The national hymn became Bande Mataram, a Bengali hymn addressed to the Mother (kālī); and India itself was figured as a Mother. The geographical limits of India were more consciously too in people's minds. Vivekānanda, among other things, had stimulated the building of a temple on a tiny island just off the coast at Cape Comorin (Kanyakumārin) at the tip of India. It was a recognition of the unity of India: this was not—as earlier Bengali pilgrims might have thought—a foreign country (Kerala, speaking Malayalam). Others before had made similar journeys; but the temple expresses national sentiment, not just piety. So later leaders, while not accepting all or part of Vivekānanda's teachings—men such as Nehru who was an agnostic—were still impressed with his position. And modern ideas of Hinduism flow as much from him as from any other interpreter in relatively recent times.

Hinduism as a single all-India system had been invented: and not just the Hinduism of the sacred books and philosophies (for the Upanishads were fairly far removed from ordinary practice), but a Hinduism that embraced all its florid aspects—images, processions, pilgrimages, temples, fasts, holy men, bathing, ashes, caste, and all: for Vivekānanda had struck upon a fine way of justifying the whole ritual dimension of Hinduism, save perhaps some which tied in with social discriminations. All rituals were imperfect responses to an only fragmentarily seen divine Reality.

## Dimensions of Modern Hinduism

If we look to the middle-class expression of the Hindu tradition in this century, what does it look like from the perspective of the various dimensions?

First, in *doctrine*, we have noted that a predominant place has been given to Śankara's philosophy: equally important ones such as that of Rāmānuja have been comparatively neglected, at least in public rhetoric. They were supposed to have been taken care of under the synthesizing umbrella of nondualism. The doctrines of rebirth and *karma* as the working out of the effects of your actions in other lives were still affirmed; but small problems were beginning to arise about how such a belief blended with modern biology, e.g. genetics. If I owe my characteristics to my two parents, how is there a place for a third force (the effects of previous actions)? The most canvassed response was: my soul homes in on my parents in order to have the proper effect of previous lives. A good soul will home in on holy and prosperous parents, a bad one on disaster-prone parents. So it turns out in India that, though there is little problem about belief in God, there may be growing doubts about rebirth.

In regard to the *mythic* or narrative dimension, much that was there simply stays in place in the modern ideology. Stories of the gods, especially of the great incarnations of Viṣṇu, are edifying. It was noted that the importance of sexual themes contrasts with the very inhibited views of nineteenth- and twentieth-century Britons. However, a new puritanism had spread among the educated elite especially. Stricter emotional controls on sex were more important as higher education stretched beyond youth into early womanhood and early manhood, particularly in a country where marriages tended to be dictated by families and within the framework of the caste system. Indians tend to defend such a system as producing better relationships than the unstable Western ethos of love-marriages.

As Indian contributions to civilization and modern thought became more openly expressed on the world scene, so there was a recognition of some kind of destiny in history which India had: perhaps to teach the materialist West some of the spiritual ideas and techniques and values which she could draw from her long history. Among the heroes of this new destiny was Vivekānanda: but there were to be others, notably Mahātma Gandhi.

As to *ethics* and social life, Vivekānanda appreciated the need for change and modernization of attitudes. Caste was a sensitive issue: mostly it was defended as a division of labor system which had alas been turned into a hereditary affair, and hedged round by unnecessary religious scruples. It was Gandhi who was to do most on this front. Already some changes had come about socially. The most pure castes, who worried most about contamination and pollution from others, did not do so well as others under the new system, where contact with the British and with other castes in offices and on railways became closer. But the hardest aspect to change was in regard to intermarriage.

Regarding *ritual* life, the modern era has produced changes, but largely through nonideological forces. The railway and then the bus network has greatly increased pilgrimages and mounted heavy pressure on centers such as Banaras. But the general principle of the modern Hindu ideology was to leave as much in place as possible.

Regarding emotion and *experience*, the modern period saw the growth of national sentiment, as we have seen. Sometimes such feelings found outlets in extreme political pro-Hindu organizations which interpreted the Hindu tradition in a much less pacifist sense than Vivekānanda, Gandhi, and others: for instance the R.S.S. (Rastriya Svayamsevak Sangh), founded in Maharashtra by Dr. K. B. Hedgewar (1889–1940), which combines revived Hinduism with military exercises (Sanskrit and arms drill) and has a dedicated celibate leadership with wide influence in youth organizations.

However, Vivekānanda and others have stressed the importance of inner spiritual experience, which has always been more important ultimately than patriotic feelings, and which realizes a person's true divinity. This aspect of modern universalist Hinduism was taken up by a number of Western writers, notably Aldous Huxley. The wide diffusion of Śankara's ideas in the West tends to cause more emphasis to be placed on this liberating experience than the actualities of Hindu life would dictate, for in India *bhakti* and the adoration of a personal God mythologized in various ways is much more dominant. Still, Hindu Yoga was new to the West, and it was something which India could offer as central to its culture, on which the Indians, both Hindus and Buddhists, had spent much effort in the past, and which might be illuminating for the West. This sometimes reinforced an often expressed opinion among modern Hindus that India has an essentially spiritual culture, while the West has slipped into a crass materialism.

From the point of view of *social* organization, the modern period has seen some erosion of the position of Brahmins. This was partly because it became common to translate Hindu scriptures and to congeal them in books rather than to rely on the sacred memory of trained Brahmins and the haunting tones of chanted sounds. The new middle class might itself importantly contain Brahmins, but many others besides, and the new knowledge was from a foreign source and different from the traditional authoritative sources of Hindu sacred knowledge. Also, some of the revivalist movements were anti-Brahmin. In the old days it was maybe the Brahmins with their Sanskrit knowledge who had formed a net of cultural unity on the subcontinent; but now there were stronger bonds—the railways, the British Rāj, the English language. Indeed, the whole status of Sanskrit was in doubt. What part would it play in a modern India? The fact was that the influential books written in India in the late nineteenth and early twentieth centuries were all in English. For these reasons there was some disturbance of the social hierarchy. But caste has remained a powerful force hard to deal with, for any revolt against caste still simply produces a new one.

As to the *material* side of Hindu life, there is not much to say in regard to the modern Hindu revival. Craftsmanship of the old kind in fashioning temples and statues is doubtless on the decline. But there has been no absence of pious people to put up temples and monuments that help to celebrate the new India. We have noted for instance Vivekānanda's temple at Cape Comorin. After his time we would have to note developments such as the mythological movie—long translations into film form of the great epics—and new styles of the printing of holy pictures and so on. But the material things that the new ideology celebrated were the great shrines and carvings of the past, which testified to the grandeur and strength of Indian society.

## Muslim Modernism in India

Because the British defeated Mughal power in the North and a number of powerful Muslim rulers such as Tipu Sultan in Mysore, and because the old Mughal emperor had let himself be drawn into the rebellion of 1857, the Muslims initially were less adapted to the values of British rule, and less favored by the British, than the Hindus. The first major Islamic thinker to adapt publicly to the new conditions was Sir Sayyid Ahmad Khan (1817–98), who had a traditional Delhi education in Arabic and Persian sources, and who was employed by the East India Company for over thirty years. He was profoundly impressed by the events of 1857 and 1858. He saw in them the inevitability of British rule, and indeed in some sense a justification. He saw the new scientific knowledge as good and ultimately proceeding from God: drawing on old Islamic philosophical principles, he saw reason and revelation as functioning in parallel. But he thought that Islam had been overgrown with foreign life, much of it unfortunately embodied in the *shari'a*, the Law. He took in this matter a neofoundationalist view: that is, he distinguished between the teachings of the Holy Qur'an and the mass of *hadith*, which he considered to be very unreliable, having been orally transmitted over long times. So he was a modernist in the sense that he urged legal and social reform, and in seeing the harmony between Western science and Islamic religion. Besides, Western science owed its initial impetus to Islamic sources, through the transmission of Greek ideas and Islamic scientific developments to the medieval West. After, a visit to England in 1878–80 he established the Mohammedan Anglo-Oriental College in Aligarh, thus beginning the process of opening up to young Muslims the possibilities of English-language higher education. He urged Muslims not to join the Hindu-dominated Indian National Congress, fearing that Muslim minority status in a nationalist movement would be perpetuated.

But though Khan's modernism pointed one way forward, it did not of course eliminate the causes of friction between Hindus and Muslims. In a revived Hinduism there was a call for protection of the cow: yet Muslims traditionally slaughtered cows at certain festivals. The Hindus agitated for Hindi, written in Devanagari script, to have equal status with Urdu (much the same language but peppered with more Arabic and Persian words), written in Arabic script. Such causes of conflict, in north India especially, must be seen as a constant background noise in the history of modern India.

The drums of violence may at times have been muffled, but their beat was still to be heard.

Some Indians have blamed the British for a "divide and rule" policy, and there were undoubtedly some British actions which helped to fuel the conflict, notably the partition of the province of Bengal in 1905. It sparked off terrorist bombing and some degree of communal violence. But the religions were at the ritual level remarkably incompatible. Muslims considered *shirk* or idolatry as the most heinous sin, and they were surrounded by Śiva statues and Ganesh and heaven knows what among the impenitent Hindus. Every statue was an offense, especially when it was carried in procession in front of the mosque. For the Hindu, Muslim cow-slaughter was an offense against their very deeply felt veneration, from time immemorial, for the cow. And if Muslims should think it their duty to smash an idol, or if Hindus were to stop Muslim sacrifices, then mayhem would break loose. So there was a constant problem of the peaceful coexistence of these two great religions.

In so far as the tensions could be resolved by intellectuals, then Sir Sayyid Ahmad Khan's position, influenced by Sufism, could help in a better understanding with Hindus. But he himself was strongly attacked by many of the *'ulama*, and his modernism was out of tune with the feelings, under threat, of many of his coreligionists. We shall take up the story of Islamic responses, later: but we may note Sir Sayyid as being a forward-looking thinker who made the move to modernism with self-conscious confidence and strong educational interests.

## The Early Twentieth Century

### Gandhi: A New Force in Hindu Response

If there was a criticism that could be made of the modern Hindu ideology it was that it could be left at the theoretical level. But with M. K. (Mahātma) Gandhi (1869–1948) we meet someone who solidly combined practical and theoretical ideas. He was raised in Kathiawar, and had close contacts both with Hindus and non-Hindus. His mother's religion was a kind of evangelical devotionalism, within the *bhakti* tradition, somewhat influenced by Islam. The area he came from was one of the main Jain regions, and he was influenced by the Jain ideal of nonviolence.

At the age of nineteen he went to London to study law, and there came into contact with the Theosophical movement, which combined Eastern motifs with a concern for comparative religion. Annie Besant (1847–1933), a leading Theosophist, was to play a notable part in Indian nationalist politics. He also was in touch with followers of Tolstoy. After his return to India he practiced law unsuccessfully in Bombay before being offered a job in Durban, Natal, South Africa. He went there in 1893 (a significant year, since it was also the date of Vivekānanda's trip to Chicago).

He worked twenty-one years in South Africa, until 1915. It was in South

The ethical dimension: Mahatma Gandhi gave a new ethical and political value to the principle of non-violence, characteristic of the Jain, Buddhist and, to some extent, the Hindu traditions.

Africa that he worked out the methods of nonviolent political resistance which he was to use to good effect against the British in India. It was in South Africa that he took on the garb and mien of a saintly holy man. But he was not a recluse: he was always in the thick of events. What he did in effect was to give the old Jain and Indian idea of *ahiṃsa* (non-violence) a political context and meaning. He also gave the notion of renunciation a new social context. The main point of his practices of austerity and simplification of life was to prepare himself spiritually for the struggle against oppression and injustice. The most important single thing that he taught was that our motives in such struggle must be pure. It is no use being outwardly nonviolent if you hate your enemy in your heart. In this he was influenced by the Christianity of the Gospels: "Love your enemies" became for him a prime precept.

In general principle the line which he took on religion and religions was very like that of Vivekānanda, but it was stated imprecisely. He made much use of the word Truth (*satyam* in Sanskrit), and for him Truth was God and God was Truth. His method of passive reisistance he called *satyagraham*, or holding fast to truth.

In his prayer meetings, Gandhi used devotional prayers and hymns, including Christian ones. Thus in *practice* he held to some view about the unity of religions; but he did not wish to spell out a highly systemized philosophy or set of *doctrines*. Nor did he make much of the *narrative* and *ritual* dimensions of religion. Yet he was very observant of his own rules of abstinence, in order to train himself better. The main locus of his action was at the *ethical* and *social* level, and he was less interested in the formalities of religion. But he was undoubtedly influenced by the monastic ideal, both Indian and Christian (in South Africa he was in touch with Trappists). His ashrams or communities were a creative adaptation of the Indian model to the purposes of the modern struggle. Round him he gathered dedicated followers who helped him organize his boycotts and strikes and other forms of action.

He struggled initially for the rights of Indian workers in South Africa. These had been brought mainly to work the sugar plantations, being reckoned more amenable to that kind of work than the local Africans. Gandhi set up two ashrams, one called Phoenix near Durban, the other Tolstoy Farm near Johannesburg.

Because of the publicity from his leadership of the Indians in South Africa he was already famous when he got back to India after over twenty years, in 1915, where he joined the nationalist movement, now burgeoning during World War I. It was in 1919, after the war in which Indian troops had loyally fought, that a most disillusioning event occured, for those who counted on British gratitude. In the Jallianwalla Bagh in Amritsar, in the Punjab, a British general fired on a crowd with great bloodshed. An official enquiry was held, but General Dyer went unpunished. The Rāj was nervous. This helped to spark Gandhi's first great noncooperation campaign, a year later. At this time Gandhi was cooperating with the Islamic *khilafat* movement, arguing that Muslims should get autonomy because they owed allegiance to the Caliph in Istanbul. However, the Caliphate was abolished by the Turks in 1924. The Muslims of India were to follow a different vision.

Gandhi, in and out of jail between the Wars, conducting fasts, marching to the sea against the Salt Tax, meeting with Viceroys, managing to be the leading voice in the Congress movement, was a major factor in the struggle for independence, which ended—successfully in one way, and unsuccessfully in another—in 1947. A Socialist government in London had decreed the end of the Indian empire. But the Muslim alternative vision had meant that India was to be divided, and it was a division that sparked massacres by Muslims of Hindus and by Hindus of Muslims, along the troubled borderlands of the new states and far beyond. The population, the heat, the poverty, the multiplication of rumors—these things make India volatile at the best of times.

This end to the national struggle deeply upset Gandhi, who, however, immediately set about trying to bring peace to the troubled areas. It was his concern that Hindus should respect Muslims that attracted criticism from fiercer nationalists, one of whom gunned him down at a prayer meeting in Delhi in 1948. But Gandhi with his spiritual power, his wiliness, his humor, his kindliness and creativity of life, was to influence many others, including Martin Luther King. There are many Christians who look to his example (maybe asking themselves the question of how it came to be that the best Christian in this century, as some think, had to be a Hindu?) He represents the practical poise of the new Hindu ideology.

## *Muhammad Iqbal and the Idea of Pakistan*

It would have been surprising perhaps if no one had sketched out an alternative to a united India, because of the strong Mughal heritage in the north and northwest. Also, for Muslims there was always the nagging question of how to arrange the law when under foreign or non-Muslim domination. Sir Muhammad Iqbal (1877–1938) was a noted poet who had been knighted by the British government for his works in Urdu and Persian. His philosophy was one which looked to a true, morally dynamic Islam, toward which Islam as it is must reach. He saw history and life in terms of an evolutionary process towards the higher ethical life. He also, significantly, in his presidential address to the Muslim League in Allahabad in 1930, urged the creation of a Muslim state in the northwestern parts of India. Only where Muslims were free to put the law into operation freely could a true Islam be realized.

His ideas on this front were a bit vague. It was Rahmat Ali, living in Cambridge, England, who gave them more precision. He invented a name for the new country, Pakistan, which consists of the first letters of some of the key provinces: Punjab, Afghan Province (or Northwest Frontier Province), Kashmir and Sindh, plus the last portion of Baluchistan. Later Rahmat Ali added the idea of another Muslim state in Bengal, far away to the east, which he called "Bangistan." Actually Pakistan at first included East Bengal, but after a civil war this did evolve into a new state, that of Bangladesh. Rahmat Ali's ideas at first put off the Muslim leader, Muhammad Ali Jinnah (1876–1948), but after 1936 he was won round, and it

Muhammad Ali Jinnah, though not a very pious Muslim himself, was concerned, as President of the All-India Muslim League, to protect the interests of Muslims, and took a large number of them out of India to form the new State of Pakistan.

was his intransigence in fighting for this new state which meant that in 1947 Partition was inevitable.

Pakistan turned out not to be a very stable country, even after the civil war in 1971 which led to the separation of Bangladesh. A succession of military regimes replaced the early civilian administrations, save for a period after the Bangladesh war. It has introduced Islamic law into its system, but is rather far from the vision of a revived Islam which was what Iqbal had looked to.

### Some Other Religious Movements in India

Though Vivekānanda represents the mainstream of Indian modernism, there were other movements of some interest and importance in the modern period. There were those like the R. S. S., which took a much harder line in promoting Hindu values. There were also movements which involved trying to improve the lot of the less favored groups. Gandhi himself, from 1935 onwards, devoted much effort to help the untouchables, whom he dubbed the Harijans (literally Sons of Hari, i.e. God; this name, once favorable, is more recently less approved by Harijans themselves, who find it somewhat patronizing). But for some the future did not lie within Hinduism at all: this is in evidence in the life and work of Dr. B. R. Ambedkar (1891–1956). He made impressive educational and academic progress as a young person, aided by caste Hindus among others, ending up with a doctorate from Columbia University in New York and another from the University of London. From the 1930s onwards, most of his energies went into mobilizing the untouchables of his region, Maharashtra. Shortly before he died he converted formally to Buddhism, though he had written about the Buddha in a book published five years earlier and he had long seen in it a faith which was a fine alternative to the Hindu tradition. Four million of his followers also converted at that time, so that now there is a whole scattering of Buddhist temples across Maharashtra.

Very different in import and style was the attempt to synthesize East and West very radically in the life and writings of Aurobindo Ghose (1872–1950). He had been educated in England from the age of seven till he was twenty-one, and only on his return to India did he discover his native land. But he had come into contact with the evolutionary philosophy of Henri Bergson (1859–1941) and in India he made a synthesis between this and Upanishadic thought. But this was only after a phase of nationalistic activity, including a spell in prison. In 1910 he moved to Pondicherry, French India, and did not further engage in politics but set himself to write and meditate. After a few years he was joined by a French woman who helped to organize his ashram and to realize his ideal of Integral Yoga. His theory was that Spirit first descends into the material world and then conversely begins its evolution upwards. This evolutionary process begins with what looks like inert matter, but this secretly contains consciousness. Integral Yoga is a means by which human beings can, at this crucial stage of history, assist the evolutionary process and be drawn upwards to a higher level of spiritual existence. This movement has drawn many Europeans to it, and is mellifluously expressed in Sri Aurobindo's many writings and above all in his masterwork, *The Life Divine*. His views have an uncanny resemblance to those of the Catholic writer Pierre Teilhard de Chardin (1881–1955).

These were movements of the rich period in Indian life between the 1920s and the 1950s, when the main struggle took place for the reassertion of Hindu and Indian values. Something different has to be said in regard to a later period, when new Hindu movements tended to become global in scope, because of the opening up of international communication after World War II and the increased interest in Eastern thought among Westerners.

### Buddhism in Ceylon: A New Modernism

Meanwhile a somewhat differing evolution of events had occured to the south, in the administratively separate island of Ceylon. The British had taken the central kingdom of Kandy in 1815, and for a while, in terms of the treaty settling the war, were obliged to support the Buddhist establishment of the Sangha. But the interpolation of Christian missions led to other pressures, and for a while Buddhist morale was depressed. In the latter half of the century a number of public debates between Christian missionaries and Buddhist monks revived interest in the defense of the faith, and Buddhists were satisfied of the greater rationality of their traditional religion.

Also important from the angle of reinvigorating Ceylonese self-esteem was the visit by an American, Colonel Henry S. Olcott (1832–1907). He had been involved originally in the formation of the Theosophical Society in 1875, with the charismatic Russian woman, Madame H. P. Blavatsky (1831–91), in New York. Olcott became a Buddhist, and the Theosophical Society always had Buddhist leanings, though its headquarters were established in Adyar, Madras. His support of Westerners who saw deep value in Eastern spirituality was of incalculable encouragement to Sinhalese Buddhists. And Olcott himself was very vigorous. He and the Theosophical Society helped to found Ananda College, the leading Buddhist school in Ceylon, and he prepared the way for the renewal of Buddhist scholarship, though himself not a scholar.

There is some analogy to Olcott's effect in Ceylon with that of Annie Besant (1847–1933), another Theosophist, and feminist—a brilliant speaker and organizer, whose work in India included being so involved with the Indian Congress movement that she was elected its first woman President in 1917, and the foundation of the institution which grew into Banaras Hindu University, one of India's foremost universities and enshrining Hindu values. Interestingly, she adopted a gifted Hindu boy, Krishnamurti (1895–1986), who was expected to be a Theosophical World Teacher. After Besant's death he struck out very much on his own, and in fact taught ideas very similar to those of Mādhyamika and Zen Buddhism, on the inability of concepts to capture the real world.

At the turn of the century, Westerners like Olcott and Besant did great service in helping the people of South Asia to see, in a period of great cultural arrogance on the part of the British and other Westerners, the vital meaning and importance of the indigenous religious traditions. Also important was the work of editing and publishing the Pali texts. This was greatly due to the impetus of the British scholar T. W. Rhys Davids (1843–1922), who founded the Pali Text Society. This helped to give Ceylon Buddhists a clear view of their own basic heritage.

The introduction of Western-style education into Ceylon had similar effects to those we have noted in India. But the transition to independence was much gentler in Ceylon than in India. The cosmopolitanism of the Ceylonese found Western democracy congenial, and a great deal of home rule was already established before World War II.

Two major forms of Buddhist modernism arose in this context. One was neofoundationalist, treating the Buddhism of the Pali canon as the norm—or rather seeing the Pali canon when suitably censored as being the norm. It was thought that rather a lot of the matter in the canon, about gods and spirits and so on, was the result of mythologizing the Buddha's original message, which had been purely rational and spiritual. Shorn of these supposed accretions, the Canon was seen philosophically as much in line with modern science (which sees the world as evanescent atoms in motion) and philosophy (for was the Buddha's teaching not empirical?) The difference from some Western forms of rationalism was that Buddhism admitted the importance of paranormal, illuminating experiences. If there was room for doubt it might be over the doctrine of rebirth, but that too could be accommodated with modern thinking provided we did not think about it naively. Naturally, this highly slimmed-down Buddhism was not the religion of the masses: for them color and myth were more important than philosophy. But Buddhism had the merit of teaching an ethical path, which could be conveyed to the masses. Such a Buddhism of course was quite attractive to an English-speaking elite: and for Europeans this Buddhism gave one the possibility of spirituality without having to believe in God (a belief which many Westerners had come to find incredible and even tiresome, with its tendency to childish anthromorphism, as they saw it).

Among other signs of revival and modernism was the work of the reformer Anagarika Dharmapāla (1864–1933), who did much in Buddhist education, and worked to restore the Buddhist pilgrimage sites of India, especially Bodh Gaya, the site of the Buddha's enlightenment: to which end, in 1891, he founded the Mahabodhi Society, which received support from Buddhists in other parts of Asia and was a factor in the rise of ecumenical Buddhism, issuing in the creation of organizations such as the World Fellowship of Buddhists.

Though nationalism was a strong ingredient in Buddhist revival in Ceylon, its impact was muted by the relatively easy transition which the country made to independence. It was mostly after independence, achieved in February 1948, that the strongest period of national resurgence came among the Sinhalese. This was expressed in the election campaign of 1946, when

The pious layman: here a Sinhalese does homage at the feet of a vast Buddha statue in Sri Lanka.

many Buddhist monks were involved on the side of the newly formed Sri Lanka Freedom Party. What it wanted was a reestablishment of something like classical Sinhala Buddhism, from the great days of Parakrama Bahu the Great and the high tide of Buddhist civilization. Its aim was now not so much modernist, philosophical Buddhism but a new arrangement in which Sangha and State would once again have a close relationship.

For a major problem in Theravādin countries—not only Ceylon—was how to reconstruct the world once the king had been removed by conquerors. In the old days there had been a reciprocal relationship between king and Sangha, with mutually defined roles. Now that we were in a democratic age with modern institutions (and moving from under a foreign monarchy), what was the system to be? The ideal of Sinhala as the only official language (the main slogan of the 1956 campaign) reinforced the concept of a Sinhala Buddhist culture. Of course there were Sinhalese who were not Buddhists, mainly Christians, and their position was not easy. But the vast majority were Buddhist. Sri Lanka (it changed its name in 1972 with a new constitution) embarked on a period of neoclassical Sinhalese revival, in which the Buddhism of the chronicles was more stressed, and money was poured into reviving the architectural glories of Anuradhapura and Polonnaruwa and in fostering Buddhist schools and universities.

All this caused great unrest among the Tamils, mainly Hindus of the Śaiva Siddhanta school, whose ancestors had been brought in as laborers in the nineteenth century. It was a conflict that ultimately led to the civil war of the 1980s. The Buddhist revival in Ceylon did not generate a clear ideology of toleration, such as that created by modern Hinduism. This was despite the generally tolerant character of the Buddhist tradition and the possibility of calling on such an ideal figure from this point of view as the emperor Aśoka. The majority Sinhalese moreover felt themselves really to be a minority, because of the large number, over fifty million, of mainland Tamils in the Indian state of Tamil Nadu.

Despite these problems, the period after independence was one of great cultural vigor. Buddhist philosophy, especially, flourished through the writings of such vital figures as G. P. Malalasekara (1911–68) and K. N. Jayatilleke. A new parliament building in traditional Sinhalese style near the place of the old capital at Kotte was created, and the general favoring of Buddhist arts saw a considerable revival of the material dimension of the tradition. Buddhist monks traveled abroad, and the influence of Sri Lankan Theravāda on world spirituality has been great, in part because of a vital renewal of the practices of meditation. At the same time Buddhism has involved itself in social work. In this it has been influenced by Christian organizations, which are also reflected in such institutions as the Young Men's Buddhist Association.

# After Independence

## India since Partition: Some Trends

The principles of pluralism were built into the Republic of India's Constitution. India became a secular state, in the sense that there was a separation between religions and the State (the only exception being a clause about cow-protection among its guiding principles). It was important to achieve some kind of political balance, so a Muslim and a Sikh as well as Hindus have been President (a largely ceremonial office, but important symbolically).

One of the Presidents, in office from 1962 to 1967, was Sarvepalli Radhakrishnan (1888–1975), who had been at the forefront of popularizing Indian philosophy in the West, and in working out a coherent account of what I have called the modern Hindu ideology. He stressed the importance of work in the world, and criticized the view that an idealist view of life is detached from the processes of this world. In this he modified some versions of Advaita Vedānta. He was also influenced by south Indian Vaiṣṇavism. He was critical of Western scientific materialism in so far as it left no space for the intuitions and experiences of religion.

Independent India reformed women's law in the traditional Hindu context, but was less bold in relating to Muslim law. There were other social changes, including the attempt to moderate the impact of untouchability by using various means of what in the United States came to be called "affirmative action." The impact of rapid modernization in various sectors was to expand the Indian middle classes, and some of the religious movements which began to have an impact in the West had their impact too among Indians. It was, from the 1960s on, a favorable period for the export of Indian gurus, yoga, and objects of devotion. With the spread of a greater prosperity through the Green Revolution, industrialization, and other factors (though poverty was desperate too), access to travel increased the popularity of a whole number of pilgrimage centers and intensified religious worship throughout India.

While the Vivekānanda-Rādhakrishnan style of modern Hindu ideology stayed important, some of the non-Advaitin schools of Vedānta, plus some of the regional schools, such as Śaiva Siddhanta in Tamil Nadu and Sri Lanka, made their public voices heard. Publications drew attention to these various strands in Indian theology and philosophy. A richer perspective on the Hindu tradition could be had. There was also the development in Indian politics of a more conservative kind of Hindu attitude, which looked more to the founding of what was seen as a genuinely Hindu State, rather than the pluralistic version which came to be in 1947. But India is such a tinderbox of ethnic, communal, and linguistic tensions that the pluralistic alternative has so far proved to be necessary. The Republic moreover carved itself up into states built primarily on a linguistic basis, and this helped to stimulate indigenous poetic and religious traditions in the various regions. It also brought a position where it was divided fairly evenly between Sikhs and Hindus, and this led one faction of the Sikhs to agitate in the 1970s and 1980s for a separate State.

*Minority Religions and Their Adaptation to Modernity*
It is useful at this point to look to the minority religions and see how they have dealt with modernity and life under a Hindu majority: religions such as the Parsis, Jains, Christians, and Sikhs. About the Muslims (to whom we shall return in Chapter 20), suffice it to say here that they have been very substantially loyal to India in its wars with Pakistan, and indeed India helped Muslim Bangladesh in its struggle for independence. But there have also been sporadic and sometimes intense local communal clashes.

The Jains had of course long integrated into Hindu society and found no special problem in the withdrawal of British rule. They had experienced something of a renaissance in modern times. They were always well represented in the merchant class, and the modern epoch gave them new opportunities. The stimulus of Western Orientalism in reviving traditional Indian studies led to the revival of Jain appreciation of their own scriptural and cultural tradition, through publications and the founding of such institutions as the Lalphai Dalpathbhai Institute of Indology in the western city of Ahmedabad.

During the eighteenth century, Bombay began its rise to become the major port of India and eventually one of its greatest cities. The Parsi community, which was largely to be found on the west coast, began to collect in Bombay, to learn English, and to work with the British. Nevertheless, some of the large figures of the Indian Congress and nationalist movement were Parsis, men such as Dadabhai Naoroji (1828–1917).

After 1947 the community was loosened up somewhat, in so far as non-Parsis were employed more in Parsi businesses. It remains well respected, though not without its crises. One has to do with mixed marriages: do the offspring of non-Parsi wives count as Parsi? Indian law confirmed the community's traditional directive, which was in the negative. But though this has led to a weakening of the group (a crisis not unlike that among Orthodox Jews in the United States), new impulses have come from the overseas Parsis. Many migrated, after World War II especially, to London, Canada, the United States, Hongkong, and elsewhere. This overseas group is less traditional in outlook and may in due course have a modernizing effect on Indian Parsis themselves.

The traditional Zoroastrian way of dealing with the dead, by exposing the corpses on towers of silence or *dkhmas*, is also for practical reasons in decline, and in most areas Parsis are buried. A growing Western scholarly interest in Zoroastrianism has helped to stimulate, partly among the Parsi diaspora, a revival of Parsi studies and the presentation of the religion in a newly sophisticated way.

In some ways the reactions of Christians to the Indian nationalist movement are the most interesting. Obviously Christians were suspect in some quarters because they belonged to the religion of the colonial power, though many Christians associated themselves with the national struggle and were close associates of Gandhi. The pressure was the greater for Christianity to show its indigenous destiny: and both Protestants and Catholics have introduced Indian styles into their ritual, their spiritual training, and their modes of thought. It is common to make use of Indian *bhajans* with *bhakti*-style singing. Catholics have experimented with Indian-style Masses, dispensing with many European practices such as the use of pews. They have been assisted in this by the reforming mission of Vatican II. At Dharmaram College in Bangalore, which is associated with a study center in Rome, much use is made of Indian philosophy in trying to expound Christian faith. One could look to various other such experiments and trends, which has given Indian Christianity a strongly Indian flavor. Dharmaram, as it happens, belongs to the tradition of the Thomas Christians, to whom we can point as showing the antiquity of the religion in India. They, like various other Christian groups and ashrams, make use of Hindu and Buddhist methods of Yoga and meditation in the quest to deepen Christian spiritual life.

The Sikhs had been involved in a struggle in the Punjab in the 1920s and 1930s over the matter of the control of their temples. The danger from a Sikh point of view was that an increasing number of them would drift back into

*Opposite* A festival inaugurating a Jain temple in Rajasthan.

the Hindu environment. In the late nineteenth century the Singh Sabha had been formed for educational and religious purposes, and had in some degree checked that drift. But the Temples remained in the hands of the *udasis* who were not outwardly conforming Sikhs. This had come about in part from conservatism dating right back to the formation of the Khalsa by Gobind Singh: the pre-Gobind type of holy person was still in charge of temples. The struggle was promoted by a militant party, the Akali Dal.

During Partition, the Sikhs found themselves existentially on the same side as the Hindus, and were regarded as such by Muslims. This gave most Sikhs a loyalty to the new Republic of India. However, as time went on there were problems, as the Sikhs saw it, in preserving their distinctive rights in law and elsewhere, and so agitation grew for a Sikh state in the Punjab. This the Indian central government has resisted. It was because of this that Indira Gandhi was assassinated by her own Sikh bodyguards in 1984. A few months previously she had ordered the Indian army to storm the Golden Temple complex in Amritsar, which a rather extreme young leader, Jarnail Singh Bhindranwale, had turned into a stronghold.

The Indian constitution looks on Sikhs as Hindus from a legal point of view, but there are many Sikhs who wish to set forth Sikhism as a separate religion in its own right. In this they are supported by many Sikhs now living overseas, especially in Britain and Canada, where a vocal minority believe in a separate Sikh state, known as Khalistan, independent from the Republic of India.

### Tibetan Religion and the Communist Takeover

Up to World War II, Tibet, because of its geographical situation, was remarkably little affected by outside cultural forces. It is true that in 1903 a British expedition under General Francis Younghusband—later, ironically, a founder of the World Congress of Faiths—captured Lhasa and forced on Tibet a treaty opening it up to British diplomatic and commercial access, a protocol which was reluctantly signed by China in 1906. The move was part of the British plan of forestalling Russian moves southward in the region. The Communists, heirs to Chinese nationalism, took over Tibet after their victory in 1949, very firm in the conviction that China had sole rights over Tibet in principle. In 1951 an agreement was made whereby the existing ruler, the Dalai Lama, should continue his theocratic rule; but from 1956 there were increased pressures for social reform and economic restructuring, and preparations to constitute Tibet as an autonomous region of China.

In 1959 a revolt started among the eastern Khambas, which was put down quite easily by the Chinese: but the Dalai Lama and thousands of monks and others fled Tibet into India, and eventually the Dalai Lama, a gifted and charismatic young man called Tenzin Gyatsho, established his headquarters in northern India, at Dharamshala. As time went on, he became an internationally famous and respected figure in world spirituality, and at the same time a symbol for Tibetan national identity. Subsequently, suppression of

The Dalai Lama, spiritual and political leader of most Tibetans, and in exile in India, hoping for the restoration of autonomy for his people.

religion and the destruction of monasteries, manuscripts, and artwork were the outcome in Tibet, till 1976. An effect of the exile of so many Tibetan monks has been the foundation in many countries in the West, as well as in India, of communities, and the teaching of Tibetan forms of Buddhism throughout the West. It has led to a great revival of Himalayan studies and a deepened knowledge of Mahāyāna Buddhism, in so far as many key Greater Vehicle texts exist in Tibetan translation though lost elsewhere. The consequence has been to add to the forces behind the advance of Buddhism as a viable religion for the West.

Buddhism of a Tibetan kind is of course also extant in such areas of India as Ladakh in the northwest and in parts of Nepal and along the Himalayan foothills. In Nepal there has been considerable change since 1959, when the country was opened to free access from the West, and its old Hindu-Buddhist society in the Kathmandu Valley has been subjected to pressures of tourism (often hippie tourism in the heyday of the 1960s Counterculture) and economic development. It is interesting as a society, in giving us some insight into the coexistence of the two religions during the classical and medieval periods of Indian history—in fact the normal state of religion in the subcontinent until the eleventh century.

## Reflections on Religion in South Asia in Modern Times

The chief culture and religious change in the last two centuries has been the introduction through most of the area of the English language and British higher education systems, often under missionary control, and accompanied by the idea that modern thought and Christian faith go naturally together. In fact, as Western history in modern times shows, they by no means do naturally combine, and there are tensions between scientific humanism and Christianity. For the inhabitants of India and Ceylon it soon became possible to evolve new ways of uniting Hindu and Buddhist values on the one hand and the need to adapt to modernity on the other. The preference in these societies was for a way of developing nationalism with traditional religion blended in. This called for the formation of ideologies which could do this, while at the same time dealing with the questions of science, liberalism, and the like. This was achieved by the modern Hindu ideology of Vivekānanda and Rādhakrishnan, and by the compatible practice of Gandhi. In the case of the Muslims, the modernism of Iqbal led them along the road to Pakistan, which has yet to evolve a stable system other than military dictatorship and a somewhat superficial Islamization. This is a topic that belongs within the wider context of modern Islam (see Chapter 20).

In the case of Sri Lanka the values of Buddhism and of minority Hinduism were able to adjust to the principles of democratic openness, and Buddhism was easily able to show its compatibility with modern scientific thinking. Socialism had attractions too: old-established Marxist parties have been a feature of the democratic political scene in Sri Lanka since the 1920s. Likewise some of the Indian nationalisms were attracted by Socialist methods. The problem in Sri Lanka was how to realize the nationalist ambitions of the Sinhala Buddhist majority without unsettling the minority Tamils. Unfortunately the vision of a revived Classical Buddhism of the glorious days of Sinhala civilization did not mesh with the need for federal-type institutions in the island. The expectations aroused for the young by the Sinhala education system of high schools and universities could not be fulfilled, and the rising of 1971, under the aegis of an ideology, superficially Marxist, but calling for self-sufficiency and Communism (similar to the ideology of the Khmer Rouge), was a symptom of this frustration. Nevertheless the postwar period has been, as we have seen, a creative period in Sri Lankan history.

The Indians were fortunate in having in their heritage the materials for forming a sophisticated ideology which did not alienate the masses, but was able to harness their religious feelings to political ends (above all through the charismatic figure of Gandhi). They were thus not forced, in the interests of national independence, to change so drastically that many of their traditions had to be jettisoned. They reached back into their tradition, reshaped it, and gave it modern force.

Part of this new Hinduism was the self-confident claim that after all Hindu ideas have universal application, and Hindu practices have much to show the

A woman sadhu
venerating the goddess
Sarasvati, at Puri in
Orissa.

world. In the 1960s and 1970s, particularly, this fact became evident, through
ways in which elements of Hinduism were taken up in the West. There were
first and foremost the gurus. There was the whole complex of yogic
practices, sometimes simplified as in Transcendental Meditation (popularized
in part by the Beatles). There were *bhakti* movements, such as ISKCON
(International Society for Krishna Consciousness). The general theory of
Hinduism in this modern form—that all religions point somehow to the same
truth—is attractive to many in the West, and there has certainly been an
increase in ecumenism and friendship between liberal religious leaders. So a
sort of neo-Hindu ideology may itself become more widely believed in the
future. All these developments mean that the Hindu tradition is a universal

religion in the world today, with its own positive message. It is not just a religion for those born within the caste structure of the Indian subcontinent.

We may note, too, that in the last century and onwards there has grown up an increasing Hindu diaspora beyond India—in East Africa, South Africa, Fiji, Mauritius, the Seychelles, Guyana, the West Indies, Malaysia, Singapore, and elsewhere—largely as a result of the export of labor to plantations. More recently a middle-class wave of doctors, scientists, and other specialists has reached the Western world, as for example in Los Angeles (in Malibu Canyon a lovely recreation of a south Indian temple has been built by the subscriptions of well-to-do Indians in Southern California). This diaspora Hinduism has tended away from the stricter requirements of caste, and toward a greater concern with such movements as the Ārya Samāj, the Divine Light Movement and the Rāmakrishna Vedānta Mission. These Hindus have also been prone to move into Pentecostalist and other emotionally charged forms of Protestantism, which supply some of the feel of *bhakti* religion. But they will constitute a more and more important part of the voice of modern Hinduism, and will probably reinforce the message of the Hindu tradition as a universal faith.

In brief, the Republic of India, and Indian culture more widely, has been able to make good use of its resources, selectively of course, in order to create a Hinduism which makes sense both of pluralism and of unity, and to have something which is both ancient and modern. At the same time the smaller religions in India have been able to make their way in the new India, thanks in part to the pluralism implicit in the secular constitution. Hinduism has entered on the world stage. So has Buddhism, which has created an attractive Theravāda modernism, even if Sinhala neoclassicism has not found a theory within itself for the accommodation of minorities: there is as it were no "theory of Hinduism" among Buddhists, but there is a "theory of Buddhism" among Hindu intellectuals.

Buddhism has also benefited on a worldwide basis through the tragic Tibetan events, since its ideas and tradition have become very widely diffused through the work of the Dalai Lama and many other Tibetan monks and refugees. We shall return to some of these issues in discussing diasporas later on. And we shall have a deeper look at the Islamic component of the South Asian scene when we deal with modern Islam and its predicaments and achievements in Chapter 20.

*Above* A scene from the inauguration of a Siva temple.

*Left* Pilgrims arriving for the Kumbh Mela festival at Prayag (Allahabad) at the sacred confluence of the Jumna and the Ganges.

# China and Korea in Modern Times

## The Chinese Predicament in Colonial Times

It was an irony that the eighteenth century in many ways was one of the most glorious in the history of Chinese civilization, particularly under the rule of the Ch'ien-lung emperor (1711–99), whose on the whole efficient administration (marred by later corruption) and wide patronage of the arts was the high point of the Ch'ing or Manchu dynasty. Contacts with European powers tended not to be of the threatening proportions that the nineteenth century brought. There was widespread admiration among European intellectuals for Chinese culture and the Confucian tradition. Earlier, the famous Jesuit Matteo Ricci (1552–1610) had made a great impression at the Chinese court for his astronomical and other knowledge, though the Jesuit plea that Chinese Christians should be allowed to continue ancestral rites in the Confucian mode was rejected by the Vatican on the pleas of the Franciscans and Dominicans; and this decision weakened Christian influence at the court, owing to the displeasure of the K'ang-hsi emperor (1654–1722), who had favored the Jesuit view. It was in the nineteenth century, though, that the real conflicts between China and Europe, and then America, were to develop.

The East India Company benefited from the British naval supremacy established in the Seven Years War (1756–63) by dominating the trade with China. China had various goods to offer, including china; but the most important commodity was tea. The demand for it in Britain had taken off. There was no comparable thing which the Chinese wanted from Europe or from India. But in time the opium trade increased, though the sale of opium in China was illegal. When in 1839 an imperial commissioner terminated all trade through Canton (Kwangtung) and confiscated opium held in store, the

*Opposite* Two relatives burning imitation paper money at a Taoist funeral: such practices were to be largely rooted out during the period of the Cultural Revolution in the 1960s and 70s.

British decided on war. By the Treaty of Nanking which brought the Opium War to an end in 1842, various ports were opened to British trade and British consuls permitted there, Hong Kong was ceded to Britain, and the way was open to a whole series of unequal treaties, whereby extra territorial concessions were granted to European powers in a whole series of cities along the coast of China. The Chinese gradually lost control over their customs operations, and the Western powers, later to be joined by resurgent Japan, had China more or less at their mercy.

There were other problems that China had to face: Muslim rebellions in Sinkiang, which was formally incorporated into China as a province; rivalry with an advancing Russia in Central Asia; persistent peasant rebellions; and problems in Manchuria from Russia and Japan. But it was mainly the problem of how to cope with the Western seapowers which exercised the imperial mind, especially after the burning of the Summer Palace in the Anglo-French war with China of 1856–60 and the flight of the emperor from Peking. It was also the time of the beginning of the main missionary era from the West, especially among Protestant missions. The Chinese traditional philosophies and religions were under pressure both from Western technology (through which European naval forces could be so successful) and from Western spiritual ideas. An attempt to resist these forces, but in an intuitive way and with little comprehension of what lay behind them, was the so-called Taiping rebellion (1850–65), a protean upheaval with millions killed in bloody conflict. This movement was itself patterned in some ways on other revolts of the era, but it has many lessons to teach about Chinese response to the West.

### Hung-hsiu Ch'üan and a New Religion

The Taiping movement was both religious and political. It was named after the concept of the T'ai P'ing or Great Peace, which was an old Chinese millenarian ideal, used by Taoist revolutionaries from time to time. In origin the notion of the Great Peace or Great Harmony (as it may also be translated) referred to a past Golden Age, in the Confucian classics. Often new emperors looked on it as their mission to restore this great harmony. But it was also harnessed as an idea to millenarian expectations, especially among Taoists: it figured in the great uprising of the Yellow Turbans, in 184 C.E., which overthrew the Han Empire. It was used by Manichaeans and Taoists in their ideologies of uprising against Confucian order and of the coming of a new society in which harmony would be promoted by minimalist government.

It was now used in a new context by Hung-hsiu Ch'üan (1813–64). He was a Hakka, a minority linguistic group in Kwangsi and Kwangtung provinces. Feeling oppressed by neighboring groups, they were already being organized in militias, when Hung's revelations gave a direction and ideology to the movement. Hung had tried the national civil service examinations but had failed several times. He had come into contact with Christian missions through some tracts by the convert Liang Pa (1789–1855). The turning point was his visionary experience of the Father (Jehovah) and Jesus—Hung himself being addressed in the experience as the younger brother of Jesus. He was granted a seal, sign of imperial status, a sword to drive out demons, and scriptures. He proclaimed himself to be the new Messiah and took the title of T'ai-p'ing T'ien-tzu (Heavenly Emperor of the Great Peace), joining with his cousin Feng Yün-shan (1822–52) in organizing military congregations with a revolutionary and anti-Manchu slant. They also drew on the thinking of some of the southern Chinese secret societies known as Triads.

The Taiping ideology was vigorous and included many elements introduced about a century later by the Communists: equality for women, colloquial language as the literary norm, the banning of the Confucian classics, the smashing of idols and other aspects of the old religions, the State holding of land and its working by groups of families, the fusion of military and political commands at all levels. Not all these programs were realized in the chaos of civil war, but they represented a remarkable ideal of the radical reconstruction of China. In all this there was of course some Protestant influence, especially in the violent campaign against what was seen as idolatry. Some missionaries, when the upheaval began to be successful—and the scope of the revolution was very great: the southern capital of Nanking was captured in 1853, and a northern expedition to take Peking was only with some difficulty repulsed at Tientsin—saw in it a force for the Christianization of China. But closer inspection of its syncretistic character caused disillusion; and, in the eventual suppression of the movement, Western auxiliary forces under the command of General C. G. Gordon (later to die in Khartoum during the Mahdist uprising) took part.

The Chinese government forces operated with great skill, and were fortified ideologically by Confucian values which they saw to be threatened by the rampaging Taipings. In 1864 Nanking was retaken. Hung had died of sickness during the siege. A year later the huge rebellion had been suppressed, but not before in all some twenty million people had died.

Hung perhaps had an intuitive understanding that, with foreigners defeating China in the ignoble Opium War, a new dispensation was called for, with the reshaping of the Chinese political and social order. But his Protestant shamanism, though it made for powerful new revelations, was not geared to any intellectual alternative to the Confucian ideology. At the *ethical* and *social* levels, the Taipings were effective, with their energetic puritanism (banning opium, tobacco, liquor, and so on, and their emphasis on the equality of the sexes, etc.) They provided, with their system of God Worshiping Societies, an effective and simplified *ritual* of devotional religion. With their attacks on tradition and their smashing up of temples they hoped to give a new sense of the future. In their appeal to the myth of a new age of harmony and their assumption of a messianic role in history, they had the *narrative* material which could consolidate a new and optimistic sense of destiny. But *doctrinally* and intellectually the movement was—to say the least—very weak. They did not have any real sense of what lay behind Western power—of the meaning and nature of science and of the necessity for a new education system. Though they substituted for the Confucian examination system an alternative one based on the Christian classics (the Bible), this was not much of a challenge to reflective thinking about China's problems.

In short, the Taiping style was insufficiently analytical and too mythological to attain any permanency. For ultimately revolution, as opposed to peasant rebellions, has to have a defined direction and a sense of how to train people for coping with the modern world. Theirs was a halfway house: it was much more than a peasant rebellion, but it fell short of being a true revolution. It was—as in many societies—a thrashing about of forces which sensed the need for change, but had not the right eventual message or the ultimate means of institutionalizing it. But it was for China, on top of its troubles with foreign powers, a sapping experience; and it made more urgent the search for ideas and a program which could restore Chinese power in a period of rapid disintegration. There were moreover other serious uprisings at the same time—that of the so-called Niens in central China, and a serious outbreak of Islamic rebellion in the northwest because of discrimination against Muslims.

### The Self-Strengthening Movement

The penetration of China by Western powers was such that by the early twentieth century there were over fifty treaty ports designated for foreign residence and trade, from Manchuria to Kwangtung and from Tientsin to Yunnan. These places provided a kind of intellectual and commercial stimulus, though they represented an unequal balance of power. They created a beginning of industrialization and of Chinese capitalism, but such that capitalists were often inextricably linked to foreign concerns. The capitalists were what the Communists were to call the *comprador* class, using a Portuguese term (the "buyers"). Missions also played their role: although missionaries were often arrogant in relation to Chinese religion and culture, they did play, as in India, a vital role in the setting up of higher education on the Western model in China. This introduced some of the fruits of Western scientific education.

The basic problem for China was how to combine the insights of Western science and of traditional beliefs. Was it possible, as a famous tag had it, for Chinese learning to provide the basis and Western learning the practical use? There were various attempts to sketch of how this could come to be.

A movement known as "Self-Strengthening" was one outcome of China's weakness. It had been started by Feng Kuei-fen (1809–74) in the 1860s, following the words of an earlier scholar who had said "learn the superior barbarian techniques in order to control the barbarian." The movement was responsible for the starting of various programs and projects—the Foreign Ministry's language school, various arsenals, dockyards, sending students for education in America, merchant shipping, and so on. But such a piecemeal program was not enough. In this sense the instinct of the Taipings was right. You cannot bring modernity to an antique society without modernizing the society itself. The Chinese empire remained a centralized bureaucracy, resting on ancient Confucian and other values entrenched in a feudal society; it did not understand the link between science and the critical spirit and a new conception of the nature of human knowledge.

At the least, some reappraisal of the Confucian tradition, some Neo-Neoconfucianism, was called for. This was a necessary preliminary to institutional reform. One may mention the frustrating effects of a more piecemeal approach in the life of China's great general and statesman Li Hung-chang (1823–1901), who took a leading part in the suppression of the Taipings and lent his influence to the Self-Strengthening Movement. He wanted modernization and helped it, from a rather traditional Confucian base. He could not, for all his skill, stop the defeat of China by a resurgent Japan in 1895. When he died in 1901 he felt that still the state of China was weak, despite his efforts.

Part of the frustration no doubt arose from observing the failure of the Reform Movement of 1898 and the disasters attendant on the Boxer Uprising, an anti-foreign uprising in 1900. The 1898 reforms had much to do with the life and thought of K'ang Yu-wei (1858–1927). He was born in Kwangtung province in the south, and was educated chiefly by his grandfather (his father died when he was a child). As a young man he became disillusioned with Confucianism and made explorations into Mahāyāna Buddhism and Taoism, as well as Western thought and knowledge. Eventually he became convinced that a new formulation of the Confucian tradition held the key to the process of modernization. He emphasized human-heartedness or *jen*, seeing it not only as a central value of Master K'ung, but also as the key to a philosophy of liberty, equality, and utilitarian reformism. History was to culminate in a time of selfless harmony, preceded by a time of emerging peace. In the great unity of the future, traditional Confucian values would be submerged in universal harmony, but the key to realization of the ideal was a gradualist and reforming approach. He considered that Confucianism should be the State religion, and indeed this came about under the Republic in a law of 1913.

In 1898 K'ang and his associates were admitted into government, and in a hundred days a whole set of reforms was promulgated. But the inept political behavior of the Reformers let in a conservative backlash at court, and the repeal of the legislation. At least, however, an attempt at structural change had been made. In 1911 the collapse of military support for the imperial regime led to the proclamation of a Republic, and in 1912 the last Manchu emperor abdicated (though he lived on, through various vicissitudes, to become a gardener in the imperial palace he had once occupied, under the Communists).

## Nationalism and the Various Options

The growth of Chinese nationalism in a modern sense was of course the result of the arrogant and damaging behavior of Western powers and Japan. On all sides China could feel encroached upon. In the west the British were gaining control in Tibet. In Central Asia and in Manchuria the Russians were advancing. In Korea the Japanese were consolidating themselves. In the treaty ports, some of them deep inland on the great waterways, Western powers were exercising control.

However, Chinese civilization did not provide an obvious ideological basis for nationalism. In the old days, China had no foreign ministry and did not expect to have to deal with foreigners as equals. They could come to petition the emperor and to recognize his suzerainty. The world outside China, except across the Wall, did not much engage the Chinese imagination: and only in that case because it was from the north and the northwest that invasions had come. Moreover, the Manchu dynasty itself was still felt to be foreign, so loyalty to it was not so easy to engage.

K'ang Yu-wei and his followers were in effect trying out a version of Confucian neoclassicism: a reshaping of the Neoconfucian tradition and an attempt to accommodate tradition to modernity. It was however unfortunate for this experiment that Confucianism was tied to the old education and examination system, which was abolished in 1905. Had the imperial family taken the option of modernization much earlier, as did the Japanese, then the outlook for a revived Confucianism would have been much brighter. But this was not something to expect, because the whole imperial system was built on the assumption of Chinese superiority and of the barbarous nature of foreign culture. At the same time, Buddhism was ill adapted to expressing Chinese nationalism, and the most substantial Buddhist thinker of the twentieth century in China, the abbot T'ai-hsi (1899–1947), was more concerned with a revival of meditation and piety, and with raising the level of Buddhist education, than he was with patriotism *per se*. Taoism, for its part, was more tied in to secret societies and inner Chinese revolt than to the problems of reestablishing Chinese dignity in the marauding imperialist politics of the era. Taoism as popular religion, moreover, was not very easily geared into the scientific mentality.

Of the Western ideologies, liberalism was undoubtedly attractive and could be combined, for an elite, with Confucian attitudes: but the basis of liberal politics is a strong middle class, and this was wanting for various reasons in the fabric of China. One reason was that the Chinese bourgeoisie was somewhat entangled in a foreign system. It weakened their opportunities and political powers. Second, power in the first half of the twentieth century was controlled by naked military force, and it was a time when bourgeois politics were not widely feasible. Third, the educated Chinese were divided still between those traditionally raised and those who benefited from the new strands of Western education.

In some degree the ideology expressed by the Christian nationalist leader, Sun Yat-sen (1866–1925), might supply the answer; but this too had its limitations. He was, like a number of other prominent national leaders, a somewhat marginal figure. Born near Macao in south China, he was

The Kuomintang leader Sun Yat-sen in traditional dress. His blend of socialism and democracy with some traditional elements was destined to fail.

educated in Hawaii and at American colleges. Well known internationally through his writings, he was the obvious candidate to be president when the Republic was created in 1911, and was so briefly; but he was outmaneuvered by the warlord Yuan Shih-k'ai (1859–1916), who took over the post and suppressed Sun's party, the Kuomintang. It was not till the early 1920s that Sun's Kuomintang became fully established, and this was with Soviet Russian assistance: Moscow sent advisers, notably Michael Borodin (1884–1951).

The ideology of the Kuomintang was based on Sun's Three Principles of the People—namely nationalism, democracy, and popular livelihood—and on his work on "Fundamentals of National Reconstruction for the National Government of China." Sun envisaged three stages: military unification of China, a time of tutelage, and then full democracy. It was assumed that the Kuomintang would become the party entrusted with such tutelage. In this idea he was influenced by the Communists, who joined the Kuomintang and became a constituent part of it. A military academy was founded in Kwangtung, the commandant of which was the young Chiang Kai-shek (1887–1975), whose later career was to confront China with the problem of having nondemocratic tutelage, even if it is thought of as being on the way to democracy: what happens when you are taken over by a military dictatorship? Sun died in 1925, when the future of his movement was much in doubt.

China was humiliated by foreigners, but it was not a colony. Had it been controlled by a single power, the political struggle would have been clearer. China in 1900 was half-independent and half-ruled by a committee of foreign powers. It was only on some occasions that nationalist passion could be aimed clearly; for instance during the May 4 movement in 1919, a great wave of chiefly student protest over what was seen as the betrayal of China at the treaty of Versailles. This was so particularly because defeated Germany's rights in Shantung province were not restored to China but were simply assigned to Japan, which was a victor on the Allied side.

The enthusiasm provoked by this demonstration led to greater interest in new political options, among them Marxism. The Russian Revolution of 1917 made a large impression across the world, and, as a kind of counter-capitalism and countercolonialism, had obvious attractions for many of the peoples of Asia. The foundation of the Chinese Communist Party and its growth into a part of the Kuomintang were signs of another choice that China might have in its struggle to regain national prestige and independence. As it turned out, it was the thought and strategy of Mao Tse-tung (or Zedong, 1893–1976) which proved to be so effective in rebuilding China.

It was ironic that, in order to combat the West, China had to reach out and take up a Western ideology, one which had much greater contempt for traditional Chinese values and religion than the most radical forms of missionary Christianity. Admittedly Mao made changes to Marxism, making it more adapted to Chinese conditions. But the advent of his revolution saw the curbing of Buddhism, the closing of monasteries and temples, the suppression of Taoist practices, assaults on the cult of ancestors, and a strong anti-Confucian campaign—not to mention attacks on minority religions.

## Mao and New China

### Mao's Rise to Power and the Japanese War

In 1926 Chiang launched a largely successful military campaign from south China to unify the country. In 1927, after the capture of Shanghai, he caused the execution of much of the leadership of the Communist party there. This showed that the struggle would have to be undertaken rather in the countryside than in the centrally controlled urban environment. It was Mao who clearly grasped two facts: one, that the peasants of China were bound to be the backbone of any revolution owing to their great numerical predominance; and the other, that the way forward was through military campaigning. He was to become a great theorist of guerrilla war. In all this he was moving away from Marxist orthodoxy, which saw the urban proletariat as the vanguard of the revolution, and which also saw a bourgeois phase as a necessary preliminary to the workers' revolution (for this and other reasons

Joseph Stalin (1879–1953) went on supporting Chiang Kai-shek and the Kuomintang through World War II).

From 1927 to 1934, Mao found himself leading a Soviet government in Kiangsi province, and engaged in warfare with the Kuomintang, through various encirclement campaigns. Then the Communists were forced to opt for a breakout, and there started the famous Long March, when their Kiangsi army and other groups marched to the Communist enclave in northwest China, in Shensi. It was a march of heroic proportions, with many battles, struggles for food, deprivations, and over 6,000 miles covered. Only about one-tenth of those who set out made it to the end of the March: but its effect was to preserve the main Communist leadership (Mao became chairman of the party during the affair), and to allow them to prosecute war against the Japanese, who invaded China in 1937 (by which time the Communists had settled in Yenan). The successful prosecution of guerrilla campaigns during the Sino-Japanese War left the Communists in a strong position in north China at its end, especially as the Soviets took Manchuria from Japan in 1945 and turned it over to Mao's forces. The Communists then took on Chiang Kai-shek and won the civil war in 1949.

## Mao's Thought and the Worldview of Red China

We have seen that Mao adapted Marxism in various ways. He was also much more voluntaristic in his thinking than most Marxists: that is, he emphasized the role of human willpower in shaping history. He became also more disillusioned with the intellectual life after the success of the revolution. He was to some extent inspired by Taoist ideals of anarchism and simplicity, and in the 1950s he began to turn his back on the Soviet model of development, which he thought might breed a centralized bureaucracy out of touch with the needs of the people.

Eventually, when he unleashed the movement known as the Great Proletarian Cultural Revolution (harking back to the events of May 1919, to which we have referred, known as the "Cultural Revolution"), much of the educational system simply disintegrated. Books and learning were no longer important. Millions of young people flooded into the streets and into the countryside to drag down much of the State and party apparatus. It was part of Mao's vision of keeping the pot boiling, and never letting revolution settle down. He had a fluid, restless vision of human betterment; and the Chinese, though blank and poor, yet could by their faith and efforts surpass others in building a new classless society in which men and women would join in the struggle to overcome faults.

It is not necessary here to recount the ins and outs of the power struggle during the years from 1965 to 1976, when Mao died and his Cultural Revolution formally came to an end. It had been a new, rather violent, experiment in social reconstruction. It involved, among other things, the intense adulation of Mao; the constant use of a selection of his thoughts in the so-called Little Red Book, compiled by Lin Piao (1907–71), who became his

The ritual dimension: the Little Red Book of excerpts from Mao Zedong's writings served as a sign and repository of faith. Here school children demonstrate their loyalty.

heir apparent but died after trying to escape to Russia when he allegedly plotted against Mao; and the rejection of traditional learning, both Western and Eastern, in the pursuit of intense commitment.

Particularly this phase of Mao's career, and of the history of China, presses us to ask whether here China had acquired a new religion. It is appropriate to think so. There were distinctively religious characteristics belonging to the Cultural Revolution. In one way, the question of whether Marxism-Leninism-Mao Zedong Thought is a religious worldview is not that vital: it is certainly a system of beliefs and practices which for a crucial period became, and still remains to some degree today, the norm for Chinese belief, and which has been used to try to wipe out rival worldviews which *are* religions, such as the traditional trio of Taoism, Confucianism, and Buddhism. It is useful to think of Maoism here in relation to the dimensions of religion.

First, during the heyday of the Cultural Revolution the Little Red Book was used in a *ritual* manner, like sacred scriptures. The book was carried around, held aloft at rallies, consulted for insight and as a guide to action. Moreover, there were continued rallies, public confessions in which people who had made mistakes were expected to confess to them, and reverence everywhere for the Great Helmsperson, as he was called (Mao, a very strong feminist from his early days, might have approved of this translation!) Second, *emotionally*, there was large investment in the figure of Mao as a kind of Amitābha figure, and there was repeated talk of conversion experiences in which people came to see their lives purified and renewed by their new commitments. Third, at the *doctrinal* level, there were the principles of Maoism, and in a wider context Marxism, to master, for they defined not only the way the world is but also gave directions for action. Fourth, there was the powerful *narrative* of China's historic weakness and corruption, her prostration before the great powers, the formation of the Communist party, the heroic struggle in Kiangsi, and the even more heroic Long March, the battles against Japan, the Liberation, the making of a new China. So then plenty of myth, not to mention all those stories about people being cured through positive thinking (about Mao's thought), driven to great deeds, and the like. Then, fifthly, there was the austere *ethic* of those times—the self-sacrifice which building the new China demands, the need to be alongside the peasants in their hardships, the ethos of the equality of women, the abandonment of hierarchical thinking (and even filial piety, that old Confucian virtue). It was a morality diametrically opposed to the orderly, respectful, traditional modes and etiquette of Confucian behavior. Sixth, there was a new *social* elite: the cadres, the young, those who armed with the Little Red Book would constitute a kind of counterculture and an organization against the big institutions of Party and State, a kind of new this-worldly monasticism roaring through the streets and the countryside. Seventh, there was the *art* of the new era: simple, propagandistic, largely Western in technique but

The social dimension: a collective farm. Chinese society was thoroughly reorganized after 1949.

without bourgeois ornament, serving the people, Socialist Realist, showing forth the heroics of the myth.

All this added up to a kind of new religion that harnessed some of the emotions and thoughts of Taoism (the anarchism of Lao-tzu, the alchemy of right commitment) and of Buddhism (the Pure Land, but here and now, and Mao as a celestial Buddha, but right here in Peking). It was by passing through the crucible of this religion that modern China was formed, if often by reaction.

The effects on the traditions were devastating. Monasteries were closed and turned into granaries and the like. Many manuscripts and books were destroyed. Much of religious practice was stopped. Images were destroyed. Ancestors were no longer venerated. Graves were not swept, nor holy mountains climbed. Monks and nuns worked the fields. Bibles were confiscated; Muslims were discriminated against. It was, in short, a period of religious and ideological persecution; and even now there are strict limits to the cautious rebuilding of the traditional practices.

### The Irony of the New Period in China

With the death of Mao in 1976, power reverted from the more extreme wing of the party, as represented by the group known as the Gang of Four, including Mao's wife, Chiang Ch'ing. The country entered a more pragmatic era. Even so, it was of course still to be guided by the principles of Marxism. This being so, there have been debates as to how far it is possible to combine such orthodoxy with the borrowing of Western methods of scientific education, trade, and technology. The irony is that China has come to the same position it was in one hundred years ago, but in a new form. No longer is it a matter of Confucian values for culture and Western methods for function, but of Marxist ideas for values and Western technology for function. Thousands of young Chinese have been sent abroad to study in the West, and the whole educational policy of the Cultural Revolution has been reversed as China scrambles to make up for past losses and to build a new and more prosperous society. But can it do so without the freedoms which go with Western systems (including here the Japanese)? The contrast, of course, with Japan is remarkable, and for many Chinese it is painful. So now China is plunged once again into its old debate.

Meanwhile the present era is more relaxed, and it is possible for religion to some extent to come out of hiding. There is a slow resumption of some of the older patterns. But undoubtedly the traditional threefold religious system of China has been shattered, and it will never resume its original, prerevolutionary, form. Any new synthesis, we must suppose, will have to incorporate Marxist materialism.

### Reflections on Modern China

We have noted that Marxism will have changed the face of Chinese (and Tibetan) religion permanently. During the revival which is slowly beginning in the time since Mao's death the place of religion is bound to be relatively private, in the sense that religious practices will depend largely on private decisions; so it is no longer possible to see the three religions of China as an integrated system, a kind of federation of ideas and practices. The Westernized concept of the three traditions as more or less independent religions is likely to become a reality (just as in the modern period a previously undefined "Hinduism" has actually come to exist in the self-consciousness of Indians).

In all the vicissitudes of Chinese modern history the decisive moment came perhaps during the May 4 Movement, after 1919: Chinese intellectuals turned increasingly to Marxism, there was widespread disillusion with liberalism, and little edge to modernist forms of traditional religion. The Kuomintang philosophy might have developed in a more liberal direction had not Chiang seized power, and then been involved in the struggle against the Japanese. It is however difficult to see real alternatives to the direction in which China has gone.

## The Chinese Diaspora

Meanwhile, China is not just the mainland. For one thing, the defeated Nationalists set up their alternative China in Taiwan, which does to some great degree carry on the traditions of the old China, alongside modern technology. Then there is Hong Kong, dominantly Chinese, and due to revert to China in 1997, but itself also an alternative China. There are important settlements of overseas Chinese—in Malaysia, Indonesia, Singapore, the Caribbean, the United States, and elsewhere. In some areas they have encountered severe problems, especially in Vietnam, where many of the refugees, the so-called "boat people," in the 1970s and 1980s were ethnic Chinese, and in Indonesia, where the coup of 1965 was very severe on Chinese institutions and people. In Singapore, a dominantly Chinese culture has performed brilliantly, creating a marvel of paternalistically controlled capitalist welfare. In the United States and other Western countries, the Chinese have been active and have merged successfully into the dominant cultural ethos.

There has been in the last forty years a revival of Western interest in Chinese religion—in Neoconfucianism especially, in various kinds of Chinese Buddhism, and in Tao as a religion. The new Confucianist emphasis is complemented by official teaching of its ethical values in the State school system in Singapore, and this concern with tradition may herald similar revitalizations elsewhere.

## Modern Korean Religion

The Choson dynasty in Korea during the early modern period (seventeenth and eighteenth centuries) had as its official ideology Neo-confucianism. Buddhism was excluded from the capital; and Catholicism, which, through

431

Jesuit missions to China, was beginning to interest some leading Korean intellectuals, was resisted vigorously by the court. Despite persecution, Catholicism went on growing during the nineteenth century. Following the Korean-Japanese treaty of 1876 there was more and more penetration of Korea by Japanese commercial interests, and in their wake missionaries from some of the Pure Land organizations, and later Nichiren Buddhism. Meanwhile Zen or Son Buddhism was undergoing something of a revival, primarily through the work of the teacher Kyongho (1857–1912).

The occupation of Korea by Japan in 1910 altered the dynamics of Buddhist leadership, especially when in 1926 the Japanese brought in legislation which made legal the marriage of monks (this had been advocated as part of the process of modernization). The Son organization in particular was split, a more conservative minority fighting to retain its traditional celibate way of life and to maintain the disciplines of meditation. After World War II, in 1954, in South Korea, the administration of Son monasteries was handed over to this conservative group, the Chogye-chong. This gave modern Korean Zen Buddhism a unity and strength which has made it one of the dominant religious traditions of South Korea.

Protestant Christianity has made great progress in Korea. From the 1880s on, American and other missions were very active, and the religion grew at a strong rate during the twentieth century despite the Japanese occupation. Probably there are about six million Protestants today in Korea, and proportionately it has been more successful there than in any other Asian country. The forms are chiefly Methodism and Presbyterianism, and they were left to progress pretty much under Korean leadership; an evangelical, Biblical piety is very manifest. The reasons for the relatively large success of Korean Protestantism are debated, but they arise from the following factors. First, Japanese sponsorship of Buddhism from 1910 to 1945 deprived that religion of the appeal based on national sentiment that it may have had elsewhere. Second, the processes of modernization and industrialization may have favored the spread of a "rootless" religion: Korea has produced new religions of its own, as we shall see. Third, the missionaries were sympathetic towards Korean nationalism. Fourth, in the 1970s the religion doubled its numbers, and it may be because of the impact of consumerist individualism on traditional Korean society during the economic miracle.

The result has been some tension between the more individualistic religions (of which we can name Son Buddhism and Protestantism, and increasingly Catholicism) and traditional Confucianism: this is reflected too in politics, in the divide between the democratic movement and the military dictatorship. In North Korea, religious echoes are muffled, and it is hard to diagnose what is going on there beneath the surface of the very longstanding dictatorship of Kim Il-sung, who flourishes his own brand of conservative or hardline Communism, written up in his collected works which are published in every national language in the world.

Responses both to the Confucian feudal tradition and to Christianity are

represented by various of the new religions of Korea, dating from the nineteenth and twentieth centuries. Two of the most important of these are the Ch'ondogyo and the Unification Church of Sun Myung Moon.

Ch'ondogyo was founded in 1860 by Ch'oe Suun (1824–64) as the Tonghak movement, literally "Eastern Learning" (by contrast with the Western learning represented by Christianity). He claimed to have had a revelation from God, and was shortly after martyred by the government as his teachings were regarded as subversive. The writings of Ch'oe Suun and of his two successors as leaders comprise the scriptures, and the religion came to be known as the Religion of the Heavenly Way (Ch'ondogyo). Though it now plays little overt role in South Korean politics, it was long thought subversive, from different directions: by the Korean dynasty because it led an

Korean Confucianism: burning incense at the shrine of deceased great scholars.

433

*Opposite* A Thai dance showing a demon trying to steal a magic jewel, drawn from the classical Hindu epic the *Rāmāyana*. Hindu culture became an important ingredient of Thai civilization (see Chapter 18).

uprising in 1894, and by the Japanese because it took part in the Korean independence movement of 1919. It is strongly egalitarian and criticizes the whole hierarchical character of traditional Korean Confucianism. It believes in God as pervading the world and as being present in individuals: one of its slogans is that "The human being is God" and gains oneness with God through the sincere practice of faith. Its rituals involve prayers and the calling of the divine down into the self, together with scripture reading and meditation on purity. It combines some traditional Korean motifs and Christian ones: in some ways it is reminiscent of Quakerism.

It is against the background of evangelical Protestantism that we may view the teachings of Sun Myung Moon. He was a child preacher who had an experience in 1936 which he saw as a commission by Jesus to spread a new message. He also claims visions of the Buddha and other religious leaders. In

The Unification Church combines elements from Korean culture with a blend of Confucian and Christian values. The movement sees itself as a great family with Mr. and Mrs. Moon at its head as father and mother. Here, over two thousand couples get married at Madison Square Garden in New York: interethnic and interracial marriages are the norm, and thought to be a means of combatting racism.

1954 he founded what is known for simplicity as the Unification Church. Its tenets involve a reinterpretation of the Bible; loyalty to Mr. Moon as possibly—that is, if he fulfills his destiny—the new Messiah; a new system of marriage designed to unite members in a large Family of which Mr. Moon and his wife are the True Parents; and the hope of unifying the world and the world's religions in a single harmony (in combat however with Communism, which is seen as the present chief manifestation of evil in the world). In practice the religion—which has made converts in the West, though most of its members are Korean and Japanese—favors explorations of the unity of science and religion, the promotion of crosscultural ties through intermarriage of its members across races and nations, and a whole range of modern enterprises, from manufacturing to fishing. It is an interesting synthesis of Korean and Protestant themes. It is Biblically oriented (with the addition of its own scripture, *The Divine Principle*), but its family structure has reminiscences of Confucianism, internationalized. It has a theology which combines Christian themes and those of the Yin-Yang dialectic of the East Asian tradition. For various reasons the Unification Church has attracted a lot of controversy, but it is the first major religious mission out of Korea to the West.

To sum up: in Korea, as in Japan, the concern to modernize combines with elements drawn from varied traditions, including indigenous shamanism. However, because of Korea's conquest by another Asian power, the logic of events took a different path: often Buddhism and Japanese State Shinto were presented as the religions of the rulers, and this gave Christianity a very different role from that which it had elsewhere, where it was identified with the colonial power. This may help to explain its growing success in Korea. But the full story of the evolution of worldviews in Korea cannot yet be told, because of the military and ideological divide between North and South. We may note, too, that in modern times Zen (Son) Buddhism has emerged strengthened by its experiences and represents a resource which other countries are beginning to tap.

*Opposite* The experiential dimension: a golden Buddha at the Shwedagon Temple in Rangoon calls upon the earth (as indicated by his left hand) to bear witness to his attainment of Enlightenment (see Chapter 18).

CHAPTER

# Modern Southeast Asia

## Southeast Asia and the Colonial Period

The impact of the colonial powers in Southeast Asia was rather piecemeal (see Map 12, p. 338–9). Early on, the Dutch and Portuguese, especially, penetrated the Straits of Malacca, and in due course the Dutch created a wide-ranging empire in the East Indies (Indonesia). The British came to be interested also for trading reasons in Singapore, which they virtually founded, and Malaya, with parts of Borneo left for dispute between the two European powers. The British also in the nineteenth century acquired lower and then upper Burma, as an adjunct to their Indian empire. The French, rather late in the colonial scramble, had an interest in Vietnam, and eventually annexed virtually all of Indochina, including North and South Vietnam, Laos and Cambodia (Kampuchea). The United States, after its war with Spain in 1898, rewarded itself with the turbulent Philippines. The only nation not to be administered by foreign powers was Thailand.

Burma and most of mainland Indochina were Theravādin in religion, and Vietnam also had a strong Buddhist presence. To the south, Malaya and Indonesia were predominantly Islamic. We shall deal with their development in Chapter 20. The Philippines is the only predominantly Christian, in this case Catholic, country in Asia.

The effect of colonial rule on the Buddhist countries was partly to sever the bond between the Sangha and the government, by removing the existing monarchies. It also dramatically injected into these societies the educational systems and fruits of Western culture, forcing some reappraisal of the traditions.

The colonial period did not last all that long, however. World War II brought the Japanese into the area, at first hailed as Asian liberators from European rule. Although the Vietnam War (which was a continuation of the

438

anti-French struggle resumed after the expulsion of the Japanese in 1945) did not end till the 1970s, substantially it was the 1950s that marked the main boundary between the colonial and the postcolonial eras.

The region came to evolve, in response to the colonial era, along very different lines. The Philippines' modernization came in effect through its conversion to Catholicism and occupation by Spain and the United States. The restoration of its Constitution after the Japanese occupation was not sufficient to prevent the slide into military dictatorship and the persistence of Marxist and Islamic rebellions. In many ways the country followed the pattern of Latin American countries, since the existence of large landowners has given point to Communistic ideas among the poor peasantry.

In the rest of the region there are some interesting variations. Thus, ultimately, a rather old-fashioned line in Marxism prevailed in Vietnam after many years of anticolonial and civil war. There were other, rejected options: a rather right-wing dictatorship based on Catholic and conservative Confucian support; and a Buddhist neutralism which was a significant factor in the Vietnam War. In Laos and Cambodia there were fruitless attempts to restore the stability of the old-style kingship with Sangha support in the face of revolutionary movements. That movement in Cambodia was the "Red Khmer," or "Khmer Rouge," a movement with its own ideology, which I shall call for the sake of analysis "post-Buddhist quasi-Marxism," which had devastating effects on the country, and has been replaced essentially by orthodox Marxism under the occupation forces of Vietnam.

In Thailand—which managed to escape occupation—a modernized Buddhism stayed on as the ideology of the State, despite some Marxist and Islamic rebellions. Alliance with the United States kept it importantly in the capitalist domain. Burma, on the other hand, had been affected by Socialist values, which it saw as a means of preserving the organic identity of the society, and most of the period of independence after World War II has been devoted to the practice of isolation. It has what may be thought of as a Buddhist autarkism or self-sufficiency as its aim: this ideal has some resemblance to the Khmer Rouge ideology. Finally, in the other predominantly non-Muslim regime of the region, namely Singapore, this island Republic has undertaken a rapid modernization through welfare capitalism under a vaguely Confucian paternalistic regime.

In the whole region some complications follow from the embedding within the larger ethnic groups of smaller nations or tribes, such as the Hmong in Laos and the Kachin and Karen in Burma, who have played an independent part in events—being for instance in perpetual civil war with the Burmese government and under non-Buddhist, mainly Christian, leadership.

## Thailand and the Process of Modernization

The survival of Thailand as an independent state in the 1840s and beyond, when European traders were becoming active in the area, was largely the work of two reforming kings. The first, Mongkut (1804–68), had a remarkable career. He happened (somewhat in the Thai fashion) to be in a monastery when he was passed over for succession to the throne in favor of an uncle, and he stayed on as a monk until his accession quite a time later, in 1851. During this period he became a fine Pali scholar and questioned many of the existing practices in Thai monasticism—which led him to accept reordination, together with a number of followers, in the Mon lineage (the Mon being a minority ethnic group), and in effect founded a new branch of the Sangha, which was called the Dhammayuttika Nikāya or "Branch of Those Adhering to the Dhamma"—or, in Thai, Thammayut. It gained great prestige among the Thai elite, both in towns and in the countryside, and attracted the patronage of influential laypersons, both men and women.

Later, when Mongkut became king, he had as such to patronize the whole Order, including of course the majority, the validity of whose ordination and practice he questioned. But it was the Dhammayuttika branch which still attracted his special favor, and it became an arm in his concern for the modernization of his country. His attitudes were not only spiritual and directed to the deepening and reforming of the life of Buddhist monks and nuns, and restoring Pali studies. Doctrinally he was a neofoundationalist, going back as he saw it to the canonical foundations of the faith. Like others, later, in the West, he saw the Buddhist Canon as essentially rationalist and empirical. It was from this point of view that he came to reject the old model of the universe which was used to justify the role of kings in the medieval period.

According to this model the king exists at a focal cosmological point. The universe is conceived here as being at three levels. Above is the ascending scale of heavens, to which you have access through meditation, but which more concretely are the levels where exist different gods of varying bliss and longevity. To be reborn in such a heaven is the reward for greatly meritorious work. Below the earthly realm there is the world of ghosts and demons and purgatories, where those who have sinned greatly are reborn, and where they undergo grisly fates. In the middle realm, which is where Buddhas appear, there are various sorts and conditions of living beings, and one's height in the scale of beings is again determined by merit. At the heart of this earthly realm is the *cakkavattin* or universal monarch (literally "Wheel-turner"—a title for the Buddha who began the turning of the wheel of the Dhamma or Teaching, but assigned also to the figure of the ideal ruler). The ideal is usually identified with the emperor Aśoka, who became a template for Southeast Asian monarchy. The king has a crucial role in the scheme of things, because in maintaining order and the Sangha, and in promoting virtue, he increases merit and gives humans the greater opportunity to ascend in the scale of life and to attain heavenly as well as earthly welfare.

It was a noble picture, but it was presented in an antique way. It involved, as did Christian and other traditional cosmologies, a three-decker universe, infested too in this case with gods and spirits permitting fanciful explanations of natural phenomena. It was this kind of picture which Mongkut de-mythologized. He saw the universe as essentially moral and the role of Buddhism as promoting ethical and spiritual welfare. He had his foreign minister and close associate write a book setting forth this more empiricist account. In it, heaven and hell became not so much places as states of mind and useful pedagogical devices. Scorn was lavished on the older explanations of things in terms of gods. Religion was thoroughly spiritualized. It was an early and courageous version of Buddhist modernism and was suffused with the spirit of naturalism.

The program of reform was carried on by Mongkut's son, Chulalongkorn (reigned 1868–1910), who centralized further the Sangha under government supervision, and set up Buddhist academies for the better training of the clergy. Buddhists in Thailand, and elsewhere in Southeast Asia, came to see Buddhism as compatible with (some thought prefiguring) modern science, and the law of dependent origination was seen as a way of stating the fundamental principle underlying the universe. It is true that there are many naturalistic elements in the Pali canon, and the rationality and intellectualism of the Buddha are evident in the texts. So the neofoundationalist style of modern Thai education of the clergy lent itself to the interpretation of the faith in a modern manner.

At the same time, however, nationalism was intensified, in accordance (one might say) with the very spirit of the age, but also as a means of unifying the country and bringing outlying areas and cultural groups into the national synthesis. This made Buddhism into the national religion in a more intense way, and led to some formulations of Thai Buddhism in the 1970s which are strongly chauvinist in outlook. But the spiritual improvement of the Sangha has led to a dialectic between official religion and the spirituality of outstanding and saintly men who have attained high states of meditation and to whom are often ascribed miraculous powers by the laity. They often operate at the periphery of political life, but still such saints have their overall role in reminding the laity that the Sangha is a vehicle of spirituality and not just an organization for maintaining social and national values.

The retention of the monarchy in Thailand has given the polity a certain stability through a variety of military coups and changes of regime since World War II. There remain problems here as elsewhere about the status of minority religions, particularly Islam in the south of the country, under a Buddhist establishment. It is a problem not effectively solved, either, in Burma, the other Buddhist state in the area.

One may see the Thai model as an effective realization, primarily through the genius and farsightedness of Mongkut and Chulalongkorn, of a modernist transition without the severe political disruption caused by foreign conquest, and one where the monarchy was retained, so that it could play a modernist role in the emerging national polity. But in other countries, though monarchies were kept on, it was under foreign control, as in Laos, Cambodia, and Vietnam, under the French. In due course these monarchies were swept aside in the establishment of Vietnamese Communist domination in 1975. Though there had been lay movements and Sangha reforms in Laos and Cambodia, they were not at a very developed level, because of the slow emergence of higher education. But Cambodia had benefited from Thai reforms in that the Dhammayuttika branch of the Sangha was brought in there.

## The Burmese Solution: Withdrawal from the World

Burma was absorbed into Britain's Indian empire through three nineteenth-century wars. Through the war of 1826 Britain took the coastal states of Arakan and Tenasserim, with Assam (which remained part of India after Burma was administratively separated in 1935). Through the war of 1852 Britain got lower Burma. Through the war of 1885 it gained upper Burma, right up to the Chinese frontier in Yunnan. In 1890, it added the Shan States, wedged between China and Thailand. The country as a whole never fully settled down under British rule, there being a succession of rebellions, some under Buddhist leadership. For instance, in the Saya San rebellion in 1930–31, put down with some hardship by the British army, a former monk was proclaimed king and gained support from members of various nationalist societies formed in the 1920s.

This attempt to go back to the model of kingship was not, as it happened, very attractive to the emerging intelligentsia, who were more attracted by Socialism. The attempt was made to blend Buddhist and Socialist values, especially in the thought and practice of U Nu (b.1907). He sought to establish a Buddhist Socialist regime in Burma, before being eventually removed in a coup by General Ne Win in 1962. Though the new regime did not so explicitly work towards his goals, in effect they followed the same ideology, and until the end of the 1970s Burma was largely cut off from foreign influences, travel being banned or severely restricted. A constant campaign had to be fought against secessionist forces from among the Christianized, non-Buddhist ethnic groups.

Though Ne Win repealed U Nu's ordinance making Buddhism the State religion, Buddhism remains predominant, of course; and there is a strand in Buddhist thinking which favors Burma's isolationism. In 1956 the Burmese Sangha had gained prestige by the holding there of a Great Council of Buddhism to celebrate the 2,500th anniversary of the Buddha's decease and attainment of final *nirvana*. Burmese Buddhist methods of meditation also became influential in Sri Lanka and the West in the years after World War II.

The isolationism of Burma can be explained, perhaps, by the collectivist transposition of ancient individual ideals. The notion of the hermit or forest-dwelling monk is vital in the Buddhist tradition: in Burma, it is as if a whole nation has wished to withdraw from the wider world. The ideal is that Burmese values will thus remain pure and uncontaminated, either by the destructive forces of Marxism which have done so much harm to Buddhism over so much of Asia, or by the corroding influences of Western materialism and capitalism. Buddhism in Burma will remain thus free, perhaps a bit mixed up with the religion of the spirits, the *nats*—who here as elsewhere in peasant Asia form an army of forces in the jungle, the field, the sky, and the streams, who have to be dealt with—but within the framework of the Dhamma. We note that not only in Burma but also in Sri Lanka among the J.V.P. (People's Liberation Front) and in Kampuchea there are similar ideas of withdrawal from the capitalist world, but in these cases the ideals are more secularized and politicized.

## Cambodia and the Purification of Kampuchea

In 1887 Cambodia became part of the French Union Indochinoise, after the suppression of a major rebellion. Cambodian troops fought for the French during World War I, and as a reward higher education and administrative opportunities for native Cambodians were somewhat expanded. But throughout Indochina the French somewhat alienated the intelligentsia through their insistence on purely French education, based on the assumption of the great superiority of French culture.

Though Laos and Cambodia became independent under their own monarchies in 1954, after the First Vietnamese War had ended in French defeat at Dien Bien Phu, they came to be sucked up in the general armed struggle of the region in the 1960s and 1970s. In 1975 the Cambodian capital, Phnom Penh, fell to insurgents of the Khmer Rouge under the political control of

Victorious Khmer Rouge soldiers are cheerful in their final success, but the regime they ushered in proved disastrous both to Cambodian culture and to the people, since they tried to purge the country brutally of dissent and education.

443

Pol Pot, who ruled till 1979. Then Vietnamese intervention brought in an orthodox Marxist regime under Vietnam's control; but not before there had been great changes and massacres.

These were carried out in the name of an ideology which had been sketched out first by Khieu Sampan (b.1925) and articulated by him in a doctoral thesis he wrote for the Sorbonne in Paris. In that work he analyzed the condition of Cambodia, which he saw at that time under colonial and neocolonial domination. In order to get true economic independence, he argued that it was necessary to isolate Cambodia completely and to go back to an agricultural and self-sufficient economy. It was a bold vision, which he thought out with clarity to its bitter end. Though he thought in Marxist terms, the direction was un-Marxist, for it looked backward to an agrarian past rather than forward through the smoke of the industrial revolution. As a British academic, sympathetic to the regime, put it wittily after a visit there: "I have seen the past, and it works."

In addition to the strictly economic vision of Khieu Sampan there were notions of national purity at work too. Kampuchea (the name was changed under Pol Pot) was to be rid of the impurities brought by colonialism and capitalism. One of these impurities was education, another urban living. Shortly after taking the swollen capital, the Khmer Rouge ordered everyone out. People went, thinking it a temporary measure, even if they had to rumble along in hospital beds. But it was permanent: the Khmer Rouge simply abolished Phnom Penh as a functioning city. Educated people were everywhere executed: and among these were counted the members of the Sangha. About a third of the population perished, many of them by hunger. A new, intolerant religion had taken over, what I have called a "post-Buddhist quasi-Marxism." It still persists as a minority faction in the continuing civil war that has followed on from the effective take-over by Vietnam, which retains an army of occupation both there and in Laos and has tightly curbed Buddhism.

In the Khmer Rouge ideology, Kampuchea saw the application of a secularist hermitism, a more brutal and greatly less traditional version of Burmese isolationism. And yet the logic of it all was in the last analysis nationalist: it was done in the name of the Khmer people, in the context of Khmer independence and "freedom." Ideology was ultimately at the service of the most powerful secular value of them all—the power of national feeling and the national idea.

## Vietnam and the Long Struggle Against Foreign Domination

As I have said, the French did much to alienate the intelligentsia of the region, especially in Vietnam, with its strong infusion of Confucian thought, which was scarcely ready to admit the superiority of French ideas. The diverse

Ho Chi Minh, the
Communist leader of
North Vietnam,
telling stories to
children.

tendencies in Vietnam rose to the surface during and after World War II,
when Japanese rule gave way first to the proclamation of independence by the
most organized of the wartime resistance movements, the Communists
under Ho Chi Minh (1890–1969), and then the attempt by the French to
regain their former possessions. That struggle led to the French withdrawal
and the division of the country into North and South. But this did not
prevent the fight from slowly resuming, by guerrilla means in the South; and
so eventually, for fear of Communism, the United States got sucked in,
sending troops in 1965.

It was during the following decade that the religious tensions in the South
were manifest. The population was mixed. Though there was a strong
Buddhist Sangha, there were also many Catholics: Vietnam was by far the
most Catholic country in Asia, after the Philippines. Many Catholics had fled
from the North and swollen the numbers in the South. But the ideology of

Catholics tended simply to be negative: anti-Communist. There were also in the South some new religions, like the Buddhist-inspired Hao Hoa and more importantly the syncretistic Cao Dai. There was a growing lobby of Buddhists who took a neutralist stance, wanting neither Marxism nor Western materialism (as it was often perceived: and certainly the Americans fought the war in a materialist way, supposing that military victory could be achieved by firepower, air power, the favorable body count ratio, and so on).

The Cao Dai is a syncretistic Vietnamese church which was founded in 1926, amid great éclat, by a Vietnamese intellectual called Ngo Van Chieu (1878–1932). It is highly eclectic, but may be said to be more than anything Taoist in inspiration. The name means "High Tower," which is a Taoist symbolic representation of the Supreme Being. In accord with the old Vietnamese tradition, the threefold religion of the Chinese-Vietnamese culture was incorporated into the beliefs and practices of the new religion, which nevertheless wove in other Western and nationalist strands. Its organization was modeled on the Catholic: having a Pope, cardinals, archbishops, and so forth. It is an interesting feature of Taoism—as of the Bön tradition, too, in Tibet—this tendency to mimic its rivals' organizational structures. In the old days it was Buddhist monasticism that was the model: here it was Catholicism.

In addition to the Supreme Being, the Cao Dai also reverence other spirits, such as the Buddha, Confucius, and Sun Yat-sen, not to mention Jesus and Muhammad, and great figures of the conquering French such as Joan of Arc and Victor Hugo (the task of one official was to continue the latter's writings; there is in the Cao Dai a strong spiritualist element, so communication with Victor Hugo and taking down further works by dictation presented no problem in principle). It sought the unity of religions, as may be gathered from this list of honored spirits. But in its nature it was destined to become a separate organization. It was too strongly organized to be an effective umbrella for other groups: until 1955 it even fielded its own army. It was in the North-South struggle emphatically anti-Communist. Its hope was for an independent Vietnam which would follow a middle path between the superpowers. In this it was sympathetic to the growing Buddhist movement in the South.

That movement contributed to the fall of the government of Ngo Dinh Diem, a Catholic, who was better able to organize outside support than to mobilize loyalty within the country; and during the 1960s the United Buddhist Association under the leadership of the monks Thich Tri Quang and Thich Thien Minh was prominent in the political struggle, but from a neutralist perspective. The self-immolations of Buddhist monks and nuns on behalf of their ideals were moving demonstrations of commitment and helped to highlight the essentially divided character of South Vietnamese religious and ideological loyalties. The victory of the Northerners in 1975 led to the elimination of dissent; and it was to be abroad that the manifestations of indigenous Vietnamese religion were to be continued—in the United States,

The ethical dimension: with vast self-control a Buddhist monk burns himself to death in protest against the actions of the South Vietnamese government. Generally Buddhist monks took a middle position between the two sides in the Vietnamese civil war. Though suicide is not commended in Buddhism, it had come to be a sporadic custom in China and was somewhat revived in Vietnam during the war.

especially, whither many Vietnamese fled, and where there flourish centers such as those of the Cao Dai and relevant Buddhist associations.

And so, over much of the old Indochina, there reigns in effect the Chinese system: the realization of national independence through Marxism. But in the case of Vietnam, mindful of Chinese domination in the past, it has been advantageous to ally closely with the Soviet Union, and to survive through Russian economic and military support, while fighting an occasional border battle with the Chinese. The logic of nationalism dictates this. But the logic of nationalism dictates otherwise in Laos and in Kampuchea, and no doubt anti-Vietnamese nationalist ideologies will surface there.

447

## The Singapore Experiment in Welfare Capitalism

The only other non-Muslim country in Southeast Asia is Singapore, a city-state which was essentially created by the British. It was founded by Sir Stamford Raffles (1781–1826), in 1819, as a trading post. It was for long part of Malaya, and as such had a great influx of ethnic Chinese during the later part of the nineteenth century in connection with rubber plantations and tin mines. These people made their way in commerce, and when Singapore gained independence as part of Malaysia, a wider federation, in 1963, and later in 1965 broke away under the dynamic leadership of Lee Kuan Yew (b.1923), it had a spectacular success as a hub of capitalism in Southeast Asia.

Singapore is governed by a form of welfare capitalism. Since there are substantial minorities in the small island republic, such as Indians, Malayans, and Sri Lankans, the regime is keen to emphasize its pluralism. Nevertheless a kind of education-oriented elitism is the main ideology, reminiscent of Confucianism. One might call it Economic Post-Confucianism, if one wanted a label, where learning and virtue are seen as the basis for economic success. Within this framework traditional religions such as Buddhism and Taoism have a modest place, plus Christianity and Hinduism.

Of all the Asian states other than Japan, Singapore has been the most successful in pursuing the capitalist path. It has gained immensely from independence, since the British notions of development and education were somewhat old-fashioned. Also, Singapore serves as something of a beacon for the overseas or diaspora Chinese, it being a conspicuous example of their success, while in Vietnam and Indonesia, and in some degree Malaysia, they suffer from a degree of discrimination.

## Reflections on the Southeast Asian Scene

It can be seen that varying options have arisen in relation to the religions of the region. In some cases, nationalism has led to the decisive and often bitter rejection of traditional ideas and practices and the substitution of secular ideologies. Of these ideologies the most conventional is the Vietnamese under the leadership of Ho Chi Minh. The least conventional is the alarming nationalist quasi-Marxism of the Khmer Rouge. The Buddhist variations comprise the modernizing conservatism of Thailand, through a forward-looking monarchy, and the Socialist hermitism of Burma. The most vital syncretism among all these is probably the modernist Thai adaptation, synthesizing canonical Buddhism and Western ideas, but building on a slowly evolving popular Buddhism which prizes the monks and nuns who attain high levels of spirituality, but also appreciates the modernizing spirit (as well as the practical fruits of modern technology, of course). Then there are the unresolved questions of Cambodian and Laotian culture. Meanwhile, Singapore has made a bold dash for post-Confucian capitalist prosperity, blending this with religious pluralism and a welfare state.

One major effect of the terrible history of Southeast Asia, through and after the colonial period, has been the large number of refugees. They have settled mainly in North America, but some, too, in Australia and elsewhere. They have brought their forms of Buddhism with them and so helped to plant that religion more firmly in the West. Since religion has suffered greatly in Marxist lands, and since most of these in Asia are Buddhist lands, it follows that Buddhism has suffered more than any other religion (more than any other save, proportionately and in sick drama, the Jews). It means that the center of gravity of Buddhism has shifted to the South—to the Theravādin countries—and in many ways to the capitalist West, where it flourishes markedly. Among other refugees, one may also mention tribal people such as the Hmong, many of whom have made their place in the United States, about to pioneer a quite different future for their culture.

A Buddhist three-day retreat in Laos before the country was taken over by the Communists.

# Japan in Modern Times

## Into Seclusion

### The Arrival of the Jesuits

By the middle of the sixteenth century the Portuguese had established a whole range of trading ports from East Africa through India to the East Indies. The chance shipwreck of some merchants in 1543 in southern Japan led to more regular visits to Kyushu, including that of the spectacular Jesuit missionary St. Francis Xavier (1506–52), who had already done great things in Goa and southern India. His mission, though fairly brief, allowed Christianity to take root in southern Japan, especially in and around the port of Nagasaki.

Christianity had considerable initial success, in part because the Jesuits were accommodating culturally in their presentation of the faith. Xavier had used the name of the great Buddha Dainichi for "God," and had used Buddhist titles and the like, and the promise of a Pure Land as the heavenly paradise awaiting the faithful. It could all look very much like a form of Pure Land Buddhism (and in a way this perception was the truth—the conceptions of grace were similar between the two religions, even if Xavier could complain that Pure Land doctrines were more like Lutheranism).

Xavier and his successors were helped by the fact that during the power struggle to unify Japan at the time, the main contender, Oda Nobunaga (1534–82), was angry at Buddhist resistance to his plans, burned the great Buddhist center at the Tendai monastery on Mount Hiei, and to counteract Buddhism encouraged Catholic Christianity. His successor, Toyotomi Hideyoshi (1536–98), was equally anti-Buddhist in policy, but was also somewhat anti-Catholic, because he feared that the presence of missionaries might itself begin to thwart his plans for national unity. From 1596 missionaries were banned, and in 1597 he caused twenty-six Christians, including Franciscans and Japanese converts, to be crucified.

The advent of Spain, trading between Mexico and the Philippines, was also disturbing, and when the shogunate was established in Edo (Tokyo) under the eventual winner in the struggle, Tokugawa Ieyasu (1542–1616), Christianity and foreign contact were excluded. Buddhism and the *kami* were instituted as the official religion. Persecution of Catholics was especially severe after the uprising in Shimabara, Kyushu, in which many Christians took part in 1637. The regime came to institute a parish system throughout Japan in which every family had to register with a temple. Temples were put in charge of burials and cemeteries, and this strengthened the link between temples and families. Also, with the exception of a controlled Dutch trading post at Nagasaki, foreigners were completely excluded from Japan, and the country underwent a rigorous policy of national seclusion (*sakoku*).

## Religion in the Tokugawa Era

The Tokugawa was a system of remarkable consolidation, which gave Japan breathing space until the next crisis, in the middle of the nineteenth century, when it became evident that seclusion would break down. It retained the imperial family as a sacred focus of the nation, but the administration was under the shoguns of the Tokugawa family—as it were, national and hereditary prime ministers—and devolved through a feudal system presided over by local warrior feudatories or *daimyo*. The social order was fairly rigorously defined by law and etiquette. The hierarchy in broad terms was: warrior, farmer, artisan, merchant (with one or two impure groups below). Though merchants were at the bottom, by the end of the Tokugawa period commerce and cities had expanded so that their status had improved with the accumulation of wealth.

As far as religion went, the Tokugawa system not only integrated the population with Buddhism, and Buddhism itself with the *kami*; but it expected the various ranks of society to conform to the proper norms. The warrior class had to follow the Bushido, for example: the Way of the Warrior. As a concept this surfaced at the start of the Tokugawa era, and as it came to be expounded by Confucian scholars it combined the twin ideals of learning and the martial arts. The new warriors of the era had to get involved in administration and the running of society, and so their education became important. In fact as the Tokugawa period went on they came to fulfill many professional goals, as administrators, lawyers, doctors, as well as soldiers. This was one of the ways which Confucianism was blended into the Tokugawa ethic. Another was by the combination of Zen and Confucian thought; and Zen also played its part in giving the martial arts a spiritual meaning and basis.

Theoretically it was a good period for Buddhism, but criticism of the regime was not allowed, and the only new form to emerge was Obaku Zen, brought in from China by Ingen (1592–1673) near the beginning of the

Tokugawa period. It combined elements of Pure Land and Zen practice. Ingen's stricter practice was a challenge to the other schools and contributed to their reform and revival. But the Tokugawa period also saw new views of Shinto tradition and Confucianism being developed. The Tokugawa shogun Mitsukuni (1628–1701) caused a great historiographic enterprise to be undertaken, which was the reinterpretation of the history of the imperial family according to Confucian principles. This work, the *Dainihonshi*, played a part later in the ideology of the Meiji restoration.

Also of some significance in the eighteenth century was a revival of nationalism through the so-called *Kokugaku* or National Learning movement, under the leadership of such intellectuals as Motoori Norinaga (1730–1801). This saw the history of Japan as having three periods: a first pristine period, then a period of corruption by foreign influences, and finally a period of restoration and rediscovery of the ancient past. This stream of ideas and feelings helped to reinforce national sentiment during the closing years of the Tokugawa shogunate.

## Opening Up and Inner Transformation

The period of isolation, however, could not last forever. The Western powers in the early part of the nineteenth century were already forcing China to make grave concessions. It could not be long before like demands were made of Japan. Severe disquiet caused by the sailing into Edo (Tokyo) Bay of a squadron of American ships under Commodore Matthew Perry (1794–1858) in 1853, and resentment at the imposition of an unequal trade treaty in 1858, contributed in 1867 to the overthrow of the Tokugawa system and the restoration of imperial government known as the Meiji Restoration (Meiji being the name given to the imperial reign). Though in theory a conservative act, this turned out to be a radical event, since the ideologists of the new Meiji era had a good idea of the measures they wanted to adopt.

From 1867 to World War I lay ahead a period of breathtaking change and early success in the processes of modernization and in the political expansion of Japan. The war with China in 1894–95 was followed by the Russo-Japanese War, culminating in the devastating naval victory of Tsushima in 1905; the annexation of Korea in 1910; and the joining of the Allies against Germany in World War I, confirming Japanese status as an "honorary Western nation."

The Japanese were quick to grasp that military power, necessary if they were to be strong enough to keep out the foreigners, depended on modern science and technology; and that the latter required education, which in turn demanded a modernized society. They were therefore determined to change their own society. This they did by various measures: forming a conscript army, founding Western-style universities, sending students overseas, creating modern industries, adopting the shape of a Western constitution, abolishing feudalism, and giving new roles to the warrior classes: in a revised military and navy, in the new professions, and in creating new modes of thought.

452

The foundation, however, of all this was nationalism, and the foundation of this was loyalty to the imperial family and through them to the national essence, the *kokutai*. Because Japan was an island nation and forever living in the shadow of imperial China, it already had a well-formed nationalism; and it did not have to grope around, as China had, to realize that it was a nation over against other nations (rather than being simply the central kingdom); nor, as India had, to discover its cultural unity over against a foreign power. The very principle of the now discredited Tokugawa regime had been the unification of Japan as a distinct entity and the closing up of Japan for fear of foreign influences. Now the national essence was the same, but the means were different: by a deliberate policy of opening up, the Meiji reformers would be able to control foreign influences and bend them to the task of creating a new and powerful Japan. In this they were amazingly successful.

The first large measure affecting religion was an imperial rescript or edict separating Shinto and Buddhism. This led to a series of events which weakened Buddhism—popular pressures against monasteries, the erosion of

The emperor Hirohito, whose era (from 1926 onwards) is known as the Showa era, dressed for his enthronement in traditional dress.

the Tokugawa system of parishes, some anti-Buddhist sentiment, the laicization of many monks and nuns. The separation in question was thought necessary in order to create a Shinto ritual system which was on its own and linked up to the imperial family. As it was, many Shinto shrines existed within Buddhist temple complexes. The *kami* were often regarded as forces in the world somewhat inferior to the Buddhas but not to be denied by Buddhists; and, as elsewhere in Asia, there was a continuum between practices that were in the narrow and purest sense Buddhist and others that drew on indigenous deities. However, even in the Tokugawa period there had been a self-conscious notion of Shinto as a system of gods and practices distinctive to the Japanese national essence. And so the way was prepared for this rather violent separation of Shinto and Buddhist shrines and practices; and in the popular enthusiasm Buddhist temples got damaged as a result of the separation edict (*Shin-butsu hanzen rei*).

### Shinto as a State Religion

There was more to come under the Constitution. This was based on French and German models (the Parliament was called, for instance, the Diet). In it there was guaranteed freedom of religion. What the Japanese did was to formalize what was implicit in nineteenth- and much of twentieth-century nationalism. They made all Japanese observe the rituals of official Shinto, because these related to the dominant ethic of the constitution, loyalty to the nation. In order to ensure this, however, and at the same time guarantee religious liberty, they hit upon a fine expedient—by declaring Shinto not to be a religion. In a way the situation was not unlike that in Marxist countries, where the constitution declares freedom of religion, and Marxism, which is the compulsory ideology of the State, is not of course a religion.

The original thought had been to make revival Shinto a kind of doctrinal ideology which was to be subscribed to by all citizens; but with the failure of the campaign to proclaim the ideology, fostered briefly among mostly unwilling Buddhist monks, in the early 1870s, State Shinto in effect got slimmed down. Priests were in fact forbidden to preach during ceremonies, so that Shinto could end up as a universal system of ethics and ritual, with of course myth attached, but not as a set of teachings which could divisively challenge other systems of ideas. To clarify matters, various new religious movements, such as Tenrikyo, which had some Shinto overtones, were reclassified by the State as being Sect Shinto. The consequence is that in modern times three or more kinds of Shinto are referred to: Shrine Shinto, which is Shinto as typically to be found in today's Japan, a set of practices rooted in the shrines (now separated from Buddhism); State Shinto, which existed from 1882 till 1945, when it perished as part of the aftermath of World War II; and Sect Shinto, which covers a number of new movements. Reference is also sometimes made to Buddhist and Confucian Shinto, covering syncretic forms of worldview.

In nominating Shinto as a necessary part of the ethos of Japan, the Meiji government was giving formal expression, as I have said, to the overriding importance of the nation over other values. Actually the same tended to apply in Western countries—through, for instance, the rituals surrounding the American flag or the British monarchy—even if in theory the nations in question counted themselves as Christian.

In brief, State Shinto—and the same is largely true of Shrine Shinto in the period since World War II—was a partly truncated religion, since it did not develop a set of doctrines. It did, however, form the emotional heart of a nationalist ideology which saw the expansion and the defence of the nation's power as the sacred duty of all Japanese. Its ethos linked up with a modern reinterpretation of Bushido as the way even of the conscript soldier. The stoicism and valor with which so many fought in successive wars is a testimony to the grip of such ideals.

## The Impact of the Modern Era on Buddhism

At first the Meiji restoration seemed disastrous to Buddhism. The support which had been part of the Tokugawa system was withdrawn. The loss of

A monk begging in modern Osaka.

patronage and membership was severe. The campaign of separation of Shinto and Buddhism damaged many temples and institutions. But in the new opening up to Western knowledge there were new opportunities.

Some elegant syntheses of Eastern and Western thought were attempted, the most luminous of which perhaps is that of Nishida Kitaro (1875–1945). His first important book was published in 1911, and set forth a philosophical method influenced by Kant, Bergson, and William James, in which he pioneered a method of examining experience. For him pure experience, that is experience unmixed with concepts and self-consciousness, is without the subject-object dichotomy by which we usually interpret experience. His relation to Zen ideas is obvious here. He gave a new slant on the Mahāyāna notion of nothingness, through his conception of absolute nothingness as the mirror of all individual existence. He was in such ways trying to blend some Western enquiries stemming from Kant's time, and the search for what lies beyond experience, with Buddhist categories of thought.

A not altogether dissimilar attempt was made at a later time by the famous Zen scholar D. T. Suzuki, or more properly Suzuki Daisetz Teitaro (1870–1966). The two men were friends, and from their correspondence can be discovered the closeness of their general thinking. But Suzuki's chief contribution was in editing and translating Zen works and writing about Zen in a way which related it both to science and mysticism, and so sparked a general interest in Zen in the Western world. He was an important figure in making Japanese thought global in character. The fact that Westerners have become interested in aspects of Japanese Buddhism also has stimulated a revival of Japanese concerns with Buddhism.

## Japanese New Religions

More dynamic than some of these more philosophical movements between the Meiji restoration and World War II were Japan's new religious movements, some of which have a Buddhist and others a vaguely Shinto background. Actually, some of these had their origins before the end of the Tokugawa regime and are associated with the disturbing social changes of the period: but their heydays were later, and they have flourished during the post-Meiji period. Let us take up three examples from the modern period: Tenrikyo, Omoto and the Nichiren Shoshu.

### Tenrikyo: the Center of the World and a New Community
Tenrikyo has in origin a Shinto ambience; during the reorganization of religion in 1888 it was treated as one of the so-called Sect Shinto movements, and in due course nationalistic values were forced upon it. But after World War II, under the Constitution of 1947 which ensured genuine religious freedom, it purified its teachings and resumed its onward course as a fairly successful missionizing religion both at home and in various areas abroad including the United States.

456

It was started by a woman, Nakayama Miki (1798–1887), during the stormy years of the collapsing Tokugawa era. She was in early life devoted to Pure Land Buddhism, and wished to become a nun. But in deference to the wishes of her parents she married, and subsequently was dedicated to Shinto deities. It was in her forty-first year that she received a vision which formed the center of the divine revelations to her and later to her close disciple Iburi Izo (1833–1907). Her mission was to prepare the way for a perfect divine kingdom in which human beings will share a life of joy united with God. This messianic element in her teachings led to clashes with the State, both during her lifetime (she was imprisoned on several occasions) and after her death. As a revelatory figure she was thought of as *Kami no Yashiro*, that is, the Living Shrine of God, who descended into her. The revelations were characterized by having three predetermined characteristics—being the right soul, the right place, and the right time.

The place is very important for Tenrikyo religion, since it functions as focus of its most important practices. It is the *jiba* marked by a pole installed in the shrine at what is now Tenri City, near Nara, the old capital of Japan, which is the place that the revelations indicate as being the point of origin of the human race. The large shrine there contains the space necessary for the performance of the dance ritual which sums up and reenacts the story of God's creation.

Miki the foundress showed her humility and chosenness through her compassion for others (her habit of giving landed her family in great poverty) and in healing powers. The teachings she left outlined the essentials of the new faith, while those ascribed to her disciple Inburi contain quite a number of directions about the organization of the movement. The Church is today grouped under a chief priest, descendant of Miki. It has grown somewhat and has about three million followers, and a very flourishing center at Tenri City, including the *jiba* shrine, a university, a remarkable library with some most valuable first editions and ancient manuscripts from both East and West (including Adam Smith's *Wealth of Nations*), a hospital, a publishing house, a mission headquarters, and a whole series of large dormitories for members returning to visit the *jiba*. Thus a city has grown up around the shrine.

The *narrative* dimension of Tenrikyo centers both on creation and on the life of Miki, who is thought to have remained in a spiritual state at her sanctuary, to help the faithful. Hers is held up as a model life (a contrast, incidentally, to the male warrior virtues which are so much held in esteem in Japanese society). As for the *doctrinal* dimension: God is seen as the true God and divine Parent who pervades his creation but at the same time is specially present to devotees. His desire to create is so that he may see human joy and harmony, but this is prevented because of selfishness, and the revelation is designed to overcome this. Human life is treated as something lent by God (borrowed by the human being), and this provides an ethical motif to Tenri teachings, which we shall come to shortly. Salvation also requires the purification of the heart, and this can be achieved over a period of lives, through reincarnation. This softens the impact of the particularism of the *jiba* as the holy center where one should prepare for final union with God, since good conduct and purification can help one to receive the divine gift of being reborn at the *jiba*.

The *ritual* dimension centers on the sacred dances in the central shrine. Pilgrimage to the center is a vital ingredient in the organization of the faith. As to the *ethical* side, we have noted how taking one's life as being on loan spurs devotees to be selfless and to use their talents on earth for the divine cause. Using Shinto-like language, where the image of dust obscuring a mirror is prominent, the faults of humans should be wiped away as being the so-called "eight dusts" covering up the human heart, one's true nature. They are such as hatred, anger, greed, arrogance, and so on. The general ethos is this-worldly, concerned with building up the visible life of the community.

On the *material* side we have noted the importance of Tenri City. The actual main shrine is beautifully built with expensive wood, but it is without ikons, unless one counts the *jiba* pole towards which the celebrants face. There are some patterns used on priestly robes which are reminiscent of Shinto modes, but basically the rites are separate from those used in Shinto.

The religion focuses strongly on the notion of parental love: God is loving parent, and the creation saga of Miki emphasizes this idea. It leaves out of the whole saga of creation the complex of motifs associated with the goddess Amaterasu and the myth of the imperial family. This was one of the causes of friction between Tenrikyo and the State Shinto that the Meiji system put in place. Tenrikyo has a lot to say to those who belong in nuclear families in the post-industrial age, in a Japan which has undergone headlong industrialization and other vital social changes, including the defeat of World War II.

### Omoto and Some Other Related Movements

Omoto (Great Source) never recovered from being disbanded on the orders of the government before World War II. However, it had great effects in stimulating other movements. It stemmed originally from the shamanistic visions of Deguchi Nao (1837–1910), a peasant woman. She saw in the talents of Deguchi Onisabiro (1871–1948) proof of his being a messianic messenger from God, whose coming she had predicted, and he was adopted into her family, becoming her son-in-law. The theology promulgated by the new religion was that souls descend from the divine world of spirits into this material world. The coming of Miroku (Maitreya Buddha) was prophesied, with whom Onisabiro identified himself. The movement saw the present state of Japan as evil and in need of divine reconstruction, which would come with the new age. It tended to look on that new age as involving a return to rural harmony: in such a life religion would be lived as art, with an aesthetic beauty and harmonious feelings.

The movement was a reaction against industrialization and the whole modernization of Japan, and though it professed patriotism in accord with the dictates of State Shinto its myth and doctrine were in many ways in continuing opposition to the route which the State was taking. It was right-wing in politics, but with an emphasis on village life and the repair of agriculture. Because of these heretical policies it was suppressed in the 1930s. But it had an influence on other new groups, including Perfect Liberty Kyodan or PL Kyodan as it is known, created by Miki Tokuchika (b. 1900) in 1956. This especially took up the theme of life as art. Thus the first three of its twenty-one principles read as follows: "Life is Art. The whole life of the individual is a continuous succession of self-expressions. The individual is a manifestation of God."

We may see in Omoto a somewhat turbulent attempt to explain the present problems as being due to the withdrawal of the original *kami* from Japan, and the hope of a new age in which many of the evils of our time will be swept away by a messianic figure or under his leadership. The appeal of the message lay in its revolt against the fashions of the times: against capitalism, against the Constitution, and against both World War I and World War II. It argued, too, for the essential unity of all religions and for world harmony. It was thus a strange mixture of peaceful and extreme authoritarian views.

Both Tenrikyo and Omoto have a background of Shinto, but both in effect have fashioned alternative myths. Neither conformed to the State Shinto or the official Shinto of the imperial family. But they went in different directions: Tenrikyo toward a building up in a practical way of a city and a center here on earth, Omoto back to an earlier vision of a rural paradise. They both testify to a period when the Shinto framework in a broad sense was exhibiting strong dynamics, and breaking out from under the newer Shinto which was being shaped both before and during the Meiji era (and then the Showa era, from 1912)—a newer Shinto which, while professing antiquity, nevertheless was self-consciously forming itself into a separate tradition rather than a functional correlative of Buddhism and Confucian values.

Just as China had the three religions which over much of its history served as a loose federation of spirituality and ideology, so Japan traditionally had a working combination of Confucian ideology, Buddhist doctrines and practice, and the *kami*. These forces were becoming separated out in the new Japan. Basically, Western institutions and ideas were taking the place of Confucian values; Buddhism was becoming self-consciously separate from the State; and Shinto was being formed into a separate system. In the nationalist period, up to World War II, State Shinto did not strictly teach any doctrines, as we have seen, in order to retain its power to unify people, but it had its imperial myth.

The disturbing thing about the new religious movements was above all their teaching of alternative myths. This harmonized with their origins in visionary experiences embedded strongly within folk culture. It would be only at a later stage that the need for more abstract and analytic doctrines would appear.

*Nichiren Shoshu and the Soka Gakkai*
Strictly, we are not here speaking of a new religion, but rather of the

revitalization of the older tradition which had been set in motion by Nichiren of the thirteenth century. This revival was due to the work of Makiguchi Tsunesaburo (1871–1944), who wove into his philosophy some elements of Western thought—notably utilitarianism and pragmatism. He dispensed, therefore, with the concept of truth as a separate category but stressed the attainment of benefits by present practice in accord with the general tenor of Nichiren's teaching. The supreme goal of human beings is happiness, and in his reforming of the Nichiren message Makiguchi founded an organization later to be reshaped by his most faithful disciple, Toda Josei (1900–58), as the Soka Gakkai or Value-Creation Society.

This aimed at increasing benefit to members in accordance with beauty and altruistic desires—the foundations of art and morality respectively. This is seen within the framework of a vigorous faith in the benefits of repeating the invocation to the Lotus Sūtra and in other ways following the general life and precepts of the Nichiren Shoshu. Because of the group's deviation from the nationalist norms of the war period, Makiguchi and Toda were imprisoned, and it was in prison that Makiguchi died. The Soka Gakkai is a lay organization, and it came to have considerable success in the period after World War II. It did so partly because of its rather aggressive style of proselytization, called the *shakubuku*, which can be translated as conversion by breaking the person down. Toda's reconstruction of the movement, after its banning and during the time of renewed spiritual hope after the War, was a marked success, and it went on to play an active role in politics through its political wing, the Komeito Party.

The aim of the Soka Gakkai is benefit here and now and the promotion of a worldwide organization which will eventually issue in world peace. Its rituals concentrate on the invocation of the Lotus Sūtra (or *Daimoku*). This should be chanted daily, morning and evening. Replicas of the sacred scroll inscribed by the founder Nichiren and placed in the temple at Taisekiji near Fuji-san are the focus of devotion, and Nichiren is seen as the very embodiment of Buddhahood, even beyond the Buddha Śākyamuni. But the modernization of philosophy undertaken by Makiguchi gives the Soka Gakkai essentially an up-to-date air, different from the more traditional forms of Buddhism.

In its organizational style and philosophical underpinning, the Soka Gakkai has taken Western models. In its myth and ritual it is the successor of the older Nichiren School. It is from this point of view a successful syncretism, to preserve the essence of this older tradition in the changed circumstances of modern Japan.

## Nationalism in Japan and Its Aftermath

The elevation of State Shinto into a sphere above religion, as it were, involved a blend of religion and the State which was perhaps made inevitable in the Japanese case by the special role which was assigned to the imperial family in the reconstruction of Japan. The shogunate had already prepared the way by keeping the emperor as a sacred monarch, separate from the business of actual administration. The Meiji restoration superficially gave back power to the emperor, but as the polity was evolving towards a Constitution which mirrored some European practices, the emperor's status was never unambiguous.

For the most part he functioned as a kind of sacred oracle, to be informed and consulted in matters of State but not to be involved directly with particular policies. It was a special mechanism, this, for the conduct of affairs—with the imperial family hitched to the Shinto ritual and the myth of its own descent from Amaterasu—which gave a powerful focus to national loyalty. The emperor became the personalized form of the *kokutai* or national essence. The latter was a kind of Absolute, and the emperor the manifestation of that Absolute in personal form. The various religions of Japan, including Christianity, which had emerged from secrecy and oppression after the Meiji restoration, were necessarily subordinated to the national Absolute. All this might have seemed antique, save that nationalism was the very political arrangement under which nineteenth-century capitalism had chosen to organize itself.

The warpath which took Japan on its various stages to World War II was of course the path of imperialism. This had been fashionable among the White powers. Britain, Russia, France, Germany, Italy, Holland, and in a limited way the United States, had all engaged in it in the Pacific area in recent times, and, earlier, Spain and Portugal had taken a hand. By the late nineteenth century this had come to be justified by more than bare chauvinism. It was supposed to bring the benefits of Western civilization, usually conceived as Christian, to the "natives" of the areas conquered. Japan in her actions up to the time of Versailles had acted in harmony with the overall assumed imperialism, save in so far as she could hardly represent "Christian" civilization. But the ethos changed radically thereafter. In the 1930s her attempts to take over Manchuria and her war with China were severely condemned (as indeed was Italy's attack on Ethiopia). Evidently the nineteenth century was the time to do these things, which became criminal in the twentieth! Moreover, Japan backed the wrong side in the lead-up to World War II, entering into an alliance with Germany and Italy. The penalties she paid were severe: most of her cities burned and blasted out by huge air raids, culminating in August 1945 in the atomic bombs on Hiroshima and Nagasaki (the latter, by an irony, the most Christian city of Japan).

These tragedies did not in fact halt the whole process of modernization. On the contrary they helped, in that the true capital was in the brains and skilled hands of the Japanese rather than in the factories and shipyards already in place: bombing enforced modernization on the material side. The Western models of life which had been presented to Japan were three in number, at least: there was the liberal democratic option, largely tied to capitalism, though it could be modified with welfare Socialism; the Marxist model, with central State control and a totalitarian system of regulating ideas and

461

behavior; and the Fascist model, which was totalitarian hypernationalism. It was this last model which Japan had slid into following, and it was this that was decisively defeated in 1945. Since America was the chief force of occupation and had a decisive role in shaping the new Constitution, it was the liberal model which was to prevail. At the same time the emperor was left in place as a constitutional monarch (but with undertones of sacrality, nevertheless, which remain in Japanese attitudes).

In October, 1945, the Allied Occupation abolished State Shinto, and on New Year's Day, 1946, the Emperor announced that he was not divine. The result was the dispersal of Shinto into Shrine Shinto. The transition was calm enough. The legislation which abolished counting by families in affiliation to religious organizations, such as the Buddhist parish system, meant a more individualistic stance in relationship to membership, but religious allegiance has grown. Thus, as far as Shinto goes, it is reckoned that the association connected with the great Meiji Shrine in Tokyo is over a quarter million strong. There are about eighty thousand shrines in the country, most of

Priests at the Meiji Shrine in Tokyo, which is dedicated to the emperor Meiji and is a reminder of Japan's great period of Westernization.

which are joined in the Association of Shinto Shrines, devoted to the training of priests, general education in religion, the development of shrines, and so forth. The associations or clubs of believers concern themselves with general maintenance, the fostering of Shinto music, boy scout activities, etc. So religion has moved on to a voluntary basis. Similar remarks can be made about membership of Buddhist temples.

## Does an Overall Japanese Worldview Exist?

The multiplication of new religions, especially in the period after World War II, the separation of religion and the State, the voluntary nature of affiliation with the religions, the onset of extensive Japanese immersion in Western thought, have led to an apparently very fragmented and confused state of affairs. Because of the possibility of belonging to more than one association, and the old tradition of combining different strands of faith and cultus, the total number of registered believers in Japan greatly exceeds the total population. The liberal basis of the Constitution, and of an open society devoted with great dedication to the pursuit of capitalist success, plays a vital place in the Japanese worldview, but how does it fit in with the traditional religions? Indeed, is there a single Japanese worldview at all?

If there is a central conception which prevails, it is probably that of harmony. A number of the new religious movements are keen to stress the unity of the world's religions; and, though the Nichiren Shoshu is aggressive, most Mahāyāna Buddhist groups seek harmony. Shinto, too, has an interest in maintaining its harmony with other religions, partly because it does not possess any rigid system of doctrines which might bring it into conflict with them. From this point of view democracy is a method of defusing rifts, especially between religious groups, in so far as the separation of religion and the State gives a peaceful basis for the voluntary pursuit of values. It also is in consonance with the Japanese ideal of gaining consensus before any serious line of policy is undertaken.

Religion has a role in promoting national harmony, and there is some hankering for the outward displays of royal religion which some other countries, most notably Britain, can still indulge in. But though religion has something of this public role, it is primarily concerned to satisfy the existential or emotional and physical needs of people—through meditation and devotion, and to some extent philosophical insight, in the case of Buddhism; through self-purification and the harmonies of nature in the case of Shinto; through moral improvement, as in the case of Confucian values; through tolerant attitudes, in the espousal of Western-style humanism.

In contrast to what happened in India and China, Japan's course in the face of colonialism and capitalism has been remarkable. She did not, as did the mainstream Indian nationalists, reach down into her own past for a philosophy from the classical period to adapt to the modern world and to give new shape to the anticolonial struggle. She did not, like China, reach out for a Western ideology to adapt against the West, and to express nationalism in a masked way. She did use elements of her tradition, but with a clear recognition of the role of nationalism in the modern world. By taking the Shinto motif, violently wrenching it from its previous entanglement with Buddhism, and promoting it as a ritual of national solidarity, the Japanese Meiji reformers attempted to give an explicit and sacred basis for the pursuit of the national ideal and conformity with the national essence. At the same time they took up as much in the way of liberal constitutionality as seemed necessary. The fact that there was no doctrinal baggage attached to Shinto left it apt for promoting unity in the nation but not in any way for teaching things which could seriously come into conflict with modern ideas and scientific thinking.

But from two angles the reformers were not able to avoid conflict with religion—first because some of the new movements offered powerful alternative myths to the stories of Amaterasu that formed the ultimate basis of the authority and sacredness of the imperial family; and second because religions have the habit of being universal and so not simply ready to bow to the absolute demands of nationalism. The path to war—both in World War I and more in World War II—led to the absolutizing of the national essence, the *kokutai*, and the clear subordination of religions to patriotism (similar things in practice had occurred elsewhere, in Europe for instance).

The basis that had been built in the nationalist phase could however remain, and Japan took (was virtually forced to take) a move towards

Pilgrims ascending Mount Fuji, the great sacred mountain of Japan.

A Buddhist requiem for broken telephones at the Zojo-ji Temple in Tokyo.

liberalism. This has evolved into a different sort of attempt to take over some Western ways and blend them into an overall Japanese synthesis. While this remains largely unexpressed, it centers on a vaguer notion of national harmony, to replace the more concrete feeling for the *kokutai*. Religions can fit within this harmony through a pluralistic framework of thought and practice. In these conditions, Shinto has undergone considerable revival as a focus of yearnings for harmony both within society and with Nature.

Western culture, with its heavy stress upon the arts, has some echoes in Japanese aestheticism. The Japanese have retained a strong affinity for Nature, even despite the creation of a very powerful and often dirty human environment in the course of the headlong economic revival from the time of the Korean War onwards. Society remains very crowded and formal; and the shrines and temples remain important outlets which allow human beings to see beyond their immediate milieu, the exigencies of correct social behavior, and the relentless pursuit of a growing Gross National Product.

If we look to India and China as comparisons: the Japanese have not retained as much of tradition as the Indians, but they have modernized more pervasively; they have not sacrificed their cultural traditions to the degree the Chinese have, and, again, they have modernized more pervasively. They have not had the same global influence in religious terms as the Indians, but some of their teachers and practices have migrated: individuals, such as Suzuki; traditions such as Zen and, to some extent, Nichiren Shoshu; and religious ways of treating the arts.

CHAPTER

# Islam Passes through the Shadows

## Setbacks and Responses

### The Reversal of Islamic Fortunes

The year 1683 marked the high tide of Ottoman expansion into Europe. The forces of the Turkish empire failed to take Vienna, which was relieved by an alliance headed by the Polish king, John Sobieski (reigned 1674–96). During the next century large parts of the Balkan possessions of the empire were taken by the Austrian Habsburgs—Hungary, a large part of Romania, Serbia, and other lands. Originally a small principality in Anatolia, the Ottoman empire had risen through its conquests of land formerly belonging to the Byzantine empire to a power which stretched from Central Europe to Kurdistan and south to Egypt. It stretched over most of the Arab lands, including the Holy Land, and considered itself to be heir to the great early civilization of Islam. But European techniques of warfare had gotten better, and the Ottomans had stood still.

It was not only in Europe that troubles were besetting the Muslim world. The Mughal empire in India was in complete disarray by the end of the eighteenth century, and by the middle of the nineteenth the subcontinent was dominated by Britain. During the seventeenth century the Dutch were extending their hold over mainly Muslim Indonesia. In the nineteenth century Malaysia was taken over by the British, and Islamic North Africa by the French, save that in the early twentieth century Italy gained Libya. The British dominated Egypt and the Sudan. In Central Asia the Russians were advancing into the mainly Muslim areas. Greece freed itself from Turkish rule, and the rest of the Balkans was liberated from the Ottomans, during the nineteenth century.

After World War I the Ottoman empire was broken up, and the Arab countries came under the rule of Britain and France through a League of Nations mandated territories scheme: Iraq, Transjordan (later Jordan), and Palestine to the British, and Syria and Lebanon to the French. Britain controlled the small Gulf States. Saudi Arabia was independent under its monarchy and system of Wahhabi Islam (of which more below); but Persia was intermittently under Western dominance. So virtually the whole of the Muslim world found itself occupied by the West. It was a traumatic experience for a once proud and glorious civilization.

*Wahhabi Reforms: Back to the Sunna*

The eighteenth century was a period of restlessness in Islam, and there were attempts at the social and moral reconstruction of the faith. Such restlessness was in part sparked by the recognition of the weakening of the Islamic world in the face of Europe. But the Wahhabi movement started in one of the least affected areas—Arabia, which was then seen as so poor and barren that it was little regarded by the marauding Western sea powers. Ibn 'Abd al-Wahhab (1703–92) started his studies in Mecca and Medina, where he was inspired with the task of renewal in Islam, and instructed in the Hanbali school of jurisprudence. Later he studied in Basra and began his preaching career calling for the purification of the religion.

After his return to Arabia he formed an alliance with a local ruler, Muhammad ibn Sa'ud, and after his death with his successor. The Saudi State came to control most of Arabia, but the Egyptian governor was ordered to suppress it, which he did in 1818. Later on the Saudis made a comeback and a second State was established, which however fell apart by the 1890s. However, in 1902, a dynamic leader from the Saudi family, one 'Abd al-'Aziz, usually called Ibn Sa'ud (1879–1953), captured Riyadh, and the third, and most important, Saudi State was established, which saw the country develop its fantastic oil riches, and so become a leading power in the region. Wahhabism remained the choice of the royal family and is the official ideology of the State.

The teachings of Wahhab were a call to reform and to go back to the original doctrinal and legal basis of Islam. Wahhab above all preached *tawhid*, or the Unity of God, and condemned those forms of practice which for him signified creeping polytheism, such as the veneration of saints at their tombs, which was common popular practice among Sufi-oriented people. His major writing was called *Kitab al-Tawhid* or the Book on the Unity (of God). He was radical in his interpretation of this, since anything which might come in the way of faith in the one God—anything which ascribes ultimate concern to something other than God—is polytheism in principle and so to be condemned. He rejected many parts of medieval law and custom as being innovation and went back to a more strictly Qur'anic law. He also revived the notion of *ijtihad* or informed reasoning as being a source of guidance. Such reasoning had to be directly based on the Qur'an and the early tradition or *sunna*. He

467

used it as the basis for rejecting many of the opinions of medieval jurists. In short, his renewal movement was more or less what we have described as neofoundationalist, going back to the basics of Islam and sweeping away much in medieval practice. The Wahhabi movement regards itself not as a denomination of Islam but as a call to reform, and yet it has come to accept the name (originally used by opponents) as if it were a denomination. It rejects Sufism, which has come under fire from a number of different directions in the modern Islamic world.

The alliance between Wahhabism and the Saudi royal family is institutionalized in the system by which Wahhab's descendants are made the chief religious advisers: they are the "family of the shaykh." Ibn Sa'ud used religious fervor in forming an organization of soldiers who were bonded together as the Brotherhood or Ikhwan. In 1929 they revolted, because the State had adopted a fairly pragmatic style which offended against their commitment; but the rebellion was put down. It may be said that in subsequent years a rather pragmatic style has continued to blend with the revivalist conservatism of the Wahhabi ideology, especially since World War II, when the Saudi royal family has had to struggle with the thrills and problems of large oil-based riches

It may also be noted that Saudi Arabia holds a special place in Islam because of its control of the holy places and the *hajj*. Though Wahhabism has a somewhat fundamentalist air, it does represent in its own way a revived mainstream Islam. It stands for a thought: that if Islam is suffering ravages from other civilizations this is because it has not remained true to its tradition. The egregious wealth of Saudi Arabia argues the converse: if a country prospers it is because it has remained faithful to the dictates of God and the spirit of early Islam. But its critics may fault it for having made too many compromises with modernity from the West, and for ruling through a royal family—a concept not welcome to many Muslims of more traditionalist yearnings.

In fact what the Saudis have done in a way largely unparalleled elsewhere, except in Kuwait and some of the Gulf States, is to institutionalize a vast family of three thousand members or more who are as it were the skeleton within the flesh of the nation, and keep control of most of the important functions of the State. So family and national loyalty are fused in this elite. They also have hired many people to work in Saudi Arabia without giving them political rights. So it is a system of layers of elitism: the elite of the family; the wider family; the nation; and the guest-workers. But the fidelity of the family to Islam is not in doubt, for the constitution of the country is the Qur'an.

Ideologically, too, in accord with Wahhabi ideas, the country is strongly opposed to wilful ignorance, of which a prime example is the atheism of the Soviet Union. It is strong therefore in its anti-Communism; but from this it does not follow that it is sympathetic to Western values, which furnish many examples of *shirk* or polytheism by putting things other than God before

God. We shall later come to look at some other forms of conservative revivalism within Islam, which became one option in the face of the West, and need not preclude technological modernization. Briefly, such a conservatism depends on the feeling that Islam withers because believers have not been faithful enough to its pure form.

## Islamic Modernism: Muhammad 'Abduh

Egypt was part of the Ottoman empire, which was nominally at least the main representative of the Muslim community or *umma*. But it was easily detached by the West, and the opening of the Suez Canal in 1869 showed that France and Britain had a continuing stake in the region. Anglo-French joint rule followed, and after a rebellion in 1881–82 under Arabi Pasha, in which the British fleet bombarded Alexandria, Britain took direct control. It was through this period that Muhammad 'Abduh (1849–1905) lived and worked. Probably the greatest modernist of nineteenth-century Islam, he was educated at al-Azhar, the famous medieval university in Cairo.

He also came under the influence of another reformer, Jamal al-Din al-Afghani (1838/9–97), a colorful figure who professed pan-Islamic ideals. Al-Afghani thought that the weakness of Islam was primarily because of its disunity, and during his travels in India he deeply disapproved of those Muslims who accepted British rule. Against them he wrote a powerful tract. His own position was that of the medieval Ibn Sin'a. People have through reason a natural means of the knowledge of God, but such a use of reason is not easy, and for the masses the prophets—and above all the Prophet—have given forth revelations couched in rich symbolic forms. This was a position which could adjust easily to the advance of modern knowledge: as our understanding of the world increases, so will our way of seeing the Qur'anic revelation change. Al-Afghani was a great preacher of pan-Islam, and he hoped to revive the universalist aspirations of the Muslim community in the face of the advancing West, particularly the British.

Muhammad 'Abduh partly agreed with these views. His involvement in the revolt of 1881 led to his exile. In Paris he and al-Afghani published together a radical journal calling for revolution and social reform. Later he was able to return to Egypt, and indeed became a judge and in due course *mufti* of Egypt and chief interpreter of Islamic law, from which position he engaged in the reform of Islamic law and the system of religious endowments.

In his thinking he attacked various elements which in his view had wrongly crept into Islam, such as fatalism, and the blind acceptance of tradition. He was influenced by early Islamic rationalist thinking and underlined the importance of free will in human life. As for science, this was itself developed in the West in part because of Islamic contributions, and there was no incompatibility between faith and modern knowledge. It would be fatal if Muslims for wrong reasons rejected modern knowledge, since it would condemn them to backwardness. So he wished to promote a purified Islam which went back to early days, without such accretions as obsolete medieval knowledge and the cult of saints. He was, however, somewhat influenced in this theoretical work by Sufism: the inwardness of religion showed the spiritual compatibility of faith and science. He saw early Islamic institutions as pointing towards legislative democracy. For him (in response to Christian missions and claims to civilizational superiority) Islam is the perfect religion, which takes up and universalizes what is good in the Jewish and Christian traditions.

It was under the influence of such modernism that many Islamic states, emerging from under colonial domination, including Egypt itself, were able to combine Islamic religion and reforms in the law, e.g. over polygamy and in areas such as banking and charitable trusts. The main planks of modernism were as follows. First, Islam must rid itself of medieval accretions, including Sufi rituals. Second, the Qur'an and the tradition had to be interpreted according to the spirit rather than the letter of the teaching. Modernism was influenced by the Wahhabi example in going back to beginnings, but it was liberal and antiliteralist. Thus law was to be seen under the light of reason, which included arguing by analogy and taking account of the general wellbeing of the community. Such practices as wearing Western dress and eating meat which was not ritually slaughtered were allowed by modernist decisions. Third, Islam was seen as a system which was to be realized in this world: and to build a modern Islam was to do much more than preach heavenly rewards.

Following on from 'Abduh was the work of Muhammad Rashid Rida (1865–1935), from the Lebanon, whose magazine *Al-Manar* (The Lighthouse), which he published out of Cairo, had wide influence. Though he was against what he thought of as innovations in belief and worship brought in since the time of the *salaf*—the first generation of the Prophet's followers—he was for change in regard to social norms. He thought of the Qur'an as laying down general principles rather than legal details of right action and the proper organization of society. Because of his appreciation of the central place of the Arabs in Islam, because of the language, he was somewhat identified with the Arab nationalist movement between the World Wars. Nationalism, as it happened, was a special problem in the Islamic context, which had the theory of a single Islamic community and a central leadership or Caliphate.

## Nationalism and the Islamic Anticolonial Struggle

It was clear to intelligent observers that nationalism was one of the ingredients of the Western mix and much involved in the process of modernization, in Europe and abroad. But when applied in the Islamic context it had mixed results. The Indian *khilafat* movement (1818–1924) was based on something wider than nationalism, namely Muslims' loyalty to the Caliphate (*khilafat*). The Caliphate had been maintained in a weak form by the Ottomans, and after their fall was kept on briefly as a religious office in Turkey and then abolished, which caused the collapse of the movement. Still, it did represent one strand in Islamic response to Western imperialism, a pan-Islamic movement. Modernism, however, did move in a nationalist direction, and it was possible to blend national loyalty into the wider framework. Thus the slogan was used in Algerian Muslim schools before World War II: "Islam is my religion; Arabic is my language; and Algeria is my fatherland."

In the run up to World War I and in its aftermath, Arab nationalism was widespread, but aimed in the first instance at the Ottoman empire. This blended in easily enough with modernism; but there were also some attractions in Arab Socialism, as a concept which battled somewhat against what were seen as the socially disruptive effects of Western ways. Some movements such as Ba'ath Socialism, which achieved power in Iraq and Syria in the 1960s, were explicitly secular movements.

## Turkey and the Nonreligious Solution

The most spectacular response to events was in Turkey, which under Mustafa Kemal (1881–1938) went the whole way in dealing with the problem of the West. The revolution in Turkey in 1923 followed the bitter war with Greece, which finished in 1922 and ended with the mass transfer of populations and the abolition of the Sultanate and the Ottoman system. The Ottoman empire had modernized itself in a mild way during the so-called Tanzimat (Reordering) period from 1838 onwards, and before World War I briefly under the movement known as the Young Turks. But it was Mustafa Kemal, who renamed himself Kemal Atatürk, who decisively institutionalized a major antireligious and secular revolution from 1923 onwards.

First, a Western-style constitution was introduced, in which in theory sovereignty was vested in the people. Second, secular education was introduced, in the Turkish language, and the old religious schools were abolished. Third the *Shari'a* (revealed law) was done away with and replaced with civil law. Fourth, the Sufi orders were suppressed, saints' tombs were desacralized, clerical garb was for the most part banned, as was the fez head-dress, Arabic was no longer used, Arabic script was abolished, and the language was romanized. Women were discouraged from using the veil, polygamy was stopped, and other apparent forms of discrimination against women were made illegal. Marriages were secularized.

All this profoundly shocked religious traditionalists; but superficially at least it turned Turkey into a European-style country. Nothing more drastic has happened in the rest of the Muslim world, except in those few Muslim areas which have become Marxist: Albania, the South Yemen, and Soviet Central Asia. The Turkish experiment has not been wholly successful, in part because the promise of constitutionalism has been marred with military dictatorships. A revival of religious interests has occurred, and some of the harsher Atatürk measures against religion have been modified.

## The Muslim Brotherhood in Egypt and Beyond

Egyptian nationalist hopes were in part pinned on the evolution of democratic

471

government after World War I, but this was hampered by the monarchy and by foreign control of the country. As an alternative to a moderate modernism, the Muslim Brotherhood emerged as another option, also modernizing but not in a modernist way. It was founded by Hasan al-Banna (1906–49), who was a primary school teacher. He wished to have a revival of Islam in a vigorous way and he thought of his outlook as being what was called Salafiyah, that is rooted in the religion of the first generation of Muslims, the *salaf*. We have seen how Rashid Rida made use of this concept also (and it was a theme which became prominent in North African reform movements). Al-Banna' had been attracted to Sufism, and though the Muslim Brotherhood which he formed eschewed much that has accrued to Sufism through the centuries, it did hold to the Sufi stress on individual piety.

The Brotherhood was a society which embraced a variety of activities: it was interested in politics and economics, as well as indulging in athletics. It was a typical modern urbanized religious movement in these ways, not owing much to tradition. But it was radically neofoundationalist in its doctrine and prayer practices, and it worked too for the liberation of Muslims from foreign control. The Muslim Brotherhood (*al-Ikhwan al-Muslimun*) rapidly became a highly effective organization in Egypt, with about a million members by the beginning of World War II. By its conferences, its preaching, its publications, and its general activism it made its mark. It also trained secretly in violent and revolutionary tactics.

The creation of the State of Israel provided the group with both opportunity and tragedy. Many young Muslim Brothers took part in the fighting. But on the armistice the Egyptian police chief was assassinated by a Brother, and a while later the Prime Minister. In 1949 Hasan al-Banna was himself killed, probably with official approval. The movement was proscribed by the government. Many fled to carry the organization into other Arab countries, notably into Syria. In 1951 it was legalized again, and had great expectations when the "Free Officers" under Gamal Abdel Nasser (or Nasr, 1918–70) came to power. But the Brotherhood was suppressed again. Later it was allowed to operate again under Anwar as-Sadat (1918–81); an extremist version of the movement was behind his assassination in 1981. Again, the problem was Israel: Sadat's peacemaking efforts were thought of as a betrayal of the Arab cause.

In Syria in the city of Hama, a center for the Brotherhood, as many as ten thousand are thought to have been killed, and similar events took place in other major cities in Syria, in 1982. They were regarded as a threat to the Alawi regime, based on a small sect, but secular in its ideology. It may have been offshoots of the Brotherhood who seized the main mosque in Mecca in 1979, when much bloodshed followed. So in various parts of the Arab world the group are active, and are regarded as a threat to existing government. They are, as one might expect, as severe on those Muslims whom they consider to have betrayed Islam as they are on the Western threat to Islam (as they see it), often made concrete by the State of Israel.

Colonel Gamal Abdel Nasser, a popular Arab nationalist, here being mobbed by supporters.

Though the members of the Brotherhood are modern in their methods of organization and propaganda, they are not modern in their attitude to education and the State. They consider it their duty and their destiny to struggle for the restoration of the *shari'a*. A pluralistic State in a Muslim country is a betrayal. A truly Islamic State would have the Qur'an as its Constitution. This hard line on the law is important and calls into question the possibility of Islamic modernism. And because they advocate the proper implementation of the law, they would no doubt agree with the dictum of Lord Cromer, who wrote in 1908: "Islam reformed is Islam no longer."

### Palestine and Israel

The questions of how Muslims should respond to the West has been further complicated by the contradictory promises made by Britain about a Jewish homeland in Palestine and the subsequent foundation of the Jewish State in 1948. This has sharpened Arab nationalism and a sense of solidarity with the Palestinian Arabs. Separate wars in 1948, 1956, 1967, and 1973 have kept up a strong sense of hostility.

Israel itself is the realization of the Zionist program formulated in the first Zionist Congress in 1897. But it contains religious ambiguities. Zionism was a secular nationalism. Many of its better-educated supporters were and are Socialists, and Israel was for them the heralding of a new age. In the communes or *kibbutzim* which were planted in Palestine the ideal of collective living was realized, often with a strong aura of Socialist idealism. Because of the strong connection with nationalism, Zionism sometimes took a right-wing political hue, as in the thought of Vladimir Jabotinsky (1880–1940). As

An Egyptian vendor sells tracts and scriptures in a Cairo street. In the last twenty years, Islam has undergone a revival among students and others.

for religious Jews, they were often opposed to the Zionist movement, or indifferent to it; the plans to hold the first Zionist Congress in Munich were called off owing to the objections of German rabbis.

However, there were religious supporters of Zionism, most notably Avraham Yitshaq Kook (1865–1935), a mystic and scholar who became chief rabbi in Jaffa from 1904, and who saw in the Holy Land the promise of a renewal of the faith: in this he was opposed by most of his Orthodox coreligionists. He also argued for goodness in all the major religious traditions and for an openness towards all faiths.

His son Tsevi Yehuda Kook (b. 1912) went beyond earlier religious Zionists, who had believed that the task of the Orthodox was to keep the status quo in Israel against the encroachments of the secular way of life. He was involved in the forming of a militant and activist form of Orthodoxy, concerned especially with expansion and the planting of settlements on the occupied West Bank of the Jordan (occupied after the Six-Day War of 1967). This movement is known as the Bloc of the Faithful, or the Gush Emunim.

The ambiguities of religion in Israel are perhaps most poignantly symbolized by the group known as the Neturei Karta (Guardians of the City), nearly all hyper-Orthodox Hasidic Jews, who often stone cars on the Shabbat and otherwise demonstrate strongly against violations of Jewish law in Jerusalem.

They are a close community, live in one area of the city, are permitted to govern themselves, pay no taxes, do not go to war, wear traditionalist clothes, and study the Torah. They are anti-Zionists in the new Zion.

The problems lie however more deeply in the logic of the State of Israel. Since it was formed on a national basis, it is a State essentially for Jews. But the identity of Jews has been preserved largely by religion. This leads to necessary tensions when the State hopes to separate itself from religion, as befits a democracy. Moreover, to complicate matters, the new Israel took over what was essentially a hangover from the Ottoman Turks, who gave the Jews of Palestine and elsewhere in the empire, under the *millet* system, a measure of control over their own affairs and the administration of their own law through a chief rabbinate. By a law of 1953, the rabbinate has jurisdiction over family and personal law (so there is no civil marriage in Israel). Since the rabbinate is Orthodox, it means that Reform and Conservative Jews have no status in these matters in Israel. For Jews, citizenship is by the norms of the

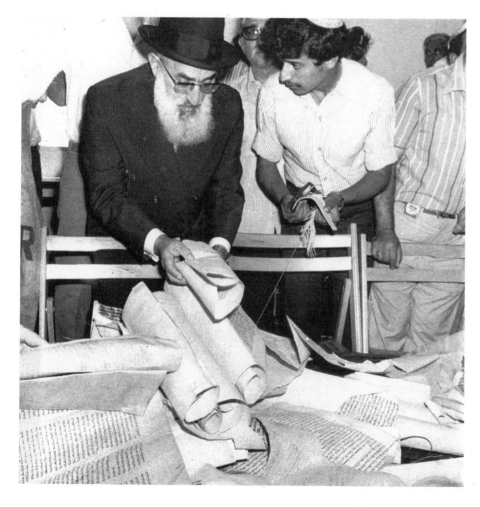

Torah scrolls defiled by Palestinians in Israeli-occupied territory being examined by Chief Rabbi Shlomo Goren, prior to burial.

*halakhah*, the law: but the State professes to be secular. That is one problem. The other relates to the status of non-Jewish citizens. It is obvious that Muslim and Christian Arabs will not be allowed to use voting-rights to overthrow the Jewish State, so in this way the status of these groups is bound to stay somewhat inferior. And yet the institutions of Israel are pluralistic and democratic, for the most part. This tension will no doubt remain unresolved. Meanwhile the Palestinians will see themselves cruelly deprived of their homeland.

An added religious tension comes from the fact that Jerusalem is regarded as a Holy City by all the three great religions, and some pious Muslims vow not to rest till they have got back Jerusalem for the Islamic cause. Moreover, it is traditional in Islam to distinguish between the Dar al-Islam, the "House of Islam," and the Dar al-Harb or "House of War," with the latter being the scene for armed struggle or *jihad*. The State of Israel is like a painful intrusion into the territory properly belonging to Islam, and it is the duty of Muslims therefore to struggle against it. From the Islamic angle, then, Zionism is like a dagger thrust at the heart of the faith. It is also a continuation, from the point of view of the Arabs, of Western colonialism, because without United States support the State of Israel, they argue, would collapse. So there remain many sources of bitterness and strife.

### The Islam of North Africa

To the west of Egypt the major part of the North African coast and its hinterland is the so-called Maghreb, from Morocco to Tunisia; it is sometimes regarded as including Libya (see Map 9, p. 278). The religion of the area came to be dominated by the marabout (*murabit*), a holy person who had wondrous powers as a saint. Such holy men came to be rallying points for centers round which brotherhoods would congregate, and with the brothers the women and children of their families. In many areas the whole population would belong to one center or brotherhood or another, and many people to more than one. All this became very much the standard religion of the Maghreb. The saint's holy power persisted beyond his life, and his tomb would be credited with the same force of *barakah*. It was a North African version of a widespread Sufi phenomenon; and the marabouts were important too in the spread of Islam across the Sahara and into West Africa.

But with the coming of French rule over the region (and, later, Italian rule in Libya), there was less influence of such religion, in that the Salafiyah movement, with its reforming neofoundationalism, came to be the more dominant perspective among the new middle classes, on whom nationalism as an ideology began to take a grip. The Salafiyah's explanation of how the Maghreb had been taken over by foreigners was that the religion had been corrupted and divided by the brotherhoods. The Salafiyah was a general movement in the Maghreb, and combined with anticolonial nationalism. But when the various countries achieved independence, religion came to be subsumed very much under the State, whether in royal Morocco, in Socialist

The blend of tradition and the institutions of modern democracy in Algeria.

Algeria, or in more capitalist Tunisia. In Libya there was also a neofound-ationalist critique of the brotherhoods: in due course Colonel Muammar Qaddafi (b. 1942) introduced his Green Revolution, which was thoroughly modernizing and Socialist in emphasis, and with a strong faith in the Qur'an alone rather than in the traditions which had accumulated in Islam. In all these countries the *'ulama* became subordinated to the State.

## Iran and the Backlash Against Modernization

In Iran, under the Safavid dynasty, from the sixteenth century, the Shi'a

A women's day demonstration, exhibiting loyalty to the revolutionary regime and the Ayatollah Khomeini.

position was consolidated, and it became the official religion. Under the reign of Shah Abbas (1527?–1628, reigned from 1587) the culture flourished greatly, with the building of beautiful Isfahan (p. 294). Religion however was beginning to be enforced, and his reign marked the start of a period of intolerance, which did however have the effect of entrenching Shi'a Islam. Eventually, in the eighteenth century, the Safavid dynasty collapsed, and a period of shifting fortunes began, which by World War I saw Russian, including Bolshevik, and British intervention in the affairs of Persia. In 1921 a coup by Reza Khan (1878–1944), who later took the title of Shah of Shahs, led to a fairly stable regime which lasted until 1979.

Reza's policies followed those of Kemal Atatürk. He abolished religious schools, modernized education, discouraged the veil for women, and set Persia (or Iran as it was called from 1935) on a path of Westernization, at least in the cities. Because of his sympathies with Hitler he was deposed in 1944 by the joint action of the British and Russians, who occupied the country; but his son Mohammad Reza (1919–80) succeeded him and took further steps, especially in the 1960s and 1970s, to aid modernization and the huge building up of the armed forces, paid for by massive oil royalties.

The Iranian Revolution of 1979 in part was a traditionalist backlash against the changes, and in part a reaction to the police repression with which the Shah imposed his regime. The opposition forces were a variety of movements—the Tudeh party which was Communist; liberal Muslims; Islamic Socialists; and the neofoundationalist Shi'a movement headed up by the Ayatollah Khomeini (b. 1900?). He had been arrested and then deported in 1963, living first in Iraq, a major Shi'a center, and then in a suburb of Paris, France. His message was a rather new one: he wanted the establishment of an Islamic Republic.

Khomeini's Islamic Republic would conform to the dictates of Islamic law, and certain constitutional safeguards for this were to be built into the system. It was to be democratic, with a parliament. Though this was in itself a somewhat conservative program, it was also radical in relation to the Iranian past, which had been dominated by kingship. Its purpose was, in the name of Islam, to remove tyranny and worldly pretensions. It was also radical in demanding an experiment in Islamic living which made the law apply to banking and the processes of capitalism as well as to marriage arrangements and family living. It was to Islamicize the universities and the whole system of education. It was to make public life obviously and consciously pious.

Negatively, the Islamic Republic was to struggle against the twin Satans of Soviet atheism and the irreligious materialism of the West. It was also to struggle against atheist tendencies in the Muslim world, as in Iraq, with its Ba'ath (Renaissance) party regime. Hopefully it would be able to export its revolutionary impetus beyond its borders. And indeed in many countries and circumstances Muslims, though they might disagree with Khomeini's postrevolutionary regime, admired the way it reestablished a kind of Islamic independence over against the West.

### Baha'i: A New Religion from Within Islam

Khomeini's Iran was not a tolerant place. It was natural that with this revivalist ideology certain groups would be hounded, notably the Baha'i. For they were regarded not as a separate religion but as Muslim heretics, on whom there could be little mercy. The Baha'i movement has become a worldwide religion, with its American headquarters in Wilmette, Illinois, and its world administrative center in Hàifa; but it can be seen also as a radically modernizing movement from within the ambit of Shi'a Islam.

It follows the teaching of Mirza Husayn Ali Nuri (1817–92), known as the Glory of God or Baha'Allah. He was a follower of the movement known as the Babis, who followed the Bab or "Gate" to the truth. Identified as the Gate was one Sayyid 'Ali Muhammad (1819–50), who was born in Shiraz in Persia. Eventually, when his followers, who looked on him as a link between them and the Hidden Imam of the Shi'a tradition, were involved in rebellion against the regime, he was executed by a firing squad in Tabriz. His teachings involved a symbolic interpretation of the Qur'an, and looked for the coming of a savior figure.

479

It was with this figure that the Baha'is identify Baha'Allah. When he came to declare his prophetic status, after having a dramatic religious experience when in prison in Tehran, most of the Babis followed him. Exiled to Istanbul, he was later banished with his followers to Palestine by the Ottomans, and settled in Acre. They are another group that looks on the land of Palestine as the Holy Land.

His eldest son, Abbas Effendi (1844–1921), also known as 'Abd al-Baha (Servant of the Glory), carried on with the work of mission and organization, and visited Egypt, Europe and America. In his will he appointed Shoghi Effendi Rabbani (1899–1957), the eldest son of his eldest daughter, as his successor; since *his* time the movement has been run by a Council.

The *doctrines* of the Baha'i are evolutionary in tone. The various religions of the world, and they were thinking primarily of the Western trio, are not obsolete or wrong but are stages on the way. Thus it is all right to think of Muhammad as the "Seal of the Prophets," but only in the sense that he has completed the work of his predecessors. Even the Baha'Allah will in due course be superseded. There is much emphasis on the inherent unknowability of God, but his Logos makes itself known. So doctrinally the Baha'is are keen to point to the relativity of religious truth and the underlying unity of all religions.

From a *narrative* point of view the Baha'is see the Baha'Allah as inaugurating a new age in which the community of the human race will become the main arena of action, moving towards world government and stressing the equality of all humans and of men and women. A world language (English) is favored, and nonviolence in human affairs. *Ethically*, therefore, the movement stresses brotherly and sisterly love, abstention from alcohol, and service to humanity.

*Ritually*, the movement asks for daily private prayers, and certain periods of fasting, but it is not a heavily ritualized tradition. The Baha'is, because of their commitment to the underlying unity of religions, are concerned with different forms of religious *experience*, including the development of meditation. *Organizationally*, they have an elective system which is nevertheless theocratic. As for their *material* expressions, the various great temples, such as the one in Wilmette, are huge and impressive structures which contain in their decorative motifs the symbols of the various world faiths.

In brief, though Baha'i arose from within the matrix of Shi'a Islam and makes uses of its eschatological themes, latching on to the idea of the Hidden Imam, it has evolved into a quite different faith with its own distinctive and modernizing characteristics. It is an example of a spiritual revolution which intuitively recognized the global state of world culture before its time and gave religious preparation for this unified world.

It is thus attractive to people around the world, especially reflective folk who are dissatisfied with the rivalry of the more traditional religions. It experienced great growth in South Asia, and in Africa, where its Islamic coloration but outward-looking message has made it attractive. In Iran it is the largest religious minority, but currently because of the Iranian revolution under a deep cloud. Its world membership may amount to about two million.

## Islam Beyond the Middle East

### Pakistan: an Islamic State?

One of the severest questions posed to the new State of Pakistan was set by the Jama'at-i Islami, created as a political movement by Mawlana Mawdudi (1903–79) in 1941. Mawdudi was suspicious of the secularizing Jinnah (p. 403), but moved to Pakistan on the partition. He was often in bitter opposition to the government. His movement was devoted to the ideal of an Islamic State in which non-Muslims would not have full rights. He foresaw the use of Islamic law in public life and took a holistic view of the religion, which fused politics, economics, private life, and public worship into a single whole. He was jailed for his part in anti-Ahmadiya (p. 487) riots in 1951–53, and even condemned to death, though the execution was not carried out. His party remained a vital force in Pakistan, though it lost a lot of ground during the civilian rule after the war with Bangladesh; and it never had much support in what is now Bangladesh, especially because it supported the Pakistani State in its war there. But its agitation for an Islamic system did bear some fruit with the adoption by the Zia ul-Haq regime of Islamic law.

On the other hand Bangladesh, founded in 1971, never really has displayed enthusiasm for the idea of an Islamic constitution.

### Islam in Central Asia

The Muslims of the Soviet Union are found in three main areas, in the Caucasus, in the middle Volga region, and in Central Asia. During the time of Russian expansion to the east there were attempts to convert many Muslims, especially in the region of the Volga. And in a sense the Soviet State has continued a like policy, save that the religion being preached is Marxist atheism. However, in Turkestan under the Tsars there had been a hands-off policy in relation to Islam; proselytizing by Christian missionaries was forbidden, and so, even, was preaching by Tatar modernists (the Tatars having been much more directly affected by Islamic modernism). Such a policy was designed to foster Islamic backwardness and to make Russian rule easier to impose. The result was that when the Revolution occurred a revolt broke out in Turkestan which was anti-Soviet and to some degree religiously motivated, and which took ten years to suppress.

Thereafter the settlement of Russians in Central Asia and the promotion of atheistic propaganda proceeded apace. Despite this, Islam has survived and indeed in its own way flourished, despite the imposition of strict controls on the mosques and the educational system. Religious education and publication is virtually banned, with the exception of minor training schools run by the government for a limited number of clerics. Yet it is reckoned that some eighty per cent of the non-Russian population still are believers. This is out of a Muslim population of some thirty million in Central Asia. It is reckoned that of the population twenty per cent are "fanatics" (the Soviet category); that is to say, they are believers by conviction. Others are more traditionally oriented. But even of the twenty per cent who are atheists, virtually all practice circumcision and Islamic burial. Yet in the whole region there are less than two hundred mosques, probably, which still function as such.

So on the one hand public Islam is more or less washed out; yet Islamic practice and belief still persist in a more private way. What is the explanation? It is partly of course due to nationalist sentiment—these peoples feel themselves somewhat under threat from what they perceive as Great Russian chauvinism—but the more immediate explanation is that the Sufi *tariqas* or brotherhoods still exist, and they are almost impossible for the regime to control, since they can operate secretly and by word of mouth, and they do not need to come into public conflict with the authorities. They represent a huge religious underground movement (the same applies in other regions such as the Caucasus).

Of the Sufi orders the Naqshbandiyah is the most important. It was founded in Bukhara in the fourteenth century and for long played a highly visible role in the politics of the region. It is moderate in its asceticism and well suited to playing its missionary role in the Soviet Union. Also important is the Qadiriya, founded in the twelfth century by the saint 'Abd al-Qādir (1088–1166), from the Caspian area, whose tomb in Baghdad is a major center of pilgrimage (incidentally, this custom of pilgrimage to saints' tombs is a major complaint of reforming, neofoundationalist Muslims, who regard the practice as a medieval innovation). In much of the rest of the Muslim world there is a reforming prejudice against Sufism. It is often seen as one of the reasons for the corruption of the faith and its straying from the true way. But in Soviet Central Asia it has been a major cause of the persistence of Islam.

The attempt, moreover, of the Soviets to make their influence firm in Afghanistan, when they moved in forces in 1979 to help the beleaguered Marxist regime after the ouster of the king in 1973, generated strong though not very united resistance from mainly Islamic guerrilla groups in that country. It has not always been possible for the Soviet Government to rely on the loyalty of its Central Asian troops in these circumstances.

## Southeast Asian Islam

In Malaysia and Indonesia, the consolidation of Islam as the religion of the area has occurred partly during the colonial period. During this time the Malay language became thoroughly impregnated with Arabic and Islamic borrowings and came to be written in the Arabic script. It is basically this language that forms the basis of the national languages of Malaysia and of Indonesia. In the latter case it is also suffused with Sanskrit and Indic expressions deriving from the Hindu culture of Java. These tongues are now written in Roman script.

The impact of Islamic modernism in the area was great, as was that of the Wahhabi reform movement. In 1912 there was the foundation of the well-organized movement known as the Muhammadiya, which was designed to purify Islam, and especially that of Central Java, of the folk elements of Javanese religion. In other words it was designed to root out aspects of the typical peasant worldview and some of the persisting aspects of the Hindu-Buddhist tradition of the area. But it came to be a pan-Indonesian movement, and it modeled itself organizationally on the methods of the Dutch Reformed Church in its missionary and publishing activity. It also did much in the reforming and modernizing of Islamic religious education.

There are also strong moves of a more conservative nature, both in Malaysia and in Indonesia. Thus in the latter country, three or four armed revolts on behalf of an Islamic State in different regions have broken out since independence in 1945. In Malaysia some of the states of the federation apply Islamic law, and there are moves to give it federal status. There is some dissatisfaction also in Indonesia with the ideology under which officially the State is ruled, which is summed up in the so-called Five Principles or *Pancasila*. This is of course originally the name given to the Five Precepts or Virtues of the Buddhist tradition.

Here Javanese influence is paramount, since Java is the hub of Indonesia and its values are often presented as applicable to the vast country as a whole. This formula seeks to create a pluralistic framework for Indonesia as a whole: the Five Principles are belief in God, nationalism, democracy, humanitarianism, and social justice. With the last four of these the Muslims have in principle no quarrel (though some see nationalism as itself something which has to be subordinated to the Muslim ethos). But belief in God is deliberately interpreted vaguely, so that the religion, say, of the Torajas of central Sulawesi is included under this head, even though from a Muslim point of view it is a polytheistic or animistic system. After all, Indonesia is a great concatenation of islands with people of many different cultures and languages and stages of economic development: for this reason the central government prefers a pluralistic ideology so as not to alienate various regional groups.

## Reflections on Modern Islam

We have looked at Islam in the areas of the world where it is dominant. We shall be considering it somewhat in later connections—in Eastern Europe (Chapter 22), in Black Africa (Chapter 23), and elsewhere. We have seen that modernism and neofoundationalism have been the dominant motifs, and in these movements there is some distancing of Islam from the past. Sufism, despite its popularity in some circles in the West, has been heavily criticized, especially by neofoundationalists, though it has made a vital contribution to the life of Islam in the Soviet Union. It was of course of great importance in the conversion of large areas of South and Southeast Asia, since it supplied a kind of bridge to preexisting religions and folk cults.

*Opposite* The ritual dimension: pilgrimage to Mecca has vastly increased with the coming of the jumbo jet. The circling of the Ka'bah, or Tawaf, is captured by this continued-exposure photograph, with people swirling round the sacred site through the night.

*Opposite* The material dimension: a recent mosque in Brunei.

Gradually, Islam is consolidating itself through reform movements and becoming more homogeneous. This is partly due to the fact that modern air transport makes the *Hajj* to Mecca much easier than it was, and this helps to cement Islamic unity. On the other hand, clashes of interest are promoted by nationalism. The break-up of the Islamic world into sometimes conflicting entities can result in bitter conflicts, for example the war which started between Iraq and Iran in 1980, partly based on different ethnicities (Iraq in attacking Iran wished to take over the southwest corner of the country, which has an Arabic-speaking majority), partly on differences of religion (though Shi'a is very strong in Iraq), and more on differences of ideology, between the secular thought of the Iraqi regime and the Iranian revivalism of Khomeini's government.

Despite such obstacles to Islamic unity, at least the infrastructure is being laid, as more areas of the world take up a renewed Islam, going back to the early days, and thinking about or actualizing the rule of Islamic law. But there

484

does remain a gulf between the religious revivalists who want to go back to early foundations and the more radical adaptors of the faith who aspire to some version of Islamic modernism. The signs are conflicting: as Islam spreads into Europe and America and reaches more places where it is in a minority, the greater is the pressure for modernism. But where it has control of the majority of the population, the greater the pressure for a revivalist imposition of the Law. And we still await some answer to the question posed by Lord Cromer: Is a reformed Islam Islam any longer?

*A Footnote on the Limits of Islam: Ahmadiya*
Finally there does remain a question about the self-definition of Islam, which maybe we can illustrate through the Ahmadiya. This is a movement which originated in India, and which has had a fairly good success in proselytizing in certain parts of the world, for instance in West Africa. It has had probably the greatest mission success of any Islamic organization, and has over ten million members in various parts of the world.

The movement rests on the teachings of Mirza Ghulam Ahmad (1835–1908), who came from a village, Qadian, in the Punjab in north India. He was a Muslim revivalist who was drawn into making special claims for his own status. He regarded himself as a *nabi* or prophet, and it was this above all that alienated many orthodox Muslims, since for them there is absolutely no need for further prophecy after the career of Muhammad: this was why he was the Seal of the Prophets. He also saw himself as Messiah in some sense, and as the returning avatar of Visnu, predicted in the Hindu system. He did not think of Messiah-hood as having some kind of transcendent ontological status, since he argued that Jesus did not in fact ascend to heaven, but escaping from the cross departed on a journey which took him to Kashmir, where his tomb is to be found in Srinagar. This idea about Jesus of course offended both Muslims and Christians, the former because the usual interpretation of the Qur'an has it that Jesus was never crucified. But in most ways, the life of the Ahmadiya conforms to Islam, though it rejects the idea of military *jihad*.

A split in the movement led to a branch being set up with its headquarters in Lahore (now Pakistan), which denied that Mirza Ghulam Ahmad was a prophet but called him merely a reformer: this branch has stayed close to formal Islam. The more radical branch, the Qadiani, set itself up in Rabwah, in Pakistan, in 1947. Its successes in the mission area were due not only to the sincerity of its exponents, who emphasized the vital part of sincerity and not just outward observances in religion, but also because of the adoption of modern Christian methods of mission—street preaching, pamphlets and other forms of publishing, good organization, and sometimes aggressive propaganda. But it has attracted enmity from the orthodox, and in 1954 it was ruled in Pakistan that it was not a form of Islam and should not use claims which suggest that it is a kind of Islam.

It will be observed from this that the tendency in modern Islam is to place a close definition on the religion in terms of doctrinal orthodoxy: a non-

*Opposite* The material dimension: the interior of a modern mosque in Bahrein.

practicing orthodox Muslim is much better placed than a practicing non-Orthodox person. By an irony the Ahmadiya movement is now much worse off legally in Islamic Pakistan than it would have been if it had stayed in Hindu-dominated India.

*Dimensions of Revived Islam*

Despite the importance of the Iranian revolution, it may well be that the future lies more with the revival movements within Sunni Islam, such as the Brotherhood. At any rate in a number of countries, such as the Sudan, Pakistan, and Malaysia, there is the pattern of Islamic law being required: and there are calls in a whole range of countries for similar legislation. This spirit of revivalism seeks to restore practice to what it was; but often its mission is conducted in most up-to-date terms. We can discern some of the dimensions of this Islam as follows.

*Doctrinally* it has a tendency towards more rather than less literal interpretations of the Qur'an. It is not hostile to science, but it rejects some of the philosophies of medieval and premodern Islam. As far as its *narrative* dimension goes, it of course accepts and focuses on the career of the Prophet: but it also sees Islamic culture as having betrayed the spirit of true Islam through various innovations, and it is because of all this that Islam has fallen into its relatively sorry current state. *Ethically* and legally it calls for the revived application of the *shari'a*. It is strict about such matters as alcohol and the conduct of women: it usually favors the use of the veil. Since it is traditionalist but not quite traditional (for it arises from the very situation in which tradition is being challenged and overridden), its espousal of tradition is a matter of self-conscious commitment, so that there is a great emphasis on being "converted" to true Islam. It has a much more notable evangelical fervor than would be typical of simply traditional Muslims. *Experientially*, therefore, it is vigorous: but it is not much oriented towards the mystical meditation of the Sufis, since Sufi practices are often what has brought Islam (in its eyes) into disrepute. *Organizationally*, revivalist Islam is much indebted to the methods of Christian missionaries, while it also lays stress on Islamic education. *Ritually*, it is pious in reaffirming the importance of regular public prayer worship. *Materially*, it is often at the forefront of the building of new mosques, especially where the Muslims are a minority; so in the lanes of Sri Lanka and the backstreets of Liverpool, England, will be found new structures, often subsidized by oil money. Islam is at a vigorous global stage.

*Opposite* In Dakar, Senegal, Muslims pray outside the overcrowded main mosque.

# CHAPTER 21

# *The Colonial Impact in the Pacific*

## The Opening Up of the Pacific by Europeans

In the early sixteenth century the Spaniards were able to sail west to the Indies from Mexico. By the end of the century they had pioneered the return voyage eastward. The Portuguese Magellan pioneered the southern route round Cape Horn. In the eighteenth century a second great wave of voyages of discovery occurred, the chief explorer being Captain James Cook (1728–79), who explored the coasts of Australia and New Zealand and touched at many of the Pacific islands, including Hawaii, where he met his death. Subsequently, whalers and colonists affected most of the Pacific, as it lay open to European imperialism. Missionaries spread through the region, especially during the nineteenth century, and Christianity came to be the dominant religion.

The Spanish spread Catholicism to the Mariana Islands in the latter part of the seventeenth century, missions coming from the Philippines which had previously been evangelized. The London Missionary Society began to work in Tahiti in 1797. Thence they moved on to the Cook Islands, Samoa, Tuvalu, and the Gilberts (Kiribati). American missionaries started work in Hawaii in 1820, and Christianity fairly soon became the official religion under the queen of Hawaii. Methodism took over in Tonga after the king (who took the name George) converted, and likewise in Fiji the islands were united under Methodism. The Presbyterians became dominant in Vanuatu. Catholic missionaries, chiefly from France, were active in many of the islands, and Catholicism became dominant in New Caledonia. New Guinea, because of its size and multitude of cultures, was not so unified as many other areas in the region: it has a patchwork of Christianities, especially in the highlands, which were not missionized until the 1950s and 1960s. In the British and German parts (taken over by Australia after World War I), Anglicanism and

490

A traditionalist in Papua New Guinea shares in a mass performed by Pope John Paul II in 1984.

Lutheranism were strongly established, but there were other Protestant denominations as well, and Catholicism is numerically the strongest of the groups now. Much of the mission work in the Pacific region was undertaken by indigenous missionaries.

It is interesting that in so many regions the whole population of a given area converted to Christianity, and of a particular sort. This helped to preserve social solidarity when the preceding religion was repudiated. But there are smaller Churches which are strong in proselytization, and they may spread vigorously at the expense of established forms of Christianity. Most notable among these is the Mormon Church, which has spread out from Hawaii; it has a great interest in, and a desire to promote, the culture of the Pacific.

The cultural effect of the missions was dramatic, chiefly through the translation of the Bible into the indigenous languages. This gave a new dimension to language, and conferred great power on the imagery and models of the Bible. So it became deeply entrenched in the thinking of many in the Pacific region. There were other outcomes: the adoption of modified dress patterns, especially by the women, the opening up of trade to the West, and most dramatically and tragically the devastating consequences of relatively mild European diseases such as measles on a population with no acquired immunity. Up to a point the introduction of Western medicine moderated the effects of this new plague.

A complication experienced in the whole region was World War II, in which many of the islands came under the rule of the Japanese and were then exposed to American, Australian, and other troops as they set about the bloody business of reconquering the Pacific region.

Also important to note is that in some areas the indigenous population itself became a minority because of the coming of settlers. Notable was Hawaii, with its Japanese and American Whites; New Caledonia, with an influx of French; and Fiji, where a large migration of Indians occurred, brought in to work the sugar plantations, and by 1980 having a slight majority of the population. Among indigenous inhabitants such inflows have caused, naturally enough, quite a lot of resentment. New Caledonia remains under French control, while Hawaii has been absorbed as a State in the United States. In Fiji an indigenous *coup d'état* threw out the new, Indian-dominated, government which was elected in 1987.

## Australia and New Zealand

Australia and New Zealand, being relatively large, have had a rather different history from that of the islands. They both became subject to a deliberate policy of colonial settlement from Britain.

Australia started as a penal colony (the American Revolution cut off the penal areas of America, and the prevailing ideology in Britain at this time was that one could cure the disease of criminality by excising the criminals from the body politic, by shipping them overseas: since many thought that there was some kind of hereditary basis to criminality, this might actually effect a permanent cure). New South Wales, therefore, came to be a convict settlement, first begun at Sydney Cove in 1788. After 1813 the colonists found their way across the Great Dividing Range, and spread out into the pastures and farm lands to the west. Other colonies were founded, such as Newcastle in 1801, Hobart in 1804, and Brisbane in 1824, all at first penal settlements. But gradually Australia became a place for settlement rather than punishment, and this was boosted by the discovery of gold in the 1850s.

It is a paradoxical country. Though as vast as the continental United States, it is heavily urban. Much of it is blank. The settlers started from the coasts and worked their way inland; but they did not have that optimism which was at a like time marking the great American drive to the West. The inner vastness of Australia is barren, blindingly hot, adapted to only the most cunning lifestyle, ill suited to Whites. As the Australian settlers moved towards the heart of Australia their hope petered out. They became more preoccupied with the mere task of surviving than with conquering any Eldorado. And so the Australian myth is more of existing than of gaining the Golden West. Moreover for much of its history Australia has unconsciously existed with its back to the ocean. It was not till World War II that Australians had to become conscious of being in the Pacific. Their shops, their customs, their suburban gardens, their beer, their religion, their language—all derived from "Home," that is to say Britain: not England, because they had a good intermixture of Irish, Welsh, and Scots. They built a British suburb on a foreign shore. The Australian mix came to be something like the British scene without the same class system.

Moreover, though the Church of England had some status in the early days of the penal colonies, it did not have an established position as in England. The major denominations all became well established in Australia, as well as others such as the Mormons, the Seventh-Day Adventists, and the Salvation Army. The Roman Catholics were always a highly significant minority, up to 25 per cent in the second half of the twentieth century. At first they were chiefly the Irish. But since World War II Australia has become a more variegated society with the arrival of so-called New Australian migrants, such as Poles, Yugoslavs, and Italians; then, in the 1970s, Vietnamese and other Asians, who had previously been kept out through the White Australia immigration policy.

A rather florid evangelical line of preaching and thinking has been strong in Australia since the latter part of the nineteenth century, advocating prohibition, a stop on gambling, and Sunday observance. There was often, especially before Vatican II, a lot of tension between Roman Catholics and Protestants, and this was a factor to take into account in Australian politics: Catholics gravitated to the Labor Party.

New Zealand was settled in a very different manner, by planning. In Christchurch, for instance, an Anglican-style community was settled; and in Otago (capital Dunedin) there was a settlement led by the Scottish Free Church, which was a reforming breakaway from the established Calvinist Church of Scotland. But New Zealand also had its gold rush, in Otago, and for this and other reasons labor became high-priced, and with that the incipient class system broke down. New Zealand had a like system to Australia, with no Church being established, though there were arrangements made for religious education in the schools. New Zealand remained rather sparsely populated, especially in the South Island, and this gave an appearance of relative prosperity, once the export of mutton to Europe became organized.

The chief difference between Australia and New Zealand had to do with the respective fates of the indigenous inhabitants. Although the Maoris came to be deprived of much of their land, they fought bitter wars with the White settlers in the 1860s. Their position was greatly weakened, but in theory they came out of it with equal rights, and partly by leaning on constitutional principle they had by the 1980s greatly improved their position. Many are by now of mixed descent; but those who have Maori descent (up to one-eighth) and wish to be Maori can be so: a point of importance partly because the close physical resemblance between Europeans and Proto-Polynesians makes merging of the races especially easy. At any rate, the Maoris at least were strong enough to fight back, and the two races can exist on a basis of equal respect (though racism of course persists in the White population). In Australia, the Aborigines were too weak and scattered, and too different in habits and culture from the White settlers. They were driven largely out of the richer parts of Australia and concentrated mostly in the north and center of the country. In Tasmania they were deliberately wiped out. Much genocidal activity took place, and many of the Whites refused to regard them as fully human.

A Maori wooden carving of an ancestor: the bounds of society include the dead and other spirits.

### Australian Aborigine Religion Today

It is against this rather melancholy background that we have to see the evolution of modern Aborigine religion. This is divided into two or three forms. First there is the indigenous religion of the Dreaming and the sacredness of the land. Second there is mission Christianity of different hues. Then there are some mixes of the two.

One may include in the latter the form of resurgent Aborigine religion during the 1970s and 1980s, when the Aborigines have taken a more overt and vigorous stance on land rights, in part encouraged by the Australian Labor Party. There is beginning to emerge a pan-Aborigine platform which has some analogies to the Native American movement in the United States. Though Aborigine religions represent a network which in the past covered the great continent in overlapping sacralities and a maze of traveled paths, nevertheless religions were also localized. Under the hammer blows of White culture, Aborigines need unity if they are to survive and gain their relevant rights; and it is from this point of view that we can think of a new pan-Aborigine ideology which is starting to emerge, emphasizing especially the tenderness with which Aborigines view the land and the total environment. There is a tendency for such views to be expressed in modern Western categories, and so to produce a mix of values, of which ecology forms a vital component. But we are only at the beginning of a process of discovering how an Australia-wide movement will shape itself.

It may be added that the concept of the time of the Dreaming is not by itself very well suited to explain change: for it fixes rites and customs in a kind of timelessness which is well suited to those who wish to maintain continuity. But the modern period, since their land was invaded by such potent outsiders, is more one of discontinuities. So far there have been rather few blends and reshapings of the tradition, though one can mention one or two. Thus, on Elcho Island, off the northeast coast, there was started in the late 1950s a movement which synthesized Aborigine ancestors with the prophets taught about in Christianity. More importantly, those who started the movement tried a rather desperate expedient: to make public the traditional secret holy objects. The rationale behind this was that their knowledge could be used to confront and combine with the knowledge displayed by the missionaries and the Whites. Aborigines had been held at a disadvantage by their very initiatory system, which helped to keep their most important powers secret. But of course the desired effect did not occur: outsiders were singularly unimpressed by the putative knowledge displayed. There were signs of adaptation: the holy objects were shown to women for the first time, a recognition that women had important rights not accorded in traditional Aborigine society. But since they were not briefed on the meanings of the objects, their status was still not equal.

The new movement petered out in the face of a strong fundamentalist Christian revival in the area, which has made strong inroads into Aborigine life, with its security, its modernizing methods and its moderate asceticism, important in combating prevalent alcoholism and other social diseases. Indeed, like other forms of Christianity, it often forms a religious net of values to take the place of the shattered webs of the old religion. For one of the effects of contact with Whites has been to alienate many of the young from tradition and to sap the morale of the elders, and through them the whole group. It is in such a situation of cultural disintegration that alcoholism becomes rampant: and one of the cures is a new universe of positive meanings.

In the Western Desert of Australia there have grown up in the 1970s and 1980s new cults which greatly simplify rituals, which are appropriate to mixed groups living in various settlements, which admit women into initiation, and which are somewhat politically active in relation to land rights. None of these has yet taken off to form a viable pan-Aboriginal complex, but no doubt the Aborigines are on the verge of such a new all-embracing reaffirmation of values, helped too by the interpretations of Aborigine religion created by writers on them, such as Mircea Eliade in his *Australian Religions: an Introduction* (1973).

## Maori Religious Life After the Coming of the Whites

In the latter part of the nineteenth century a variety of missions were active in the North Island, especially, where most Maoris were concentrated. The result was a great success from the Christian point of view. The Maoris, like the other Polynesians, converted virtually en masse to the new religion. The tradition did not have much resilience. However, two Maori Christian movements did emerge: the Ringatu, which was founded in the 1860s by a Maori warrior turned preacher; and the much more important and vital Ratana movement, named after its founder, who had experienced conversion after grappling with alcoholism. Here was a Maori-controlled Church which could also play a part in the political arena and in the struggle for human dignity and social justice.

There has also in recent times been interest in whether the old Maori religion, though now virtually dead, can supply the materials for the background to Christian faith, that is as a kind of alternative Old Testament. This move is of course very widespread in differing forms throughout the Third World. The mainstream White-dominated Churches, too, have been open to an egalitarian approach in religious matters: one former Archbishop of New Zealand is a Maori, who became Governor-General (that is, honorific President of the country and representative of the Queen in the Commonwealth system).

Auckland, New Zealand, has also become the largest Polynesian city in the world with an influx of non-Maori Polynesians from the islands, partly because some of these territories were mandated to New Zealand after World War I, and partly because of the relative magnetism of the city. Very traditionalist forms of Christianity prevail—no doubt giving a sense of certainty and rootedness in the flux of emigrant life.

## Melanesia and the Cargo Cults

The impact of German, Dutch, Australian, and Japanese rule at different times in New Guinea and outlying islands (where also British and French rule came into play) was great. The emergence, from the 1890s onwards, of so-called Cargo cults was a major response. These movements, based essentially on indigenous categories, but often mingled with Christian mythic and eschatological elements, looked to have access to the god or gods who was the source of the cargoes brought in by the Europeans. The goods, ranging from canned food to radios, were eye-opening to the locals. In the matrix of their own religious tradition, vegetables and other crops had their origin in the gods: they knew about the god who brought taro to humankind, for instance. By parity of reasoning there must be a transcendental or hidden source of the Europeans' cargoes. World War II helped to increase the wonderment of locals and their amazement at the prodigious supply of everything brought in by the Americans. Again, in terms of their ritual categories it should no doubt be possible for them too to have direct access to the divine source of these. If the Whites denied that there was such a source, or said that the goods came out of factories, no doubt they were dissembling in order to keep the cargoes to themselves.

Sometimes this kind of cult has attracted the amused contempt of the Whites. The idea that you could get lots of baked beans by building symbolic airfields in the New Guinea scrub and by performing various rituals can seem

Cargo cults, especially common in Melanesia, are well illustrated in this votive offering from the Nicobar islands in the Bay of Bengal (which have possible linguistic connections with the South Pacific). Here, the white man at the top is surrounded by goods, such as guns, pens, mirrors, etc. The next level shows a hut with a traditional and a Western ship on either side. Further down is traditional currency, namely pigs, and at the bottom, there are various creatures of the sea.

at first sight somewhat ludicrous. But the cults had a deeper meaning not so obvious to the eye of the outside beholder. The canned goods and so forth were only the concrete manifestations of what the locals perceived as a superior power and a greater knowledge. They knew the knowledge was greater, and sometimes therefore thought of the invaders as being gods. But though they knew the knowledge was more powerful, they did not have it, and so they did not know on what basis it rested: how were they, out of their civilizational horizons, to imagine the industrial revolution, the division of labor, Newton's physics, capitalism, and the thought of Adam Smith and J. M. Keynes? The incoming cargoes were signs of power and they tried to have access to it in the only way in which they knew how, by ritual means. After all, their rites worked well enough when it came to taro.

Though the conceptual apparatus of such new religious movements is indigenous, the forms vary, from purely indigenous cults, through Christian versions, to syncretic Christian-indigenous movements. In the process, awareness of tradition becomes self-conscious, and so you can have a fourth kind—the conscious return to tradition, or what may be called neotraditionalism. The importance of rites is marked throughout. In the case of Christian movements, there is emphasis on right behavior as well as the appropriate kind of revivalist services. Sometimes, especially among syncretic movements, people may destroy their own fruits and agricultural products, felling trees and digging out crops. This prepares the way for the millennium: the future myth is important in movements which have been affected strongly by Christianity. The destruction of crops does not only smooth the

The old rituals tamed: Fijians perform a war-dance in front of a Christian church.

path to a rich future, miraculously brought: it represents a great sacrifice, and is a hidden way of repudiating the gods who provided the old fare, in face of the arrival of the new fare.

Like many other new religious movements arising at the point of meeting of small-scale societies and powerful colonial powers, the cargo cults represent a first experiment using the old categories. But they will not be ultimately viable as new religions without a better appreciation of the concepts on the other side of the divide. Here the impact of Western-style education, including higher education at Port Moresby and in the University of the South Pacific in Fiji, is bound to be profound; and may introduce some newer form of syncretic blend. There are signs that this is happening, for instance in the Moro movement on Guadalcanal, which mingles Christian, traditional, and capitalist themes together. This is, so to say, "beyond cargoism," because the leap to the "other side" has been made.

## The Pacific Way

It remains true however that the overwhelmingly predominant religion of the Pacific region is Christian, and for the most part Protestant. As we have seen, in many areas conversion was by group and from the top down. This has helped to give stability to societies throughout the region. They are of course mainly very small societies, scattered in islands, from Micronesia to Polynesia. They are thus highly susceptible to the "logic of islands," which is that they are especially vulnerable to outside forces.

Because they are small-scale, and because the modern world is a place of greater amalgamations of economic and organizational forces, it is important for the islanders to combine: and to this end there is a Pacific Forum for the leading politicians of the South Seas, including New Zealand and Australia. This also leads to the question of whether there is some spiritual counterpart to this, and some have written of the "Pacific Way" to represent the values of the region. This Way seeks to incorporate some pre-Christian values; and in some ways it has undertones of revival. Thus it is often thought by people in the region that Northern Christianity has largely lost its way and will be revitalized by the fresher and more vigorous Christianity of the Pacific region. Such people are right, of course, in holding that the center of gravity in Christianity is surely moving South.

With the awakened consciousness of Maoris and Australian Aborigines in the larger southern states, and the welding of a new polity in Papua New Guinea, the region is likely to play an important part in the struggle of small-scale peoples for dignity. The western part of New Guinea was given over to Indonesia, as inheritor of the Dutch empire: this has already begun to spark another national struggle, since colonialism is of course not solely a White preserve. With its blue ocean and lovely islands, its rugged lands and beautiful bush, the South Pacific is a region not without deep problems, but with a call to shape its values to contribute to the welfare of humankind as a whole.

Огонёк

№ 52   ДЕКАБРЬ   1949
ИЗДАТЕЛЬСТВО «ПРАВДА»

# Eastern Europe and the Soviet Union

## Russia: Expansion and Revolution

The Russians have played an important part in global colonialism, but it is not always noticed because their empire spread across the land; being in the great hinterland behind European Russia (itself vast enough not to be easily grasped by those further to the west), it is often conceived by outsiders in the vaguest possible terms. Even in the late nineteenth century, when Britain, for instance, was much preoccupied by the Russian threat, it was a threat which moved south from Central Asia towards India and in the direction of the warm waters of the Arabian Sea. The great extent of Russian advance to the east into Siberia was little comprehended. And in the twentieth century, when other colonial powers have been on the defensive, the Russian empire, suitably modernized and reshaped as the Soviet Union, scarcely seems to count as a colonial power at all (see Map 12, p. 338–9).

By the end of the seventeenth century, virtually all of Siberia was in Russian hands. The vast territories were fairly thinly occupied by various Siberian peoples such as the Yakuts and the Tunguz. In Central Asia, the drive south had begun, and by 1900 Russia was up against the frontiers of Persia and Afghanistan, having subdued the Kazakhs, Uzbeks, and Tadjiks, together with several other peoples. By 1800, moreover, their drive through the Ukraine to the Black Sea and the Crimea was complete, and in Odessa they built an important harbor. There were to be more gains in the late nineteenth and early twentieth century at the expense of China, but the basic shape of Russia had formed. It was this empire which the Bolsheviks were to take over.

It had in the meantime been modernizing—through for instance the abolition of serfdom in 1861; the building of great railways, including

*Opposite* Secular ritual: Stalin replaces the Christmas star; from the cover of *Ogonek* magazine.

501

*Opposite* The experiential dimension: an evangelical preacher on Waikiki Beach, Hawaii, hoping to induce conversions (see Chapter 21).

the Trans-Siberian, started in 1891; the opening up of mineral and industrial development; and the consolidation of large towns, from St. Petersburg to the Urals. Russia was on the brink of great economic advances in 1914; but the rigid bureaucracy and centralized Tsardom were unable eventually to cope with the hammer blows of war. Liberal revolution in 1917 was swiftly followed by the Bolshevik seizure of power and the beginning of the Russian Revolution under the initial guidance of Vladimir Ilyich Lenin (1870–1924). In due course the direction of the revolution was taken over by Joseph Stalin (1879–1953), who took the path of "Socialism in one country;" he collectivized agriculture, promoted intense industrialization at a headlong pace through various five-year plans, erected the apparatus of a thorough police State, and pursued for the most part a policy of suppressing religion. After World War II, which Stalin prosecuted with overwhelming, ultimate success, Soviet armies controlled most of Eastern Europe, and the Marxism which he espoused was imposed on Poland, East Germany, Hungary, Romania, and Bulgaria; but not on Yugoslavia and Albania, which had not in the same way been occupied by Soviet forces. But in all of them Marxism became the State ideology, often in place of a previous State religion.

## Varieties of Marxism

The Stalinist model, though much criticized since Stalin's death, was long regarded as the pattern wherein a Communist State should be developed and organized. The Yugoslav and Albanian parties provided initial alternative modes of operating in the European context. Albania pursued a policy of strong isolationism with an alliance with the Chinese for a period, as a counterweight to Soviet power. It lays claim to be the only fully atheist State in the world, having crushed Islam, which was the majority faith, as well as Christianity. It is doubtless too early to say whether this claim is true, for it could be that the same phenomenon applies as in Soviet Central Asia, namely the survival of Islam among the people through the clandestine work of Sufi orders. In Yugoslavia the chief preoccupation has been with maintaining the unity of its federation of diverse peoples. But it has also experimented with a nonaligned Communism and close commercial relations with the West.

The varying patterns of the period that followed World War II in part reflect the ways in which religion is present in the different countries. Poland is a dominantly Catholic country, the more so after the terrors of the Holocaust which wiped out virtually all of Poland's large prewar Jewish population. Also the move of the boundary westward has meant that the Ukrainian part, with its Orthodox and Uniate (that is, Vatican-affiliated Orthodox) populations, has been absorbed in the Soviet Union. Poland is thus monolithically Catholic. Before the War the Catholicism often was right-wing politically; but in the events of the 1970s, culminating in the Solidarnoś or Solidarity movement, it has taken up roughly a social democratic posture. Though Solidarity is not itself a Church organization and

# 1917 ОКТЯБРЬ 1920

Товарищ! Утроив энергию свою,
Сквозь строй орудий, штыков щетину
Радостно встретим в кровавом бою
Октябрьской Революции Третью годовщину!

Она—залог нашей близкой победы,
Рабами нам больше не быть никогда!
Чрез временные неудачи и беды
Мы шествуем в светлое царство Труда.

Мечем пролетарским сражен издыхая
Дракон империализма разинул пасть...
Советская, федеративная, социалистическая, мировая
Республика—да здравствует ея власть!

is keen to demonstrate its independence and religious openness in practice, there is a great overlap between it and the Church, and often it is at or after Masses that important meetings and rallies have taken place, under the leadership among others of Lech Waleska, a pious churchman.

The strength of this ultimately rather unsuccessful attempt to achieve a degree of independence for Poland was reinforced by the election of Cardinal Karol Wojtyla (b. 1920) as Pope John Paul II, the first Polish Pope, and the first non-Italian for nearly five hundred years, in 1978. The Polish Church has survived and indeed flourished while on the whole maintaining a conservative stance in matters of doctrine and ethics, but its social policy has converged with those who have wanted a more genuinely democratic way of running the unions and beyond that the State.

The other East European country where religion has flourished is Romania, but the faith here is primarily Orthodoxy (though there is a substantial minority of Catholics among the Hungarians of Transylvania). After initial persecution in the 1950s and 1960s the Church has had considerable financial support from the State, during the regime especially of Nicolae Ceausescu (b. 1918) from 1966 onwards. Romania has been independent somewhat from the Soviet Union, but in a way very different from Poland. In the latter country the government and the party have had great problems keeping the lid on popular movements from below. In Romania there has been a somewhat independent foreign policy, but it has been imposed from above. Romania is run in a rather Stalinist manner, with centralized planning and the pervasive presence of the secret police, to keep the population in line. But because the regime emphasizes nationalism and the glories of the Romanian

A crowd of farmers celebrating the anniversary of the foundation of Rural Solidarity, their free union, and giving the V for Victory sign outside Warsaw Cathedral.

*Opposite* The new Saint George: a Marxist ikon slaying the dragon of capitalism.

505

heritage; and because the Church played such an historic role in keeping alive the Romanian tongue and Romanian national identity during the Ottoman period; it has been useful and possible to let the Church flourish. It has also been a safety valve: the gleam of heaven can distract people from the rigors of earth.

However, the official ideology of the regime is still Scientific Socialism, as it is called, and party members, teachers, and other professionals are not expected to attend Church or be members of congregations. Religious dissent is banned. You cannot convert a person from one religion to another, and the system is closely watched by the relevant ministry in Bucharest. Baptists and other wandering evangelists are dealt with severely.

### The Contribution of Eliade

Romania, as it has happened, has produced the most important religious intellectual to come out of Eastern Europe since World War II, Mircea Eliade (1907–86). As a precocious and brilliant young scholar in prewar Romania he plunged into Renaissance studies and from there branched out into Oriental learning, for he went to India and studied at the feet of India's best-known historian of philosophy, Surendranath Dasgupta (1885–1952) from 1928 to 1932. It was there that he began his work on yoga. But on his return to Romania he engaged in a wide range of literary activity, from scholarly works to novels. He saw the consonance between varieties of folk religion the world over, and sought a new humanism which would do justice to the universal archetypes and symbols which well up from the human unconscious cross-culturally. He was in some ways a Romanian populist, seeking salvation among the peasantry whose intuitive knowledge and values were of the widest human significance. He therefore was not distant from the Romanian right wing and the so-called Iron Guard, part of which later collaborated with the Nazis. During World War II he was in the Romanian diplomatic service, and after the occupation of his country he stayed in exile. Between 1945 and 1955 he wrote his major works, and in 1957 he became a professor in Chicago and extended his influence widely over the American continent.

His orientation was Orthodox, a religion which combined the eternal values of human archetypal religion and the Christian break with timelessness and plunge into the historical process. In a way all his writings, even those that seem on the surface the most detached and scholarly, are aimed at a kind of redemption in which something is done to remedy the exile which deprives us of the saving symbols.

### Democratic Socialism as an Alternative

In Poland in 1980 (with the formation of Solidarity), in Hungary in the revolution of 1956, and in Czechoslovakia in 1968, there were spontaneous movements which can be represented as the demand for "Socialism with a human face," or in other words democratic Socialism. They were crushed by the reality or threat of Soviet tanks. These impulses combined nationalism and the desire for freedom in ordinary life, both of which were conspicuously crushed by the regimes imposed after World War II by Stalin.

Czechoslovakia had been a democracy before the war, so there was some rootage of these desires in nostalgia: before the cruel events of the Nazi and then the Communist regimes was something of a golden age for the well-organized Czechs. But the other States had been right-wing. Indeed, the prevalence of such thinking in Poland, Hungary, Romania, Yugoslavia, and Bulgaria was a reflection of the nationalism which had been given free rein by the Treaty of Versailles. It was very much a charter for a new, nationally oriented Eastern Europe. These more rampant forms of national politics lent themselves ultimately to takeover by a hard-line regime from Moscow which was bent on making Eastern Europe an extension of its empire. Meanwhile however Catholicism had become politically more mature in Western Europe through its espousal of a new and moderate Christian democracy, and to some degree therefore became the bearer of democratic ideals in the East. The Orthodox Church in the countries of Bulgaria, Romania, and Yugoslavia has used its experience under the Muslim Ottomans to bow its head and weather the storms of Communist rule.

Thus throughout Eastern Europe and in the Soviet Union, the Communist Party in effect has become the true Church. Those who wish to gain promotion and do well in life, and to take part in the ruling of the country, need to join. Citizens need to subscribe to the official ideology. And so it is that instead of the old Lutheran arrangement whereby the ruler's religion is made into that of the subjects, according to the old tag of *cuius regio eius religio*, we now have *cuius regio eius ideologia*, "Of whom the rule, of that person the ideology." It is only because we draw a line, rather arbitrarily, between religions and ideologies that we do not notice how the old Protestant-Catholic carve-up is now repeated in a new form in Eastern Europe.

The Eastern bloc countries are not pluralist. Marxism becomes the *de rigueur* religion, which is yet other than religion, much as State Shinto was entrenched in the Japanese Constitution before World War II. But even that was less pervasive, because it had no doctrines: now in Marxist countries there is an attempt to make the official line a set of ideas which has to be internalized. So the religion begins to reach down into academic life, science, the arts, and every intellectual activity.

More recently, however, such rigors have been unenforceable or thought to be inappropriate, and in Poland and Hungary particularly there is a much more relaxed rule, while in the Soviet Union the late 1980s have seen the policy of "openness" or *glasnost*.

## Religion in the Soviet Union

### The European End
We have already in the previous chapter noted some of the vicissitudes of Islam in the Soviet Union: and we shall a little later on say something about

the position of small-scale religions in Siberia, both before and after Soviet predominance. Meanwhile let us look briefly at the situation in European Russia, amid the traditional Christian Churches and other groups. The Revolution itself in 1917 altered the picture greatly, since all private property was nationalized and this included the landholdings of the Orthodox Church. Religious education was at the same time banned. But it was not until 1929, during a period when peasant and religious resistance to the new measures of collectivization was at its height, that the severest restriction was placed on religion: the only right which a religious organization had was to conduct worship.

In 1926 the League of the Militant Godless had been set up, which carried on vigorous propaganda against religion. It charged that traditional religion was unscientific because it rejected Evolutionary Theory and thought that God was in the sky, and so forth (this was more an attack on literalism than anything). It also charged that traditional religion was right-wing politically and antirevolutionary. It was superstitious, corrupt, manipulated by priests, hypocritical, and so on. Meanwhile, campaigns to close churches or turn

The Anti-religious crusade: ikons being carried away in 1930.

them into grain stores, museums of atheism, and the like were vigorously pursued, so that the number of buildings still operative and the number of priests declined by up to ninety per cent by World War II.

However, World War II posed new problems. Many Russians thought of Holy Russia as the focus of their loyalty. The Orthodox Church particularly had in its bones a nationalism which Stalin had need of. There were memories of Russian Orthodox beating off attacks by Teutonic Knights and Polish Catholic chauvinists. So for patriotic reasons, Stalin allowed the Churches greater latitude, and this period of greater relaxation lasted until about 1956.

But the Uniate Churches of Belorussia and the Ukraine were forcibly suppressed and had to merge with the Orthodox: in other words they had to renounce their ties to the Vatican. The Catholic Church always had the stigma of being a transnational organization, and so its adherents were therefore looked on with suspicion as being possibly unpatriotic. So, too, Judaism was seen as an international faith. Generally speaking nonpracticing Jews have been able to do reasonably well within the structures of Soviet society (despite a beginning of pogrom in the last days of Stalin). But practicing Jews have had great obstacles placed in their path. Persecution has been the norm, with, however, a certain proportion being granted exit visas to go to Israel. Also, toleration such as it is has never been extended to the evangelists of Baptists and other Protestant organizations. The wandering and underground evangelical Christians are subject to severe persecution because they break the Soviet norms. These imply a publicly controlled and evident form of religious organization.

The leaders of the official Churches have had to walk a tightrope in trying to keep the limited independence of their flocks and at the same time to adhere to the official Soviet line in world affairs. All these remarks apply not only to the mainstream Russian groups but also to national minority Churches such as the ancient Armenian Church.

## The Small-Scale Religions of Siberia

The Russian spread eastward had its profound effects, of course, on the peoples of the vast regions of Siberia. European contact, as elsewhere, could spell disease. Many of the peoples were subject to Orthodox missionary activity. The 1917 Revolution had rather ambiguous effects. The Bolshevik ideology was sympathetic to these peoples as the objects of prior Tsarist repression. The Communists were keen on the expression of national sentiment through folklore, the language, indigenous art, and so on. On the other hand, they were opposed to religion and wished to impose a Marxist ideology on these peoples. Part of the problem was how to detach folklore and the like from religion.

Some customs, such as that of the domestic hearth, can survive in the new conditions of Soviet society. In the Soviet Far East there are still evidences of shamanism among the Tunguz people, while the Buryats have effected some kind of synthesis of Buddhism, shamanism, and Marxism, retaining thus a mélange of customs in the life of the State farms and collectives. (In some respects the collective character of Soviet agricultural life helps the identity of tribal groups.) As elsewhere, much of the older shamanic worldview persists, sometimes disguised in Orthodox language—where Christianity and indigenous religions have merged—and sometimes by itself.

In more recent times Soviet anthropologists have made more sympathetic investigations of Siberian religions and have uncovered a much greater survival of religious ideas than had been thought. Here again, Soviet atheism is not an all-conquering force.

## Soviet Atheism

Atheism does, however, represent an important branch of the human array of worldviews. Probably we can say that Marxist atheism is the most important of the various worldviews of the Soviet Union, and despite the vigor of traditional religions in Eastern Europe it still has an important following there too. For many it has expressed revolt against the corruptions of the older world which the Revolution has replaced. Admittedly much unnecessary suffering has occurred since the Revolution; but nevertheless the Communist system has its achievements, and so can express in its own way a sense of Soviet and in particular Russian patriotism. Despite a lot of disillusion with the system, it would not work at all if it were not for the fact that Soviet-style Marxist atheism does represent a worldview to which many citizens can be loyal, no doubt with many critical qualifications. Let us sketch briefly this worldview in its dimensions.

*Doctrinally*, scientific Marxism persuasively puts a form of materialism at the center. It has two important characteristics. First, it is not a crude materialism in saying that conscious events and mental products are simply material: they are derived from the material, but their existence can and does have important reflexive effects on the material world, ranging from the way my mental state may affect the health of my body to the manner in which revolutionary consciousness may build up the material production of society. This materialism is also highly dynamic, containing its contradictions which so to say propel it into motion. Lenin could argue that this inescapable dynamism is what gives the universe its independent life and so causes us to dispense with the idea of an outside God who imparts motion to the cosmos.

In terms of *mythic* history, the Soviet system has a crucial part to play in the whole pattern of events which will ultimately issue in world revolution and the achievement of universal human social justice. The Revolution of 1917 was the forerunner of others, and so other countries such as China should recognize the seniority of the Soviet example.

In the *ethical* dimension, the Soviet system in eliminating unemployment achieves great social justice which is not evident in the capitalist countries, still less in the colonialized peoples of the Third World. The lack of certain individual rights is unimportant besides the great steps that have been made in

Crowds lining up to see Lenin lying in state, 1924.

Marxist countries to give workers a dignity and status that they had not had before. The new Soviet person is hardworking, cultured, forward-looking, devoted to science and to the realization of Marxist ideals.

In the *ritual* dimension, the Marxist rejects the old mumbo-jumbo, but there are the courtesies and ceremonies of the new State. In the pilgrimage to the tomb of Lenin, the rites of Marxism merge imperceptibly into those of the nation-State. As to the *material* dimension of the new order: Soviet art is supposed to reflect the nature of the new society, and so is rather iconographical, showing the heroisms of daily life and achievements of the party and State. With a shining and luminous kind of literalism, it may not figure greatly as art; but like religious painting it is meant to inspire. Similarly, the great writers are supposed to be Social Realists; although it happens that most critical opinion favors the achievements of the dissident writers: the Soviets have found no way to regiment great art into existence. Their great musicians, Prokofiev and Shostakovich, managed to survive the system since their craft was less easily controllable. But the achievements of the material

511

dimension are also to be seen in hydroelectric power, rocketry, factories, and all the buildings and inventions which can be ascribed to the Soviet State.

All this adds up to a still credible worldview. Often it is this worldview which is the focus of criticism, but often too, the criticism itself starts from within the worldview. It is not to be neglected as a major form of atheism in today's world, and its variations are held from Tirana, Albania, to Peking (Beijing), and from Moscow to Havana. *Organizationally*, Marxism remains strongly embedded, even in countries like Poland, where the grip of its other dimensions are loosened.

Alexander Solzhenitsyn visits a Buddhist temple in Taiwan: the spirituality of Russian Orthodoxy has something cognate with Mahāyāna Buddhist faith.

This raises questions as to how far Marxist atheism of this kind can admit into its fabric older forms of religious experience. What is the role of the spiritual life of human beings? Some of these questions are being asked by newer Marxists; such as Milan Macovec in his 1972 book, *God Is Not Quite Dead*, who saw that there are analogies between Christian faith and Marxist commitment. We shall see, too, that the social analysis and program of Marxism still can inspire new thinking, as in Latin American liberation theology (see Chapter 24).

In Western countries the Marxist strand is often carried on in a very vigorous (and sometimes very intolerant) way by those who follow that stormy petrel and theoretician of the Revolution, the great hero of the early Red Army, Leon Trotsky (1897–1940). His more fluid account of revolution has attracted many in the West who are disillusioned by the heavy centralism and bureaucratic sluggishness of the Soviet system, which can also be seen in its actions as another version of imperialism.

Finally, it is fairly obvious to Soviet sociologists as well as to outside observers that religions have by no means withered away in the Soviet State. The modern intellectuals of the Soviet Union have by no means always conformed to Marxist orthodoxy; and the two most vital of recent writers, Boris Pasternak (1890–1960) and Alexander Solzhenitsyn (b. 1918), have expressed an Orthodox viewpoint in the face of militant atheism. Even Buddhism, which was the religion most heavily hit, seems to have staying power. Statistics vary, but as many as twenty per cent of European Soviet citizens continue to attend churches. As we saw in regard to Islam, the rate of belief here is very high indeed. So were complete *glasnost* and relaxation to occur, there would no doubt be a wide and open expression of religion which would be counted as a great revival. The comfortable social democratic values of Sweden are probably a stronger menace to traditional religion than the harsher realities of Soviet atheism.

CHAPTER

# *Africa in the Modern World*

## The European Impact

*The Slave Trade*

In 1800 Africa was still substantially unaffected by foreign conquest. There were some Portuguese trading posts on the coast, and some other settlements of European powers involved in the slave trade. There were Dutch farmers and settlers, not to mention Indonesians imported by them for labor, round the Cape, and British influence there was about to expand. But the great bulk of Black Africa retained its traditional powers and social patterns.

In a number of areas social life was disrupted by the slave trade, carried on by various Western nations and also substantially by the Arabs, especially in East Africa and across the Sahara. The profits of the trade were great. Its origin lay in plantations, of tobacco, sugar, and later cotton, which became vital ingredients of the economy of the New World—in Brazil, in the Caribbean and in North America. Over ten million slaves arrived in these and other territories, mainly from Senegambia and the Gold Coast, but also from East Africa, and in the nineteenth century from Madagascar and Mozambique. The numbers of arriving slaves (for many, maybe up to thirty per cent, perished in the crossing) were about a million and a half each for Spanish America, the British Caribbean, and French America; a bit over three and a half million for Brazil; half a million for Dutch America; four hundred thousand for British North America and the United States combined; and something under two hundred thousand for Europe. It was a great movement of human beings for those days. Its effects in West and Southwest Africa were by no means negligible, and it left a quite new stamp on the cultures of the American South, the Caribbean, and Brazil particularly. Reflexively it affected Africa because many of the new ideas which underlay the independence movements in Africa came from across the seas in the New World.

In some degree the religious effects of slavery were deeply shaped by whether the importing culture was Catholic or Protestant. If it was Catholic, as in Haiti and Brazil, then it was possible in some degree to integrate African religions with the cult of saints. On the other hand, in Protestant North America saints were disapproved; and it had to be in other ways that African values were brought into the practice of Christianity. The ritual of baptism, the idea of being possessed by God, and the imagery of spirituals were ways of expressing a mixed culture. In North America the increase in the population was predominantly natural, rather than by the importation of successive waves of slaves, and this brought distance from the African experience. Of course, elements of folklore and music would persist and enter into creative synthesis with White culture.

Catholicism, in providing a more hospitable context for the transmission of African religious values, also helped to create new religions, to which we shall return in the next chapter.

## The Settlement of South Africa

In 1652 the Dutch East Indies Company, wishing to establish a staging post for the resupply of ships on the way to the East Indies, started a small base at the Cape of Good Hope. The settlement became Cape Town. At first there was no thought of a colony. But, as Dutch settlers came and undertook farming, the occupied zone was gradually extended beyond the bounds of Cape Town into the wild areas beyond. By the late eighteenth century the farmers had extended as far as the Kei river.

The British took over the Cape as a result of the Napoleonic wars, and later sent a substantial number of settlers to Natal. The Dutch-speaking farmers (or Boers) engaged in wars beyond the Kei, along the Fish River, and became at the same time greatly annoyed by what they thought of as outside interference, especially with the missionary lobby urging the abolition of slavery. In 1835 the Boers began the movement known as the Great Trek, and in due course occupied the regions known as the Orange Free State and the Transvaal, which became independent republics. Meanwhile the genius of Shaka (1787?–1832) had welded together a new nation, the Zulus, with whom the Boers and later the British came into collision. Their defeat in 1879 brought British control over the whole of Natal.

The British now faced two wars with the Boers, the second very bitter, from 1899 to 1902. The Boers were incensed by the methods by which the British confined their women and children in concentration camps—the origin of the term—and by the destruction of their homesteads and farms. Their revenge was to work away politically within the new State which the British set up in 1910, comprising Transvaal, the Orange Free State, Natal, and the Cape Province. Britain's interest in the first two was gold and diamonds. The vision of Cecil Rhodes (1853–1902) had seen British rule

515

stretching from the Cape to Cairo. The South African system in fact extended somewhat into Rhodesia, though this stayed a separate colony (later it was renamed Zimbabwe, after the massive ruins of a prior African culture).

By 1948 the Boers (now Afrikaners) had gained power democratically within the chiefly White electorate, and began to implement the policy of separateness or *apartheid*. That is, they tried to separate as far as possible the different races, namely Black, so-called Colored (or mixed race), Asian, and White. The assumption of White control and superiority was at best thinly veiled. This system greatly deprives Blacks of educational, business, and other opportunities, and rests in part on an ideology of separateness entangled in Dutch Reformed Church theology.

This theology was Calvinist. The Afrikaners derived part of their Calvinism from their Dutch heritage, but there was also a good infusion of French Huguenot religious refugees, who added strong commitment to the traditional beliefs. In addition after the Trek—which had not, by the way, been much approved by the Church, and the Trekkers had no ministers with them— Scottish Calvinist ministers worked in South Africa with the Boers. Calvinism preached predestinationism and encouraged the Afrikaners to believe that they were a chosen people, who modeled their life and warfare on that of the ancient Israelites. Their defeat of the Zulus at the battle of Blood River in 1838 they saw as due to divine help, and made a covenant to remember the day ever afterward. They thought their own culture to be unique and free, and they did not want contamination with other races. All this was welded into a powerful myth for their edification; but it also justified racial superiority and the system in which the Black and Colored populations, plus the Asians (Indians and others, mainly in Natal), would have a much lesser stake in South Africa than the Whites. Later we shall see some of the Black reactions to all this.

### The Colonial Scramble

The early settlement of South Africa preceded the main colonial conquest of African territories. Much of the initiative in this came from the French, who stimulated the British to rival action. The Germans and Belgians also put their hands into the tub. The partition of Africa was virtually complete by 1900. It remained for the Italians to take over Libya and the French and Spaniards to divide Morocco between them. Only Ethiopia remained free, having seriously defeated the Italians at Adowa in 1896. Germany lost her share of Africa after World War I; Tanganyika was taken over by the British and Namibia (Southwest Africa) by South Africa (see Map 12, p. 338–9).

In 1881 the Mahdi, a messianic leader, mixing Islamic eschatology and the politics of revolt, had started his struggle in the Sudan, then under Egyptian control, and the British intervened. But in 1885 Khartoum fell and General Gordon (1833–85) was killed; it was not till 1898 that the Mahdi was crushed at the Battle of Omdurman, when Egypt and Britain jointly took over the Sudan as a condominium.

The scramble for Africa grew out of European rivalries. The boundaries were drawn for the most part without any regard to the linguistic and cultural divisions of the continent. When Africa became decolonized in the 1950s and 1960s these boundaries were held by the Organization for African Unity to be sacrosanct (mainly because of their absurdity: call one into question and the whole house of cards might come tumbling down). The successor States have had to fashion their myths of identity as best they can.

## The Penetration of Christianity into Black Africa

Undoubtedly the greatest change to come over the African continent, and that was primarily in the twentieth century, was the massive spread of Christianity. It is now the majority religion of Black Africa. One might at some preceding stage have expected that Islam would become the dominant faith. It has indeed made some progress, but rather small compared with that of Christianity.

In the eighteenth century, apart from the rather few Christians around the coasts where Europeans had settled or established trading posts, there was little Christianity at all, except in the ancient kingdom of Ethiopia. But towards the end of the century Christian opponents of the slave trade arranged for a group of emancipated slaves of African origin to be settled in Sierra Leone, at Freetown, and thirty years later a college, Fourah Bay College, was set up, to be Africa's first modern institution of higher education. It became a center for the spread of Christianity, as Black missionaries went out into the region. The most important of these was a Yoruba, from what is now Nigeria, Samuel Ajayi Crowther (1809?–91), who became Anglican Bishop on the Niger.

Already before the main partition of Africa missionaries were making progress, though the most famous White missionary in Africa, David Livingstone (1813–73), was more successful as an explorer than as a winner of souls (he only converted one person, who fell away). But during the colonial period there was especially strong activity in the translation of the Bible into vernacular languages, and this had a powerful influence on people. Christianity and education were closely connected, not just because in fact so many schools were run by missionaries, but because African societies saw the need for modernizing—if only often intuitively—and school was the main agency for this. And more than this: Christianity did supply something to rely on in a period of sudden and disturbing change. As classical African religion wilted, so Christianity provided an alternative.

The Bible seems to have had great potency. The missionaries were rather short-handed, and made much use of local catechists who were often poorly trained. But they could carry the Bible around with them: for most Africans the first and often the only book in their own language that they knew. Its power was the more numinous in that it could bring forth the very sounds of language—it was a miraculous score from which the person who could read could play a wonderful set of musical pieces. Also, its themes rang true to the African condition. It spoke of circumcision; of the witch of Endor; of Mount Carmel and the contest in rainmaking; of prophecy, healing, and the sufferings of the people of Israel. With much of this the Black African could easily identify.

As has happened at other times and places in Christian history the Bible was at odds with perceived practice. It had revolutionary potential. The mission Churches were almost completely in the control of Whites until the end of the 1950s; and it was not surprising if many Blacks saw in this some contradiction with the spirit of the Gospel. Part of the expression of Black resentment at injustices was found in the independent Churches, which proved to be so potent a phenomenon in most of Black Africa. It should on the other hand be noted that many missionaries supported independence movements. Still, there was until the 1960s a feeling of paternalism which was pervasive. Vatican II on the Catholic side, and various revolutionary changes "back home" among Protestants, altered this picture.

### The Mainstream Churches in Black Africa

In virtually all of Africa, Catholicism has come to be the majority religion, and not only in territories formerly colonized by, say, France or Portugal. But it is, in most areas, very short of priests. Similarly, Protestant Churches are short of trained people. The result is that much of African Christianity follows on with the use of catechists, as in the days of the missionaries. This has meant that even when the Whites were in control at the top, at the bottom things were more fluid and not easy to keep a strict eye on. The strength of the system is that it leaves a lot to the work of the laity, and so it engenders a lot of active piety. Increasingly the leadership has become Black, with six African Cardinals. South Africa, with many White Anglicans and Catholics, has Black Church leaders, Archbishop Desmond Tutu, of Cape Town, being the best known example. Such figures have begun to play leading roles in Church policy-making through ecumenical and other global organizations.

Some differing strands of thought are evident in these Churches. On the one hand there is a greater interest in Liberation Theology, because of the struggle in South Africa and also elsewhere, in so far as the Churches are concerned with global injustices and a possible Marxist analysis both of how things are and of what should be done. More conservatively, there is interest in an African theology, which is the effort to make use of classical African categories in the statement of Christianity. It is the attempt to see in indigenous ideas something of a forerunner of the Gospel, and so to find in them an alternative or a supplement to the Old Testament. Some make the distinction between African theology and Black theology, the latter being a version of Liberation Theology.

### The Notion of Africanness: A Modern Phenomenon

It is notable that much of African and Black theology is based on the sense

The social dimension: the churches play a notable role in both sides of the South African struggle. Here Bishop Desmond Tutu, later Anglican Archbishop of Cape Town, addresses a press conference about a government ban on a conference on religion and peace.

that there is a common African or Black experience. This was scarcely true before the colonial period. The lack of communications in many areas, the divisions of language, the lack of a living "other" to promote a sense of solidarity among Blacks—these and many other factors worked against any unitary vision of Africa. It was above all through the colonial experience, and the growing realization of the nature of Black history and the sufferings and contempt so often lavished on Africans, that such a new sense of identity grew.

This is where of course the contributions of the Churches are ambiguous, for the fact of the matter is that many missionaries came to Africa with an ideology which was something like this: the Africans are inferior; they need Christianity and civilization; the means to this will be conversion and education; and then the African will be able to take his place proudly with the White person. Images were projected of "darkest Africa," and European and American readers thrilled to pursue the voyages and hardships of Livingstone or the adventures of the ebullient H. M. Stanley (1844–1904). Africans were represented as savages, sometimes noble no doubt.

These images have not gone away: though racism is everywhere to be found, it is especially strong against the Blacks. So it was not unnatural that, with self-consciousness, Africans should seek to define an African identity. A major contribution in this was the school of writers, somewhat under

519

the stimulus of Jean-Paul Sartre (1905–1980) and Leopold Sedar Sengthor (b. 1906), who defined Négritude.

It was in the same milieu of a more embracing consciousness that indeed conceptions of African religion as a whole emerged. Thus in 1945 a Franciscan, Placide Tempels (b.1906), published his *La Philosophie bantoue*, which described a pan-Bantu worldview, seeing the universe as a dynamic system flowing from God and animated by a whole hierarchy of vital forces, some benevolent and others hostile, which play upon each other and appear at differing times as weakened and strengthened. Other writers, and not just from the region where the Bantu live (equatorial and southern Africa), saw this same structure. After World War II, especially, classical African religions thus came to be seen as an integrated whole. In this sense African religion is so to speak a modern invention, and itself a way of looking at classical religious phenomena from a new point of view.

The advantage of a pan-African approach is that it combines values in a large enough unit to deal with the influx of such forces as science, capitalism, theories of economic development, Christianity, etc. And yet an indigenous African worldview has not yet emerged which has quite the edge and complexity needed to embrace modern social and technological change. On the whole, the process of modernization has occurred through conversion to the Christian Churches, and to a lesser extent to Islam.

## Islam South of the Sahara

During the colonial period Islam continued to spread into Black Africa from the north. Important agents of conversion were the various Sufi orders and the marabouts, who played a leading role in West Africa especially. One of them, from Senegal, Ibrahim Niass (1900–75), was especially important in stressing the universal character of Islam, over against the particularist trends which often emerged in the blends of Muslim and local cultures and values. But it was especially the Salafiya movements, led by men who were educated in Cairo and in North Africa, who introduced the more radical anticolonial and anti-Western impulses. They were highly critical of marabout and Sufi leadership in tending to play upon the ignorance of the masses: they wanted a reformed, neofoundationalist Islam firmly rooted in the Qur'an. At the same time, they saw this Islam as able to stand up to the West both in values and in intellectual strength.

In East Africa, Islam played little political role. But Swahili culture was important: the language itself reflected a mixed Afro-Arab society, fluid at its edges, which established itself in various centers along the coast and inland, partly as a result of the vigorous trade in slaves conducted by the Arabs in the nineteenth century. Islam got a foothold too in Uganda, among the Baganda nobility, and this was one area of fierce struggle between Islam and Christianity—with more power going to the Christian missions since they were aided by the British.

The ritual dimension: implanting the Qur'an in the hearts and minds of the young, in the Western Sudan, under the guidance of a religious leader or sheikh.

Though syncretism between rituals particularly is widespread in Black Islam, this tends to be a temporary phenomenon, as Muslims on the *hajj* to Mecca come to perceive orthodox Islam and return with ideas of reform. The Salafiya movement, too, has tended to root out tendencies to syncretism.

Another ingredient in Islam in Africa comes from the migrant populations of Asians in East Africa and South Africa, brought in to work in the plantations during the colonial period. A minority of these are Muslims, as are some of the Indonesian settlers who are a part of the so-called Colored or mixed race population in the Cape Province of South Africa. There have been tensions between Asians and Blacks, notably in the events of the 1970s leading to the emigration of most Indians from Uganda under the rule of Idi Amin; and in the Zulu-Asian riots of 1947 in Durban, South Africa, and sporadically since that time. Such tensions partly explain why the example of Gandhi, who was a very effective fighter for rights in South Africa during his twenty-year period there from 1893, has not been easy to popularize among the Black populations of South Africa.

## Ethiopia and its Ancient Christian History

Of special fascination to many Africans, especially in overseas revival movements, is the heritage of Ethiopia. The situation has however been complicated by the overthrow of the imperial system under Haile Selassie (1892–1975) in 1974 by a Marxist revolution. (Marxism, incidentally, has had some appeal in Africa, since Marxist regimes have been set up not only in Ethiopia but in the former Portuguese territories of Angola and Mozambique,

*Opposite* A float at the Rio festival, Brazil (see Chapter 24).

and in one or two other places.) Ethiopia's long Christian history and independence over nearly all its history from foreign domination creates a vital myth in Africa. Ethiopian Christianity dates from the fourth century or earlier. It has strong Semitic connections. The monarchy is traced back to Menelik, who was supposed to be son of Solomon the Great and the queen of Sheba; the use of dance in its ceremonial and the vital role of the Psalms recall consciously the minstrelsy of the period of David; circumcision of males is practiced; and the Sabbath is kept on Saturday. The attempt in the seventeenth century by Portuguese Jesuits to change the religion and romanize it was at first seemingly successful, through the conversion of the emperor in 1621. But his effort to impose the new religion was ultimately a failure: it met too much resistance. So it was that Ethiopian Christianity kept its independence, with its ancient structures. It retained its archaic language of Ge'ez in which the scriptures were written, its hierarchy, linked to the Coptic Church of Egypt, its scribes, painted shrines, monks in high rocky hermitages and monasteries, its magical rites, its ancient and particular saints, above all St. George and the Virgin Mary, its music and dancing, its minstrelsy and psalms: it was essentially *theirs*, and this familiarity arose from its integration into the culture and bones of the Christian Ethiopians. The dynamic Jesuits left an imprint on Ethiopian literature and architecture: but the ultimate prize managed to elude them.

Because Ethiopia has such a long history of Black Christianity it has often been looked on as a model for new Black movements both in Africa and overseas. There are Churches in America and the Caribbean which use the prefix Abyssinian or Ethiopian, and sometimes conduct liturgy in a mixture of Ge'ez and English. The mix is complicated by the emergence since 1974 of refugees from the new Marxist regime in Ethiopia itself, which has established its control over the Church.

## New Religious Movements in Modern Africa

By far the most dynamic phenomenon in the modern period has been the growth of independent Churches or new religious movements in a number of regions, which have produced variations chiefly on Christian themes but have tried to adapt religion to the African condition rather than accept the foreign structures of Western missionary religion. They form a bridge between classical African religions and Western thought, and between indigenous values and those of the modern world. Estimates of the number of new religions vary, but probably there are about 10,000, spread over such regions as Nigeria, Ghana, central Kenya, Zaire, and South Africa, but less evident in Uganda and Tanzania. Perhaps fifteen per cent of all Christians in Africa belong to such groups, though as we have noted the situation at the edges of Christianity is very fluid in Africa.

There were a number of problems in Africa for Blacks in regard to the White religion. One was the general question of control: mission Churches tended to be very paternalistic. Another was the role of ancestor cults, which were important socially in the African scene, but seen as superstitious or idolatrous by the missionaries. Another was the problem of polygamy, which was fairly widespread and built into social structures. There were great injustices caused if a man had to give up all but one wife. Another very potent issue was that of health. In some matters so-called Western medicine was seen to be effective, but in other areas it was much less so, and so a reversion to classical African modes of treatment was reasonable. There were analogies, too, with faith-healing in the Christian context.

In some degree the new religious movements dealt with these problems, by for instance splitting off from mainstream Churches under Black leadership; or by focusing on a Black Prophet or Messiah figure; or by otherwise establishing Black control. They could incorporate methods of faith-healing or more traditional medicine; and they could allow polygamy (with the Bible at their disposal Africans could easily see that polygamy was part of the fabric of ancient Israelite religion). They could reintegrate other features of African society and religious practice.

The first example we shall look at is the one founded through the example of the prophet Simon Kimbangu (1889–1951). It is an interesting case, because it was a breakaway movement which nevertheless became a member of the World Council of Churches in 1969, thus attaining a kind of ecumenical "respectability." It is a case of Christianity rejoining the mainstream.

### The Church of Jesus Christ on Earth Through the Prophet Simon Kimbangu

Simon Kimbangu was born in what was then the Belgian Congo, later to be named Zaire, and was baptized a Baptist after his marriage. He was not able to become a pastor, failing his examinations, though he was trained as a catechist. He received visionary calls to be a healer, and eventually started to heal. He rapidly gained converts, and the colonial administration saw in this a threat. His arrest was ordered in 1921, but he eluded his would-be captors, until later in that year he voluntarily surrendered. Though he was sentenced to death for possible/alleged subversion against Belgian rule, the sentence was commuted by the Belgian king on the petition of missionaries, who favored more lenient treatment. He stayed in prison for the rest of his life and died in 1951. His imprisonment in some ways increased his appeal as a Prophet, and the movement continued to spread despite the exile and imprisonment of many of his followers (over two thousand). After his death his Church was reorganized by his youngest son in accordance with his wishes, and eventually came to join the World Council and to be one of the officially recognized Churches of Zaire, with over four million members.

In some ways of course Simon Kimbangu's career reminded his followers of the life of Jesus: here too there was a call, a healing ministry, a large following, condemnation to death by a colonial regime. It is notable that the themes of the Bible could reverberate in this way, and cause the Prophet to recognize in his own healing powers the work of the Holy Spirit.

### The Prophet Shembe and South African Zionism

Many of the new religious movements in South Africa have to do with healing. They also emphasize the charismatic powers of their leaders. They were influenced to a greater or lesser degree by an American Church which had some presence in South Africa, the Evangelical Christian Catholic Church of Zion City, Illinois: for this reason these new movements are often classified as Zionist. Since they often look forward to earthly liberation, the name has a deeper significance too.

One of the most notable of these was founded among the Zulu by the Prophet Isaiah Shembe (1870?–1935). At a time when the Zulu people had been deprived of much of its land, and not long after the Zulu rebellion of 1906, Shembe had visionary experiences; in one of these, at the mountain of Inhlangakazi, he underwent twelve days of retreat, temptations, and final victory, through which he got new powers both of casting out evil spirits and of healing. He set up his center at another mountain, Ekuphakameni outside Durban, which is the scene of a great annual gathering. Shembe's career made many of his followers look on him as Messiah. At any rate the Nazarite Church which he founded was deeply imbued by his remarkable creativity in composing a body of hymns, which welled up from him, and which he committed to writing, having learned to read in his early forties for this

The experiential dimension: the prophetic and shamanistic experiences of this man, Isaiah Shembe, drove him to form the Nazarite Church in Natal province in South Africa. Such independent forms of Christianity are a marked feature of the Black African scene.

purpose. This body of hymns was embedded in lovely rituals of solemn dancing and singing, with his followers dressed in the Zulu style. It was a religion of renewal and revival, among a people who had been crushed in war and deprived by colonial rule.

## Some Catholic Separatist Movements

The two examples we have taken of revived Africanism and Christianity draw on Protestant sources. Father Placide Tempels, whom we have noted as a writer on Bantu philosophy, helped to found a movement known as the Jamaa (a word which means "family" in Swahili). It was intended to express a sort of African Catholicism from within the Church, but came under unfavorable judgment by the authorities, and part of the group became a separatist organization, which is still working in some areas of Shaba and Kasai in Zaire. In both Kenya and in Zambia there were other breakaway Catholic movements. But Vatican II, with its great encouragement of vernaculars, its call for dialogue with other religions rather than their repression, and its call to indigenization, made it less important for groups to try to break away.

## Some Other Movements

An important strand of African religiosity is represented by those Churches which stem from the Aladura movement founded in the 1920s in Nigeria and prominent along the West African coast, stressing the importance of prayer and spiritual healing. They incorporate charismatic visions and the virtues of an ethos of Biblical self-reliance.

A more eschatologically oriented movement was that founded by the Prophetess Alice Lenshina (1919?–78) in Zambia (p. 528). She, too, had a vision in which she believed that she had been especially favored by God. She broke away from the Presbyterian mission to baptize her own followers. She emphasized forms of music that were attuned to her and her followers' ethnic background. Eventually they got into conflict first with colonial authority and then with the new government of independent Zambia. The Lumpa Church (Excellent Church) saw the end of the world as near, and refused to pay taxes. In battles with the authorities her followers with their primitive weapons were easily overcome. Their very puritanical communes, outside of the sphere of the Devil who controls the world, were totalistic organizations that were bound to come into conflict with the new authorities. Though Christian in much of its ethos, the movement did not deny the existence of witchcraft, which it regarded as evil but as something which the Lumpa Church afforded protection against. By contrast, the rationally minded Presbyterians simply denied the very existence of witchcraft.

Some other movements were revivalist of classical African religion, using mission means of organization and propaganda in order to express their ideas, such as the Église de Dieu de Nos Ancêtres (The Church of God of Our Ancestors) in the southwest Belgian Congo (Zaire), founded in the 1950s.

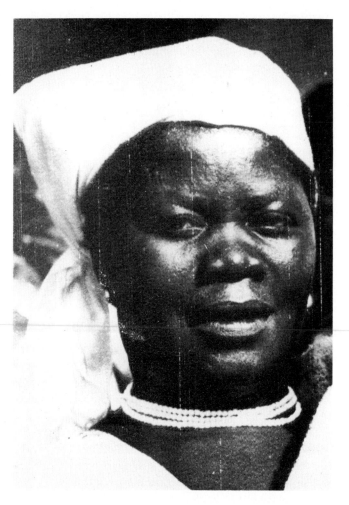

Alice Lenshina of Zambia formed her own movement known as the Lumpas: another instance of new indigenous religions in the twentieth century.

In the various new Churches and movements we can see several patterns. One is where traditional functions are transferred but traditional content is rigidly rejected: for instance in movements where healing, but not traditional methods or theories, is prominent. Another mode is more explicitly syncretist, where classical motifs such as belief in ancestors are woven into Biblically based teachings. In many of the movements visionary experience is important. This is something that is hard for Protestant groups, especially, to control. It has brought to prominence many folk, both men and women, who are looked on by their followers as Prophets and sometimes as Suffering Servants who have followed the path of Jesus. The similarity of many of the motifs in the new movements to those which are found in the New Testament is quite striking.

As responses to the various powerful forces coming into African society the new movements are often effective within a limited context. They have produced some striking and beautiful forms of piety. Their great weakness, which in some degree the Kimbanguists have overcome, is that these new religions, as well as the classical forms, need some kind of doctrinal or philosophical underpinning if they are to digest successfully the impacts of modern science, economic change, urbanization, and Christianity. They have a choice to turn back towards the mainstream Churches, in which case they will become distinctive African contributions within that context: or they will more explicitly turn away in order to create a new African synthesis which draws both on African classical religion and Western concepts, including Christian ones.

All this bears on the general question of whether a pan-African philosophy is in the making. Or is it that Africa is too quickly being sucked into a global situation in which the dominant Western modes of thinking and organization will constitute a new form of mental colonialism? This is where Négritude and other forms of the search for an African philosophy are important. The new movements have great force in welling up and boiling round the frontiers of Christianity and Islam. But their very number does represent a fragmentation inherent both in the plurality of African societies and in the diversity of Biblical Christianity.

## Reflections on Black Africa

The scene in Africa is one of great dynamism. The future will no doubt see the continued spread of Christianity and Islam at the expense of classical African religious forms. The societies in which they are based are on the whole too small to be able to bear the full impact of modern social changes, especially the magnetism of the cities. This last phenomenon will no doubt favor those new movements which can give people a new sense of identity in larger, more impersonal contexts. The struggle over the colonial heritage is by no means complete: the battle in South Africa to get rid of apartheid is still in full flow and probably will last for many years. And Africans still have to put up with the low value placed on their cultural achievements and styles of life by the West. An important ingredient in the attempt to break free from these limitations, and to spell out Africa's distinctive contributions to a world civilization both in the future and from the past, will be the formation of a philosophical framework in which we can view African ideas and institutions. Meanwhile Africa overseas is important, in South America, the Caribbean and North America particularly. There, too, religious dynamism is evident.

### Dimensions of African Spirituality
We can finish by looking briefly at the dimensions of African, and especially Christian, religion. Naturally there is great variety, as we have seen, but some patterns emerge.

First, as to *ritual*: forms of Christianity, both mainstream and new religions, have stressed African forms of worship. This is most notable in the hymns and devotionalism of some of the new movements, in the dance of

Shembe's Church, for instance, and in the use of vernacular languages. Impetus to indigenization was given by Vatican II. For many Africans, because of the shortage of priests and pastors among the mainstream Churches, and for other reasons, the Eucharist is not so central. Vital is the imagery of baptism, partly because of the purificatory symbolism of water in the classical African background and because of the often numinous character of streams.

In the *experiential* dimension, there remains an important place for dreams and visions in the formation of new movements; and because of the affinity between African classical religion and Pentecostalism the latter has widespread life. Commitment becomes more important in the shifting choices of urban life and transformations of rural economies, and in these circumstances conversion experiences are important.

As for *ethics*, there is still heartsearching about marriage customs and the role of polygamy in African society. There are also issues about duties towards the ancestors. Very important in the African scene is a sense of solidarity, brotherhood and sisterhood, which some of the new religious communities wish to express with intensity.

As for the *doctrinal* dimension, there is some way to go in formulating the characteristic African holism in its modern cosmological setting: how can we combine some traditional African views of the interrelation of forces in the universe with a modern scientific worldview? There is also the problem of providing the philosophical basis for religious pluralism in the African setting.

The dimension of *myth* leaves much to reflect on in telling the story of Africa in the perspectives of world history, and the relation of Christianity in Africa to that: it looks as if there is a story emerging which emphasizes the sufferings of Blacks, through the slave trade and the colonial era, as providing a parallel with the life of the Israelites in the Old Testament and the role of the Suffering Servant.

In *art*, African carving and painting has already made its first major impact on Western imagination, and is poised to express more deeply the new spiritualities which are flourishing in Africa.

Africa is an exuberant as well as a problem-haunted continent. The dimensions of its religious life match the contributions of other areas, but it may be that deeper creativities also are yet to come.

*Opposite* The ritual dimension: water has played a prominent part in classical African religion and is given new significance in new forms of African Christianity.

# 24

# *Latin America and the Caribbean*

## The Spirit of the Conquest

Although the original aim of sailing west from the Iberian peninsula was to reach Asia, and it was not until about 1520, nearly thirty years after Columbus' first landing, that the Spaniards were fully convinced that what they had found was really a New World, the discovery of these vast lands and their exploitation were taken up with a kind of crusading zest. The expulsion of the Muslims from Spain had been an arduous business, but it fired the Spaniards, and to a lesser degree the Portuguese, with a Catholic zeal. And to complicate matters, there was the Reformation, causing Europe to disintegrate religiously but reinforcing the value of commitment to the Catholic cause. The fact that the Spaniards acted in the New World with great cruelty and greed should not blind us to the fact that they thought themselves to be doing God's will. The Church followed on the heels of the Conquistadores, and there was held up before the eyes of the faithful the prospect of a great extension of Christ's work.

The general attitude to indigenous religions, such as the Aztec and the Inca systems, was one of horror and disdain. The Aztec practice of human sacrifice was not easy to take. But the true horrors lay in the general idolatry of the New World's inhabitants. The gods were often seen by Catholics as creatures of the Devil. So much, therefore, of the native culture had to be rooted out. Disentangling culture from religion was itself a problem, and so much of the indigenous literatures and creations were simply destroyed.

The spirit of the conquest was one of dedication to a sacred cause at the same time as the opportunity for hugely exploiting the conquered population. And because of the advent of the Counter-Reformation the Church had the motivation and the apparatus to carry orthodox Catholic faith to the New World. The conquest was then in its own way a crusade.

The astonishing ease of some of the conquests was uncanny. It lay in the fact that the two great empires the Spaniards encountered were so centralized. The Spaniards struck at the brain of these empires and paralyzed their bodies. Their superiority lay in their horses and muskets, and their ships and cannons. The rapidity and glory of the conquests boosted the self-confidence of the victors and their belief that their civilization and religion were immensely superior to those of the peoples they had come to dominate.

By 1700 the Spanish domains in the New World were immense, running from California and Texas to Patagonia and from Ecuador to the Caribbean. The Portuguese ruled over the huge area of Brazil, after some fighting with the rival Dutch (who kept a base in Surinam). But certain areas were highly important and others thinly populated and marginal. The rich and densely populated places were Peru and Mexico (known as New Spain), together with part of the Caribbean. It was during the period leading to the consolidation of power over so great an area that the way of life of the New World was worked out and in this the Church played a leading part.

## Disputes Over the Treatment of the Indians

For better or worse the natives were called *indios*, or Indians, because the theory was that Columbus and his successors had reached India. Indians the native populations would remain. There was indeed some question as to how they should be treated. Were they to be regarded as fully human? The effect on the Indians of the conquest and its aftermath was to be devastating. This was not merely because so many were virtually enslaved, and worked in unspeakable conditions in the silver mines of Peru and elsewhere. It was also because of the incidence of European diseases, and above all smallpox. Estimating populations from the data available is not an easy job, but it may be that by 1700 the population of New Spain was only a tenth of what it had been in 1500. An important question was how the Indians were to be treated, both by the Church and by the civil powers.

In this debate a crucial role was played by Bartolomé de Las Casas (1474–1566). He had been born in Seville and gone overseas to take part in the subjugation of the large island of Hispaniola (now divided between Haiti and the Dominican Republic). He became a priest, but went on to take part in the bitter conquest of Cuba. In both islands he got lands under the *encomienda* system. It was a kind of feudalism, in which land with villages would be acquired by a Spaniard, usually as a reward for campaigning and conquest. At the age of forty, however, he was converted to a deep concern over the plight of the Indians and from that time on became their unwavering defender, speaking out boldly and plainly against the atrocities being committed against them. He gave up his own estates. His energies were considerable, and he was involved in various struggles and projects, including a colony in Venezuela that unsuccessfully tried to blend Spanish and Indians in agricultural work.

*Opposite* The mythic dimension: a narrative of significance for Indians focused upon the Virgin of Guadalupe who spoke in the indigenous language, Nahuatl, and thus became a reminder of how the Divine speaks to the Indians as well as to the Spaniards. Here she is seen returning after being taken in procession through Sucre, Bolivia.

Las Casas was successful in his advocacy of Indian rights at the court, and agitated against a number of abuses. He was a force for adopting the New Laws in 1542, which in some measure protected Indian rights. He passionately advocated the equality of all human beings, and in his great *History of the Indies* he catalogued some of the major cruelties and hypocrisies that had been used in the extension of the faith: for him, mission should be a matter of preaching and gentle exhortation, not of violence and enslavement. There were those who argued, on a nakedly racist basis, that the Indians were inferior and as one put it "almost as monkeys to humans." He with vehement passion argued that the Indians had souls as much as the Whites. His career, and his tireless hostility to the abuses of colonialism, helped somewhat to mitigate the plight of the indigenous peoples of the New World.

### A Religion for Both Peoples

The New World was a place for many Spaniards to settle. It gave vast opportunities for them. It was also of course the place of the Indians, and much of later history concerns the relations between these parties. But there was also a growing class of people of mixed descent. These *mestizos* were differentiated from the Whites, who held control over much of Latin American history. The latter themselves were divided into *criollos*, that is, those who were born and raised in the New World, and home-born Spaniards. Essentially, the liberation of the New World from Spain at the beginning of the nineteenth century was a *criollo* revolt against metropolitan control, and largely left the institutions in place.

The pattern which emerged in much of Mexico and Peru was that the Indians were organized into their own villages, where missionaries from various orders—Franciscans, Dominicans, and others—would labor, teaching them by means of vernacular languages. The secular priests (that is, ordinary priests not belonging to any of the orders) would minister to the Whites, and, after a generation or two, to the *mestizos*. So a form of segregation was practiced. It had the advantage from the colonists' point of view that the Indians if settled into villages were easier to control. They could also be the more easily incorporated into the system of *encomiendas*, and so into the pattern of forced labor. In outlying areas priests and monks would wander from village to village preaching Christianity, and this corresponded to the Church's growing ideal of mission work, following the prescription of Las Casas.

Much in the conversion of Indians was forced, and little compunction was shown in uprooting indigenous religion and destroying the gods of the conquered. In some degree the Catholic cult of saints helped to cover the reemergence of some of the old gods, however: or at least to provide alternatives to them. The most important saint in Mexico came to be Our Lady of Guadalupe: here, just outside Mexico City, the Virgin had appeared to an Indian and spoken to him in the native language of Nahuatl. She became a symbol of a religion which was now itself *mestizo*: the Mary of the Spaniards also spoke the language of the Indians. Throughout the great

regions of Latin America there remain pockets of indigenous culture and religion which have not much been touched by the missionary enterprise; but it is remarkable, even so, how wide the net of Catholicism was cast. Much of the conversion took place after the Council of Trent, so a kind of reformed Catholicism could work with greater effectiveness, and it was a highly ornate baroque style of art and architecture which was brought to the New World. Some of the great edifices of Catholic cathedrals in the many cities were built over pre-Christian sites, such as the site of the Templo Mayor in Mexico City, where once the Aztec emperor had performed his human sacrifices.

The Indians came to perceive that, great as was the catastrophe of the arrival of the Spaniards, it was not the end of the world. Were the old sacrifices really necessary? The invaders seemed to trample the gods with impunity. In the second half of the sixteenth century the Inquisition was also at work in the New World, rooting out idolatry, heresy, and Judaism. It was able to deal with captured Protestant seamen among others, and initially was somewhat directed at backsliders among the Indians; but a more paternalistic spirit later prevailed, for they were reckoned to be too naive to be held fully responsible. For a long period, indeed, it was impossible for non-Spaniards to be priests, so that what was institutionalized was a thoroughly paternalistic system.

### Paternalism in Paraguay and California

This paternalism can be illustrated by a Jesuit and a Franciscan example. The Jesuits had been admitted to the New World from the mid-sixteenth century on, and in the seventeenth and eighteenth centuries they began to organize what were called Reductions, or regimented villages, on great estates that had been given to the Order either by royal grant or in some other way. In these settlements the Indians were taught useful crafts and skills. Schools were opened and the local languages preserved and reduced to writing. It was a kind of benevolent dictatorship: complete obedience to the Jesuit fathers was enforced, and for the rest the Indians shared everything in common, on a basis of equality. It was religious communism. The Indians were there, not by choice on the whole, but because they had been born into the system or put there in recompense for some wrongdoing.

The great discipline of the Jesuits was matched by their devotion to education, but this was very narrowly conceived. In their universe education was a matter of hierarchy. The Church had the *magisterium* or teaching function. As soldiers of the Pope, they would hand down the truth. It was not a mode which in any way encouraged self-reliance, independent judgment, or free expression. Consequently, when the Jesuits were expelled from the New World (for European political reasons), the Indians of the Jesuit Reductions were at a great loss and the whole system fell apart. The most famous part of that system was the area of modern Paraguay, which had been a mini-State handed over to the Jesuits in deference to their marvelous method of control.

In California a chain of mission stations, from San Diego in the south through to beyond San Francisco, was set up from the late eighteenth century onward, on the initiative of a Franciscan, Junípero Serra (1713–84). These mission stations gathered in the local Indians, such as the Chumash, in order that they should pursue agricultural and other pursuits. The missions would often have a place for a small garrison of troops, who would help to keep order and pacify the regions of Alta California which had hitherto been scarcely occupied by the Spanish. With independence for Mexico in the early nineteenth century, and the subsequent takeover by the United States, the system fell apart. The concentration of Indians, and their exposure to White people's diseases, had a devastating effect on Indian life, as did also the destruction of their traditional culture.

One of the ironies of the Franciscan mission chain is how in the Spanish-style churches (which are in their own way pleasing) there is fake marble painted on by Indians who did not know what it was they were imitating. But Our Lady of Guadalupe is also present here and there: a symbol of the inherent worth of Indian life, though that life was culturally despised by the Whites.

### The Layering of Latin America

The net effect of the population and religious policies of the New World was that the people were arranged in three or four layers. There were the two kinds of Spaniards, European-born and *criollo*, on the top; then a swathe of *mestizos*; then the Indians. In parts of the area the Indians had virtually gone, from some islands of the Caribbean for instance, and slaves from Africa had been introduced. Much of the importation of Blacks was in the nineteenth century: slavery was not abolished in Brazil until 1888. We may also note that in the nineteenth and twentieth centuries there was massive migration from Europe in some countries.

This has produced a variety of racial patterns. The classic pattern is an ascending scale of population between Whites, *mestizos* and Indians, of roughly the proportions 1:2:4 or 1:2:3. This applies in Mexico, Central America, and Peru. Then there are areas where the larger number are *mestizos*, as in Colombia and Venezuela. Then there are countries with a predominance of Blacks, such as Brazil and Cuba (the latter has lost its Indian population, however; and in Brazil it is the smallest section of the population). Then there are countries, notably Chile and Argentina, which are over-whelmingly White. In Argentina, more than half the migrants were from Italy, but there are significant Spanish, French, and other groups; while Brazil has a fair number of Germans and a significant group of Japanese descent: of all the countries of Latin America Brazil is the most colorfully variegated. In some areas, such as Amazonia, part of Central America, central Argentina, and southern Chile, there are extant unconquered Indian populations. In (formerly British) Guiana, a substantial population was brought in from India as indentured laborers in the latter part of the nineteenth century, and there are East Indians elsewhere in the English-speaking Caribbean.

*Opposite* Africa meets
Catholicism in the
Voodoo of Haiti.

Central America and the northern states of South America have the classic layered pattern, with the Indians at the bottom. This has given edge to economic and social struggles, as also in a different way in Brazil with its great Black population. This situation was not affected by the wars of independence, which lasted from 1810 to 1826. The resultant political pattern has with relatively minor changes stayed on till modern times.

## The Liberation of Latin America

The revolts of the colonies were essentially a matter of the White elite. There had of course been independence wars on behalf of the Indians, but they had been crushed—most notably the campaign fought by the Inca prince Tupac Amarus (1742–81), who led a large Andean uprising which was put down with great cruelty. The motives of the colonial Whites in seeking independence were similar to those of the North American colonists a generation earlier. There was also strong influence from the liberal thinking of the Enlightenment, and the pervasion of British support for a new system which would widen the possibilities of trade and investment. But the change in government did not as yet involve any essential change in the system of land tenure, nor of the primary facts of a kind of race-oriented class structure.

In Brazil no war was necessary: a separate monarchy in Brazil was established in 1815, later turning into an empire, and giving way in due course to a republic in 1889. In Cuba independence from Spain did not arrive till 1888. In the British Caribbean the islands achieved independence only after World War II. In Haiti, however, a slave rebellion established Black rule in 1804. Panama was not created till 1903, mainly as the bread of a sandwich of which the Canal was the filling.

The dominant motif of the anticolonial struggle among the elites of Latin America was liberal, and often this involved some anticlerical sentiment. But mostly the Church still exercised its traditional functions, even if in some countries religious orders were expelled. In a number of constitutions the nominal separation of Church and State was effected. The growth of various forces, such as the influence of Freemasonry, the work of Protestants, positivistic philosophy from Europe, liberal theories of government, and the arrival of large numbers of migrants from Europe, put pressure on the Catholic Church, which remained remarkably conservative up to World War II. Because of population increase, Latin American influence also grew within the Catholic worldwide community.

Protestantism, which was often effective in proselytizing tribal groups, and had its footholds in many new immigrant communities, was sometimes looked on as alien and even as an agent of North American imperialism. There was indeed quite a lot of traditional hostility against the Yankees or Gringos, as they were called, both among the elite—because of aesthetic philosophies stressing the superior culture of the Latin South, such as the philosophy known as Arielism, at one time moderately fashionable—and

among the ordinary populations, because of the perceived exploitation of the masses by the forces of modern capitalism, emanating by the twentieth century chiefly from the United States.

Before World War II the Catholic Action movement, coming from France and Italy, stimulated new concerns for democratic action and service to the poor: a moderate social reformism spread its ideas through the creation of Christian Democratic parties. But many Churchmen wished to see a solidarity between Church and society, harking back to the old days: such dreams were helped by organizations such as Opus Dei, a new clerical and lay movement with extreme right-wing leanings. Such dreams of going back to a harmonious body of Catholic Christians (which may never have existed) were, however, interrupted by Vatican II. After this period there was an explosive period of doctrinal innovation and new social thinking, identified with what is known as Liberation Theology.

## Liberation Theology

This set of ideas was heavily influenced by Marxism. It blended a Marxist analysis of the social situation with the Catholic and Christian values evident in the New Testament. Vatican II had given a great impetus to Biblical scholarship, and the new thinkers saw in the New Testament especially a revolutionary concern for the poor on the part of Christ. They argued that the Church's prime duty was to raise the life of the poor. They were often critical of older attitudes which glossed over present miseries because the faithful could be sure of the joys of heavenly bliss in the life after this one. The movement was thus very critical socially, revolutionary in spirit, concerned with altering the structures of existence, and anticapitalist. It led some priests into actively participating in revolutionary struggle, as in the case of the Sandinista revolution in Nicaragua.

The Liberation Theology movement also emphasized some other things, apart from the analysis of the present condition of the poor of the Third World. They were very keen on a practical approach (they used the Marxist word "praxis" here as a slogan for their commitment to realizing ideas in practice); and they were keen on starting at the grass roots, thus inverting the traditional Church approach, which was from the top down. They wanted to raise the consciousness of the poor (and this often meant the Indians), who too often were imbued with a kind of fatalism which traditional Catholicism did very little to puncture. So it was with "base communities" that the movement realized its ideas—the creation of small communities of lay and clerical people organizing social betterment, Bible-reading and the raising of local consciousness. Over two hundred thousand such communities have been set up in Brazil and elsewhere in the continent.

Liberation Theology has come to have a wide influence beyond the Latin American scene, being of some especial attraction in the Third World and also among those involved in the Church struggle in South Africa. Among the prominent exponents are Gustavo Gutiérrez of Peru, Juan Luis Segundo of

*Opposite*
Revolutionary impulses are important in much of Latin America as is indicated in this mural by Diego Rivera celebrating the Mexican revolution.

Archbishop Romero
assassinated in San
Salvador, March 24,
1980.

Uruguay, Leonardo Boff of Brazil, Hugo Assmann of Costa Rica, and
(among Protestants) José Miguel Bonino of Argentina.

### Protestantism in Latin America

Protestantism has had a spectacular increase during the twentieth century. Its
three roots are, first, migrant Churches in such countries as the Argentine,
Chile, and Brazil, with a large number of German and other European

immigrants; second, more important, Protestant missions especially out of the United States, who have worked both among Catholics and among Indian tribes, where Biblical evangelical preaching has made large inroads; third, spontaneously arising Protestant groups from within Latin America, especially Pentecostals. Pentecostalism has also had some prominence within Catholicism, as elsewhere in the world after Vatican II. There may be as many as eighteen million Protestants in the Latin American region, compared with a few hundred thousand a century ago. But the statistics are hard to find.

The success of Protestant preaching was worrying enough at one time to be put on the agenda for Catholic Bishops' conferences, together with the impact of Freemasonry and other matters: until fairly recently relations between Catholics and Protestants have often been bitter, with Catholics trying to hold on to old monopolies and Protestants often taking a severe evangelical line against Catholic superstitions (as they saw them). The reasons for Protestant success, in Latin America as elsewhere in the Catholic world, are varied. One is that the individualism of Protestant religion makes sense in a capitalist, urban environment. Second, Protestant emphasis on religious experience and conversion is direct, appealing and promising for togetherness, for feeling becomes the glue of new communities. Third, it is natural that people should awake to the essential pluralism of the religions and within the religions of the world. Catholicism can no longer claim to be the sole possibility.

All this is part of an increasing ferment in the Latin American scene. Among Catholics the meeting of bishops at Medellin in 1968 is commonly regarded as a turning point, when the voices which roused the social conscience of the Church were significant and loud, and when the Church seemed to acknowledge the need for new structures both in Christian life and in society. This call, with the attendant Liberation Theology, has made the Latin American Christian scene central to the religious history of the world.

# Religion and Race

## The Churches in the Caribbean Region

The islands of the Caribbean are culturally really a creation of the colonial era. The major part of the indigenous Indian populations in the region was wiped out by disease and oppression. Economically the islands came to depend on plantations, especially sugar, and to work the fields Blacks were imported from Africa. So in differing regions we have peoples of whom a rather small minority are settlers from Europe—Spain, France, Holland, Denmark, and Britain above all. The majority are Blacks; and there is a mixed-race intervening layer of folk. But as we have noted, some colonial powers also later imported Indians and Chinese as indentured laborers. On the mainland the colonial possessions of British Guiana, French Guiana, and Dutch Surinam were important too, and contained Indians too; and similarly with Belize (formerly British Honduras) on the Central American mainland.

Because the island populations were so much a creation of European colonialism, they are predominantly Christian: but there were other influences than settlement and mission at work. For one thing, in one or two areas, notably Barbados, it was for long illegal to try to convert the Blacks. In other areas there were African ideas and rituals mingled in with Catholic practices, as in Haiti. There was a large trend in the British dominated islands for Church of England (for a time established as the official Church) to be interested only in the White settlers, and from the 1800s on the void among the Blacks was largely filled by nonconformist Churches of varying kinds, Baptists, Methodists, and others. In the last twenty years or so the fastest-growing group in the Caribbean has been Pentecostalism, fired in part through fundamentalist American missionaries.

In Cuba, the victory of Fidel Castro (b. 1927) in 1959 led to pressures against religion. By 1980 only about a third of Cubans claimed to be Catholics, and there was a big overlap with the movement known as the Santería. This compares with a large majority claiming to be Catholic during the pre-Castro years. No doubt there is a feeling that certain answers are favored or expected in such polls: and the results reflect the change in ethos and regime. Castro's is the only genuinely successful Marxist regime in the Western hemisphere: though Nicaragua's Sandinista government, dating from 1979, may eventually attain like stability.

### Black Religions in Latin America and the Caribbean

There are a number of religions in the Caribbean which serve to express some Africanness. In some ways the Santería in Cuba (and, since Castro, in various centers in the United States, among exiles) is the most interesting because it has imported so directly so many features of Yoruba religion and Yoruba rites. Its deities are Yoruba, but are also identified with Catholic saints: Shango, god of thunder, becomes St. Barbara; Orunmila, of divination, becomes St. Francis; Obatala is Our Lady of Mercy; Elegba is St. Peter. In this way the two religious traditions are integrated, and the Catholic saints no doubt provide a kind of cover for the other faith, which has persisted thus after the dislocations of forcible removal to the plantations. Similar remarks apply to the father like group of cults known as Shango (from the god) in Trinidad.

Interesting also is a kind of holding together of religious traditions, which however is not syncretistic in the proper sense, as represented by the system known as Winti in Surinam. It may be that because of the predominance of Protestantism, derived in part from Moravian missions, there was less ease in blending traditions. In any case, those who practice Winti most often behave in other contexts as straightforward Christians, whether Protestant or Catholic. Winti conceives the world as being shot through with various spirits and forces—gods of the air and earth and water, presided over by a High God—very much in the classical African way. Various rites both evoke and propitiate the varied gods, with spirit possession being a marked feature of the religion: it deals with everyday affairs including illness, and involves shamanistic cures.

Two forms of spiritism have been powerful in Brazil. One is known as Kardecism, after the French thinker Allan Kardec (1804–69). He propounded a view that there are spirits who are in process of reincarnation, and one can have communication with them through mediums. There is a hierarchy of such spirits, who ultimately derive from God. Happiness and unhappiness are the result of previous actions. The greatest virtue is Christian love, and we should cultivate this and other means to spiritual perfection: we are free agents and can alter our destinies, therefore. The belief-system of Kardecism ruled out miracles and a magical view of the world: for Kardec it was all based on science. His ideas were introduced into Brazil in the 1870s and 1880s and began to attract a large following among the urban middle class. It continued to gain support, despite a Catholic campaign against it in the 1950s.

Kardecism came to have a lot of influence upon an earthier, more symbol-laden movement which started in Rio de Janeiro in the 1920s, the Umbanda religion, a loose, African-based conglomeration of cults led by shamanistic women and men with their own groups. There is a strong Yoruba admixture here also. The groups are especially important in the great and often squalid urban shanty-towns, because they give a sense of belonging. The gods often are identified with Catholic saints, and there is a strong overlap between membership of the Church and of Umbanda.

Before and during World War II the government made attempts to stamp out the cults, but without success. In the period after World War II some blending between Kardecism and Umbanda occurred, because Kardecism provided a good doctrinal and intellectual framework for the cults; while the latter helped to give color and force to an otherwise too polite religion.

A somewhat analogous system to the Santería of Cuba is Haitian Voodoo (so-called: it is a term applied by outsiders). In this belief system and practical way of ritual, Catholicism is not rejected, but used as a framework within which the African gods and spirits (some from Nigeria, others from Benin and Zaire) may be approached to help with the ordinary problems and tribulations of life. The Christian God, the Bondye in Haitian Creole, presides and sends down his angels, the spirits, nearer to human beings on earth: but generally speaking we do not seek for him to do anything. He functions therefore very much as the High God of classical African religion. More immediate concerns are taken to more immediate spirits. Rituals range from the simplicity of lighting candles to animal sacrifices, and in the cities small temples are available. Drumming and singing are designed to bring on spirit-possession, which is an important function, for it serves as a main means of communication between spirits and humans, and enables spirits to participate in the celebrations. In general this religious system was created by slaves out of African materials, supplemented by some of the categories of Catholicism.

All the systems considered here give Black people dignity, in so far as they emphasize African roots. But some others also project connections to the future. Important among these is the Rastafari movement, which had some of its origin in the work of the Jamaican leader Marcus Garvey (1887–1940), in forming the Universal Negro Improvement Association in 1914. The coronation of Haile Selassie in 1930, coinciding too with the miseries of the Depression, helped to stimulate interest in a millennial return to the paradise of Ethiopia, a symbol of the riches of the Black tradition.

Rastafarianism by the early 1950s was strongly anti-White. It saw Whites as inferior to Blacks, thought of the coming of the Blacks to the West Indies as some kind of punishment, looked to the hope of return to Ethiopia, saw Haile Selassie as the living God, and believed that Blacks will soon be able to rule over Whites. Some of these beliefs have been modified: and some externals have been acquired since that time by the Rastafarians, such as the wearing of dreadlocks (which however, in a polite form, have become fashionable in a wider circle, as has the Rastafari music) and the smoking of marijuana. There came to be a greater emphasis on self-help among the Blacks of Jamaica, and less reliance on the actual help of Haile Selassie, especially as he was overthrown in 1974 and died in the following year.

### Problems for South American Small-Scale Groups

In some areas of Latin America—in Nicaragua, for instance; but above all in the Amazon basin—the opening up of the areas to government control or commercial exploitation causes severe distress to the independent groups of Indians still subsisting outside of Latin culture and society. Logging and mining in Amazonia, and its development for pasturing cattle and growing crops, have had a severe impact on the environment of tribal peoples. Also, there are widespread evangelizations by Protestant groups which are changing patterns of life. It is doubtful whether many tribal communities will long survive in the present ways of life. On the other hand many who were long ago loosely integrated into Catholicism, such as the Quechua speakers of the high Andes, retain much of their preconquest culture and religion, but with a Catholic superstructure.

## Reflections on the Latin American and Caribbean Scene

The dynamism of this highly varied region of the world is evident. There remain social problems which are most severe in those countries which have a high number of Indians. But some of the stratification into race-based classes has been overcome. Thus, in Mexico, the Revolution of 1910 harked back to leaders who were themselves Indians, most of all Benito Juárez (1806–72); and it commissioned the great murals of Diego Rivera (1886–1957), which combined a vision of indigenous liberation with Socialism. The Institutional Revolutionary Party (a nice contradiction, some think) has provided Mexico with stability and a secular anticlerical State, despite the Catholicism of most of the population. But poverty remains.

The role of the Catholic Church has bifurcated between its old conservative support for established regimes and elites to the new revolutionary cast depicted by and encouraged through the new Liberation Theology. In many areas, Protestant evangelization is making progress, while Black populations have devised religions which in one way or another link to African roots. In the great republics of the far south, White societies have struggled with political problems and options, but the desire for pluralistic democracy seems stronger than ever after the dreadful killings of the military regime in Argentina in the 1970s and the violence and militarism of contemporary Chile, the Pinochet regime in Chile after 1973.

## Dimensions of Caribbean and Latin Religion

We can perhaps single out some of the most significant items from the different developments as a sampling of the Latin American and Caribbean spirit. In regard to *doctrine*, the most vital contribution has been Liberation Theology; but it may also turn out that Kardecism too will spread, because "Spiritismo" is also well developed among Mexicans and Hispanics in the United States. As to *myth* and the narrative dimension, there is a growing sense of Latin America as having a special part to play in human civilization; and there is the great popularity of Our Lady of Guadalupe, who supplied a mythic missing link between the religion of the conqueror and that of the conquered.

In regard to the *experiential* dimension, there is as elsewhere an emergence of emphasis on Pentecostal experience and the religion of being "born again." We may note, too, the persistence of shamanism at the level of the small-scale societies; and this also wells up in the concern with mediums among the Black religions. The interest in hallucinogens also continues, for instance in the use of coca among Andean Indians and in the employment of marijuana among the Rastafaris. As to the *ritual* dimension, the greatly simplified Catholic rites after Vatican II, and the use of the vernacular languages, represent a great shift away from the older colonial Baroque style. The setting up of "base communities" under the influence of Liberation Theology has revived the use of the Bible as a central element in the *practical* dimension of religion.

As to *ethics*, there is too a growing sense of identification with the poor, as in the preaching of John Paul II, and through the more revolution-oriented aspects of Catholicism. Protestantism imports a more individualistic ethos, which is encouraged too by the growth of capitalism and the beginnings of consumerism in the southern republics and elsewhere. *Organizationally*, there are greater conflicts in some areas between Church and State—latently in Mexico, more overtly in Cuba and Nicaragua—and a general weakening of the authority of the Church in a period of more obvious pluralism; but again, Liberation Theology's concern with the grass roots gives a vivification of Church organization from below.

An Indian waits in line
to greet Pope John
Paul II in Guatemala
City in 1983.

At the *material* level, the gradual diminution of the external signs of
Counter-Reformation Catholicism does not remove the vast church buildings
which are a glory of the Spanish colonial period, brooding over the cities
which the Spaniards above all loved to found, to bring their own version of
Christian civilization, in a highly confident period, to a whole great continent.
It is this Spanish and Portuguese architecture, and that of the dusty towns in
the plains and the Andes, on river sides and by the great oceans, that stands as
the largest testament to the colonial spirit which is now beginning to fade.

CHAPTER

# Some Final Reflections on Global Religion

## The New Forms of Religion

From out of Europe arose two major forms of humanism: one was the liberal pluralistic tradition, the other the Marxist. The Marxist tradition has defined itself for the most part as a rival of traditional religions: it is itself a new political religion, which has become the State orthodoxy in many countries. Pluralistic humanism has, as we have seen, blended with a major kind of Christianity, namely liberal Protestantism and finally at Vatican II with Roman Catholicism. It is nibbling at the edges of Orthodoxy too. This modernist Christianity is not unchallenged, for it has stimulated a backlash in a neofoundationalist or fundamentalist Christianity, which is also powerful. Liberal or modernist Christianity has a crisis of authority, because it erodes the absolutes of both Bible and Papacy. But it has continuity and it is able to talk to modern science, liberal democracy, capitalism, and nationalism as the major forces of the modern world. In regard to nationalism there are some reservations, especially because also the capitalist system has become global and transnational in character. Modernist Christianity is not only critical of nations, but it also seeks to take a prominent part in the curing of some of the evils which in part flowed from colonialism. It is most suited, however, to be the religion of a middle or professional class; and developed countries do tend to expect everyone to move in that direction, within the modern consumerist and democratic condition. The question is as to how far the same process will spread to the so-called Third World.

Modernist Christianity is a new form of the faith. It is very far from the assumptions of the Middle Ages or the ancient world, and far, too, from the early days of the Reformation, though it is part descended from the Reformation. Because the backlash evangelical Christianity involves a self-

Pope John Paul II praying before Our Lady of Peace in Stoczek, Poland, in 1983.

conscious reference to the absolute authority of the Bible, it too is a modern phenomenon. It has great power in mission and other work; but it has problems with gearing into a genuinely modern intellectual worldview, though it fits well with modern Western economic individualism and technical progress.

Liberal Judaism, both Reform and Conservative, is also a modern version of the faith, mindful of ancient roots, but modernist in emphasis. As for Orthodox Judaism, that too has a modern aspect in being also self-conscious in its reaffirmation of the authority of the Torah. But all Jewish forms of religion have also been reshaped in modern times by the foundation of the State of Israel. Even many of the Orthodox, who do not like the sense of forcing God's hand in the restoration of Israel, support either the State or at least the project of living in Israel.

Another religion profoundly affected by modern times has been Hinduism, which has in effect defined itself during the colonial period. Its new Hindu ideology, pioneered by Vivekānanda and Gandhi among others, proved to be a highly effective way of synthesizing ancient roots and modern values; and it played a vital part in the Indian national struggle for independence and for the imposition of a religiously pluralistic and democratic constitution upon the Republic of India.

# Reactions to the West

## Reactions in Asia

There were several ways of dealing with the challenge of modernity during the latter part of the colonial period. The modern Hindu ideology was one of them: of all the Asian countries India perhaps preserved most of her tradition in the transition to the new world. Japan also was very successful in the conservation of many elements of her tradition, by a modernizing strategy which was brilliantly conducted. By first of all turning in on herself and keeping out foreign influence for as long as she could; and then by embracing the necessary Western institutions wholeheartedly, but within a nationalistic framework, she succeeded in reshaping herself to meet the Western colonial powers on equal terms. This of course led her disastrously into World War II, but the mental structures of modernity remained embedded in the nation, and the destruction of her cities and factories, though painful, in fact helped in the processes of remodernizing. Japan's economic success goes with a Buddhist heritage, enriched with various new religious movements, which fits easily into scientific thinking.

Buddhism, indeed, did not have great difficulty in showing its modern power. This was because of the essential congruence of Theravāda and some dominant aspects of the Mahāyāna with scientific thinking; but also Buddhism's emphasis on meditation was revived and proved important to the Western world, especially during the 1960s. In that decade the West first began to feel itself in a global context; and Buddhist and other forms of yoga were a vital ingredient in a revived spirituality. In Buddhist countries in South and Southeast Asia, however, Buddhism combined with nationalism, especially in Sri Lanka and Burma, which took, however, different paths, one of self-isolation and the other of cosmopolitanism.

Southeast Asia got caught up in the violence of the struggles between Marxism and Western capitalism. The result has been that three Buddhist countries, Vietnam, Cambodia, and Laos, have come under Marxist domination, with all that that implies for the free expression of the faith. We saw how in Cambodia the new isolationist ideology of Khieu Sampan and Pol Pot destroyed the middle class and deeply wounded the practice of Buddhism.

If we ask why Marxism made such strides in Asia, the answer lies primarily in China. There the country did not "benefit" from being colonized by a single power. That might have made the struggle for independence a good deal milder. As it was, it had to fight its way to an ideology which would be powerful enough to restore national pride. The Confucian tradition, which can function as a support of modern nationhood, as in South Korea, was too entangled in the old imperial system to be easily geared to the project of creating a modern China. (More recently, though, a purged Confucianism has undergone an overseas revival.) Buddhism was not sufficiently militant within the framework of a national ethos. And Taoism, which had served as a

Chinese regimented health: a consequence of the Maoist revolution.

revolutionary ideology in uprisings and rebellions against central government, was not ready with a modern version which could rally the Chinese. Moreover, the old system of China had been a threefold religion, which divided its theoreticians though not its practitioners. The obstacles to a religiously based nationalism were too great in China. Liberalism demanded a better-developed middle class. It was therefore necessary for China to reach out for a revolutionary, anticolonial ideology from the West, and to adapt it through the writings and praxis of Mao. This was highly successful up to the point of independence and the initial restructuring of Chinese society; but since that time China has been somewhat floundering. Can one combine Maoism and a modern, technically adequate and economically potent society?

Because Marxism is antireligious, the effects of this new ideology on China and especially upon Tibet were most serious. There has been great oppression of Buddhism and other religious traditions. The flight of the Dalai Lama to the West has helped to reinforce the potency of the Buddhist movement in the West, but signalizes the break-up of the old Tibetan system.

552

We can see the victory of the Bolshevik revolution also in the context of the spread of modern Western institutions and ideas. The weakness of Russia was exposed by World War I. Its problems lay in part with its very late emergence out of feudalism, with the liberation of the serfs only occurring in the second half of the nineteenth century. In part, its problems lay in an excessive centralization and an unreformed religious heritage. The conservatism and subservience of the Orthodox Church were to some degree mitigated by the flowering of Orthodox intellectuals such as Dostoyevsky. But nationalism was not so sympathetic to the liberalism that might have guided Russia in a different direction. It modernized itself, as did China, through a version of Marxism.

But Marxism left in place the old Russian empire: because it had a revolutionary and anticolonial ideology in Marxism-Leninism it was easy to think that the Soviet Union is not, after all, modeled on the old colonial empires. It has tried to resolve the nationality problem by dividing folklore and language, as aspects of culture, from religions, and favoring one while repressing the other.

## Reactions in the Islamic World

The impact of the West on Islam led to several different reactions. One was the Turkish: simply to reject Islam, and to reform society on a totally Western model, according to the precepts of secular democracy, with an antireligious bent. Another was to adopt some form of Socialism, without suppressing religion or reining it back particularly, but essentially Westernizing within a nationalist framework: we see this formula in Ba'ath socialism in Syria and Iraq. In Afghanistan and South Yemen, Marxist regimes have come in. In all these cases we may look on the reaction as essentially Western in style and non-Islamic.

Some other countries have tried to reconstruct religion within a State framework by pursuing a version of modernism, but with Salafiya overtones, claiming that the new ideology is after all faithful to the earliest Islam. This is the typical North African reaction. It was foreshadowed in modernist Islam as expounded by 'Abduh, and applied in Egypt and elsewhere. Another form of reaction is a more neofoundationalist one, which strives to resurrect the purity of early Islam through the institutionalization of Islamic law: most notably through the Wahhabi movement in Saudi Arabia, but also in a weaker form in Islamic revivalism in Pakistan and the Sudan. Such moves have a problem with religious pluralism: the persecution of the Ahmadiya in Pakistan and of Baha'i in Iran, and the civil war in the Sudan, all reflect this. The most serious revivalist version of Islam in recent times, because it incorporates a well-thought-out ideology, is the Iranian revolution, which works with the notion of Islamic law within the framework of a partly democratic republican system with theocratic attributes.

Generally speaking, Islam is resistant to Marxism because of its atheism. In modern times, in trying to clean up its fabric in order to deal with the challenge of the West it has tended to reject Sufism. But it is mainly through the Sufi orders that Islam has survived so well in the Soviet Union, where it is remarkably adhesive in Central Asia.

The problem of pluralism cannot go away in Indonesia. Javanese Hinduism also contains strands of thinking which have proved vital in today's post-colonial Indonesian society. The ideology of *Pancasila* permits a pluralism of religious practice, on the theory that all religions really point to the same God. Many Muslims resent this as too compromising, but it has provided a viable ideology for ruling so complex a nation.

In general there is, then, a divide between liberal or modernist Islam and revivalism in the shape of neofoundationalist forces. The latter are growing round the world at the moment, as Islam digests further its experience within a global framework. However, there are many countries, including Western ones, where Islam is an important minority, and Islam has to live in such circumstances and find a viable mode of operating. Modernism seems to be attractive in this context.

### The Small-Scale Peoples and Christianity

In the modern period, it has been chiefly Christianity which has spread among the small-scale societies of Africa, among the Aborigines and Polynesians, Melanesians, and others of the Pacific regions, and among tribal folk who exist in many pockets of North and South America and elsewhere. However, though Christianity has transformed the culture of many of these peoples, there are about two hundred and fifty million members of such small-scale societies in the world who maintain their traditions or belong to new religious movements which lie beyond the margins of mainstream Christianity.

The experience of indigenous religions and cultures is that they often get picked off one by one, because they are individually too weak to stand up to the massive cultural, religious, and economic forces which impinge on them. So there are tendencies towards regional thinking, often crossing the borders between Christian and non-Christian cultures. So we see in the modern period the growth of pan-Africanism, of pan-Indian religion among the Native Americans, some political coalescence among the Aborigines in Australia, and the formation of the idea of the Pacific Way. Such regional notions are vital to the survival of such cultures.

It may be that in due course the whole world's tribal groups will form some sort of alliance, to argue for an ideology of the unity of close-to-Nature religions, and for the recognition that within a general framework of piety every group can look most fruitfully to its own tradition for guidance. But such a move, by making small-scale religions self-conscious, would already have changed them; and in any case the conditions of modern life—including methods of agriculture and fishing—will have altered the concepts used in ritual and in shamanism.

# Religion and Global Communications

## The Existence of Multiple Diasporas

There has been great migration during the colonial and postcolonial period, not merely to countries which have long been used to immigration, such as the United States and Australia, but also to other countries, such as the major European ones, which have not. There has also been the transfer of large numbers of Blacks to the New World, and Indian and Chinese migrant worlds beyond the shores of their homelands. So in much of the globe there are culturally plural communities. They have to find a way of living together, and the cultural diversity often causes conflicts. Racial and ethnic riots are experienced in many cities of the world: Chicago, Boston, Durban, London, Karachi, Ahmedabad, and Auckland, to name a few. Moreover, where minority aspirations are not met there may be civil wars, as in Cyprus, Sri Lanka, the Philippines, Northern Ireland, again to name only a few. This remains one of the most important issues in the world today, how to cater for minority rights—or occasionally, as in South Africa, for majority rights.

But diasporas have other effects. First, in modern conditions there is good communication across the globe among people of a particular religious tradition—between Hindus in South Africa and India, and in Fiji and India, and so forth; between Parsis in Hong Kong and Bombay; between Sikhs in Toronto and the Punjab; between Muslims in Indonesia, Arabia, New York and Egypt; between Rastafaris in Jamaica and London; and between Spiritists in Mexico and Chicago. Such good communications tend to unify the

Some Tibetan Buddhist monks at their makeshift temple near Greenham Common, site of a prolonged demonstration against nuclear weapons at an American base in Britain.

religious traditions more (consider the case of the Nation of Islam and its assimilation to mainstream Islam, for instance). It also often means that new resources are put at the disposal of diasporas—as with Saudi grants for mosque-building in Sri Lanka—or conversely flow from the outlying populations towards the center, as when propaganda and money for a Sikh independent State is sent from Canada to India.

All this invigorates religious and national movements. It also means that what many scholars have been denying has become actual. Many modern historians of religion wish to deny that there is some one thing called Hinduism or Buddhism; they think that these are at best labels for a whole slew of differing religious movements, cults, beliefs and so on. But modern conditions have made religions more self-consciously global in character. They have increased a degree of homogenization through mutual contact, and have also bred ecumenical movements which are quite influential in the exchange of ideas and mutual feelings of support. So though Buddhism may not quite have existed before, it does now; and the same for all the other religions. Self-definition is becoming the order of the day.

## New Religions and Blends

The interactions between traditions have spurred the growth of new religious traditions which incorporate elements from differing worldviews. Moreover, we have noted how old religions are in new places not just because of the migration of traditional members—say Sri Lankans in California—but because of the conversion of people who have not traditionally belonged, such as White American Protestants who become Hare Krishna followers, or Jews

Western devotees of Krishna in the Hare Krishna movement.

The Gion Matsuri Shinto festival at Kyoto. A figure dressed as the goddess Amaterasu is paraded in the street.

Buddhist monks performing a ceremonial for the installation of a relic at a peace temple in Battersea Park, London.

who become Zen Buddhists, or Scots who convert to Islam. Since the 1960s there has in the West been a great mingling of themes within religious and secular traditions. One can expect this to go on. Thus there simultaneously is some trend in the global context towards homogeneity, but there is also great plurality in the regions of experimenting with new religious ideas and practices. In general, most societies have—through migrations, the relaxing of Church or other religious establishment ties, new religions, and the blending and exchange of ideas and practices—seen a great increase in pluralism.

*Opposite* Sikhs at the dedication of a temple in Kenya.

## A Single Religion?

There are those who predict that with a single global system in the making we can look forward to a single federal religion based on an ideology like that of Vivekānanda. It is worth repeating at this point that we have to deal not just with religions but more broadly with worldviews, including Marxism and scientific humanism. These are in differing degrees hostile to religion and incorporate a vision of human progress not unlike that of Auguste Comte (1798–1857), who saw atheism as a higher stage beyond polytheism and monotheism. His general view has been influential in a number of continents, notably in Latin America and in Europe. So for those who reject religion, atheism is the higher and predestined form of belief. And it is true that especially among intellectuals in Western countries atheism is a strong option, and it is of course *de rigueur* among Marxists in the Eastern bloc countries, and where the ideology is the "established religion."

And even if we look among traditional religions there are obvious obstacles to the theme of unity. For one thing many conservatives in reacting against modernism react too against a soft view of other faiths. This is especially true among scriptural conservatives in the three great Western religions, but can be paralleled elsewhere. For another thing, it is quite hard to make the conceptual adjustments necessary to fit *bhakti* Hinduism and Theravādin meditation into the same framework, let alone Christian theism and Jain nontheism. But there are those, as we have seen, who have managed to satisfy themselves as to the transcendental unity of all religions, and it is an attractive idea: it means that human beings are divided by externals and not by essentials. It is true that Buddhists and Sufis can find a place to talk, as can devotionalists from the Pure Land and Methodism. There may not be absolute unity, but there are without doubt overlaps of theme and experience in the religions.

In general, then, it is unlikely that a real unity of worldviews can be found, except as a minority view. There will foreseeably be a degree of struggle and conflict between worldviews, though a majority of societies may in time come to opt for a pluralistic mode of letting different worldviews live together. In a way this will reflect the nature of world society as a whole. Even if some religion or ideology is dominant and exclusive in one or more countries, it will still turn out to be in the minority on a worldwide scale. The major religions will have to get used to this thought, even if they often start from a central position in the home culture and view that as the norm for the whole world.

But though a single religion or worldview for a single world is unlikely, and there will remain the differing commitments of human beings, a loose framework of thinking may become universal: one which is committed to scientific and technological development, transnational economic arrangements, and easy travel and communication between different parts of our planet. Around this loose framework the differing value systems will need to fit, though each will in some ways transcend that network of ideas and the structures of global action.

## Worldview Analysis and the Future of Education

The understanding of differing worldviews, including religious ones, ought in these circumstances to become an integral part of human education, so that neighbors can understand neighbors' ideas and practices. This book, in trying to set forth the nature and history of religious and other beliefs, is doing just a little to help this process. But, of course, to achieve such a pluralistic education you need to have a relatively open society; so there is a political edge even to the study of religions.

Such education may be the more important because of the typical breakdown of authority in worldviews. We have noted the gradual protestantizing of the Roman Catholic tradition. This is only one among a number of cases where the obvious presence of alternative modes of interpreting the world is bound to have a disturbing effect, in presenting choices where there were no choices before. It is not an easy world in which there is so much choice of an uncertainty about values. It is a situation, though, which we cannot get out of: its impact is likely to grow rather than to diminish.

The net effect of pluralism is that each group will need to present its own worldview as a vision. Is such a vision appealing? To whom does it appeal? Does the appeal enrich the possibilities of human living? The educated person, to begin to think about these questions, will need to feel for and know something about alternative religions and worldviews. We live at an exciting time when all the worldviews of the world are in motion against one another, throwing forth new possibilities of living and new combinations of symbols and living themes.

So long as humans are brought up in different paths, so they will see the world differently, and for each path some things will seem natural and right and others not. But the paths cross. We can benefit from that. Social justice, which Marxists struggle for; human freedom, which liberals emphasize; love of God and fellow humans, which Christianity preaches; brotherhood, which Islam promotes; calm and mysticism, which go with Buddhism; devotion and pluralism, which Hinduism points to; harmony with nature, which Taoism commends; the cultivation of interpersonal behavior, which is a lesson from Confucianism; holism in life, which we find in Africa; finding meaning through suffering, which Judaism has had to emphasize; the importance of inner sincerity, which we find among the Sikhs: these and many other spiritual and moral values are not of course mutually incompatible. In that respect, though we may not achieve a global religion, we may achieve a global civilization in which values from the great traditions are woven together in a glittering net. Perhaps it will turn out like the jewel net of Indra, of which Hua-yen so eloquently speaks: each stone reflecting every other.

East comes West: a child practicing a form of
Indian yoga in America.

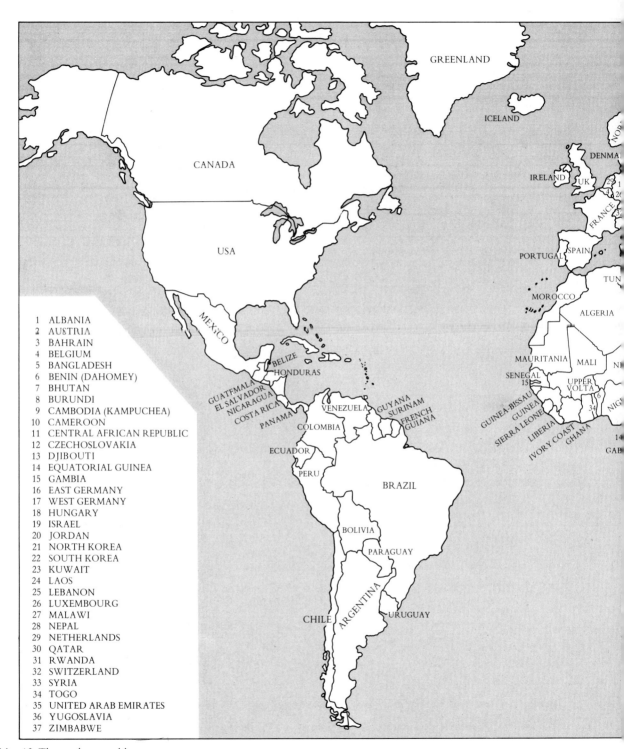

GREENLAND

ICELAND

CANADA

NOR

DENMA

IRELAND    UK    29
                        26
USA
                                    FRANCE

PORTUGAL   SPAIN

                        TUN
MOROCCO
              ALGERIA

MEXICO                              MAURITANIA    MALI    N

                                    SENEGAL
                                    15    UPPER
                        BELIZE       GUINEA-BISSAU   VOLTA
                    HONDURAS                    6
GUATEMALA                                GUINEA   34
EL SALVADOR                          SIERRA LEONE      NIG
NICARAGUA        VENEZUELA   GUYANA          LIBERIA
    COSTA RICA               SURINAM        IVORY COAST
        PANAMA          COLOMBIA   FRENCH      GHANA   GAB
                                GUIANA              14
            ECUADOR

            PERU
                        BRAZIL

                    BOLIVIA

                        PARAGUAY

                    ARGENTINA
        CHILE           URUGUAY

1   ALBANIA
2   AUSTRIA
3   BAHRAIN
4   BELGIUM
5   BANGLADESH
6   BENIN (DAHOMEY)
7   BHUTAN
8   BURUNDI
9   CAMBODIA (KAMPUCHEA)
10  CAMEROON
11  CENTRAL AFRICAN REPUBLIC
12  CZECHOSLOVAKIA
13  DJIBOUTI
14  EQUATORIAL GUINEA
15  GAMBIA
16  EAST GERMANY
17  WEST GERMANY
18  HUNGARY
19  ISRAEL
20  JORDAN
21  NORTH KOREA
22  SOUTH KOREA
23  KUWAIT
24  LAOS
25  LEBANON
26  LUXEMBOURG
27  MALAWI
28  NEPAL
29  NETHERLANDS
30  QATAR
31  RWANDA
32  SWITZERLAND
33  SYRIA
34  TOGO
35  UNITED ARAB EMIRATES
36  YUGOSLAVIA
37  ZIMBABWE

Map 13  The modern world

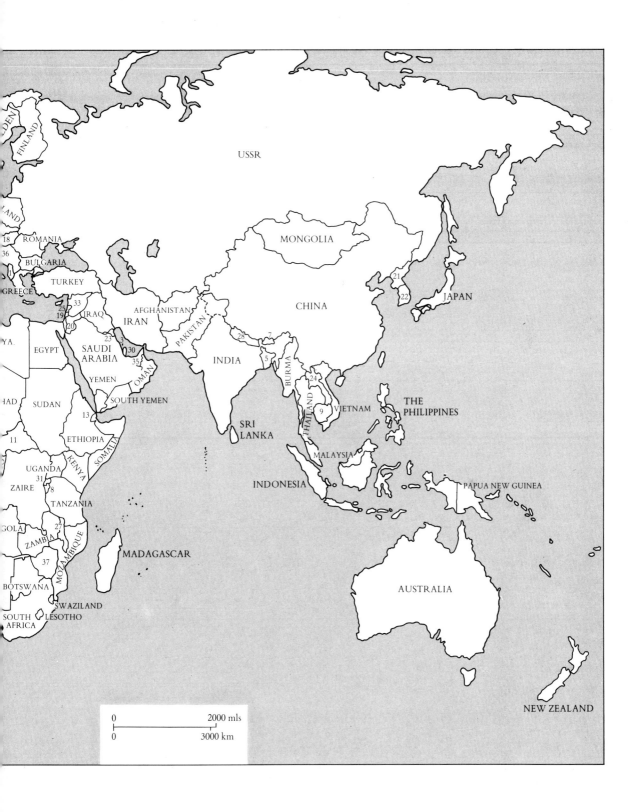

USSR

FINLAND

18 ROMANIA
36
BULGARIA
1
GREECE

TURKEY

MONGOLIA

25 33
19 IRAQ
20

AFGHANISTAN

CHINA

21

22 JAPAN

EGYPT

SAUDI
ARABIA

23 3
30
35 OMAN

YEMEN

SOUTH YEMEN

13

HAD

SUDAN

11

ETHIOPIA

UGANDA
31
ZAIRE 8

KENYA

SOMALIA

TANZANIA

27

GOLA
ZAMBIA
37

MOZAMBIQUE

BOTSWANA

SWAZILAND
SOUTH LESOTHO
AFRICA

IRAN

PAKISTAN

INDIA

28

7

5

BURMA

SRI
LANKA

24

THAILAND

9

VIETNAM

MALAYSIA

THE
PHILIPPINES

INDONESIA

PAPUA NEW GUINEA

MADAGASCAR

AUSTRALIA

NEW ZEALAND

0                    2000 mls
0                    3000 km

# Bibliography

Mircea Eliade, ed., *The Encyclopedia of Religion*, 15 vols., N.Y., 1987
E. E. Evans–Pritchard, *Theories of Primitive Religion*, Oxford, 1965
John R. Hinnells, ed., *A Handbook of Living Religions*, Baltimore, 1985
Rudolf Otto, *The Idea of the Holy*, London, 1950
E. G. Parrinder, *Worship in the World's Religions*, London, 1961
Eric J. Sharpe, *Comparative Religion — A History*, London, 1976
Ninian Smart, *The Religious Experience of Mankind*, 3rd edn., N.Y., 1984
Ninian Smart and Richard Hecht, eds., *Sacred Texts of the World*, London, 1982
Ninian Smart, *Worldviews*, N.Y., 1983
G. van der Leeuw, *Religion in Essence and Manifestation*, Princeton, 1987
R. J. Z. Werblowsky, *Beyond Tradition and Modernity: Changing Religions in a Changing World*, London, 1976
R. C. Zaehner, ed., *Concise Encyclopedia of Living Faiths*, London, 2nd edn., 1971

## Earliest Religion
E. O. James, *The Beginnings of Religion*, Westport, Conn., 1973
Johannes Maringer, *The Gods of Prehistoric Man*, N.Y., 1960
Alexander Marshack, *The Roots of Civilization*, N.Y., 1972
Elizabeth Shee Twohig, *The Megalithic Art of Western Europe*, Oxford, 1981

## South Asia
A. L. Basham, *The Wonder That Was India*, London, 1971
E. O. Cole and P. S. Sambhi, *The Sikh Tradition*, London, 1978
Edward Conze, *Buddhism: Its Essence and Development*, N.Y., 1984
Cromwell Crawford, ed., *In Search of Hinduism*, N.Y., 1986
S. N. Dasgupta, *A History of Indian Philosophy*, 5 vols., Delhi, 1976
Louis Dumont, *Homo Hierarchicus*, Chicago, 1970
Richard Gombrich, *Theravada Buddhism*, London, 1988
Mircea Eliade, *Yoga: Immortality and Freedom*, 2nd ed., Princeton, 1969
Friedhelm Hardy, *Viraha Bhakti*, London, 1981
P. S. Jaini, *The Jaina Path of Purification*, Berkeley, 1979
Winston L. King, *Buddhist Meditation*, Philadelphia, 1980
Wendy Doniger O'Flaherty, ed., *Karma and Rebirth in Classical Indian Traditions*, Berkeley, 1980
Trevor Ling, *The Buddha*, London, 1978
Walpola Rahula, *What the Buddha Taught*, N.Y., 1962
Giuseppe Tucci, *The Religions of Tibet*, Berkeley, 1980
Ninian Smart, *Doctrine and Argument in Indian Philosophy*, London, 1964
Benjamin Walker, *Hindu World*, 2 vols., London, 1968
A. K. Warder, *Indian Buddhism*, Delhi, 1970
R. C. Zaehner, *Hinduism*, N.Y., 1966
Heinrich Zimmer, *Myths and Symbols in Indian Art and Civilization*, Princeton, 1972

### China and Korea
D. Bodde, *Festivals in Classical China*, Princeton, 1975
Kenneth Ch'en, *Buddhism in China*, Princeton, 1973
F. H. Cook, *Hua–yen Buddhism*, Philadelphia, 1977
Theodore de Bary and JaHyun Kim Maboush, editors, *The Rise of Neo-Confucianism in Korea*, N.Y., 1985
Stuart R. Schram, *The Political Thought of Mao Tse–tung*, rev. edn., N.Y., 1969
D. Howard Smith, *Chinese Religions*, N.Y., 1968
D. Howard Smith, *Confucius*, N.Y., 1973
L. C. Thompson, *Chinese Religion: An Interpretation*, 3rd edn., Encino, Ca., 1976
Holmes Welch, *The Practice of Chinese Buddhism*, N.Y., 1967
Holmes Welch and Anna Siedel, eds., *Facets of Taoism: Essays in Chinese Religion*, New Haven, 1979
Feng Yu–lan, *A History of Chinese Philosophy*, 2 vols., Princeton, 1952-3

### Japan
H. Dumoulin, *History of Zen Buddhism*, N.Y., 1965
H. Byron Earhart, *Japanese Religion*, 3rd edn., Belmont, Ca., 1982
Raymond J. Hammer, *Japan's Religious Ferment*, London, 1957
S. Murakami, *Japanese Religion in the Modern Century*, Tokyo, 1980
D. T. Suzuki, *Shin Buddhism*, N.Y., 1970

### South East Asia
Georges Coedes, *The Indianized States of Southeast Asia*, Canberra, 1968
Clifford Geertz, *The Religion of Java*, Glencoe, Ill, 1960
Melford E. Spiro, *Burmese Supernaturalism*, 2nd edn., Philadelphia, 1978
Donald Swearer, *Buddhism and Society in Southeast Asia*, Chambersburg, Penna., 1981
Keith W. Taylor, *The Birth of Vietnam*, Berkeley, 1983

### Oceania and Australasia
Mircea Eliade, *Australian Religions: An Introduction*, Ithaca, N.Y., 1973
Peter Lawrence and M. J. Meggitt, eds., *Gods, Ghosts and Men in Melanesia*, Melbourne, 1965
Roslyn Poignant, *Oceanic Mythology: Myths of Polynesia, Micronesia, Melanesia, Australia*, London, 1967
Jean Smith, *Tapu Removal in Maori Religion*, Wellington, 1976

### Indigenous American Religions
Walter H. Capps, ed., *Seeing with a Native Eye*, N.Y., 1976
Ake Hultkrantz, *The Religions of the North American Indians*, Berkeley, 1979
Walter Krickeberg, et al, *Pre-Columbian American Religions*, N.Y., 1968
J. H. Steward, ed., *Handbook of South American Indians*, vol. 1, Washington, D.C., 1949

### Ancient Near East
W. F. Albright, *From the Stone Age to Christianity*, Baltimore, 1958
J. Gray, *Near Eastern Mythology*, London, 1969
S. N. Kramer, *History Begins at Sumer*, N.Y., 1963
S. Morena, *Egyptian Religion*, N.Y., 1973

### Persia and Central Asia
Mircea Eliade, *Shamanism*, Princeton, 1965
John R. Hinnells, *Persian Mythology*, N.Y., 1971
John R. Hinnells, *Zoroastrianism and the Parsees*, London, 1981
Geo Widengren, *Mani and Manicheism*, N.Y., 1965
R. C. Zaehner, *The Dawn and Twilight of Zoroastrianism*, N.Y., 1961

### The Hellenistic World and Northern Europe
Peter Brown, *The Making of Late Antiquity*, Cambridge, Mass., 1979
Hilda Davidson, *Gods and Myths of Northern Europe*, Baltimore, 1964
E. R. Dodd, *Pagan and Christian in an Age of Anxiety*, N.Y., 1970
G. S. Kirk, *The Nature of Greek Myths*, N.Y., 1975
M. P. Nilsson, *A History of Greek Religion*, N.Y., 1964
A. D. Nock, *Conversion*, N.Y., 1961
A. and B. Rees, *Celtic Heritage*, London, 1975
H. J. Rose, *Ancient Roman Religion*, N.Y., 1948
Kyrosslava T. Znayenko, *The Gods of the Ancient Slaves*, Columbus, Ohio, 1980

## Judaism

Joseph Blau, *Modern Varieties of Judaism*, N.Y., 1966
E. Kedourie, ed., *The Jewish World*, N.Y., 1979
C. G. Montefiore and H. Loewe, eds., *A Rabbinic Anthology*, new edn., N.Y., 1974
J. Neusner, *Early Rabbinic Judaism*, Leiden, 1975
H. Rabinowicz, *The World of Hasidism*, Hartford, Conn., 1970
D. Rudavsky, *Modern Jewish Religious Movements*, 3rd edn., N.Y., 1979
G. G. Sholem, *Major Trends in Jewish Mysticism*, N.Y., 1961
S. Singer (tr.) *The Authorized Daily Prayer Book*, 2nd edn., London, 1968
Alan Unterman, *Jews: Their Religious Beliefs and Practices*, Boston, 1981
J. Weingreen, *From Bible to Mishna*, N.Y., 1976

## Christianity

Catherine Albanese, *America: Religion and Religions*, Belmont, Ca., 1981
A. S. Atiya, *A History of Eastern Christianity*, N.Y., 1970
D. B. Barrett, ed., *World Christian Encyclopedia*, Nairobi, 1982
Peter Brown, *Augustine of Hippo: A Biography*, Berkeley, 1967
Owen Chadwick, *The Popes and European Revolution*, N.Y., 1981
C. H. Dodd, *The Founder of Christianity*, N.Y., 1970
R. S. Ellwood, *Religious and Spiritual Groups in Modern America*, Englewood Cliffs, N.J., 1973
W. H. C. Frend, *The Early Church*, Philadelphia, 1966
W. J. Hollenberger, *The Pentecostals*, London, 1972
Paul Johnson, *A History of Christianity*, N.Y., 1976
C. Lane *Christian Religion in the Soviet Union*, N.Y., 1979
J. N. D. Kelly, *Early Church Doctrines*, N.Y., 1978
Y. Meyendorff, *Byzantine Theology*, 2nd edn., 1978
Timothy Ware, *The Orthodox Church*, Baltimore, 1980

## Islam

Clifford Geertz, *Islam Observed*, New Haven, Conn., 1968
Ernest Gollner, *Muslim Society*, Cambridge, 1981
S. Hussain M. Jagri, *Origins and Early Development of Shi'a Islam*, London, 1979
Bernard Lewis, *The Emergence of Modern Turkey*, London, 1963
Richard C. Martin, *Islam: A Cultural Perspective*, Englewood Cliffs, N.J., 1982.
Marmaduke M. Pickthall, *The Meaning of the Glorious Koran*, N.Y., 1930
Fazlur Rahman, *Islam*, 2nd edn., Chicago, 1979
Joseph Schacht, *An Introduction to Islamic Law*, Oxford, 1974
Anne–Marie Schimmel, *Mystical Dimensions of Islam*, Chapel Hill, N.C., 1975
Wilfred C. Smith, *Islam in Modern History*, Princeton, 1957
H. Montgomery Watt, *Muhammad: Prophet and Statesman*, London, 1974

## African Religions

Roger Bastide, *The African Religions of Brazil*, Baltimore, 1978
Adrian Hastings, *A History of African Christianity*, 1950–1975, N.Y., 1979
J. S. Mbiti, *Concepts of God in Africa*, N.Y., 1970
E. G. Parrinder, *African Traditional Religion*, 3rd edn., London, 1979
Benjamin C. Ray, *African Religions*, N.Y., 1976
H. W. Turner, *Religious Innovations in Africa*, Boston, 1980
E. M. Zuesse, *Ritual Cosmos: The Sanctification of Life in African Religions*, Athens, Ohio, 1979

## Secular Worldviews

Frederick Copleston, *A History of Philosophy*, Vol. VIII, London, 1966
Lescek Kolskowski, *Main Currents of Marxism*, 3 vols., Oxford, 1978–1981
John Macquarrie, *Twentieth Century Religious Thought*, 2nd edn., N.Y., 1981
David Martin, *A General Theory of Secularization*, San Francisco, 1979
Peter Merkl and Ninian Smart, eds., *Religion and Politics in the Modern World*, N.Y., 1984
David Roberts, *Existentialism and Religious Belief*, N.Y., 1960

# Credits

The author, publishers and John Calmann and King Ltd wish to thank the following institutions and individuals who have provided photographic material for use in this book:

**Colour illustrations**
65 G. Bauer/Barbara Heller Archive; 66, 117, 136 Victoria and Albert Museum/Michael Holford; 83, 135, 557 (top) M. Macintyre/Alan Hutchinson Library; 84 (bottom) National Gallery of Prague, W. Forman/Barbara Heller Archive; 84 (top), 293 British Library/Michael Holford; 118 (l.) Wellcome Musuem/Michael Holford; 118 (r.) British Museum; 153, 383, 435, 436, 485 Douglas Dickens; 154 G. Clyde/Michael Holford; 171, 207 (bottom) W. Forman/Barbara Heller Archive; 172 A. Singer/Alan Hutchison; 189, 208, 249 Michael Holford; 190 Museum für Völkerkunde, Basel/W. Forman/Barbara Heller Archive; 207 (top), 312 (top), 417 (bottom), 486, 503, 521 (top and bottom), 557 (bottom), 558 Alan Hutchison Library; 250 British Library/Fotomas Index; 251 (top) Bibliothèque Nationale, Paris/Sonia Halliday; 251 (bottom) Bibliothèque Nationale, Paris/S. Corr; 252 Sonia Halliday; 294, 539 Barnaby's Picture Library; 311 (top) Wallace Collection, London; 311 (bottom) Museum of Mankind, London/Michael Holford; 312 (bottom), 418 S. Errington/Alan Hutchison Library; 337 The Toledo Museum of Art, Toledo, Ohio; Gift of Edward Drummond Libbey; 340 Kunsthistorisches Museum, Vienna; 365 Enrico Ferorelli/DOT/Colorific!; 366 David Burnett/ Contact Press Images/Colorific!; 384 Ann and Bury Peerless; 417 (top) P. Goycolea/Alan Hutchison Library; 504 David King Collection; 522, 540 Tony Morrison/South American Pictures.

**Black-and-white illustrations**
FRONTISPIECE E. T. Archive
INTRODUCTION
12 Novosti Press Agency; 14 Alan Hutchison Library; 15, 20 Victoria and Albert Museum; 16 Sarnath Museum/JCK Archive; 18 John Topham Library; 19 Popperfoto; 22 I.W.M./Robert Hunt Library.

CHAPTER 1
32, 34 JCK Archive; 37 Institut für Urgeschichte Universität Tübingen; 38 Mansell Collection; 40 Jerico Excavation Fund/JCK Archive

CHAPTER 2
46, 56, 69, 86 (l. and r.) Douglas Dickens; 47 Musee Guimet, Paris; W. Forman/Barbara Heller Archive; 60 Freer Gallery of Art, Washington/JCK Archive; 70, 87, 90, 94, 101 Victoria and Albert Museum; 72 Alan Hutchison Library; 78 Ann and Bury Peerless; 87 (r.) W. Forman/Barbara Heller Archive; 102 Rietburg Museum, Zurich.

CHAPTER 3
107, 116, 123 Victoria and Albert Museum; 108 John Topham Library; 113 Mansell Collection; 119 Barnaby's Picture Library.

CHAPTER 4
132 P. Montagnon/Alan Hutchison Library; 134, 147 Douglas Dickens; 140, 157, 158 Barnaby's Picture Library; 143 John Topham Picture Library; 145 Robert Hunt Library.

CHAPTER 5
152 Douglas Dickens; 157, 158 Barnaby's Picture Library.

CHAPTER 6
165, 168 Museum of Mankind, London; 168 Alan Hutchison Library; 175 Australian News and
Information Bureau.

CHAPTER 7
180 Rietburg Museum, Zurich Collection: von der Heydt; 181 British Museum/Mansell Collection;
184 Harvard University Museum; 184 (top) Douglas Dickens; 187 Photo James Mooney/Smithsonian
Institution; National Anthropological Archives; 192 John Topham Library/JCK Archive.

CHAPTER 8
194, 198 Mansell Collection; 200 W. Forman/Barbara Heller Archive; 202 Alan Hutchison Library;
203 Giraudon/Mansell Collection; 203 British Library/Mansell Collection.

CHAPTER 9
218 Edinburgh University Library; 220 Douglas Dickens.

CHAPTER 10
230 Mansell Collection; 235 Ronald Sheridan Library; 236 London Museum/Mansell Collection; 240,
244 Anderson/Mansell Collection; 241 JCK Archive; 243 Pont. Comm. di Arch. Sacra, Rome.

CHAPTER 11
248 Alinari/Mansell Collection; 257 JCK Archive; 259, 266 Mansell Collection; 260 Victoria and
Albert Museum; 267 N. D. McKenna/Alan Hutchison Library; 269, 270 JCK Archive; 272 British
Library/Mansell Collection.

CHAPTER 12
283 (l. and r.) Victoria and Albert Museum.

CHAPTER 13
299 Black Star/Robert Hunt Library; 304 John Topham Library; 305 W. Forman/Barbara Heller
Archive; 307 J. Highet/Alan Hutchison Library; 309 Barnaby's Picture Library.

CHAPTER 14
314 Anderson/Mansell Collection; 317, 327, 335, 342 Mansell Collection; 321, 322, 332, 343 Fotomas
Index; 328 Rijksmuseum, Amsterdam; 345 Popperfoto.

CHAPTER 15
355 Fotomas Index; 357 Mansell Collection; 359 Barnaby's Picture Library; 369, 374 John Topham
Library; 379 Popperfoto.

CHAPTER 16
386 Victoria and Albert Museum; 383 Ann and Bury Peerless; 401 Popperfoto; 403 John Topham
Library; 407, 410, 415 Douglas Dickens; 413 Barnaby's Picture Library.

CHAPTER 17
425, 428 Alan Hutchison Library; 429 Douglas Dickens; 433, 435 John Topham Library.

CHAPTER 18
443, 447 Popperfoto; 445 Robert Hunt Library; 449 Black Star/Robert Hunt Library.

CHAPTER 19
453 Mansell Collection; 455, 462 Barnaby's Picture Library; 464, 465 John Topham Library.

CHAPTER 20
474, 488 Barnaby's Picture Library; 475, 478 Popperfoto; 477 Black Star/Robert Hunt Library; 484
Mohammed Amin/Camerapix.

CHAPTER 21
491 John Topham Library; 494 National Museum of New Zealand; 497 Rijksmuseum voor Volken-
Kunde, Leiden/W. Forman/Barbara Heller Archive; 498 Black Star/Robert Hunt Library.

CHAPTER 22
500, 511 David King Collection; 505, 512 John Topham Library; 508 Popperfoto.

CHAPTER 23
519, 523 John Topham Library; 526, 528 Popperfoto; 530 Black Star/Robert Hunt Library.

CHAPTER 24
535 Barnaby's Picture Library; 542 Popperfoto; 548 John Topham Library.

CHAPTER 25
550, 555 John Topham Library; 552 Alan Hutchison Library; 556 Barnaby's Picture Library; 561
J. Highet/Alan Hutchison Library.

# Index

572

574

Ugarit 201, 202, *203*
Ulfilas 256
'Umar 285
'Umayyad dynasties, 285, 288
Umbanda religion 545
*Umma* 283, 284
Unitarianism 358
United Buddhist Association 446
Upanishads 44, 56, 67, 72–4
Urban II, Pope *251*
'Uthman 285

Vairocana, Buddha 91, 137
Vaisnavas 71, 87
Vajrayāna, the 57, 91
Vanuatu Island 161, 490
Vardhamāna *see* Mahāvīra
Varuna 54
Vasubandhu 82
Vatican Councils: I 344; II 345,
   351, 371, 372, 527, 531, 541
Vedānta 88
Vedānta Society 394
Vedas, the 46, 53–5, 72
Venezuela 533, 537
Venus 234
Vestal Virgins 234
Vietnam 149, 150, 152, 158–9,
   438, 439, 441, 444–7
Vietnam War 350, 371, 372, 377,

438–9, 443
Vijñānavāda School 82
Vikings, the 275–6
Vīraśaiva *see* Lingāyata
Visnu 45, 47, 55, 71, *85*, 86–7, *87*
Vivekānand, Swami 392–3,
   394–6, 397, 398, 399, 400, 401,
   404
Vladimir, Prince of Kiev 262
Vogelherd Cave, Germany *37*
Voltaire 330
Voodoo, Haitian *538*, 545

Wahhabi movement 467–9, 483
Waleska, Lech 505
Wang Kon 128
Wang Yang-ming 126
Watts, Alan W. 372
Weber, Max 321
Wesley, Charles 357
Wesley, John 19, 356
Whitby, Synod of 261
White, Ellen Gould 363
Whitefield, George 356
Whitney, Eli 330
Williams, Roger 354
Winti system 544–5
Wise, Rabbi Isaac 362
World Council of Churches 351

Xiuhtecuhtli 183

Yahweh *see* Jehovah
Yamato emperors 133
Yamm 201
*Yang* 106, *107*, 108, 115, *118*
Yang Hsi 119
*Yasasna* 215
*Yazatas* 215, 219
Yehoshu'a *see* Jesus
Yellow Turbans, the 116, 420
Yesha'yahu *see* Isaiah
Yeshiva University 362
Yggdrasil 276
Yi Yulgok 129
*Yin* 106, *107*, 108, 115, *118*
Yirmeyah *see* Jeremiah
Yisra'el ben Eli'ezer 333
Yo T'oegye 129
Yoga 45, 47, 63, 64, 73, 74, 85,
   404–5, 415, *561*
Yohanan *see* John the Baptist
Yoruba, the 303, 304, 305–6, *311*,
   544, 545
Young, Brigham *359*, 360
Younghusband, General Francis
   412
Yü Huang Shang Ti, Emperor
   124
Yuan Shih-k'ai 425

*Yüeh Ching* (Classic of Music) 109
Yugoslavia 502, 507

Zaire 297, 300, 308, *309*, 524,
   525, 527, 545
*Zakat* 282, 283, 284
Zambia 527
Zarathustra 215–17, 219, 220, 222
Zealots 238
*Zen* 131
Zen Buddhism *18*, 131, 133,
   142–5, 147, 148, 451–2, 453,
   454, 455, 456. *See also* Son
   Buddhism
Zeno of Citium 233
Zeus 227–8, 229, 231, 233, 234,
   *235*
Zimbabwe *14*, 297, 516
Zinzendorf, Count 357
Zionism 334, 335, 350, 362–3,
   473–5
Zoroastrianism 100, 104, 127,
   214–22, 223, 224, 411
Zulu, the 309–10, 515, 516, 523,
   526–7
Zurvān 215, 220
Zurvanism 214, 220, 221
Zwingli, Ulrich *336*